Coffee

The Political Economy of an Export Industry in Papua New Guinea

Coffee

The Political Economy of an Export Industry in Papua New Guinea

Randal G. Stewart

Routledge
Taylor & Francis Group
NEW YORK AND LONDON

First published 1992 by Westview Press, Inc.

Published 2021 by Routledge
605 Third Avenue, New York, NY 10017
2 Park Square, Milton Park, Abingdon, Oxon OX14 4RN

Routledge is an imprint of the Taylor & Francis Group, an informa business

Library of Congress Cataloging-in-Publication Data
Stewart, Randal G.
Coffee : the political economy of an export industry in Papua New Guinea / Randal G. Stewart.
p. cm.
Includes bibliographical references and index.
ISBN 0-8133-8525-3
1. Coffee trade—Papua New Guinea. I. Title.
HD9199.P252S74 1992
382'.41373'09953—dc20 91-37452
CIP

ISBN 13: 978-0-3671-5778-4 (pbk)
ISBN 13: 978-0-3670-0791-1 (hbk)
ISBN 13: 978-0-429-03777-1 (ebk)

DOI: 10.4324/9780429037771

Contents

Illustrations

Tables

Figures

Map

Preface

This is a study of the particular forms of production and exchange in the coffee industry of Papua New Guinea. It is an historical and critical study, examining (1) the pre-independence period of the industry from its establishment in 1952-53 to 1975 and (2) changes in the post-independence period to the outbreak of coffee rust in the industry in 1986. The post-independence study includes a detailed account of an important new program (established in 1982), the 20-hectare development, which aims to change the predominant form of production, farm plantation and smallholding, to small plantations.

The study of the Papua New Guinea coffee industry is placed in the context of the International Coffee Agreement (ICA), the world's longest surviving commodity agreement. Commodity agreements are generally thought of as cartels established by producers for their own benefit. However, this study shows that the ICA actually disadvantages small, new producers like Papua New Guinea.

The methodology used to penetrate the economic and technical complexities which reveal the underlying structure of interests and some of the dynamics of change at work make this study relevant to all those interested in material outcomes in Third World development. The findings reveal a hitherto neglected facet of Third World exploitation - - in the simple act of production and exchange of a commodity - - which may not be as dramatic as war, terrorism, apartheid or patriarchy, but which nevertheless may be as damaging to the future of vast numbers of Third World people.

Randal G. Stewart

Acknowledgments

Many people help put a book together. It is a social product even though one person must in the end take responsibility for it. The social contribution includes assistance with and critique of the material itself and friendship and support when the going gets tough.

I was fortunate to have the support of John Ballard, who was both a critic and friend when I needed him. It is certainly true to say that without his faith in and commitment to the project it might never have been completed.

This book is for Georgina. Those who read material and offered helpful criticism or support include Amos Anyimadu, Henry Bernstein, Dianne Bolton, Hugh Collins, Diana Giese, John Girling, Christine Jennett, Colin Leys, Daudi Mukangara, Anabel Murray, Michael Oliver, Bill Standish, and Vincent Warakai.

Karen Davis, University of Queensland, laboured long and hard on the preparation of the manuscript for publication. Technical assistance was provided by Tony Bunney, Department of Government, University of Queensland, and is much appreciated. Amos Zubrow of Westview Press was patient and supportive in the production process.

Fieldwork was funded by the Australian National University with valuable assistance from the University of Papua New Guinea.

Finally, to all the bureaucrats, business people and coffee growers who gave their time for interviews, I offer my thanks.

R.G.S.

Introduction

Why Study the Coffee Industry?

Coffee is second only to crude oil as the most important internationally traded commodity in value. In 1984 it was reported that coffee had an annual turnover of about US$10 billion (*South*, October 1984). The coffee industry is chosen because coffee is also an important commodity in the domestic economies of many Third World countries.

Coffee is not the world's main agricultural crop - - its total volume of production is less than that of wheat and rice - - but its importance in world trade is due to the fact that almost all of it is produced for export. Coffee is the main source of foreign exchange for some of the world's poorest countries. In 1979 Uganda (98 percent), Burundi (92.8 percent), Rwanda (76.5 percent), Ethiopia (68.6 percent), El Salvador (63.6 percent) and Colombia (58. percent), relied heavily on coffee for their total export earnings as did Guatemala (34.1 percent), Ivory Coast (31.1 percent), Tanzania (27.1 percent), Kenya (26.8 percent), Papua New Guinea (18.1 percent) and Brazil (15.3 percent) (Mwandha, Nicholls and Sargent 1985:12). The top world producers in 1981–82 were Brazil, with 21 percent of total world production, Colombia, 17 percent, and Ivory Coast, 8 percent (Mwanda, Nicholls and Sargent 1985:152–153). But even in countries which are small producers in world terms, coffee provides a source of cash income for numerous smallholders, and jobs for many others in the importing countries in trade and manufacture. It has been estimated that coffee provides employment for about 20 million people in 3–4 million enterprises in the 70–80 countries in which it is produced (Payer 1975:154). There are few commodities which have such domestic and international importance.

If coffee is grown in some of the world's poorest countries, it is consumed in some of the richest. Those who grow coffee rarely drink it, and those who drink it almost never grow it. Coffee has thus always been dependent on world trade for its market, and much attention has been lavished on regulating its international trade. Many consider liberal, negotiated, institutionalised commodity agreements to be the ideal way to overcome underdevelopment. But have these worked in the favour of coffee-producing nations? Has regulation of international coffee trade through the long-surviving International Coffee Organisation (ICO) benefited small producers? These questions are taken up in Chapters 11, 12 and 13 of this book.

A study of the coffee industry inside peripheral countries also sheds light on general and historical state and class processes in coffee-producing countries. Colonialism provided the impetus for the establishment of coffee industries in many countries. Under its different forms, different industry structures were established. However, in almost all cases, because coffee was a rich crop, it was grown in highly productive areas on rich soils and in moderate climates. A study of coffee is, then, also a study of some of the most advanced capitalist areas in a country. As capitalism developed rapidly, so too did attendant processes of class formation. In coffee-growing areas, because of the surpluses generated, the basis is laid for the establishment of more advanced economic activity, including service industries, and for more complex forms of social organisation. It is also in advanced capitalist areas that the domestic capitalist state displays its most developed form.

Any study of coffee must also deal with the complex problem of household commodity production. In many parts of the world, coffee is produced in households, on small plots of 1 to 2 acres, and in rambling gardens in which it is interspersed with food crops. The process of its production and exchange brings into focus peasant-state relations in the political economy of Third World agriculture.

A brief history of pre- and post-independence Papua New Guinea

Papua New Guinea is often seen as the 'last frontier'. Viewers of world explorer-type documentaries can watch semi-naked men and women, and hear stories of cannibalism. This is the tabloid image of a country undergoing complex, rapid social change.

Papua under British rule and New Guinea under German administration were colonised in the 1880s at the same time as the 'scramble for Africa'. As in the African case, the motives for colonising Papua and New Guinea (hereafter called Papua New Guinea) are clouded by *post hoc* rationalisation. Commerce was an incentive, but defence the main motive of the British, who were pressured by the Australian colony, Queensland, to annex Papua, in 1884. After World War I, Australia was given responsibility for both territories under a League of Nations mandate, converting to a United Nations Trust Territory after the World War II. Curiously, both territories remained formally under separate administration, although both reported to the Department of External Territories in Canberra until independence was granted to the nation of Papua New Guinea in 1975.

As in Africa, the colonists found a complex indigenous culture in Papua and New Guinea, which they did not understand. Papua and New Guinea societies were small-scale and self-sufficient. They practised agriculture and had developed complex cultural rituals related to life crisis events. On the coast, trade took place, and there is evidence that a form of money was used and that trading relations penetrated remote mountainous areas. Most groups developed complex forms of leadership and social hierarchy, gender relations, hunting and cultivating practices. It is difficult to generalise because the overwhelming feature of pre-contact indigenous society is the isolation of groups one from another, all over the island. Such isolation produced regional and tribal diversity reflected in more than six hundred languages -- not dialects -- spoken on the island.

One reason for isolation is topography. Papua New Guinea is an amazingly diverse island. The coastal and island areas are classic postcard tropical islands, while Papua is dry and uninviting. The country is split by the massive range of highlands which form the backbone of the country. High mountains, deep ravines, rushing rivers and a temperate climate create patterns of life dramatically different from the coast and the islands. Social organisation has also played a role in isolation. There can be no doubt that pre-contact Papua New Guinea was a dangerous place, although colonists and anthropologists have probably overemphasised the extent of war and tribal fighting.

The indigenous culture has created a robust, independent, creative people. Papua New Guineans have always shown an eagerness to develop, although arguments that traditional acquisitiveness made them 'pre-adapted to capitalism' (Finney 1973) are not correct. This book shows that capitalism in Papua New Guinea, as elsewhere, had to be imposed by white settlers and the colonial state. Nevertheless, for people who have so recently begun to experience development on a large scale, progress has been truly remarkable. The acquisitiveness and competition evident in indigenous society, as well as the independence and self-confidence generated by isolation, has created a dynamic capitalism in Papua New Guinea.

When Mick, Dan and Jim Leahy, Australian-Irish prospectors, first contacted the one million people living in the highlands of Papua and New Guinea in 1930, it is difficult to know whether they, or the indigenous people, were more surprised. Moving pictures taken of this fully-filmed first contact show the no-nonsense whites setting up camp and roping it off to assert their authority. It is the indigenous people who seem confused and awed by the trinkets -- and the gramophone -- which the Leahys brought with them. But the Leahys also had problems. What had begun simply as a gold prospecting expedition had turned into one of history's great journeys of exploration. The Leahys were ill-prepared. They bought shovels to prospect for gold, but had neither the cultural or administrative ability to understand the people they found -- one million of them in the immensely fertile Highlands.

Australian administrations were, arguably, even less prepared than the Leahys to appreciate the massive responsibility and opportunity presented by the Highlands and its people. Two of the Leahys did manage to adapt. They put their prospecting days behind them and squatted in the Highlands to help establish the coffee industry, founding a tribe of mixed-race Leahys who are today influential in coffee business and politics.

The Australian administration, by contrast, remained confused well into the 1960s. At first, land was alienated for white settlement, but this stopped abruptly in the mid-1950s. Australian colonial administrators were less practised in the art of "divide and rule" than their British counterparts, and far less sophisticated in their expectations of colonial rule. Australian colonialism in Papua New Guinea was a neglectful, penny-pinching, paternal business. Neglect caused its own problems in limits to education and health improvement, although it also meant that the excessive cruelty and exploitation of other styles of colonialism were avoided. Australia did not seem to know what to do with the Highlands, so it operated a night watchman administration with minimal outlay and rudimentary administration based on the legendary *kiap*, the single district officer, the lone white man in the bush.

The coffee industry, as we shall see, grew up almost by accident without administration tutelage, and pioneered by rough, entrepreneurial white settlers. Coffee-growing soon spread to smallholder, indigenous cultivators despite administration discouragement and the withdrawal of technical and agronomic assistance. There were never any clear objectives for the industry. The administration's attitude seems to have been: 'coffee-growing is a matter for you commercial chaps'. There was not the same hostility to capitalism displayed by the British administrative caste, although a similar battery of 'native' regulations and restrictions on enterprise were in place until the 1960s. The administration assisted the industry with regulations when it needed them as requested by white growers -- but never with money. Essentially, the industry was treated with the same benign neglect adopted for the territories as a whole.

There was, however, no stopping the spread of an industry which was aptly described as 'money which grows on trees'. For both planter and smallholder alike, coffee was abundant, easily grown, and required virtually no agronomic experience or special cultivation skills. When coffee cherry was ripe, it was ready to be sold for instant cash. Its ease of cultivation and hardiness caused it to quickly become one of the great industries of the country.

Though white settlers very profitably ran coffee and other industries in the colonial period, their tenure was very insecure. Without the support of a forceful administration, their social and political power was weak. By the end of the colonial period indigenous people were showing that anything the whites could do, they could do better. And white settlement and administration was built on a house of cards in Papua and New Guinea. Without purpose or direction in the late 1960s and early 1970s it quickly collapsed, as both external opinion and indigenous self-determination were exerted. Colonial rule and white enterprise simply fell apart all over the country, although white expertise was, and still is, required and hired.

How much of this broad colonial history affected the coffee farmer, the cocoa grower, the bosboi's and the village teacher is a moot point. But the opportunities for enterprise and development enticingly displayed in the colonial period were openly sought and coveted in the post-independence one. Rural life in the Highlands was transformed by the 450 or so coffee trees at the bottom of the smallholders' gardens. Coffee meant cash: cash for goods, for matches, for beer, for education, for trucks, for video players. Cash and individual and group economic advancement is a basic desire of Papua New Guinean people all over the country.

By the 1980s, a visit to any main town in the Highlands such as Goroka or Mount Hagen showed the wealth, and contradictions which the 'money which grows on trees' had brought to the Highlands region. In the mud main street of Mount Hagen, Papua New Guinean men in boots and cowboy hats would tether their four-wheel drive trucks like horses. Video stores and computerised banks competed with ragged *buai* sellers in the main street.. In Goroka, a customer in the modern bank building might turn from the impeccably groomed, white-shirt-clad teller with a 'Good-day', to brush past the next customer, an old woman in traditional dress with a mud-packed face to indicate mourning, waiting to have her passbook processed. Papua New Guinea, a land of immense contrasts, is also a land of acute economic contradictions, most particularly in export industries like coffee.

The achievement of self-government in 1972 and Independence in 1975, has heightened interest in Papua New Guinea's social, economic and political development. Independent Papua New Guinea is most interesting politically because, since Independence, it has been able to maintain a functioning competitive political system. This is rare in the developing world. The transition to independence from Australia was achieved peacefully after some eighty years of colonial rule.

Since 1975, Papua New Guinea has held three successful post-independence elections, in 1977, 1982 and 1987. Each was conducted by secret ballot and was based on free speech and multi-party competition. The Parliament functions as a political cauldron; twice, in 1980 and 1985, governments have been defeated on the floor of the House. Each time the defeated Prime Minister, Michael Somare, leader of the independence party, Pangu, and father of the nation, has gone quietly into opposition. In Papua New Guinea, unlike some developing countries, politics does matter because access to state institutions and policy influence is a reward for those who succeed in political competition. But is competition in the formal political institutions a major source of social change or is it a mere reflection of social change and competition that has occurred elsewhere?

Papua New Guinea has not attempted to drastically alter its inherited political or economic structures. The removal of colonial control required the new government to carry out a large number of technical alterations to the machinery of state, e.g., the setting up of a foreign affairs department; the establishment of a national currency and a central bank; and policy development in a whole range of other areas, most importantly in macro-economic policy, co-ordination of government functions through the establishment of the Budget Priorities Committee, and localisation of the public service. Apart from the establishment of provincial governments in its nineteen provinces, itself a response to threatened instability and fragmentation, no significant restructuring of state institutions has occurred in post-colonial Papua New Guinea.

Today, the Papua New Guinea economy is highly dependent. Trade is heavily concentrated on four main export commodities, copper, coffee, copra and cocoa, all subject to severe price fluctuations on the international market. With 73.9 percent of its GNP provided by trade, Papua New Guinea ranks very high in the world on this indicator. Of those countries ranking higher, most are either very small or are oil and mineral exporting countries (Taylor and Jodice 1983:226). Trade dependence shaped the macro-economic policy adopted by Papua New Guinea in the 1970s, the policy known as the 'hard kina' strategy. It required the monetary authorities to maintain the value of the currency in order to ensure its international purchasing power. The strategy was based on the belief that above all else Papua New Guinea needed a stable income in its early years of independence and, as a new country with a new currency, had to exercise financial responsibility in order to establish itself in international financial markets. This could be achieved by using fiscal mechanisms such as stabilisation funds to smooth out fluctuations in international prices and the exchange rate.

Papua New Guinea was extremely fortunate in attracting a steady inflow of aid. It also benefited from an inflow of mineral rents from the giant Bougainville copper mine in the 1970s. The adoption of the 'hard kina' strategy did, however, have its costs. It maintained an open economy and reinforced the division of labour within the country. It facilitated the import of processed and luxury items from Papua New Guinea's developed country trading partners, Australia and Japan, and the export of unprocessed primary products. It had a negative impact on the domestic economy in at least three ways. First, it did not encourage the restructuring of the economic base. Second, the fiscal and monetary mechanisms were not considered suitable for the encouragement of industry, for example, and the basic premiss of the strategy was that Papua New Guinea would remain a dependent country. Third, it discouraged government intervention in the domestic market, and government ownership of the means of production except where, as in the case of large mineral resource projects, such ownership was vital for management of the nation's finances. The 'hard kina' strategy may also have inhibited the rate of growth of Gross Domestic Product in Papua New Guinea in the period 1976–83, which has increased only by 1.4 percent a year compared with an average for all developing countries of 2.6 percent a year (Goodman, Lepani, Morawetz 1985:35).

All these features of Papua New Guinea - - political competition, differentiation in the state, private enterprise in a market economy, an open economy - make it an ideal case study for the analysis of capitalist development in the periphery. If such development is to occur along the lines of its own premisses, then it should certainly occur in Papua New Guinea.

Papua New Guinea's population is still small: 3,700,000 in 1987. Its Gross Domestic Product in 1987 was US$3030 million. Its Gross National Product per capita is around US$700, which gave it a ranking of fiftieth poorest country in the world in 1987 (World Bank Development Report 1989). Gross National Product per capita is not to be taken as an indicator of development progress, as it was by early development economists. However, Gross National Product figures, or more properly Gross Domestic Product (GDP), disaggregated even in quantitative terms, can give a quite useful understanding of the way in which people live in certain countries and where and at what they work. In Papua New Guinea, for example, the percentage of Gross Domestic Product provided by agriculture is very high. With 30 percent of GDP accounted for by agriculture, it ranks thirty-first in the world (Taylor and Jodice 1983:217). The importance of agriculture in Papua New Guinea is much more evident when one looks at the percentage of the labour force in this sector. In 1977, the country ranked equal thirteenth in the world on this measure, with 84 percent of its labour force in agriculture. This was almost double the mean of all countries in 1977 (Taylor and Jodice 1983:208).

The coffee industry of Papua New Guinea remains the nation's most important agricultural export crop, and Papua New Guinea's second earner of foreign exchange after copper. It is of immense local and national importance. In 1976, during the coffee boom, coffee earned K132.6m, some 25.6 percent of the country's export earnings; by 1980 this figure had fallen to K118.6m. Coffee is produced on large-scale European-style plantations, averaging about 100 acres and by smallholders whose average 450 trees are interspersed with subsistence gardens. Scope for accumulation in the coffee industry occurs not only at the level of production but also in roadside buying and dry processing and exporting -- all activities which come under the jurisdiction of the Coffee Industry Board (formerly the Coffee Marketing Board).

A number of conclusions follow from the importance of agriculture in Papua New Guinea. The first is that it is one of the least urbanised countries in the world, ranking one hundred and eleventh on urbanisation (Taylor and Jodice 1983:202). The second is that industry plays a very minor role in its economy. In 1985, manufacturing in Papua New Guinea provided about 10 percent of GDP, with a similar share of formal employment in the economy. Total employment in manufacturing was only 26,000 in 1983 (Goodman, Lepani, Morawetz 1985:9). In economies where industry is of little importance, small-scale non-farm growth and employment usually takes place in two other main areas, the services sector and government. This is also the case in Papua New Guinea. In 1974 service activities accounted for some 45 percent of Gross Domestic Product. Despite this growth, service industries are not large employers, and in Papua New Guinea services employed only 7 percent of the labour force in 1977 (Taylor and Jodice 1983:216). The government sector has grown in the country in the period since independence, government employment has increased and provision of government services has improved. Primary and secondary school enrolments as a percentage of the school age population is low, Papua New Guinea ranking one hundredth, with 37 percent of the school age population in school (Taylor and Jodice 1983:164), but the growth rate in enrolment has been steady and great improvements have been made in the number enrolled in higher education. Public health is another area where Papua New Guinea performs well, ranking twenty-ninth in the world (Taylor and Jodice 1983:31). All these figures suggest that any analysis of Papua New Guinea must focus on life in the countryside, where most people live and work on small household production units, or in rural towns, where they are engaged in service activities and government.

Methodological and Theoretical Considerations of the Study

This book is about production and exchange in the coffee industry of Papua New Guinea. A rural industry is examined because if we are going to deal seriously with the problem of development, then our analysis should be applied to the concrete reality of life in the countryside, where most people live and where the bulk of the surplus is produced and exchanged. However, this is not an agricultural economics textbook. It aims to penetrate the economic and technical complexities of the coffee industry to reveal the underlying structure of interests and some of the dynamics of change at work. In particular, it aims to uncover the social and political processes, as well as the economic, which determine why some people do better out of the organisation of the industry than do others. It is appropriate, therefore, to elaborate at this point on the methodological and theoretical devices used in the study.

The Third World countryside is the home of that awkward class, the peasantry. Three recent publications, all on Africa, and with no counterpart in the Pacific, open up the prospect of a critical political economy of Third World agriculture. The books are Robert H. Bates, *Markets and States in Tropical Africa* (1981), Keith Hart, *The Political Economy of West African Agriculture* (1982) and Dianne Bolton, *Nationalisation – A Road to Socialism? The Case of Tanzania* (1985). All three attempt to deal with the economic and political processes in agriculture, and the historical circumstances that shaped them. They move far beyond economists' limited concern with short-run micro-economic efficiency which, as Ellis (1983) notes, is by 'default' the main approach to the study of agricultural marketing systems in the Third World. Each book recognises that agricultural marketing systems are something more than a set of purely functional activities and that the object of interest in their study cannot exclusively be the minimisation of costs (Ellis 1983). Rather these books argue that state marketing boards in Africa are largely geared to extract from a mainly agricultural population a reliable income sufficient to support the expenditure needs of the regimes in power. Their focus is on state and social processes rather than micro-economic ones.

The three books attempt to deal with the role of the state and social structure but they all do this in a rather unsystematic and unsophisticated way. Hart's focus is upon state formation. He regards the maintenance of viable rule as problematic and sees the African state engaged in the struggle to assert its authority, as well as to increase its revenue, in the African countryside. Bates tries to inject a political dimension into his analysis of agriculture by generalising about the groups in society which benefit or lose as a result of the operation of state marketing boards. He writes:

> The agricultural policies of the nations of Africa confer benefits on highly concentrated and organised groupings. They spread costs over the masses of the unorganised. They have helped to evoke the self-interested assent of powerful interests to the formation of a new political order and have provoked little organised resistance. In this way, they have helped to generate a political

> equilibrium. But in the longer run, the costs inflicted by these policies are being passed on to members of the policy-making coalition and the configurations that were once in equilibrium are now becoming politically unstable. (Bates 1981:129)

Bolton's book is focused on a single industry, sisal in Tanzania. She attempts to provide a class analysis of its state and social processes. In her conclusion, she endorses the view that the state largely intervenes in the sisal industry in a way that advances the interests of the powerful, or the 'governing class' as she calls them. Bolton sees nationalisation as a defensive radicalism which does not benefit workers and peasants in the industry. Further - and this may be her main contribution to the political economy of African agriculture - - she emphasises the continuities between colonial and post-colonial Tanzania in the sisal industry. Despite talk of socialism there are striking similarities between the nationalised and remaining private sisal plantations. But Bolton's class analysis is not highly developed or linked in a sophisticated way to state processes.

All three books admirably attempt to deal with the politics of African agriculture, but do so by applying fairly simple models of state and social relations to the complex state and class patterns and structures of rural Africa.

Part of the problem is methodological, as a comparison of Bates and Bolton make clear. Bates makes a bold attempt at a broad analysis of agriculture throughout sub-Saharan Africa, including an analysis of interlocking food and export markets. It is probably because he uses such a broad canvas that he makes simplistic political assessments. Bolton, however, provides a more rigorous treatment of state and social processes in African agriculture, mainly because her focus on a single industry allows her to make a detailed analysis of state initiatives and class response. A single industry approach overcomes the level of generality inherent in broad sectoral approaches and, at the present stage of theoretical development, is probably the only way to study the political economy of Third World agriculture. That is why single industry approach is adopted in this study.

The method I propose to adopt for coffee can be called the commodity chain approach, which

> take[s] an ultimate consumerable item and trace back the set of inputs that culminated in this item - the prior transformations, the raw materials, the transportation mechanisms, the labour inputs into each of the material processes, the food inputs into labour. (Hopkins and Wallerstein 1982:59-60)

The linking of these processes offers at least three major advantages for the study of the political economy of a single industry. First, it is an historical approach. By studying the transformation of items through the various stages of production and exchange, one is also studying the enduring structure of the industry. How have these processes of transformation changed over time, and why? Is the industry marked by continuities in production and exchange from the colonial to the post-colonial period, regardless of regime change or rhetoric? What has the social impact of this process of transformation been over time, and how has the state intervened in the process in the industry?

Second, the commodity chain approach is simultaneously a study of production and exchange processes. The industry must be studied in its totality, from the input of raw material to the final, consumed product. Such a method brings state and class process into the analysis in a way that is consistent with the Marxist scheme for locating classes in production. In most agricultural industries this brings the focus sharply upon the major producers in the Third World, the peasantry. The commodity chain approach ensures that markets are not treated as epiphenomenal. Clearly, market processes affect the fortunes of producers and are more easily manipulated by the powerful than the production processes in peasant societies. In addition, the commodity chain approach forces the analyst to deal in a subtle way with the role of the state because the analyst must deal with a particular marketing board in a single industry rather than marketing boards in general. Thus the simultaneous study of production and exchange which the approach demands also helps to analyse in a sophisticated way state and social processes in a single industry.

A final advantage in adopting the commodity chain approach is that if the industry chosen is an export one, then the impact of the form and type of international capital in it is important. Many agricultural industries in Third World countries are export ones, so the commodity chain ends with the First World consumer after international capital has played its role in transforming the item. The commodity chain approach enables the analyst to situate the particular forms of production and exchange in an industry in their international context.

This book is a critical, not a descriptive, study of the coffee industry in Papua New Guinea. Critical means that precise, rigorous terminology such as "state", "class" and "imperialism", is used to analyse the social, economic and political relations of the industry. Some will find such terminology odd in a Papua New Guinea context, others will object to its Marxist heritage, and some will find it redundant. However, this terminology, though subject to sectarian disputation, has a long pedigree.

The book is dedicated to developing an analytical approach which shows precisely how external factors, such as international trade and regulation, and internal factors, such as 'state and class', are linked, reciprocal and mutually constitutive, and how they define and shape each other. The starting point is a recognition of this link but one can proceed only by developing a sound analytical framework. This is Skocpol's point when she argues that:

> instead of exclusively pursuing Wallerstein's world system approach, we should investigate the world–historical emergence and development of capitalism in terms of hypotheses about variations in both 1) institutionalised class relations of production and exchange, and 2) patterns of state structures and interstate relationships, without simply reducing the latter to the former. To be sure, markets and patterns of trade are bound to be part of the picture, but it seems unlikely that they can be understood in their origin, functioning, or effects except with reference to changes in class and political structures. The alternative picture of world capitalism that is likely to emerge from historical analyses pursued along these lines will probably pertain to intersecting structures (e.g., class structures, trade networks, state structures and geo–political systems) involving varying and autonomous logics and different, though overlapping, historical times, rather than a single, all–encompassing system that comes into being in one stage and then remains constant in its essential pattern until capitalism as a whole meets its demise. (Skocpol 1976:1087–1088)

This book aims to deal with these 'intersecting structures' (e.g., class structures, trade networks, state structures and geopolitical systems) involving varying and autonomous logics and different, though overlapping, historical times, as outlined by Skocpol (1976).

The theoretical position taken is that development and underdevelopment are caused by a complex interweaving of external and internal factors. This view recognises that underdevelopment has been caused in many developing countries by external forces and factors, but it considers external influences to be only one level of the complex process of development and underdevelopment, and is not prepared to state that underdevelopment must always be the outcome of external intervention. Rather, this view asserts that the form and type of international capital which enters the developing country must be analysed in its particularity, and in the context of the history and structure of the developing country itself. One crucial outcome however, of the entry of international capital, which this view regards as fundamental, is that the structuring of developing economies around the production and export of unprocessed primary commodities during the colonial period has made households vulnerable to changes in the world economy. In particular, the advent of external trading capital has left the household at an intermediate stage, short of full proletarianisation. Peasant commodity production at household level is a new form of production in which commodity production has entered the household reproduction cycle but which has not, at the same time, become directly vulnerable to exploitation by internal and external dominant classes.

This simple fact has created a myriad of complex class and state patterns and structures in the Third World. The most general outcome of external structuring and peasant household production is the fragmentation and weakening of resident capital and national dominant classes in Third World countries. The development of social formations is retarded by three main factors. First, their linkages to the world economy limit their accumulation, usually by unequal exchange but sometimes by international regulation, as we will see in the case of coffee. Second, their own patterns of production are usually restricted to production in industries (such as crops for export) where it is only possible to appropriate absolute surplus value (increasing profit by lengthening the working day or devalorising labour) and not relative surplus value (increasing profit by increasing the intensity or the productivity of labour). Third, the survival of households as production units and the difficulty of extracting land and labour from them, and the impossibility of directly appropriating surplus value from them, limits exploitation of those engaged in household production.

These three factors weaken and fragment resident capitals and dominant classes and impose significant limits on the self-expansion of resident capitals. This has the most profound implications for the whole society. For one thing, accumulation is a much more political process because in such circumstances capital cannot rely on its own impetus to expand. The state therefore becomes of central importance in development and underdevelopment. It is important because it sets the framework for accumulation. It is also important because it adjusts patterns of production, market relations, public political and economic institutions to the changing demands of class forces as they struggle against one another and against the limits imposed by retarded development. The state in the Third World takes a complex form; it is a hydra-headed monster ever-changing or never-changing, depending on whether the class struggle requires it to be an *instrument* in the hands of the dominant classes, a *Bonapartist* state, one which functions in no particular class interest but which is transcendent over dominant and subordinate classes, or a *partisan* state, soaking up surplus to fill its own treasury coffers. In this study, the coffee industry in Papua New Guinea is analysed to demonstrate the validity of these more general theoretical propositions.

Summary of the Book

The first chapter traces the origin of the coffee industry in Papua New Guinea focusing particularly on the area around Goroka in the Eastern Highlands where the arabica coffee industry began and which remains an important centre. The spectacular growth of the industry is demonstrated. In the beginning, growth was led by white planters and later by small growers cultivating garden coffee. The development of the industry enriched many planters and also gave them a base for demands on the colonial state. It is shown that, despite small grower enthusiasm for "money which grows on trees", the precise administrative and exchange relations established in the industry were imposed and controlled by white planters. The first chapter foreshadows the structure of the book and its analytical approach which on the one hand examines exploitation and change occurring as a result of the production and exchange of coffee as a commodity and, on the other traces the political and administrative changes engineered by the powerful in the industry to further enhance their interests.

It is implicit in the analysis that the manner in which a commodity is produced determines the nature and form of political and administrative control which can be exercised over the industry. Chapter 2 examines the form of production in coffee at both the planter and smallholder level. It shows that neither can change the production system very much, due to the rudimentary nature of technology employed and the low level of skill. Hence, both groups face limits of accumulation and experience difficulties in making the "agrarian transition" -- the formation of a rural capitalists class and a rural proletariat of wage labourers completely separated from the means of production (Goodman and Redclift 1981:25). The powerful planters cannot drive the smallholders out of business and thus concentrate production and exchange on themselves because coffee grows easily and neither the planters nor the state have ever had the resources to police control of smallholder production. This point is very important because it means that the 'politics' of the coffee industry revolves around the attempt by the powerful to control exchange processes and/or to modify the level of competitiveness in the industry to enhance their own interests via assistance from, and utilisation of, the state.

Chapter 3, on the exchange of coffee in the colonial period, and Chapter 4, on colonial administration of the coffee industry, show this 'politics' in action. Chapter 3 shows how white planters established a cartel of exporters which gave them power over exchange of coffee in the colonial industry. This was done by controlling key 'pinch points', in the marketing chain, the points in the commodity chain that form bottlenecks through which raw material must pass on its way to becoming a saleable item, particularly at the processor level. Chapter 4 shows how the administrative state supported white planter control by establishing a marketing board, ostensibly including smallholders but, in reality controlled and run by white planters for white planters. Illustrating the limits to white planter power in the industry and showing their political cunning, was their attempt to promote a social buffer between themselves and smallholders by sponsoring a richer, élite group of indigenous growers on to their own plantations. This 'social surgery' is reminiscent of many late, colonial conceptions of 'partnership', often in reality an attempt to help whites survive the transition to independence. This strategy did not appeal to the colonial state, for it had a policy of 'gradual development' for Papua New Guineans, designed to prevent an élite of this kind emerging anywhere. In any case, the attempt to modify the existing racial division of the industry into white planters and black smallholders was half-hearted, and came too late to prevent the collapse of the white planters.

Chapter 5 and 6 show how the coffee industry was beset by two major crises in the late colonial period and in the run-up to independence. First was the 1966-67 crisis when the squeeze on plantation capital, caused in part by Papua New Guinea's coffee exports being governed by the colonial clause in the 1962 International Coffee Agreement (ICA), resulted in, on the one hand, an attempt by foreign owners of PNG plantations to enlist support from the metropolis and, on the other, in their determined support for a continuous ban by the colonial state on smallholder coffee development. The second crisis occurred in 1972-74, when low prices and uncertainty in the international industry due to breakdown of the 1968 agreement, coupled with the coming of Independence, led to an exodus of white plantation owners. The result was that the plantation segment of the industry came under almost total national ownership and control.

These crises, which had the effect of wiping out the white planters, show dramatically how vulnerable the coffee industry in Papua New Guinea is to volatility in world markets. They coincide with the collapse of the colonial state. This coincidence underlies the importance of a stable state for powerful groups in the industry, to help them cope with externally-generated crises and fluctuations. Chapter 6 examines the broad changes which took place in the transition to Independence in Papua New Guinea. In relation to the coffee industry itself, we see in Chapter 7 that a complex struggle for ownership and control of the industry emerged between groups of black élites and technocrats in the independent state of Papua New Guinea. Would the independent state become an instrument in the hands of the powerful black élites of the industry? Would it modify their power by adopting a 'public interest' perspective and instead advance the interests of smallholders in the industry? Or would the black technocrats have a program of their own to pursue, regardless of élite and smallholder interests? These questions are taken up in Chapters 8, 9 and 10. It is shown that despite talk of nationalism and the rhetoric of the new black élites and technocrats who took over from white planters, the convulsive changes occurring at Independence in the industry offered few benefits for smallholders. Chapter 8 shows that, despite intense competition between black élites, the post-colonial marketing mechanisms remain virtually unchanged from the colonial period. In the post-colonial period, new élites have struggled to replace white planter control of export and processing but have not succeeded in restructuring the institutions in their own interests. New institutions in the industry have been established, such as the stabilisation fund, but these are accepted as technical structures, not the subject for political competition and control. Curiously, in a Third World context, the new technocrats have also attempted to use the new institutions in a technocratic way and not, as a 'bureaucratic bourgeoisie' might, to expand the power of the state. The technocrats do exercise influence in the restructured Coffee Industry Board (CIB), but do not use their power to alter the structure for exchanging coffee inside the country.

The answer then, to questions about the role of the state in the post–colonial coffee industry, is that it is a complex one, reflecting the diverse interests at stake. The dominant interests identified are black élite groups of commercial coffee growers, processors and exporters, and two such groups are identified in Goroka. These are labelled a *petit bourgeoisie* class fraction and a big peasantry – – and a technocracy which operates as an arm of the public administration in a liberal–democratic state. The technocracy is unable to impose solutions on the industry and must work with the interests in the industry. The subordinant interests are labelled the smallholders. A consequence of this complex social structure is, as Chapter 10 shows in two case studies, that the role of the post–colonial state – labelled Bonapartist – – is both confined to delivering handouts to powerful interests in the industry and restricted to disciplining the smallholders, through the use of technical instruments, through tightening control of production and exchange in the industry, as the 'coffee rust' case aims to demonstrate.

The role of the state underwrites a competitive capitalism in the industry. It also creates instability and bitterness. There is an increasing danger that the state will become more and more involved in production and exchange, either because it has become captured by either of the two dominant class fractions, or because the technocrats will resort to coercive measures to reduce instability in the industry. One advantage the technocrats have (which is why they are sought as a partner by each class fraction) is the administrative and informational vantage point they have in relation to the external market. This is crucial during those periods when the world coffee market is regulated. Ultimately, the world market determines the fate of all the actors in domestic coffee industries. Hence the structure and performance of the world market is a crucial determinant of domestic political and economic outcomes in the coffee industry of Papua New Guinea.

In Chapters 11, 12 and 13, the world market in coffee is discussed, with special emphasis on the International Coffee Agreement (ICA), the world's longest surviving commodity agreement. Commodity agreements are generally thought of as cartels established by producers for the benefit of producers. This perspective would suggest that a producer country like Papua New Guinea must continue to benefit from the ICA. In the final chapters, two main questions are considered. The first asks why the international coffee agreement has survived when other agreements have collapsed. The Second has to do with its impact on small coffee producers like Papua New Guinea, both at the level of national aggregate performance and in its effect upon the domestic structure of the Papua New Guinea coffee industry.

Chapter 11 explains why the ICA has survived, principally because coffee is unusual as an internationally traded commodity in that it is not easy to substitute one variety for another. Thus, unlike many primary commodities, the importance of taste and consumer reluctance to experiment with different tastes creates quite inflexible import/export relations in world coffee trade. International regulation of coffee through the International Coffee Organisation (ICO) not only complements, but reinforces, this already tightly structured circulation of coffee. This is achieved, it is argued, by the informal establishment under the ICA of sets of bilateral alliances made up of importers and exporters. These alliances can be ranked hierarchically according to the amount of world coffee which they control. The influence of the big importer/big exporter alliance of USA and Brazil is greater in the ICO than lesser strata such as European importers and African exporters of Robusta coffee. Chapter 12 shows how, despite the many changes to the agreements, for many years these fundamental bilateral alliances have been preserved. It is a measure of the importance of these bilateral alliances to the survival of the ICA that developments in the late 1980s, when Brazil and Colombia could not agree with the USA on the structure of a new agreement, began to cause international coffee regulation to collapse.

The effect of the structure of world coffee, and its international regulation, has been to enhance the interests of members of dominant bilateral alliances -- big producers like Brazil and Colombia and big consumers such as the USA -- rather than, as a cartel might, small producers such as Papua New Guinea. In aggregate, Papua New Guinea is disadvantaged by the ICA. Yet, like many small producers, it retains its membership of the ICO. The explanation for this curious situation is that the ICA does co-opt domestic states to police ICO quotas. It is the technocrats in the small producing states which favour membership of the ICO. The reason this co-operation occurs is because the agreement works on policing of coffee trade at state borders and therefore requires country membership. This arrangement is favoured by technocrats because it does not interfere in the domestic political and economic outcomes in any particular country.

Thus, while membership of the ICO does underdevelop the coffee industry of small producers it does not equip any particular group, except technocrats, with a power to dominate the domestic industries. International regulation and trade determine the aggregate limits of coffee development but they do not predetermine domestic political and economic structures and outcomes.

1

The Origin of the Coffee Industry in Colonial Papua New Guinea

Australian Colonialism in Papua New Guinea

Australian colonialism in Papua New Guinea was administered initially under a League of Nations mandate and, after World War II, under a United Nations Trust Territory arrangement. These international arrangements had an important impact on Australian-Papua New Guinea colonial relations. But this impact was not direct. It was felt less in what was done by the coloniser and more in what was not done. Australia did not commit atrocities in Papua New Guinea. However, nor did it display much interest in developing the territories. Exploitation did occur but this was within the boundaries of indentured labour and administrative regulation. Thus, Australia's impact was felt in the way it imposed an administered structure of taxation requirements, labour contracts, encouraged free contributory labour on roads and other civic projects, and through the colonisers' mild pressure to consume and produce for the market. This was exploitation of a kind, and racist, but it was exploitation of a type that could allow the whites, then and now, to think they were simply doing a job in an underdeveloped territory.

The Australian colonial regime was above all, administrative in structure and purpose. It focused more directly on social considerations -- education, health, law, etc. -- rather than on economic development. When industrial and economic development was considered at all by the colonisers, it was usually as infrastructure, rather than in terms of the need to construct a self-sustaining economy. Indeed, there was resistance to economic development among the administrators especially if this meant fostering aggressive, indigenous entrepreneurs. The Australian Department of External Territories, which administered Papua New Guinea from Canberra after World War II until Independence in 1975 was not run like the British Colonial Office.

It did not develop a core of Oxbridge-trained administrators who were hostile to capitalism. Rather, the colonisers' resistance to capitalism, expressed in the policy of gradual development -- which proposed that all indigenous people should develop at the same pace -- was a pragmatic response to the circumstances. It made a 'virtue' out of a necessity, because a financially strapped Administration, in a colony of virtually no interest to most people in Australia, with Paul Hasluck, a Minister of undoubted ability but who was relatively lightweight in the Menzies cabinets, had little choice. Hasluck was reduced to begging each year for increases in the territories' meagre budget.

Such entrepreneurial drive as was allowed to exist was provided by a small number of white settlers. They were to be backed by infrastructural provision from the Department. At least, this is the relationship the Department of External Territories would have liked to have had. The parameters of this relationship were, however, contested. Colonial politics revolved around the pull of resources from a penny-pinching Administration and the push of the whites to have it go beyond the provision of minimal infrastructure. The outcome, in the economic history of Papua New Guinea, was a colonial experience that caused even greater regional fragmentation and diversity than already existed geographically and culturally. Benign neglect occurred in regions not attractive to white settlers. Stunted development occurred in those regions where white settlers could 'make a quid'.

The Administration, adopting the economic way of thinking of the period, usually favoured development in Papua New Guinea which was complementary to Australia's stage of industrial development. This meant that Papua New Guinea's exports should match Australia's exports. Invariably, this dogma placed the colony in the role of supplier of raw material for Australian transformation and consumption. This economic way of thinking was influential in Britain in the period after the war and found a receptive audience in the Menzies government. It was, of course, a misguided approach. It represented less a fear of colonial competition and rather more a conceptual belief in linear development -- that countries pass through stages of growth -- and a commitment to the crudest analysis of comparative advantage. It was racist but benign when applied to economies. However, when applied to people it was racist and malevolent, especially when, as so often happened, it turned into its opposite and became a policy for suppression of development and discouragement of individual improvement.

Arabica coffee is an industry in which white settlers found they could both 'make a quid' and get Australian assistance to develop a raw material required by Australian industry and coffee drinkers. Arabica coffee is grown in the Papua New Guinea Highlands (see map). The term 'Highlands' refers to the complex of mountain ranges, intermediate valleys and plateaus of the central

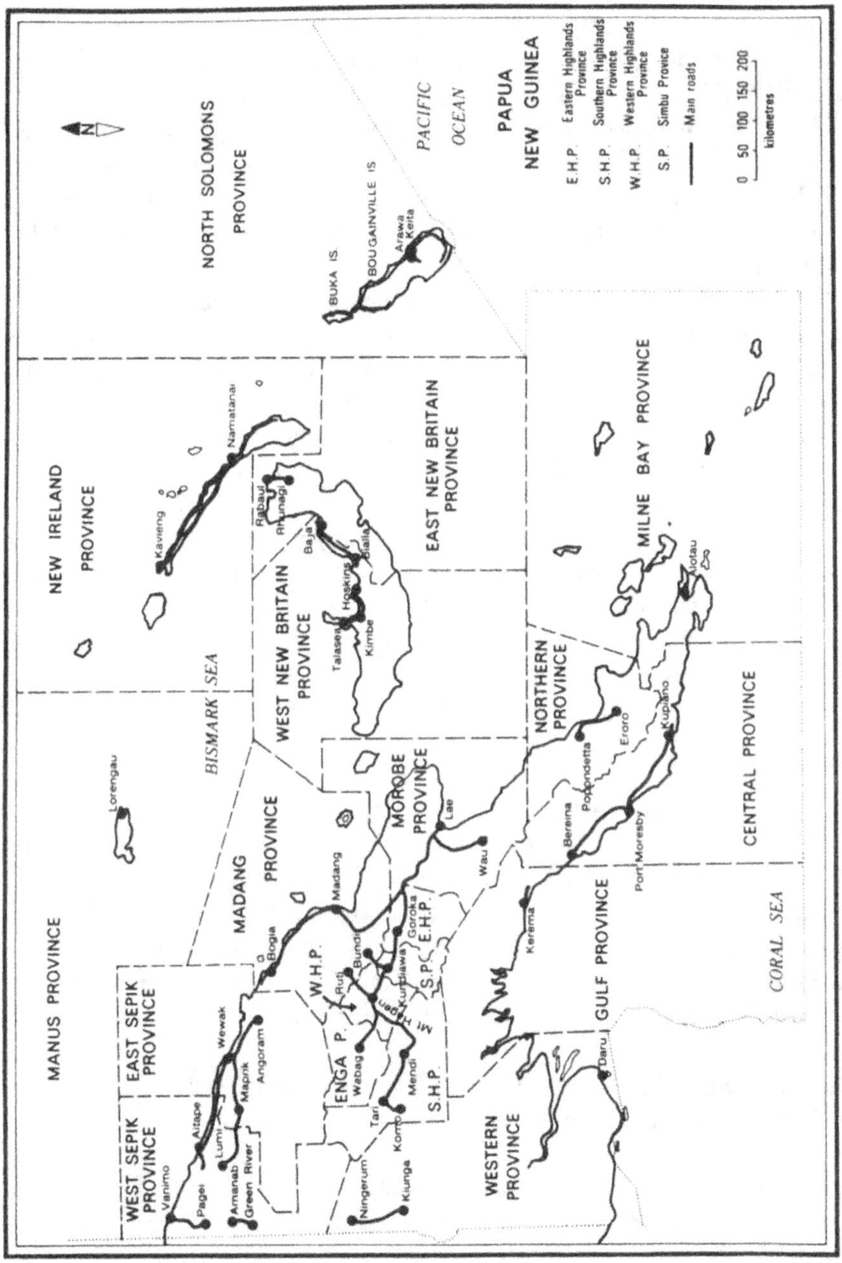
MANUS PROVINCE
NEW IRELAND PROVINCE
NORTH SOLOMONS PROVINCE
PACIFIC
OCEAN
PAPUA NEW GUINEA
E.H.P. Eastern Highlands Province
S.H.P. Southern Highlands Province
W.H.P. Western Highlands Province
S.P. Simbu Provice
Main roads
0 50 100 150 200
kilometres
BUKA IS.
BOUGAINVILLE IS.
Arawa
Keita
Namatanai
Kavieng
Rabaul
Lorengau
BISMARK SEA
WEST NEW BRITAIN PROVINCE
EAST NEW BRITAIN PROVINCE
Talasea
Hoskins
Kimbe
Bialla
MILNE BAY PROVINCE
Alotau
NORTHERN PROVINCE
Popondetta
Kupiano
CENTRAL PROVINCE
Port Moresby
CORAL SEA
GULF PROVINCE
Kerema
Daru
WESTERN PROVINCE
Kiunga
Ningerum
MOROBE PROVINCE
Lae
Wau
MADANG PROVINCE
Madang
Bogia
Goroka
E.H.P.
S.P.
W.H.P.
S.H.P.
ENGA P.
Wabag
Mendi
Tari
Mt Hagen
EAST SEPIK PROVINCE
Wewak
Maprik
Angoram
WEST SEPIK PROVINCE
Vanimo
Aitape
Lumi
Amanab
Green River

cordillera, among which are the Hindenburg, Kubor, Schrader, Bismarck and Kratke ranges of mountains, the Wahgi, Chimbu, Goroka and Bululo valleys and the Kainantu plateau. The physical characteristics of the Highlands region make it highly suitable for coffee production. As described by Howlett, "the terrain is characterised by steep, often sheer slopes, sharp ridges, the scenes of innumerable landslides and swift rivers in the steep narrow valleys". (Howlett 1967:33–34) The high altitudes and the accompanying temperature and rainfall patterns make the Highlands climate "on the whole regarded as favourable for coffee production". (Barrie 1956:4)

The Goroka valley and the Kainantu plateau, which together make up the Eastern Highlands Province, contain the optimal physical and climatic conditions for growing coffee. The Goroka valley is really a series of valleys which occur between mountain ranges, such as Mount Otto and the Asaro ranges. It is drained by two rivers, the Asaro and the Bena Bena. The Goroka valley is known for its mild temperatures -- much lower than those on coastal lowlands -- relatively low humidity and cool nights. Goroka town was the first Highlands town to be established (1939) and it became an important transport and market centre both because of its strategic location at the heart of the highlands and because of its attraction for white settlers. Goroka also became and remains the centre of the Highlands coffee industry. The Coffee Industry Board (previously the Coffee Marketing Board) is located in Goroka as is the country's largest coffee exporter, ANGCO. Goroka was the area in which pioneers of the coffee industry, Jim Leahy and Ian Downs, settled and established the first coffee plantations. For these reasons, the empirical work for this study is based on the Goroka valley.[1]

The development of the commercial coffee industry in Papua New Guinea Highlands was from the beginning marked by the same distinctive historical circumstances as foreign penetration of the Highlands itself. In particular, the key role played by white individuals and the administrative state, the backwardness of existing social relations and the lateness of penetration were characteristic of both penetration and the development of the coffee industry.

The 'gold that grows on trees': white planter success in the early days of the coffee industry

Small areas of Arabica coffee were first planted in the Highlands at Kainantu and Korn farm (Mount Hagen) as early as 1935. Little more was planted before 1939 except at Wau. Many of these early plantings were by missions, hence in very small quantities. During World War II, it appears that the Australian New Guinea Administrative Unit (ANGAU) may also have experimented with small areas of coffee production. In addition, robusta coffee has been grown in coastal areas of Papua New Guinea since the turn of the century. Coffee exports from New Guinea in the years preceding the war were slowly increasing but still totalled only 74 tons in 1940–41.

The first person to grow coffee commercially in the Highlands was Jim Leahy. He and his brothers, Mick and Dan, were the first white men to explore the Eastern Highlands, in 1933. Jim later took up residence at Goroka where a village west of the township offered him 150 acres, and the Administration, although it had misgivings about encouraging white settlement in the Highlands, granted him residency and finally an agricultural lease. This was in 1947, the year he planted his first six acres of coffee. Dan and Jim Leahy were not rich men. Dan recalls that the money he spent on the failed Kuta coffee plantation -- £40,000 to £50,000 -- almost broke him. Jim stated that the main reason he went in for coffee and not tea was because it could be grown economically in practically any amount and because coffee processing machinery was relatively simple and inexpensive. (Finney 1973:44)

The period 1948–51 was the trial period for white settlement in the Highlands as far as the Administration was concerned. It was not then encouraging alienation of land from indigenous ownership and only about half a dozen plantations were established in this period. But in 1952, the Administration abruptly changed its tune and in May of that year it publicly opened the Highlands to applications for land alienations. (Finney 1973:44–45) In the following July, Jim Leahy harvested coffee from his original six acres. It was "a year of world shortage, and the price he was paid, seven and ninepence a pound, has never been equalled in Papua New Guinea since. Then everyone started to plant it." (Ashton 1978:191) The land rush was on. Ian Downs, then Acting Director of the Department of District Services and Native Affairs, was sent to Goroka to investigate. This land rush, with which Downs was later to become personally involved, resulted in the alienation of dozens of agricultural properties in Goroka, totalling 3,550 acres between 1952 and 1954, a tenfold increase over the acreage alienated during the previous three years.

The amount of land leased to Europeans in the years 1952–54 was also high. "Prior to 1952, 4,833 acres was leased to Europeans in the central highlands but with the lifting of the last restrictions on settlement in 1952 in the next two years nearly three times this amount, 13,109 acres, was leased" (Donaldson and Good n.d.:146), although this was still a small area compared with the total area of the Goroka valley. (Finney 1973:45) It was, however, enough to ensure that by 1955 the plantation section of the industry was basically established in the form in which it exists today and that plantations would dominate the coffee industry in the early years of colonialism.

In 1955 there were 55 European holdings in the Eastern Highlands, out of 76 in the Highlands as a whole. Today there are 44 large plantations in the Eastern Highlands and 88 in the Highlands overall. In 1955, plantation holdings in the Eastern Highlands covered 14,642 acres of land although only 2,026 acres were under cash crop cultivation. Today 12,800 hectares of land are covered by large plantations, of which some 10,800 hectares are under cash crop cultivation (mainly coffee). In 1955, 45 non-indigenous and more than 2,000 indigenous workers were employed on these plantations. By 1954, although the plantations had only been established in the previous four years, the Highlands had established itself as the second largest coffee-bearing area in New Guinea.

Today Highlands coffee totally dominates the coffee industry and the plantation sector remains proportionally an efficient and important part of that industry. While the bulk of coffee is produced by smallholders, and they own by far the bulk of coffee trees, the high productivity of plantations makes their contribution to production an important one.

The settlers lost little time expanding their influence beyond production into both marketing and the political sphere. Jim Leahy bought out a number of other plantations in partnership with his Collins and Leahy nephews. In 1960 he led a syndicate of three in buying Asaro plantation from Jim Taylor, a move west which culminated in Collins-Leahy setting up and managing the first coffee processing factory in Chimbu at Kundiawa. In the east, Collins-Leahy spread as far as the purchase of Mick Leahy's Markham Valley property, and established trade stores and marketing channels in Kainantu. (Ashton 1978:192) Jim Leahy was primarily interested in the commercial and agricultural development of the coffee industry, though he was responsible with Jim Taylor and George Greathead in founding in 1953 the first political association in the industry, the Highlands Farmers and Settlers Association (HFSA). In 1956, Ian Downs resigned as District Commissioner and

> with a feeling of relief . . . I entered the private sector as a beginner to join in the expansion of the coffee industry and face the marketing problems that would have to be overcome before coffee could make so much more possible for the Highland people . (Downs 1978:246-247)

Downs became the key political figure in the development of the coffee industry in the 1960s, as founding Chairman of the Coffee Marketing Board to February 1965 and then as President of the HFSA from 1956 to 1968.

Much of the work of Downs and the HFSA was intensely political. The need for political action and organisation began virtually with the first substantial quantity of coffee production in Papua New Guinea. The problem was that of finding a market for a crop that had increased from 87 tons in 1953-54 to over 2,000 tons in 1960. When a panic about markets began in 1959-60 the estimated 1961 crop was 3,000 tons, with a carry-over from 1960 of nearly 300 tons. (Cartledge 1978:54) The HFSA began a campaign in January 1959 to ensure that the coffee industry in Papua New Guinea would not be inhibited due to its inability to find a marketing outlet for the crop. Related to this campaign was the Administration's change of policy to discontinue active promotion of coffee planting by smallholders, though assistance was still given freely when sought and plantings continued at a high rate.

The main activity of the Administration and the HFSA in this period was to establish a most-favoured nation agreement with Australia for Papua New Guinea coffee. The 1959–60 season was the first year that many trees would come into bearing and it was also the first that a lot of coffee from Papua New Guinea had to be marketed(Cartledge 1978:52) The HFSA argued for a 1 shilling per pound duty on coffee coming into Australia from places other than Papua New Guinea. This would, according to the HFSA, allow Papua New Guinea to take its rightful place in the Australian market. The Australian Treasury and Department of Trade were against any attempts to apply new duties, and argued that any such measure was contrary to the International Coffee Agreement (ICA) and also to GATT. (Cartledge 1978:67) However, they did offer Papua New Guinea a remission of the existing duty of threepence per pound for new coffee. The offer was made at a somewhat acrimonious meeting in March 1961 and was grudgingly accepted by Papua New Guinea in August 1961 as a temporary measure pending Tariff Board enquiry. The Papua New Guinea growers were of the opinion that the threepence remission did not provide sufficient incentive to clear the market and in any case did not offer an incentive for Australian manufacturers to take increasing amounts of Papua New Guinea coffee as production continued to expand. The HFSA began an intensive lobbying campaign during the period between August 1961 and the Tariff Board enquiry of April 1962, and achieved great success. Not only did the HFSA manage to have existing duty on coffee raised, but Papua New Guinea coffee was given very high levels of remission on other coffee if large quantities of Papua New Guinea coffee were taken. (Cartledge 1978:64–65)

Coffee production in Papua New Guinea was also given special treatment when Australia entered the 1962 and 1968 ICAs on behalf of its colony. The 1962 and 1968 ICAs in coffee made specific allowance for the colonial relationship. Article 67 of the 1962 ICA stated that: "Any government may, at the time of signature or deposit of an instrument of acceptance, ratification or accession, or at any time thereafter, by notification of the Secretary–General of the United Nations, declare that the agreement shall extend to any of the territories for whose international relations it is responsible, and the Agreement shall extend to the territories named therein from the date of such notification."

The wording of Article 67 does not make clear in what manner the dependent territory's exports are tied to the metropolitan country's imports. Is it the case, for example, that the dependent territory's *de facto* export quota under the agreement is the amount of coffee it can sell to its metropolitan power (i.e. the contracting party to the agreement)? Is the dependent territory forbidden under Article 67 to export to other countries? Or, conversely, is it the case that a dependent territory's export quota is the same amount of coffee as the import quota of the contracting party to the agreement? In other words, can Papua New Guinea under Article 67 export 156,000 bags, regardless of what portion goes to Australia? Finally, what happens under the agreement when the exports of the dependent territories begin to exceed the imports of the contracting party to the agreement? Is this extra coffee non-market coffee? Is it time for the colony to be given its own export quota, or can the contracting party to the agreement with its dependent territory become, in effect, an exporting group and be given a joint export quota? If so, does the importing country receive votes in the International Coffee Organisation (ICO), according to its importing status or its exporting status by virtue of its tied relationship with an exporting dependent territory? These problems became central to the 1966–67 crisis in Papua New Guinea -- when its production increased beyond the limit allowed to be exported to Australia -- for they gave rise to the phenomenon of netting, the belief on the part of planters that Papua New Guinea could export to member markets an amount equivalent to the import quota given to Australia. We will see in Chapter 5 how the politics of the 1966–67 crisis drew the planters in Papua New Guinea into conflict with the metropolis and the Administration over the extent to which the former as guardian of the international agreement should interpret it in a way that put a squeeze on plantation capital in Papua New Guinea.

The HFSA supported a policy, embodied both in the International Coffee Agreement and in the most-favoured nation remissions of duty, which would link territory production with Australian imports. The HFSA argued that such a linkage was necessary because the coffee industry in Papua New Guinea was in the early stages of development and because marketing conditions were difficult in the early 1960s. The HFSA argued strongly "that in theory and practice New Guinea may never produce sufficient coffee to meet the total Australian requirements". (Cartledge 1978:29) However, the establishment and reinforcement of a linkage between Territory coffee production and Australian importers -- both through the ICA and through the remission of import duty in Australia -- created a much more complicated political situation in the industry. This was 1960, a time when most of the rest of the world was being decolonised and newly independent nations were eager to see the process of decolonisation completed throughout the world. The process of structuring Papua New Guinea's economy to be complementary to Australia's, firmly accepted by all political actors in Papua New Guinea, was regarded with suspicion in other places. Thus, the linkage between Territory production and Australian imports had to be made on the basis that this was good for the industry as a whole and was not a result of collusion between white planters and metropolitan or colonial state officials. The high profile taken by the HFSA did not help to lend legitimacy to the idea that the linkage was in the interests of the industry as a whole. For these reasons, and because the operation of the ICA demanded it, there developed in the early 1960s a need to establish a Papua New Guinea coffee authority of some kind.

The establishment of the Coffee Marketing Board (CMB) and the outline of its functions was done within the framework of political relations as described. It was the metropolitan Departments, the colonial Administration and the planters who discussed the CMB and decided on its future. After some discussion and confusion as to what powers the authority should have, it was finally set up in August 1964.

It is difficult to determine whether the push for a PNG coffee authority came from inside or outside Papua New Guinea. Cartledge claims that the initial push came from the HFSA, though he notes that "the Tariff Board Report of April 1962, released in November 1962, also favoured the establishment of a Coffee Marketing Board (CMB)". (Cartledge 1978:71) Presumably the Department of Trade, signatories to the agreement, realised that the policing of the agreement required the regulation of exports through the allocation and licensing of exporters and the issuing of coffee stamps, and that this could be properly done only by an agency within the dependent territory. It does appear, at least according to Cartledge, that the colonial Administration and the Department of External Territories were 'cool on the idea'. (Cartledge 1978:71) Perhaps the Administration was fearful that the CMB would be captured by the HFSA and that the Administration's authority over the industry would be reduced. They were certainly opposed to the suggestion of the HFSA that the CMB take compulsory control of the marketing of territory coffee. (Cartledge 1978:32) This idea was quickly shelved and it seems certain that the Department of Trade would also have been opposed to a CMB function of this kind.

Although it was not given authority to undertake marketing of Papua New Guinea coffee overseas, the CMB was expected to exercise a good deal of control over exports. The CMB has always been seen in Papua New Guinea as being primarily concerned with international coffee relations, with exporters and the ICA, and there have rarely been serious suggestions that the CMB monopolise or delegate monopoly control at the internal level.

Nevertheless, this section shows that the Administration and the white planters moved quickly to cement their control over the industry. They were guided by ideas of complementarity in economic development of Papua New Guinea with Australia which justified their tight control of the industry and which had implications for the role of indigenous Papua New Guineans in the coffee industry. The HFSA stated that while failure by 'native' people (at the time owning about 55 percent of total trees in Highlands) to sell coffee will not impair their actual subsistence, such failure will amount to a government blunder in encouraging a vital avenue of economic development. The HFSA believed that the future economic development of New Guinea should be integrated with the Australian economy and that in the case of coffee, a crop which could not be grown in Australia, New Guinea "growers should receive the same support and encouragement customarily given to the Australian producer on the mainland". (Cartledge 1978:29–30)

The spread of coffee production to black households

The first indigenous plantings of coffee in the Highlands in the Asaro valley of the Eastern Highlands, was in 1952. The smallholder industry really began, however, in 1954. From the beginning, the growth of the smallholder coffee industry was spectacular,

> plantings by indigenes soon exceeded those of Europeans so that by 1961–62 over 60 percent of all coffee acreage and about 43 percent of the output was under indigenous control. On the assumption that in most cases 'native' coffee units are one quarter of an acre (and the average is probably less than this) a large number of 'native' families obtained a cash income from coffee production after only 8 years of planned extension effort. (Cartledge 1978:42)

However, the halt in extension around 1960 hardly affected the growth in smallholder production. Smallholder coffee production had shown a steady upward trend in the 1960s. From 1966–67, when smallholders were producing 10,600 tonnes, to 1975–76, when they produced 29,900 tonnes, the growth of smallholder production was about 12 percent per annum. (Anderson 1977:71) By 1977 the major producers of coffee were the smallholders, whose average 450 coffee trees were added to their subsistence gardens. By then there were over 200,000 smallholder coffee growers who were producing over 70 percent of the total coffee crop. (Anderson 1974:4)

The smallholders who began growing coffee in the 1950s in the Highlands were not producing commodities for sale in a market in the period before penetration. Coffee was, in most cases, the first commodity they produced. They were extremely 'backward' societies, a term used in a technical sense to indicate first, that the unit of production was based on the household and usually on a gender or age division of labour rather than one of skill, and second, that socio-economic authority was both vertically and horizontally contained. This was done horizontally in the sense that the spread of exchange relations was limited in a given territory by its kinship nature, and vertically because authority could be exercised only at the level of exchange and not production. I will show in this section that coffee, despite its commodity status, was incorporated into 'backward' households.

Prior to penetration, development was based on the rudimentary development of the productive forces and a division of labour based on gender and age, not skill (Salisbury 1962:49). The principal food crop in the Highlands was sweet potatoes which formed about 90 percent of the diet of

Gorokans. (Howlett 1967:66) According to Finney (1973:10), the sweet potato revolution was the main reason the population has always been high in the Highlands, because good conditions allowed it to mature in as little as four months. The raising of pigs also helped population growth. The households and the clan which they made up were expected to be self-sustaining, while the producers were expected to consume the fruits of their production. They were able to do this because the producer was not alienated from the land and the labour required to produce food. The major exception in the Highlands to the production of things for use was, as Gregory shows, the production of things for gifts and ceremonial exchange, especially pigs. (Gregory 1982:91) Leadership in Highland societies took place at the level of the clan and principally in relation to ceremonial and gift exchanges. Some Big Men could amass wealth and prestige, i.e. pigs to lead the clan in these exchanges with other clans. There was no formal office of leadership.

It is clear that neither the rudimentary nature of the organisation of use-production and gift exchanges, nor the social structure based on the role of the big man, as clan leader, proved a barrier to the introduction of cash crops. However, what is not clear is precisely why this should be so and, once commodity production for exchange in market is introduced, precisely what changes occur in the system of use-production and gift exchange and the system of leadership as a result of this. The standard answer to this question is to focus on the role of the Big Man, and argue that, as his status was achieved through the amassing of ceremonial and wealth gift-things for exchange, the traditional culture was pre-adapted to the amassing of money from the sale of commodities by modern entrepreneurs. (Finney 1978:108)

It is the entrepreneurial skill pre-existing in traditional society which Finney argues explains the growth of the coffee industry. There are a number of objections to this argument. A major one, as Standish has argued, may be that the belief that Big Man status is *achieved* is an overstatement: Big Men are often Big Men because they have 'hereditary advantage', there being advantages for members of certain lineages and even instances of succession to leadership in Highlands societies. (Standish 1978:33) While the question of ascription or achievement is important for the general question of leadership in Highlands society, it may not be very important at all in terms of the spread of coffee production.

What would seem more important than leadership in the spread of coffee production is the capacity for it to be incorporated into existing production units. The spread of coffee occurred throughout the Highlands very rapidly and in many cases long before the benefits of its exchange were known. This is because coffee takes some three to four years to bear. Obviously those who planted it expected a return, but its success as an innovation may be less to do with the demonstration effect of leadership and more with the fact that coffee production could be incorporated into the existing household reproduction cycle. Coffee could be produced on customary land with a marginal improvement in rudimentary tools. Because it could be produced at the household level where the division of labour was ascribed and therefore not under the influence of the Big Man, the incorporation of coffee into the household reproduction cycle did not, in the first instance, disrupt established social and political roles in the clan. I will show in a later section just how rudimentary and limited is coffee production at the household level.

Smallholder coffee production does not appear to threaten existing power relations, for it is incorporated into the householder reproduction cycle. As Bernstein (1977:63) shows, the peasant household can continue to produce use values[2] alongside its production of commodities. Indeed, the plot of coffee may be so small as to appear irrelevant and to have little or no bearing upon the household's social relations. Bernstein shows how quantitative measures -- say only 20 percent of labour time spent on commodity production -- also give the impression that production of the commodity is merely an adjunct to subsistence. However, once commodities have become incorporated into the household reproduction cycle, so also do the conditions necessary to produce the commodity (i.e. supply of seed, land) become internalised in the reproduction cycle to the extent that reproduction of the whole household can no longer take place without the production of the commodity side of its activities

> in other words, commodity production becomes an economic necessity. To meet its needs for cash the household produces commodities which become, through the circuit of exchange, material elements of constant capital (raw materials) and variable capital (food). (Bernstein 1977:63)

This has a profound effect on the relations of the household to other social actors. Instead of being subsumed under a clan, the household comes to relate to capital. In the long term this leads not to an enhancement of the role of Big Men, as Finney would argue, but perhaps to a demise in their status if that is based on exchange of use values. The Big Man's authority is supplanted or at least shared by authority exercised by various interests in the production and supply of cash crops such as coffee buyers, processing plants, exporters and the state.

The production of commodities by the household brings the household into indirect struggle with capital. Capital aims, as always, to appropriate the surplus from the exchange of commodities. Struggle in this case is 'silent', muted by the fact that the conditions of backwardness still apply at the level of production of the smallholders. In a smallholder industry, by definition, production is taking place at the household level. The household producers cannot be as easily disciplined as wage labourers because they continue to own the means of production. This is the second aspect to the continuation of backwardness which exists in the smallholder industry. Short of destruction of an entire stratum of an industry, capital has no possibility of increasing its share of the surplus in the orthodox and most durable way, through re–organisation of production along the lines of a division of labour based on the sale of labour power in a market. Capital is thus reduced to three main ways of increasing its share of the surplus: (1) intensification of household labour in producing the commodity through a deterioration of the domestic terms of trade; (2) plundering the surplus through export taxation; or (3) freeing one of the productive forces, land, from household control. The role of the state is crucial for all three ways. The aim of the private actors in many developing countries is to link their demands with the banner of the state.

The analysis of smallholders borrowed from Bernstein posits a dual contradiction in primary producing developing countries: firstly, the capital–labour relations in which the owners of capital aim, usually with assistance from the state, to realise greater profits by extending the working day (absolute surplus value) and/or improving technology in the workplace (relative surplus value); secondly, the petty commodity–state relation in which small growers face a state which aims to increase its share of the surplus by intensifying exchange relations (by artificially lowering the price of the commodity from the grower by monopoly purchase, taxes, etc.). Bernstein's analysis has the advantage of putting 'the state' and the huge group of 'smallholders' (both aspects neglected by Marx himself), visible to all who visit the Third World, at the centre of the analysis. It has the disadvantage of complicating the analysis beyond the two–class schema and introducing ambiguity into key terms like 'capitalism', 'exploitation' and 'class'. This occurs because the peasant–state relation is one based on price, not on production.

Gibbon and Neocosmos (1985) object to Bernstein's approach (as has MacWilliam [1984] to the author's work in another context), arguing it is capitalism which brings the smallholders into existence, not states, and that the smallholder is similar to the *petit bourgeois* element in Marx's work, merely displaced to a developing country environment. The shoemaker and the tailor are no different from the smallholder, they argue. They regard the term 'peasant' used by Bernstein for smallholder as a throwback to its subjectivist usage, pioneered by Chayanov. It must be acknowledged that Bernstein's terminology is often subjectivist and classificatory. Gibbon and Neocosmos's most serious criticism, however, is that the approach leads to a proliferation of class labels – – interest groups by another name – – and loses the rigor of Marxist analysis.

It will be argued here, however, that there is indeed a great difference between the tailor in the developed country and the smallholder in the developing country, a difference not based on subjective assumptions about 'peasantisation', but a difference as fundamental as the difference between capital and labour. Capital owns the means of production, and this gives it the power to accumulate. Accumulation is based on investment in plant and equipment and other factors to turn money into capital. A tailor can certainly borrow and invest but a smallholder cannot or does not. When, of course, a smallholder does invest and/or employ labour, he/she becomes a middle peasant or a big peasant which is certainly equivalent to the *petit bourgeoisie*. This outcome is neither a weakness in the analysis nor bound to lead to a proliferation of class categories but merely a recognition of the unique features of Third World capitalist accumulation in agriculture. Bernstein's work is based on this empirical location and it is to be preferred to the more dogmatic views of his critics.

A colony built on coffee beans: the important role played by the colonial administration in the origin of the coffee industry

The colonial state played a role in supplying seed and keeping Papua New Guinea coffee free of disease. (*New Guinea Highlands Bulletin*, October 1965) The state also had an effect upon the factors of production -- land, labour and capital -- in the early coffee industry. Land is the most important factor of production then and now, the most difficult to regulate and the area of most vital concern to the plantation and smallholder sectors of the coffee industry (and indeed all other agricultural industries in Papua New Guinea). Until World War II, land in Papua New Guinea was regulated by the Regulation Ordinance of 1888 which prohibited private buyers from dealing in land.

However, after the war, dealing in land began. In the Highlands, regulation of this trade devolved upon the District Commissioner who, at the time of the establishment of the plantation industry in Eastern Highlands, was Ian Downs. Hasluck (Minister for Territories, 1951–1963) wrote:

> strictly in conformity with policy, no acquisitions were to be made in disregard of the present and prospective land needs of the native people themselves, but in fact we were back to the days of 'Have a yarn with the district commissioner and he will fix you up'. In practice the district commissioner with the best of intentions and with an undoubted idea of bringing benefits to the native population had become a promoter of settlement. (Hasluck 1975:121)[3]

Hasluck intervened to stop the land rush which resulted but the land problems were never solved by the colonial Administration. The package of land bills presented finally in 1963 were not workable in terms of detailing the processes of inquiry into customary lands. The Bills aimed to speed up land tenure conversion to freehold and leasehold suitable for use as large-scale agricultural units, i.e. plantations, but all they achieved was policy dominance from the centre and virtually no change in customary land tenure patterns.

Labour was the other vital productive force which was affected by the role of the colonial state. The colonial labour laws were complex, covering almost every conceivable aspect of the contract under which labour was recruited, employed and repatriated and the conditions under which labourers lived while they were at their place of work. (West 1958:90) Colonial labour laws, like land, were affected by changes occurring during the war but this had less to do with the disruption to labour caused by the war and more to do with the economic growth which followed it, as in the coffee industry, where labour was in short supply in the time after the war. In labour legislation, there was also a move toward centralisation and control of labour -- most evident in the Highlands Labour Scheme -- though the initiative in this area seems to have lain less with Hasluck and the metropolis and more with the Administration. Perhaps related to this fact is the point that, unlike colonial land laws, colonial labour laws actually worked, achieving their purpose. This was the prevention of full proletarianisation not, as the Administration often claimed, to ease indigenes through the transition from village to modernity, nor even to ensure the village would subsidise the labourer, but rather, via manipulation of conditions and contracts, to ensure that wages would remain fixed at low levels. It became especially important after the war, in conditions of labour shortage, that wages remain unaffected by market determinants such that labourers might find alternative, non-regulated employment. In achieving this purpose, colonial labour legislation and the requirements of the planters in the coffee industry were compatible in a way that colonial land policy was not.

The effect of the colonial state on the other major productive force, capital, was also significant but largely because of the neglect of state expenditure on agriculture in colonial Papua New Guinea. In New Guinea, where coffee was grown, only some $2,771,433 was spent by the Department of Agriculture, Stock and Fisheries (DASF) in the year to June 1966. This was almost double the $1,361,702 spent by DASF in the year to June 1962. This increase clearly reflects the 'development push' that began in the colony in the mid-1960s. But the amount spent on agriculture in New Guinea in 1966 was far below that spent on Public Health ($6,118,632), Education ($6,901,761), District Administration ($2,939,632), Stores and Supplies ($4,949,349) and Capital Works and Services ($7,750,725). Thus directly productive areas were neglected in favour of infrastructural development and social services as late as 1966, and agriculture -- the sector that provided a living for most people in the country -- was receiving only some 5 percent of expenditure from revenue in New Guinea and only 4 percent of expenditure from revenue in the territories combined in 1966. (Territory of New Guinea Report for 1965-66:291; Territory of Papua Report for 1965-66:251)

The Administration intervened in the coffee industry more directly often in ways smallholders found difficult to understand. At the time the CMB was being established, ostensibly because controlled marketing was "particularly in the interests of the local people" (Cartledge 1978:76), the Administration was acting against their interests by withdrawing its support for smallholder coffee production. This withdrawal of support was presented by the Administration (through its functional agency for coffee, DASF) as merely a failure to stimulate the smallholder industry. It was emphasised by DASF, however, that smallholders would be offered assistance should they request it. (Finney 1973:66) This decision came after great pressure was applied to the Administration by planters, and the CMB to close down the smallholder industry because planters "felt that the surplus stock and marketing problems had arisen largely because of governmental policy to allow continued expansion of indigenous plantings". (Cartledge 1978:202)

The description of the origin of the coffee industry does not provide convincing evidence that the colonial state acted as an instrument in the service of white planters. Thus, while this state called a halt to smallholder expansion, it did not back this up with its full coercive power, as it might have done. The land policy of the state also generated a degree of hostility toward the state from planters. Downs labelled the Administration as 'indifferent and incompetent' in its approach to agriculture, and felt administrative structure and policy were interfering with any possibility of agricultural officers in the field getting results. (Downs 1967:12) To complicate matters further, the closeness of the metropolis to the colony has meant that an explanation of the role of the state must include the fact that the metropolitan state was active in pursuing interests which sometimes conflicted with both the Administration's and planters' interests. This was undoubtedly the case in land policy, but it was also the case in other areas where the metropolis intervened in policy either to enhance its direct control or to restrict its capital outlays in the Territory. In other instances, as in the case of the Tariff Board Inquiry, the metropole could accommodate the demands of the Administration and the planters providing this did not conflict too seriously with the metropolis' international interests and the interests of its bourgeoisie, in this case instant coffee manufacturers in Australia. All these factors make the task of explaining the role of the state complex, an issue to which we will return in Chapter 4.

Notes

1. This is an important point for it should not be assumed that what follows, in its specific detail, can apply to the Papua New Guinea Arabica coffee industry as a whole. In Chimbu, for example, where the terrain is much steeper and population density much higher, and where a plantation industry was not established in colonial times, the development of the Chimbu coffee industry has taken a very different path. (See B. Standish [1981] for some detail on Chimbu coffee.)

2. Use values: the 'characteristic' of usefulness, that is, satisfaction of human wants. This can be contrasted with exchange values. Commodities are goods, possessing use value produced by human labour. Exchange commodities, therefore, have a value which is quite distinct and different from their use-value; they have a value in exchange, or exchange value.

3. Hasluck, as Parker (1966) shows, had taken advantage of the geographical proximity to Australia of Papua new Guinea to 'centralise' administration. The Administrator's role however, was confined within much narrower limits than that of the Governor in a British colony. Parker writes: "Though his [the Administrator's] administration is responsible in New Guinea for nearly the whole of the functions which are carried out in Australia by state and federal governments together, his administrative discretion and authority are in practice scarcely equivalent to those of a single department in Canberra." (Parker 1966:196)

2

Producing Coffee

Introduction

The first chapter has shown many interesting features of the colonial coffee industry in Papua New Guinea. It also raised some challenging questions. How powerful were white planters in the industry? Would smallholders go on to become planters themselves? Why did the colonial state seem to operate in such a contradictory way, sometimes assisting the white planters and sometimes not? The answers to these questions about social and political outcomes in an industry is to be found, this book argues, in the 'hidden abode of production'. That is, in order to explain social and political relations in an industry, it is necessary to know how a commodity is produced. This is certainly not the way industries are usually examined. It would be more common to analyse them in terms of price competitiveness, relative efficiency of smallholders compared with plantations, or the price responsiveness of smallholders. Such an analysis would find that the coffee industry in Papua New Guinea is highly competitive at the level of production and exchange. (World Bank 1981:6) This competitiveness is often taken to mean that smallholders benefit from the operation of the market in a way they do not benefit in other state-dominated coffee industries.

This rosy picture does not describe an industry which many smallholders would recognise. By ignoring production and politics, it fails to describe the antagonistic social and political relations which most smallholders experience as enhancing the development of the powerful while frustrating them. These unequal relations are established at the level of production. The following sections examine the technicalities of plantation production in the colonial period, though these conditions are little changed today and thus also apply as a description of contemporary plantations. Plantation production is contrasted with the techniques adopted by smallholders in their gardens.

How a plantation operated in the colonial period

The original white planters were attracted to the production of coffee because of the low level and inexpensive nature of the means of production. The BAE survey (1961) showed that the major investment made by the white planters in coffee was in land and plantings and plant and machinery. Capital outlay was small: "for the 30 plantations [surveyed by the BAE in 1959] the average capital investment per acre of total coffee planted was 444 pounds with a range between 277 and 853 pounds". (Cartledge 1978:46) The white planters were competitive capitalists. Their location in production imposed severe limitations on their self-expansion and accumulation.

The original thirty settlers were particularly fortunate in their acquisition of land for they managed to obtain agricultural leases in Goroka ranging from 36 acres to 410 acres - - though the optimum area for European settlement was 200 acres - - before the land rush and before the authorities clamped down on the alienation of land. (Finney 1973:51) The alienated land was obviously valuable but, due to the low and regulated price at which they acquired it and the fact that transactions in land soon ceased to be legal, it became difficult to put a value on plantation land. The clampdown on land did not seem to adversely affect the original settlers in the pioneering phase. (Finney 1973:48) A feature of plantation development, according to Beckford (1983), is under-utilisation of land on the plantation for, where land is low in cost and the future reasonably bright, planters will attempt to secure more land than they need or have the capacity to use. This was the way in which the coffee plantation industry developed also. (Cartledge 1978:117)

The second main area of investment undertaken by white planters in the pioneering phase was, according to the BAE survey, investment in plant and machinery (12 percent), mainly in processing equipment. The purpose of processing is to separate the green coffee bean, the bean of 'commerce' as Haarer (1962:256) calls it, from the berry (or 'cherry' as it is called in Papua New Guinea). 'Cherry' is the name for coffee which is ripened on the tree ready for harvesting and for coffee sold without any processing whatever. There are a number of stages to processing and a number of different methods which can be used to extract the green bean from the berry. It is important to understand the various stages of the processing of coffee because the degree of processing undertaken determines the amount of equipment required by various production units and thus influences investment. Processing is also important because its stages more or less determine the domestic marketing structure and thus the mode of appropriation of surplus which exists in coffee marketing chains. In explaining the various stages of processing, it is simplest to begin with the beans of 'commerce' which are most familiar, and work back along the processing chain to the berry itself. The beans have a very hard outer casing or hull which is retained at the 'parchment' stage of coffee processing. The beans in their hulls are separately enclosed in a mucilaginous substance which is sweet to the taste, and immediately surrounding this is the somewhat thick skin of the fruit. (Haarer 1962:256)

The process is one of stripping away the outer layers of the berry in order to recover the green coffee bean, which is the form in which coffee is sold for export to roasters or instant coffee manufacturers. The greatest overburden is to be found between the cherry and the parchment stage with a recovery rate in Papua New Guinea of only 0.18 kg of parchment coffee from 1 kg of fresh coffee cherries. Between parchment and the green coffee bean, the recovery rate is much higher, 1 kg of parchment coffee giving 0.83 kg of green coffee on largeholdings in Papua New Guinea. The recovery rates affect all calculations made in relation to coffee and will be used throughout the text (see Table 2.1).

The two different methods of processing Arabica coffee are known as the 'dry' method and the 'wet' method. The 'dry' method is used in Brazil for about 80 percent of its output and turns out low quality base beans. The 'wet' method is used in Papua New Guinea and many other places to produce high quality washed Arabica coffee. The 'dry' method is used where water is scarce and consists of spreading the beans in the sun for about three weeks. The beans go through a process of fermentation through the loss of moisture. The harder shrivelled cherry is then hulled after imperfect cherries are separated out. As Wellman notes, 'Drying may take days or even weeks depending on the cherry'. (Wellman 1961:373) The 'wet' method involves a good deal more skilful handling and specialised equipment. The 'wet' method requires that the cherries be picked when they a ripe, so as to be suitable for the next stage, pulping. The principle of pulping is to squeeze the ripe oval fruit so that the encased beans fly out under pressure from the berry. The skin of the berry can then be pulled back and discarded. At this stage the encased beans are covered with the mucilaginous substance which must be removed, otherwise the encased bean can become sticky and can pick up a taint which can ultimately dry on the parchment and affect taste. The mucilaginous substance, which can affect taste, is removed by fermentation in a vat. Fermentation does not affect taste, nor does it loosen the parchment casing. Fermentation merely removes the sticky substance. The encased bean is then washed and sun–dried, at which stage it is known as 'parchment'. The process of hulling or curing then begins with an extensive drying programme, either by sun or rotary, which takes about eight days. (Haarer 1962:271)

The beans are then ready to be hulled. Hulling is the separation of the parchment casing from the green bean itself. The hulled beans are then polished, sorted, graded and bagged for export. The principal argument in favour of the wet method is the higher quality, superior taste and therefore higher market value of the washed Arabica bean. The main argument against the 'wet' method is that it is very labour intensive. In most countries there is

TABLE 2.1 Coffee Recovery Rates

1 kg fresh coffee cherries	= 0.18 kg parchment coffee = 0.15 kg green coffee beans
1 kg parchment coffee	= 0.83 kg green coffee beans (largeholdings) = 0.80 kg green coffee beans (used by the Tariff Board)
1 kg green coffee beans	= 0.84 kg roasted coffee = 0.33 kg soluble (instant) coffee
1 kg soluble (instant) coffee	= 3.00 kg green coffee beans
1 tonne green coffee beans	= 17 bags at 60 kg net

Source: Papua New Guinea, *Rural Industries 1979*, National Statistics Office, Port Moresby.

not really a choice between 'wet' and 'dry' methods because climatic conditions can preclude the dry method as, in many countries, cherries would become mouldy or could not be properly dried in the sun. (Wellman 1981:373)

The amount of capital invested in machinery clearly depends on the stage to which processing is done on the production unit. Smallholders who sell cherry make no investment in processing equipment. Smallholders who sell parchment need to invest in a hand-operated pulper (costing currently about $A280), some concrete or wooden (but not steel) vats and blue canvas or plastic upon which to dry the seeds after fermenting. For a plantation, equipment must be bought for each stage of the processing chain and housed in a separate building. Pulper, vats, driers, garers, polishers, baggers and drying trays must be provided. The initial outlay must be substantial, but the equipment is durable. At Erinvale, Jim Leahy's old property, most of the original processing equipment was still in use in 1982. However, the investment cost is not so much in the original purchase price of the equipment but in the fact that for much of the year -- between harvest times -- the equipment lies idle.

A further problem is caused by what is known as the coffee flush, the regular tendency of Arabica coffee to bear much more heavily in alternate years. It is described by Ford as: "the biological two year bearing cycle that affects Arabica trees in particular although it is relatively unimportant for robusta trees. It has been observed that Arabica trees have a tendency to bear heavy and light crops in alternative years which has given rise to the concept of 'off' and 'on' years in the coffee producing countries of Latin America." (Ford, in Adams and Klein 1978:37)

This means that provision of processing facilities has to be made on the basis of high yielding years. This can be an expensive and wasteful outlay, especially in colonial Papua New Guinea where most colonial plantations also processed smallholder coffee to export stage. This required each plantation to maintain a processing capacity far beyond the requirements of the plantation itself. A further unusual feature of the processing on plantations in Papua New Guinea is that most plantations had the capacity to process coffee to the export stage. This meant much over-provision of equipment, but control of processing was an important factor in raising plantation returns as well as in gaining a good deal of control over the industry itself. It is perhaps a testimony to the political strength of the planter class that the right to process to the export stage was never challenged by the Administration in colonial Papua New Guinea.

Plantation agriculture is capitalist agriculture for it is the process of putting labour to work with the means of production -- land, machinery, specialised inputs such as fertilisers -- to produce a crop for sale in a market. The intensive use of labour in production of high quality washed Arabica is not confined to the plantation preparation stage, nor to specialist functions like processing. The planter's task is essentially what is 'commonly known' as management.[1] Management involves the working out of arrangements whereby labour is combined with the means of production in the most efficient manner possible. Efficient operation does not necessarily mean reducing costs. In the production of a quality product some inputs cannot be curtailed. In the case of washed Arabica production, every aspect of production has intensive labour requirements including routine maintenance work, weeding and harvesting. Also, each aspect of the processing of washed Arabica has a quality dimension (unlike 'dry' processing in Brazil) so that great care must be taken not to sacrifice quality for economy.

Most of the full-time labourers are employed in non-harvest times on routine maintenance work and weeding. Weeding is especially labour-intensive in the coffee industry for, unlike crops such as cocoa, weeding in coffee has to be done throughout the year. Adequate weeding is essential for healthy plant growth in coffee since weeds use up water and plant foods, and can cause root competition which crowds out the coffee feeder roots. This can result in stunted growth and lower yields. As Wellman says: "one thing is certain, that good coffee growing will always require attention to weeding. If coffee trees are at proper spacings, with an adequate amount of sun, on good fertile soil, weeds will necessarily flourish." (Wellman 1961:198)

Weeds are usually removed by hand, either spaded out or slashed with a bush knife. The weeds thus gathered can then be mulched and placed around the plant. This has been shown to be good for yields no matter how good the fertiliser. (Wellman 1961:201) Weeds can also be removed by chemicals (herbicides) but these need to be handled carefully by trained labourers. A large workforce is still needed for hand weeding and mulching.

Pruning is a task that also needs to be carried out if high yields are to be maintained. The objective of pruning is to remove all dead and diseased wood and maintain a balance between vegetative and flowering vegetation whereby maximum cropping is obtained without any debilitation. (Department of Agriculture, Stock and Fisheries, Territory of Papua and New Guinea 1970) Under Papua New Guinea Highlands conditions, trees give excellent yields from about the fifth to the seventh year after planting but thereafter, unless pruning is carried out, yields decrease steadily as the bulk of lateral branches and excessive vegetation growth increase. (Dick 1977:47) Pruning is done only once a year on Papua New Guinea plantations. The recommended method, which most plantations have adopted, is the multiple-stem method. A Department of Agriculture, Stock and Fisheries (DASF) pamphlet describes the multiple stem method:

> Multiple Stem -- the vertical framework is developed by capping the young seedling at about 15 inches from the ground. Two suckers then develop on either side of the immediate cap cut and usually other suckers will appear below. These suckers form the vertical growths.
>
> The usual practice is to obtain 3 or 4 sturdy growths and have them growing up together about the same size and of equal strength. Should only 2 verticals develop from capping either one or both of the verticles may be capped to produce 3 or 4 verticles as desired. As the verticles develop upwards the branches will be interlaced in the centre of the tree. However, as the verticles become taller, the weight of the crop on their upper branches and the pulling of the pickers to reach the fruit soon forces the vertical stems to bend away from each other. Thus the centre of the tree is opened up and the interlacing branches are pulled apart. (Department of Agriculture, Stock and Fisheries, Territory of Papua and New Guinea 1970, see also Downs 1966:9-13, for a detailed description of pruning methods.)

This is a more economical method of pruning than the single-stem method which requires much more attention and time for each tree. In Papua New Guinea: "pruning is generally carried out after the main crop harvest, say September-December period. A skilled pruner can prune ½ acre a day." (Department of Agriculture, Stock and Fisheries, Territory of Papua New Guinea 1970) Thus pruning is not as labour intensive as other activities on the coffee plantation.

The most labour intensive of all the activities undertaken on Papua New Guinea plantations is harvesting. This is particularly the case where high quality washed Arabica coffee is produced. The main reason this is labour intensive is that berries have to be picked when they are ripe so that they can be pulped. Once picked, the berries have to be processed within twenty-four hours or they deteriorate. Picking is very slow and cyclical for, while coffee cherries ripen mainly during a short period called the flush, which in Papua New Guinea extends from April to August, they can continue to ripen in small quantities over many months. (Papua New Guinea Coffee Industry Board 1980:8) Thus: "pickers of quality coffee must return to the same tree time and time again to pick only the ripe cherries -- an inordinate amount of labour for the two pound of clear green beans which is an average yearly yield for one tree". (Roden 1977:49)

A modest level of human skill is required to identify and pick ripe, as opposed to unripe, berries, and little investment is devoted to developing it, though poor harvesting techniques can clearly cause damage and waste.

The object of plantation agriculture is profit, an increase in monetary return and accumulation. Profit and accumulation are conceptually distinct. Unlike accumulation, profit can be realised at the level of exchange as well as in production. Profit can be realised in various ways such as reducing the relative cost of the means of production, increasing its relative efficiency, manipulating the market or taking advantage of market fluctuations. Profit is simply money return and thus can be realised without reorganising the relations of production. Accumulation, which occurs only at the level of production, is a process based solely on the appropriation of surplus labour. Surplus labour is the excess value created in the course of the capitalist production process. Marx argues that this comes from the fact that capital pays labour the amount socially necessary to ensure the reproduction of labour power, but in return has the right to consume labour power for a period well in excess of that needed to create its use value.[2] It is the ratio of this unpaid labour time (surplus labour) over that part of capital represented by labour power (variable capital) which gives the rate of surplus value, the source of the capitalist's profit and the true measure of exploitation. Accumulation is a process by which the capitalist attempts, through organisation and reorganisation of the production process and through reinvestment of the profits in newer and more efficient plant and machinery, to widen the gap between the amount paid to the labourer and the value of the product labour power produces.

The production of surplus value suggests certain definite forms of production relations. In particular, the production of surplus value requires the existence of a pool of labour, although contrary to Marx's famous dictum that capitalism presupposes the complete separation of the labourer from the ownership of the means of production, experience shows that labourers need not be entirely free nor divorced from dependence on the household.[3] The production of surplus value takes place within a production unit which combines labour with the means of production, usually in some form of factory organisation, with the aim of maximising the efficient use of all these resources.

Within this framework -- the combining of labour with the means of production -- Marx shows theoretically that there are two possible ways to increase the rate of surplus value in capitalist production, the production of absolute surplus value and the production of relative surplus value. The production of absolute surplus value is the most obvious, and historically the earliest form of increasing the rate of surplus value. The production of absolute surplus value occurs when the capitalist aims either to extend the length of the working day or attempts to eliminate wasteful labour time through an increasingly sophisticated and complex division of labour (Taylorism). It can be shown that the proportionate increase in the rate of surplus value is large, even when the actual time by which the day is increased is fairly small and even when labour power is paid its market value or above for this extra time. (Kay 1979:46) But there are natural limits to the production of absolute surplus value, i.e. the lengthening of the working day. Labour power is obviously also living labour so there are natural limits to the amount of time a labourer can work (the labourer must eat and sleep to renew labour power). Even when, in the course of a single day, spent labour is replaced with renewed labour as in shift work, the production of absolute surplus value runs up against the natural limit that there are only twenty-four hours in a day. These natural limits have forced capitalists to attempt to increase the rate of surplus value by the production of relative surplus value, by increasing the intensity (or productivity) of labour during whatever time it is at work.

The two main ways in which relative surplus value can be produced is by putting labour to work with new and more efficient techniques embodied in complex machinery or through the development of new skills which act to reduce labour time. (Kay 1979:46) Kay reminds us that, in practice, the distinction between absolute surplus value and relative surplus value is blurred empirically, that these two modes of appropriation are usually combined in practice and that there exists great variety in these combinations from industry to industry. (Kay 1979:51) In certain industries it may be that there are structural limitations to the adoption of new techniques such that the production of absolute surplus value dominates the combined mode while in other industries the production of relative surplus value will be the main way in which the rate of surplus value is increased.

TABLE 2.2 Correspondence Between Average Earnings in Rural Industries and the Rural Minimum Wage, 1959 to 1978

	Kina per Week	
	Rural Industries' Average Earnings (Papua New Guineans)[a]	*Rural Minimum Wage (Including Rations and Issues)*[b]
1959	3.33	-
1960	2.79	-
1961	3.01	3.01
1962	3.18	3.15
1963	3.22	3.56
1964	3.31	3.00
1965	3.30	3.61
1966	3.44	3.34
1967	3.45	3.29
1968	3.78	3.59
1969	3.87	3.57
1970	4.02	3.56 (4.48)[c]
1971	5.02	3.60
1972	5.12	4.27
1973	5.52	5.90[d]
1974	6.14	5.90
1975	8.26	8.00
1976	9.84	8.90
1977	10.68	9.43 and 9.90
1978	11.37	10.73 and 10.98

(a) Current price average annual earnings divided by 365/7.

(b) Minimum wage (including rations) lagged one year in order to get as close an approximation as possible to the average earnings 'year' for which it was in force.

(c) Figure in brackets is an alternative estimate for this year.

(d) All-cash minimum wage.

Source: Jackson (1981)

TABLE 2.3 Average Earnings in Rural Industries, 1959–78

Year	Chained consumer price index, 1962=100	Export price index, 1973=100	Average annual earnings (kina): Papua New Guineans: Current prices (a)	Papua New Guineans: Constant 1962 consumer prices	Papua New Guineans: Product wage (b)	Expatriates: Current prices prices	Expatriates: Constant 1962 consumer prices	Percentage change over previous year: Papua New Guinean average earnings: Current prices	Papua New Guinean average earnings: Constant 1962 wage	Product	Papua New Guinean employees
1959	–	–	173.8	–	–	2,400.9	–	–	–	–	–
1960	–	–	145.4	–	–	2,509.9	–	–16.3	–	–	11.5
1961	–	–	157.0	–	–	2,554.3	–	8.0	–	–	6.4
1962	100.0	–	165.6	165.6	–	2,763.2	2,763.2	5.5	–	–	0.6
1963	99.8	–	167.7	168.0	–	2,940.1	2,946.0	1.3	1.4	–	1.9
1964	102.6	–	172.4	168.0	–	2,916.3	2,842.4	2.8	0	–	4.7
1965	106.7	–	172.3	161.5	–	3,065.4	2,872.9	–0.1	–3.9	–	–0.9
1966	111.9	–	179.2	160.1	–	2,945.0	2,631.8	4.0	–0.9	–	–1.0
1967	114.7	–	180.0	156.9	–	3,347.7	2,918.7	0.4	–2.0	–	4.7
1968	116.0	–	197.0	169.8	–	3,811.1	3,285.4	9.4	8.2	–	1.3
1969	115.6	–	201.8	174.6	–	4,131.4	3,573.9	2.4	2.8	–	2.3
1970	117.5	116.8	209.4	178.2	179.3	4,246.1	3,613.7	3.8	2.1	–	4.0
1971	125.1	112.5	261.6	209.1	232.5	5,062.8	4,047.0	24.9	17.3	29.7	–7.7
1972	132.72	94.0	267.1	201.3	284.1	4,921.1	3,708.4	2.1	–3.7	22.2	–1.4
1973	143.7	100.0	287.7	200.2	287.7	5,097.2	3,547.1	7.7	–0.5	1.3	–2.7
1974	177.1	163.3	319.9	180.6	195.9	7,239.6	4,087.9	11.2	–9.8	–31.9	–0.9

continued

TABLE 2.3 *continued*

Year	Chained consumer price index, 1962=100	Export price index, 1973=100	Average annual earnings (kina) — Papua New Guineans: Current prices (a)	Constant 1962 consumer prices	Product wage (b)	Expatriates: Current prices prices	Constant 1962 consumer prices	Percentage change over previous year — Papua New Guinean average earnings: Current prices	Constant 1962 wage	Product	Papua New Guinean employees
1975	195.6	173.9	430.9	220.3	247.8	6,806.2	3,479.7	34.7	22.0	26.5	-5.9
1976	210.6	145.5	513.0	243.6	352.6	8,363.1	3,971.1	19.1	10.6	42.3	-14.8
1977	219.9	277.2	556.8	253.2	200.9	9,172.4	4,171.2	8.5	3.9	-43.0	3.8
1978	232.6	286.1	593.1	255.0	207.3	9,443.2	4,059.8	6.5	0.7	3.2	14.5

(a) Estimated form using employment total (Column 4) and wage and salary payments to Papua New Guinean employees (Column 7).

(b) Current price average earnings deflated by the product price as measured (approximately) by the export price index excluding copper concentrate.

(c) Estimated by reducing total wage and salary and contractors' payments of K8,184 thousand by 0.8 per cent to deduct contractors' estimated payment; 0.8 per cent estimated from 1967 figures.

Source: Jackson (1981)

To ensure profit, white planters in colonial Papua New Guinea were concerned to reduce the costs of production, of which labour was the principal cost. Labour costs accounted for about 45 percent of total costs on plantations in the early 1970s. (Densley n.d.:14) In the pioneering phase, labour costs proved not to be a serious burden for the white planter because, during this period, most labour was contract or agreement labour and was paid at very low rates or not paid at all until termination of the contract. This meant a considerable wage saving over time for planters. In the early 1960s, however, planters had to contend with the emergence of a rural minimum wage. The minimum wage concept was formalised in *The Report of the Board of Inquiry Investigating Rural Wages and Related Matters, April 1966* which recommended *inter alia* that the food, clothing, housing, fuel and other material components of the wage be retained, resulting in a substantial increase in the rural minimum wage in 1967–68.

The white planters, through their association, the HFSA, opposed the concept of a rural minimum wage. It argued that a minimum wage is actually a maximum wage because it puts a lid on wages. (*New Guinea Highlands Bulletin* October 1966) The minimum wage did, however, offer planters some stability in their production costs structure. Also, the real test of the extent to which labour costs impaired planter fortunes is whether or not they were so high as to inhibit certain aspects of production. There is no evidence of this occurring for plantations in colonial Papua New Guinea and indeed the situation seems to have been that coffee prices have frequently been substantially greater than marginal harvesting costs, resulting in the optimal response being to harvest the available crop. (Ford 1978:37)

However the real problem white planters faced in the operating phase was not rising costs of production but the fact that accumulation in the industry, due to the plantation form of production and the nature of the coffee bean itself, could be realised only through the production of absolute surplus value and not through the production of relative surplus value. This is the case because most of the phases in the plantation production of high quality Arabica coffee cannot be mechanised. Haarer recommended that 'every possible use of mechanisation to save labour must be devised' (Haarer 1962:232) but there are limits to mechanisation in the high quality Arabica coffee industry. Nor can new skills be developed to reduce labour time. In weeding, for example, while some progress has been made in the use of new techniques such as herbicides, there are limits to which these can be used, especially when the plant is young. In any case, the importance of mulching means that a great deal of weeding has to be done by the manual spading method carried out by unskilled labourers, even where the plants are able to tolerate the use of herbicides. There seem to be few ways in which labour required for year round hand weeding can be intensified by combining it with machinery or developing its level of skill. Pruning, on the other hand, does require specialist skills so that labour time can be saved in this activity if teams of specialist pruners are established solely for pruning. Pruning, however, is not a particularly labour-intensive task so that labour savings made on this activity are not very significant for the plantation overall.

The main area where planters would like to use machinery to increase the productivity of labour is in the most labour-intensive task of all, harvesting. Machines have been invented to harvest coffee but these are not suitable for quality Arabica coffee produced for taste, since taste is only fully developed if the cherry is harvested when ripe and processed immediately. Given that cherries ripen unevenly, it follows that an assessment must be made at the point of harvesting as to whether the cherry is ripe or not. This assessment can be made only if the cherry is hand-picked. No machine has yet been invented which can tell the difference in ripeness of various berries even if it could get them off the tree without damaging them. In Brazil, machines are used to strip everything off the tree at once (leaves, flowers, over-ripe berries, under-ripe berries), but this can be done only with poor-quality coffees at a time of booming prices for it takes the mutilated tree two years to recover from this savage treatment. (Roden 1977:49) It is also doubtful that the separation of cherries from dry leaves, etc., which is done fairly automatically in the 'dry' processing method used in Brazil, could be incorporated into the 'wet' method used for high quality Arabica. Thus, it can be stated quite categorically that the process of producing high quality Arabica coffee on plantations such that it is unlikely that increased mechanisation or the development of new skills can ever form the basis for extended accumulation in the industry.

The coffee planters' dilemma is thus easily stated. On the one hand, plantation production of coffee is extremely labour intensive and, on the other hand, planters' ability to increase exploitation of that labour is limited to strategies to extend the working day, i.e. to the production of absolute surplus value. Coffee producers must employ a sizeable labour force but, due to the agronomic features of the plant itself, they are limited in their ability to appropriate relative surplus value. So it is through attempts to extend the surplus labour time via the lengthening of the working day that coffee planters have tried to increase the rate of surplus value and therefore profits. The length of the working day during harvesting has been extended by paying pickers piece rates. Under this system the worker is paid at a specified rate per unit of output in terms of, for example, 0.5 cent per pound of coffee cherry. If a worker picks 50 pounds of cherry in a day he/she receives 25 cents; if he/she picks 180 pounds of cherry in a day he/she receives 90 cents. His/her earnings therefore vary in the same proportion as output. The most significant feature of a piece rate system under which a worker's reward varies in proportion to his/her output is that gains or losses resulting directly from changes in his/her output accrue to him/her while gains or losses in overhead costs per unit of output accrue to the employer. A variation of straight piece work is the differential piece work system in which the rate is varied at specific levels of output. For example, a system may pay coffee pickers per day, 0.5 cent per pound from output up to 150 pounds. For the next 60 pound the picker receives 0.75 cent per pound and for any output above this (i.e. above 210 pounds) the picker receives 1 cent per pound. If a picker achieved an output of 220 pounds in a day, he/she would receive a payment of $1.30 which is made up of 150 pound at 0.5 cent per pound (75 cents), 60 pound at 0.75 cent per pound (45 cents) and 10 pound at 1 cent per pound (10 cents). (For more on this see 'An Outline of Piece Rate Systems in Labour' a paper prepared by the Department of Labour, Territory of Papua and New Guinea, reprinted in *New Guinea Highlands Bulletin*, October 1968.)

Piece rates represent a time-honoured strategy which is particularly successful in the Highlands where pickers are generally local village women or wives of the permanent labourers who see no need, and no desire, to establish an agreement on what is a 'fair' working day. The aim of a piece work system is to yield increased output, to lower the cost of production through more effective utilisation of labour (less labour for the same output) and to raise earnings for employees. However, this is an idealised aim for, in practice, piece work systems come up against social realities that stem basically from the antagonism between labourers and planters. For a start, trials undertaken in harvesting at piece work rates on colonial plantations showed that the cost of supervision of piece workers was about double that for day rate supervision and day rate payment. This was due to the temptation of some piece workers to forge or steal weight receipts, to lose their copies of weight receipts or to resort to destructive or careless practices to get the berry off the tree. (*New Guinea Highlands Bulletin*, April 1965)

In circumstances where the lengthening of the working day through piece rate payment proves unsatisfactory and where the production of relative surplus value is limited, there is only one other way in which the coffee planter can realise profit from changes made to arrangements at the level of production. This is to increase production output by reducing the amount of shade on the plantation. Shade trees are a vital part of the agronomic make-up of the plantation because shade cools the soil, maintains soil moisture, depresses weed growth and keeps the coffee bush in a healthy state of growth. In the Highlands, the principal shade tree now used is a species of casuarina, because of its nitrogen-fixing abilities. (Dick 1977:45) But just as shade depresses weed growth, so too can shade depress yields. Yields, in turn, can be increased by reducing shade. However, if Arabica coffee is to be grown in the highlands with reduced or no shade, 'it is necessary to carry out a thorough programme of chemical weed control and heavy fertiliser applications'. (Kimber n.d.:2) Hence, there exists the potential for a trade-off between reduction of shade and an increase in fertilisers and herbicides for the planter aiming to increase yields. However, it appears that the reduction of shade is possible only in the short term for, in many places where it has been tried, it has resulted after a period in die-back and debilitation. (Haarer 1962:88)

Given all these limits on profit and accumulation at the level of production it is not surprising that white planters quickly realised that they faced only two main alternatives in increasing their level of prosperity. The first alternative was to go beyond coffee altogether and diversify their interests into areas where they could realise relative surplus value. The second was to increase profits at the level of circulation. This would involve a degree of vertical integration and control of the coffee-marketing chain so that profits could be realised in marketing and on produce produced at other levels of production such as smallholdings. Or, if profits could not be realised through appropriation of the surplus of smallholders at the level of circulation, then at least limits could be imposed on the extent to which the produce of smallholders would compete with the products of planters. The success of either alternative would depend on the extent to which white planters could get state support and mobilise as a class at the level of class relations. We will assess the success of white planters in these activities in later sections.

The Rise of, and Social Limits on, Rural Proletarianisation

Despite the limits on accumulation of white planters in the coffee industry, it did grow spectacularly, and became a very profitable industry. The demand for rural labour grew accordingly. The growth of indigenous wage labour in the industry has been fairly rapid since the first coffee was harvested in 1955. At that time some 2000 indigenous workers were employed on plantations. By the late 1970s there were over 11,000 full-time indigenous wage labourers in the Papua New Guinea coffee industry, of whom at least 70 percent (estimated) were employed on plantations. Employment statistics do not distinguish between employment on large acreages and employment on smallholdings. The figure of 11,000 was given by Densley. (n.d.:10) The increase is due to the establishment of more plantations after 1955 and to the fact that the demand for labour is greater as plantations reach the operating phase. The number of full-time labourers required on a plantation can vary depending on the soil, rainfall, landfall, etc. However, an average workforce for a plantation of about 20,000 trees would be anywhere from half a dozen labourers in the slack season to two dozen or more at the height of harvesting. (Finney 1973:150)

The intensity of labour and the sheer volume of labour employed on coffee plantations raises the question as to whether rural proletarianisation is occurring as a result of capitalist plantation agriculture in coffee. The knee-jerk reaction of the Marxist social scientist (e.g. Good 1979) would be to argue that proletarianisation is occurring and will continue to develop as capitalism is extended. It would be pointed out that workers in plantation agriculture share the experience of exploitation, they work under conditions that approximate factory agriculture, receive uniform rates of pay, etc. This Marxist argument would incorporate an addition to the effect that class action by rural proletarians is either hindered by false consciousness (ethnicity, kinship) which takes precedence over proletarianisation or, in a more sophisticated version, that the reality of ethnic and gender concerns allied with state intervention through the Highlands Labour Scheme (West 1958) or the minimum wage, act to disorganise the rural proletariat against the well organised white planter class. The argument is that the working class exists and is conserved at the level of class location (in production) but is dissolved at the level of class relations (in opposition).

This argument has had to contend with the orthodox argument on wage labour in Papua New Guinea (Howlett 1973 and 1980), which marxist 'articulation' theorists (Fitzpatrick 1980) also seem to endorse, that plantation labour is only partly proletarianised because its reproduction is dependent only partly on wage labour and mainly on non-wage subsidies derived from the village and subsistence agriculture. The claim in the orthodox view that rural proletarianisation is limited leads to the question of whether, and to what extent, plantation labourers do/do not depend on the wage for their reproduction. The orthodox scholars are concerned with the way in which this question might uncover the factors that influence the life chances of rural proletarians.

In Papua New Guinea the debate about the life chances of rural proletarians has been dominant in the official literature because of its bearing upon the question of what minimum wage would ensure that rural wage labour is reproduced. Reports on rural wage labour such as the Cochrane Report (Territory of Papua New Guinea 1970) and the Isaac Report (Territory of Papua and New Guinea 1970) and the 1971 Native Employment (Minimum Conditions) Ordinance were "crucial in producing a more receptive attitude to the eventual growth of a permanent rural work force [and] as a result of these reports rural wages were increased and a minimum wages tribunal established". (Howlett 1980:203–204)

The reports and the resulting wage rises established, at least in principle, that there were limits to the extent to which the reproduction of wage labour could be subsidised by the village. These limits exist, as Howlett shows, even when rural wage earners are not permanent and alternate between the village and wage labour because many are "functionally landless in that their land is economically disadvantaged by environmental or locational conditions which prevent them from earning a cash income". (Howlett 1980:195)

It is important to note at this point that official reports and legislation in the late colonial period began to recognise the growth of a permanent rural proletariat and to recognise that the life chances of rural wage earners do depend as much upon the level of the wage as on village subsistence.

Most of the academic writing on rural proletarianisation, Marxist (Mortimer 1975, Good 1979) and non-Marxist (Gerritsen 1981, Howlett 1973 and 1980) is caught in a contradiction which is well expressed by Howlett.

> Given the embyronic stage of rural proletarianisation, it is perhaps too early to decide whether a significant rural proletariat will eventually emerge in Papua New Guinea, or whether present trends are simply leading to further differentiation of the peasantry. (Howlett 1980:208)

The reason given for this confusion by Marxists is usually that rural proletarians in Papua New Guinea are not 'conscious': they do not organise. They exist, in other words, at the level of class location, but they disappear at the level of class relations. How can this be explained? What processes are dissolving the class action of this class? Is it merely in formation? Are ethnicity or, region, disorganising the class at the level of social relations?

I argue that in the case of the coffee industry in Papua New Guinea -- and perhaps in the coffee industry of other countries -- the dissolution of the class of rural proletarians takes place at the level of class location in production rather than, as is usually assumed, at the level of class relations. It can be shown that the same production processes that create a need for wage labour, and therefore for the exchange of labour power might also, in certain industries, contain processes which dissolve that wage labour as a class or a collectivity. A twin, seemingly contradictory, process is going on. This is that a rural wage labour force is being established and at the same time this is being dissolved as a class in the production process. Among the factors which cause this dissolution are the plantation form of production, the nature of plantation work, and the method of engagement of plantation labour. By far the most important factor causing the dissolution of the labour force as a class at the level of production is the nature of plantation work, particularly the fact that on coffee plantations the division of labour on plantations is ascribed. It is not based on achievement or worker skills.

Pruning is the only paid labour task on a plantation which requires a modicum of skill. The highly labour intensive activities of weeding and harvesting require little skill. In harvesting trials, for example, "those who picked well were not capable of being distinguished by any age group, experience or other similarity". (*New Guinea Highlands Bulletin*, April 1965) Skills in harvesting or weeding are not developed nor necessarily preserved or retained by the employer. The division of labour is not based on acquired skills. It thus becomes impossible to draw a boundary around a collectivity of permanent experienced rural wage labourers in coffee who are differentiated from untrained workers, peasants or others in rural areas. The situation in the coffee plantation is significantly different from production in almost all other forms of capitalist production for even the most humble workshop uses rudimentary machinery and has margins of skill which separate employees as a collectivity from untrained outsiders.

The fact that achievement is rarely a feature of the wage earning capacity of rural labourers in the plantation coffee industry means that other factors can actually influence the selection of labour in the industry. In particular, gender usually dominates the criteria for choice of pickers, as Haarer long ago recommended it should. Women rarely do other more serious or responsible work and they often do the harvesting on the plantation as a family subsidy to the earnings of their permanent labourer husband. Piece rate harvesting is the most inferior form of labour and one which pickers do not like even when they earn reasonable money. (*New Guinea Highlands Bulletin*, April 1965) But women do it. They are obviously in a difficult position. They may work in order to keep their husband employed as a full–time labourer. Doubtless also much of the pressure to labour at piece rates comes directly from husbands employed on the plantation rather than from employers. Ethnicity is also a factor influencing the selection of labour in the plantation coffee industry. This is because plantation labour is labour of last resort. It is not undertaken by groups which are not land short, or which can grow cash crops.

In the Papua New Guinea plantation coffee industry, plantation labour has not been undertaken by Gorokans despite their location at the centre of the plantation industry since the early 1950s. Gorokans have a range of ways to earn cash from their fertile land, not only from smallholder coffee growing but from the production of food crops and vegetables for local marketing. Consequently, most plantation labour in Goroka is from Chimbu province, where land is short or from the less fertile outlying areas in the Eastern Highlands. With no pressure to employ labour on the basis of achievement, planters will hire Chimbus because of the belief that they have racial qualities which make them good or 'tractable' workers. (Finney 1973:52) Added to these various ascriptive factors that determine the selection of labourers for the plantation coffee industry is the fact that for many years contract and agreement labour ensured that the planter would experience rapid turnover of even full–time staff. It becomes easy to see how the class of rural wage earners has been dissolved in the process of plantation production.

It is a curious feature of plantation agriculture in coffee – – which after all is capitalist agriculture based on the payment of labour and the appropriation of surplus value – – that the division of labour in many ways resembles ascriptive pre–capitalist systems. The division of the workforce on gender and ethnic lines is reminiscent of village organisation. This factor helps us to understand more clearly the potential for class action by rural wage earners employed on plantations. The implication of this argument is that a class of rural proletarians would require not merely the organisation of the class at the level of class relations in opposition to white planters or the state (that is, as a party to influence governemnt or in terms of a trade union movement aiming to influence wage decisions), but would require conservation of the class at the level of class location (in production), which in turn would depend upon the destruction of the coffee plantation form of production itself.

In Papua New Guinea, changes in the organisation of the plantation labour force are occurring which are liable to make the division of labour even less subject to achievement criteria. Plantations are moving to have settled married workforces on the plantation rather than employing individual male workers as in the days of agreement and contract labour. "A settled married workforce was considered to be both less expensive and more productive than the agreement system which has always involved a high turnover of single workers." (Howlett 1980:205) Howlett has suggested that this new development 'is likely to give considerable impetus to rural proletarianisation' (Howlett 1980:205), but this will only be accurate if we accept that evidence of increases in the exchange of labour power is the same as class formation. But in class action terms the new arrangements might further inhibit mobilisation or even increase dissolution at the level of production because the family labouring unit will become completely dependent on the plantation employer, creating the possibility of relations between the married unit and the employer being based more on obligation and patron–client relations than on wage labour relations.

Consquently rural proletarians will not be treated systematically in this book, as are other classes in the industry.

The unique role of the smallholders: how coffee grew wild in smallholder gardens

Outstripping the growth in rural labour, and much more significant in social terms, was the spread of coffee-growing activities among smallholders.[4] Smallholder coffee, or garden coffee, grows easily in the highlands of Papua New Guinea. The cultivator needs few skills and no investment beyond a handful of seeds and a small plot of land. Coffee growing provided, and still provides, village people with a necessary source of cash in the easiest possible way. No wonder the plant was treated almost as a divine gift, 'money that grows on trees', and that it spread rapidly throughout the Highlands. The arcane problem of limits on accumulation did not worry village people who then and now simply picked "money" off their trees, selling coffee at the roadside when they were hard up. Smallholder cultivation has not changed in its essentials, so the following account is a generalised version rather than an historical one.

On the eve of decolonisation in 1972–73, there were 45,560 indigenous coffee growers in Eastern Highlands Province, with some 5,008 hectares under coffee. This area was quite small, about 0.11 hectares, giving an average smallholder between 500 and 1,000 coffee trees. Anderson, in fact, found in a survey of coffee smallholders that 'the average tree numbers for the three provinces was 530 trees of which 450 were mature and 80 (16 percent) of the total immature'. (Anderson 1977:10)

The 45,560 indigenous coffee growers in Eastern Highlands in 1972–73 produced some 6,118 tonnes of green bean equivalent, which is approximately 140 kg or between two and three 60 kg export bags of coffee each. "Average smallholder yields in the highlands are of the order of one tonne per hectare while the average total production per grower is around 200 kg dry parchment for the highlands." (Densley n.d.:9) This is a very small volume of coffee per household. The cash return from coffee production to these producers in 1972–73 would probably have been around $45 per year or less. As Finney noted in the late 1960s, smallholder coffee returns in Papua New Guinea do indeed provide 'a low per capita cash income, putting the Gorokans well down on any scale, even one that would include other underdeveloped countries of the world'. (Finney 1973:68) It follows that for most smallholders there is very little spare cash to invest back into production so that production of coffee by smallholders is extremely rudimentary involving the most elementary and inefficient machinery (such as pulpers and hoes), limited or undeveloped techniques and unskilled labour. They rarely weed and almost never mulch. Further, pruning is rarely done by smallholders. This causes lower yields, difficulties for pickers and a failure to rejuvenate the tree by providing bearing wood. Given the absence of shade planning and official DASF encouragement of smallholder use of fertilisers,[5] the soil is quite quickly exhausted by this type of coffee production. (Dick 1977:51)

The household provides the two main inputs needed to grow coffee, land and unskilled labour. Coffee can be grown in a household unit alongside food production and in circumstances where migratory labour is sometimes withdrawn from the household. Coffee has thus fitted in with the existing division of labour internal to the household. Barnes, quoting Reay (1959), shows that the division of labour internal to Highlands households has always been gender determined. Women do the less spectacular, more repetitious work such as pulling grass, maintaining subsistence food production and the care and protection and feeding of pigs, leaving men free to build houses, make tools and exchange valuables. (Barnes n.d.:268) Though women's work is essential to the household's survival and to the man's prestige in the clan, women remain low of status and do not share ownership of the household's wealth in pigs or benefit from exchanges.

This gender division of labour has barely altered with the introduction of coffee production into the household. "Women continue to do the less skilled but most time-consuming tasks (weeding and picking) while the tasks requiring some knowledge of coffee technology (planting, shading, fencing and pruning) are mainly men's work." (Barnes n.d.:274) This requires women to put in more time than men in both subsistence food and coffee production. It suggests that coffee production in the Highlands depends less upon the diversion of male labour from other activities than upon the extension of women's labour from food production. (Barnes n.d.:175) The main point, however, is that the household does not have to drastically modify the internal gender-determined division of labour in order to be able to be engaged in the production of coffee as a commodity.

Barnes shows that the internal division of labour has been maintained on a gender basis much as it was before the household began to produce coffee. This is partly due to the fact that household production of coffee required limited technical knowledge or equipment. But coffee is not only produced by smallholders, it is also harvested and processed by them. It is these activities which link the coffee households into the larger systems and forces changes in the system of household reproduction. In general terms, two moments are involved in this process of linkage. The first is the monetisation of certain elements within the household. The second, where commodity production and preparation for the market are labour intensive, is the movement of domestic terms of trade against the household. This is the simple reproduction squeeze. Bernstein's general analysis is applicable to Papua New Guinea coffee smallholders because the main social change undergone by smallholder producers of coffee in Papua New Guinea is the simple reproduction 'squeeze'. (Bernstein 1977:64) This 'squeeze' causes smallholder coffee producers to intensify commodity relations in the household.

Bernstein sets down in theoretical terms the relationship between the simple reproduction 'squeeze' and the intensification of labour:

> The objective of the simple reproduction 'squeeze' is to act as one of the mechanisms intensifying the labour of the household to maintain or increase the supply of commodities without incurring any costs of management and supervision of the production process. (Bernstein 1977:65)

He continues:

> It is necessary to introduce the concept of intensification of commodity relations which can help distinguish the various ways in which and degrees to which, peasant production is constituted and household reproduction realised through commodity relations. In any concrete analysis this entails consideration of the extent and forms of capitalist development of the economy as a social formation as a whole, that is, examining the place of peasant production in the social division of labour, its relations with other forms of production including capitalist agriculture and industry. The overall development of the circulation of commodities and money and so on. At the level of household economy the intensification of commodity relations refers to the degree to which the reproduction cycle is realised through the production and exchange of commodities'. (Bernstein 1977:66)

Later, Bernstein adds a further aspect to the concept of intensification of commodity relations. He writes:

> Differentiation in class terms is another dimension of the intensification of commodity relations to be added to our previous observations, in that the homogeneity of the conditions of the household economy (as an economy of simple reproduction) is broken up as means of production are capitalised and labour power becomes a commodity, exchanged on a systematic basis within the rural economy. However, differentiation is not a necessary condition nor effect of intensification of commodity relations -- this will depend on the concrete conditions in which intensification occurs. (Bernstein 1977:68)

The simple reproduction squeeze thus occurs when more and more of the labour of the household is devoted to maintaining the supply of coffee to the market. Papua New Guinea coffee smallholders have been particularly vulnerable to this intensification of relations within the household partly because the production and processing of coffee in the household requires an enormous amount of labour and partly because the cost of production of household produced coffee has been rising.

The implication of the linkage of the household to larger systems is that the production of coffee in the household has penetrated the natural economy, broken its cycle of reproduction and thus caused fundamental social changes in the conditions of production and exchange in which these smallholders are engaged. (Bernstein 1977:61–62)

The monetisation of certain elements within the household, which produced a rupture in the cycle of reproduction of the natural economy, began in the Highlands with the imposition of taxes necessitating sources of cash income for the household. Cash was provided in the beginning by labour migration and later by the production and sale of coffee. But cash was also needed for coffee production even though smallholder production was limited in its technical development. Anderson (1977) found the cost of production among smallholders varied greatly depending on whether they employed labour or not. But even non-labour costs of production for coffee were not insignificant as a percentage of cash return from coffee and were higher where the smallholder processed the crop to parchment stage. Anderson found:

> Smallholder coffee producers normally incur a small cash cost for the purchase of tools such as spades, knives, saws and bags, buckets, sheets of plastic and other items. The average amount spent on such items by growers actually incurring the expense was K6 per year. In addition, growers may hire labour to assist them in the garden. Where this was incurred the cost averaged K18–40 a year. (Anderson 1977:21)

Some of these purchases (the tools, for example) were items which were also used for food production, but bags and plastic sheeting were purchased so that parchment could be produced and stored. By far the largest fixed capital investment householders ever make is the Bentall pulper introduced into the Highlands in 1965 at a cost of K175 in the early 1970s. (Good and Donaldson 1980:29) This is a major purchase, the use of which has significant impact upon internal household production though not, as is often claimed, upon the differentiation of households. Today, in the Eastern Highlands, the monetisation of certain elements within the household has reached a much more sophisticated level. Now cash is needed and desired mainly for consumption purposes. Grossman, who has recently and extensively observed and described village life in the Eastern Highlands, writes:

> Money is needed for many purposes - - school fees, taxes, transportation, clothing and entertainment, and to purchase certain necessities and items of consumption which are part of the currently accepted standard of living. Village life is also intensely social and money is required to fully participate in many aspects of social life from beer drinking and gambling to certain pig exchanges and payments of bride wealth. 'Bisnis' activity has entered into the characteristics defining a man of respect and prestige, one held in esteem by his fellow villagers . . . what is significant for the man of business is not so much the amount of money he makes though this may be important but that he is involved in 'Bisnis'. Not to be involved in any form of such enterprise invites the label of Bach- - Bainte or Rabisman in Tok Pisin, a person of no worth or consequence lacking in prestige. (Grossman n.d.:12)

Clearly, monetisation has proceeded very far when it influences social attitudes to such an extent.

Villagers have to maintain this level of consumption but their ability to do so is dependent on the price of coffee. As a hedge against falling prices, villagers have mastered the art of processing coffee to the parchment stage. This is a vital development in the industry because of the need for pulping cherry within 12 to 24 hours of picking. Village processing grew from necessity because in the early days of the industry it simply was not possible to provide the facilities for transporting cherry from each remote smallholder to a central processing plant. The system of roadside buying, in which trucks driven by coffee buyers weigh and pay cash to growers waiting at the roadside (smallholders can also sell directly at the factory door) has alleviated this difficulty. Even where transport was available, household processing of coffee to the parchment stage had its attractions because: "it was seldom possible to synchronise purchasing days with picking days as finely as this. Coffee parchment can be kept for long periods (as long as it is kept dry) and is much lighter and easier to transport than cherry". (Donaldson and Good n.d.:152) But the real advantage of processing coffee to parchment from the grower's point of view is that this gives the grower the ability to determine - - either for reasons of price or transport needs, or for household requirements - - the time of selling. The advantages of parchment are that it is a storable product:

> so that it need not be marketed immediately and can be accumulated into large amounts so that large batches of income can be received. Where access to a coffee factory is cheap, cherry has the advantage of providing a quick cash return of a day's harvesting. A grower can utilise both methods of selling. (Anderson 1977:18)

Smallholders tend to opt for the sale of parchment even though there are substantial arguments against this course. These include the fact that a smallholder must somehow gain access to a pulping machine; that when conservation rates are taken into account in comparison with cherry, parchment is definitely not an economic proposition; and also that processing is extremely labour intensive. Processing does have significant impact on the peasant household, involving coffee smallholders in an intensification of commodity relations within it. Smallholders process coffee to the parchment stage because parchment is a storable product. It can be released onto the market at a time which suits the smallholder. Processing thus offers the smallholder greater security. However, smallholders gain this control over the crop at the cost of investing an enormous amount of labour in processing. Processing is not nearly as time consuming as harvesting, but it does require labour time over and above that of sellers of cherry, and it adds to the cost of equipment and thus represents a significant intensification of commodity relations for the smallholder household.

Most processing is carried out during a four-month period between May and August. During this time, ripe coffee berries are picked and then processed in the evening of the same day. Picking and processing are not done every day in this four-month period, although Anderson found that a household with 400 mature trees would need to work about 31 days in the four months. (Anderson 1977:31) The following calculations of the overall distribution of household labour are made not solely on the basis of man-days required to get the coffee crop out. The aim of the analysis is to show that the household is poorly rewarded for a crop upon which its reproduction depends. Thus a calculation of the overall labour commitments of the household is more relevant than a calculation of labour time invested per man-day.

The procedure begins with the pulping of the harvested berries. Anderson found almost all villagers operated a Bentall pulper. In only three cases in the survey, all from Lufa village, was pulping done by the enormously tedious hand method of removing the coffee cherry skin by squeezing the cherry between the fingers. (Anderson 1977:26) Where Bentall machines were used, Anderson found the time taken at the pulpery was two hours. Water for pulping and for washing the cherry before drying must be at hand at the fermentary, and is frequently carried to the fermentary, involving extra labour time. (Dick 1977:84) The next stage in the production of parchment coffee is the fermenting and washing of the coffee. Anderson found from nineteen observations that an average time spent at each washing was 1.3 hours. (Anderson 1977:27) A minimum of 3.3 hours is thus required for pulping, fermenting and washing on any one of the thirty–one days in the four months when the household is engaged in getting the crop out.

The above calculation does not include the hours spent on harvesting the crop during the thirty–one days. This is a very difficult and highly variable process because the conditions under which coffee is harvested vary considerably among smallholders. Coffee is sometimes harvested in a very informal manner, no records are kept, and it is likely that even the most detailed study will show great variation among labour time spent on harvesting by smallholders. Despite this, calculations can be made about harvesting, the aim being not to set down an average figure for smallholder labour time devoted to harvesting but merely to roughly calculate the commitment of the household in labour time to harvesting. Smallholders in the Eastern Highlands, on the eve of decolonisation, were producing about 140 kg of green bean equivalent in gardens that were approximately 0.11 hectares. This amount of green bean equivalent is 200 kg of parchment and 1000 kg of cherry at DASF recovery rates (Table 2.1). Thus the average smallholder had to harvest about 1000 kg in the 31 days spent on coffee during the 4 months of the harvesting period. The hours of household labour time invested in picking 1000 kg can be roughly calculated using adjusted figures from harvesting trials undertaken on plantations, where the base rate of harvesting for pickers on day rates is about 45.9 pounds (21 kg) each 8–hour day:

> For smallholders picking is immensely more difficult, and slower, because their gardens are not spaced out, their trees are not planted in rows, they have to cope with weeds and other trees and they may not have buckets and proper equipment. For these reasons, it would be optimistic to consider a harvesting base rate for smallholders as being any more than one–quarter the plantation base rate. If this is the case a member of the household could not be expected to harvest coffee at a rate faster than 5.25 kg per day. But it is evident that the household is harvesting approximately 32 kg of cherry a day (1000 kg total in 31 days getting the crop out) so it seems that the household may be committed to having 6 people working eight hours a day on each of those 31 days to pick 1000 kg of cherry off the tree and ready for processing. This is a total of about 48 hours of harvesting a day to which the household is committed, making a staggering total of 1488 harvesting hours required over the four month period of harvesting. We must add this 1,488 hours to the 93 previously calculated for pulping and fermenting and washing the parchment. We must also add the labour time invested in the sun drying of parchment, a process which takes 8 days. (Haarer 1962:271)

During this time, "some person needs to be about to turn the coffee to ensure even drying, be ready to take the coffee inside if rain threatens and to prevent theft". (Anderson 1977:27)

This work is usually done by village children, thus the value of this labour is impossible and unnecessary to calculate for our purposes, even though it is an important part of the process of preparing parchment for sale. The final calculation that must be made is the labour time the household must invest in coffee production at non-harvest times of the year. Anderson calculated this to be about 8 hours per fortnight in the 8 months of the non-harvest period, which would work out at approximately 128 hours. A minimum total for committed household labour to producing parchment would appear to be about (1486 + 93 + 128) = 1709 household hours annually for a smallholder with 400 mature trees on about 0.11 acres. This estimate is far higher than the only previously known calculation of annual labour time for coffee production, in Sinasina, undertaken by Hide, who estimated that more than 2000 hours per hectare were required annually for coffee production. (Howlett, Hide and Young 1976:226) Could this estimation be inaccurate by a factor of 5? This is likely for, in at least one area of Hide's calculations of labour time – – that of non-household labour used in coffee production – – Anderson found the estimates grossly inaccurate. (Anderson 1977:31)

Returns to labour from smallholder coffee production are, as the Sinasina survey notes, even for Hide's labour time calculations, very poor indeed. (Howlett, Hide and Young 1976:226) In 1972–73 it was estimated that the smallholder coffee household with 400–450 mature trees may have earned approximately $45 per year form the sale of coffee. But if the household is committed to invest at least 1709 hours annually on coffee, we find that the return to the household per hour committed to coffee is about 2.4 cents per hour, 17.2 cents per day or 86 cents for a five–day week. This certainly makes coffee production a non–economic proposition for the smallholder. If the smallholder has to hire outside labour to get the crop out, then the household's return from coffee production is even more dismal. It must of course be remembered that much of the labour invested by the household is, as we have seen, that of women and children, and this labour would not be expected to realise a rate of return at a very high level. But equally it must be realised that the household is also dependent upon the labour of women and children. Their labour is vital if the household is to produce coffee at all; therefore, it does have a value. It may be difficult to calculate the value of this labour in monetary terms but the entire household is dependent on the labour of women and children for its reproduction, and for the production of both use values (food) and exchange values (cash crops).

The low rate of return on labour invested by the household is important for another reason, this being that the household's labour time when invested in coffee production is not only low but devalorised in relation to its other uses.

This is mainly caused by the fact that it is peasant or household labour. The 1972–73 returns to peasant household production compare poorly, for example, with returns to hired labour paid at the level of the rural minimum wage. In 1972–73, the rural minimum wage was $4.27 (Jackson 1981:117), which is much higher than the above calculated returns for the smallholder. The smallholder was better off in 1972–73 to spend labour time in rural employment than in the production of coffee.

It is also necessary to emphasise that the intensification of commodity relations in the household, caused by the production and exchange of commodities such as coffee and the exchange of labour power as a commodity, takes place in a unit where food is still produced for use by the household. Food production (use value) uses the *same* labour that goes into commodity production (exchange value). Another important feature of peasant households is the simple reproduction 'squeeze' of smallholder coffee producers which demonstrates that households engaged in commodity production have their labour time devalorised through the structure of peasant production. This means the distribution of labour time between use value production and exchange value production is difficult under even the least difficult household conditions. This affects the household's response to cash needs because it can, and usually does, purchase food in the market to subsidise household food production. A threat to the reproduction of households producing both use values and exchange values can occur if the labour time devoted to household production of food is suspended. The household depends on being able to balance the labour requirements of coffee and food production. However, the intense demands of coffee for labour make it difficult to maintain production of food. This has made purchased food necessary for reproduction.

The point of this explanation is to show that a discussion of the response of peasant households to variation in the price of a marketed commodity cannot be attempted without acknowledging that the household will consider first, the amount of food needed to be produced by the household; second, the amount of labour that goes into producing the marketed commodity as against labour time needed for food production, and third, the capacity of the household to purchase food. For example, the 'perverse' response by peasants to falling prices in the marketed commodity is possible because the household produces food for consumption. It can thus reduce levels of consumption of purchased food and, if labour is available for food production, intensify production of coffee. There would seem to be no reason not to do this when labour devoted to food and coffee can be maintained and where outside purchases can be suspended. On the other hand, when prices of coffee rise, the level of food purchases can be maintained while, at the same time, labour time devoted to either food production or coffee can be reduced. The choice for reduction between food and coffee would be coffee because, as we have shown, the labour component of coffee production is unreasonably high anyway.[6] Hence, whether price variation is high or low, the peasant response, if one assumes that peasant households produce only exchange values, might appear quite irrational but, viewed in the context of the distinctiveness of household production, they can appear quite rational.

Evidence of the intensification of commodity relations in the household is the alteration of the balance between use value production (food) and exchange value production (coffee) so that households are required to purchase food more and more rather than produce it for themselves. The effect on food production of the intensification of commodity relations in coffee is, as this section has shown, merely one aspect of how the intensification of commodity relations internal to the household works to the disadvantage of smallholder producers. In later sections I will examine peasant production in relation to the social division of labour as a whole, and show that coffee smallholder producers are forced to compete with production from plantations. Planters can, through control of marketing channels and with the assistance of the state, double or even triple the simple commodity 'squeeze'. This is done by devalorisation of peasant labour at the point of production and through an intricate set of controls and regulating mechanisms at the level of exchange, as will be shown in later sections.

This section has shown that devalorisation of peasant labour time in production is a structural feature of household production of coffee and one that continually forces households to invest more and more for a minimum return. Peasant households are 'squeezed' not only in relation to labour but also in relation to that other major productive force which is needed for coffee growing, land. It has been argued that the growth of smallholder coffee production had slowed down after decolonisation because of land shortage. (*Draft Hansard* 17 August 1978, *Post Courier*, 19 October 1976) If this is so, then the smallholder has the choice of either producing less coffee or, alternatively, as Dick argues, devoting more attention to maintaining higher yields on land already given over to coffee production. (*Post Courier*, 19 October 1976) This will involve further regeneration and maintenance of older trees at the cost of more and more labour devoted to coffee production. The situation is such that smallholder coffee producers must face the reality of greater and greater commitment to labour to coffee production where labour is devalorised in relation to alternative uses of labour time while their costs of production due to land shortage are rising. It is little wonder that smallholder coffee producers in the Highlands complained to Grossman that 'coffee imprisons us'. (Grossman n.d.:4)

Notes

1. I use the term 'commonly known' to describe the common conception that management is a learned objective skill. I do not agree with this view of the role of management for I regard management as the exercise of class interest. The impossibility of teaching management skills, though not of socialising people into class perspective, should make the 'common' definition of management suspect. I return to this point in detail in the twenty-hectare case study.

2. To say that payment for labour power is based on what is 'socially necessary' is important for this highlights a key assumption of Marxist theory: that labour power, a commodity which exchanges in a market place, does so at its full value at the level of circulation. 'Socially necessary factors include, the accumulated history of wage bargaining, state legislation of working conditions and other moral factors all of which are incorporated in the wage'. See Marx (1954:479) where the major propositions are summarised.

3. Marx wrote: "The process, therefore, that clears the way for the capitalist system can be none other than the process which takes away from the labourer the possession of his means of production; a process that transforms on the one hand, the social means of subsistence and of production into capital, on the other, the immediate producers into wage-labour." (Marx 1954:668)

4. The empirical information upon which the following section is based is drawn from a range of surveys conducted during the colonial and post-colonial period (e.g. Dick 1977; Anderson 1977). However, it must be noted that it is commonly agreed that the store of information on smallholder coffee growers is very limited. (Richard Doery, DPI, Personal Interview May 10, 1982) Each year from 1972–73 the *Rural Industries' Bulletin* from the Bureau of Statistics has contained a proviso along the following lines, 'This issue of a rural industries' bulletin contains less information on production for small holdings for some years than on others because it has not been possible for the field staff of the Department of Primary Industry to compile for all years estimates of cropping activity for the numerous, widely scattered small holdings.'

5. The reasons given for this are somewhat paradoxical. Anderson writes: "It is not DPI policy to encourage smallholder usage of fertilizer and it is unlikely whether such applications would be beneficial under the smallholders' low level of management. Were the cutting of shade to result, such actions would be disastrous for it is unlikely (and unreasonable) that smallholders would maintain sufficient fertilizer applications in times of low prices'." (Anderson 1977:15)

6. It is interesting to note how roundly smallholders are condemned by those in authority when they make such a decision. Prime Minister Julius Chan, in a 1981 speech, implied that the smallholder was 'lazy' and 'unreliable', and accused them of a stubborn reluctance to use land which holds back development 'and it is development alone that brings the good things of life?'. (Allen 1982:4)

3

Exchanging Coffee

Introduction

The production locations outlined in the previous chapter lie buried beneath the second stage of commodity relations, exchange relations (the third stage in this industry being international trade, as discussed in Chapters 11, 12 and 13). Exchange relations are more visible to most people and consequently are capable of greater overt political manipulation by powerful interests. The previous chapter showed how white planters were forced -- as a result of limits on accumulation in production -- into manipulation of the market, presumably with state assistance, to extend profits. But what form did this take in the colonial coffee industry? How extensively did the Australian colonial administration tolerate white planter manipulation of marketing channels to disadvantage black smallholders? In this chapter, I examine the marketing chain in coffee in colonial Papua New Guinea. I uncover some 'natural' or 'inevitable' pinch points -- points at which control can be exercised -- and show how control was exercised, by whom and with what implications for the various groups in the industry. These pinch points are represented graphically in Figure 3.1. This chapter shows how the white planters established a cartel of exporters which gave them power over exchange of coffee in the colonial industry.

An Industry Designed for White Planter Dominance at the Export, Processor and Coffee Buyer Levels

In the coffee industry of colonial Papua New Guinea, there were five main exporting companies all foreign owned (and mainly Australian owned) trading companies. There were ANGCO Marketing Pty Ltd, Gollin and Co. Ltd, Harrisons and Crosfield (ANZ) Ltd, E. Singer Pink and Co. Pty Ltd, Peter

Figure 3.1 Structure of the Colonial Coffee Market in Papua and New Guinea

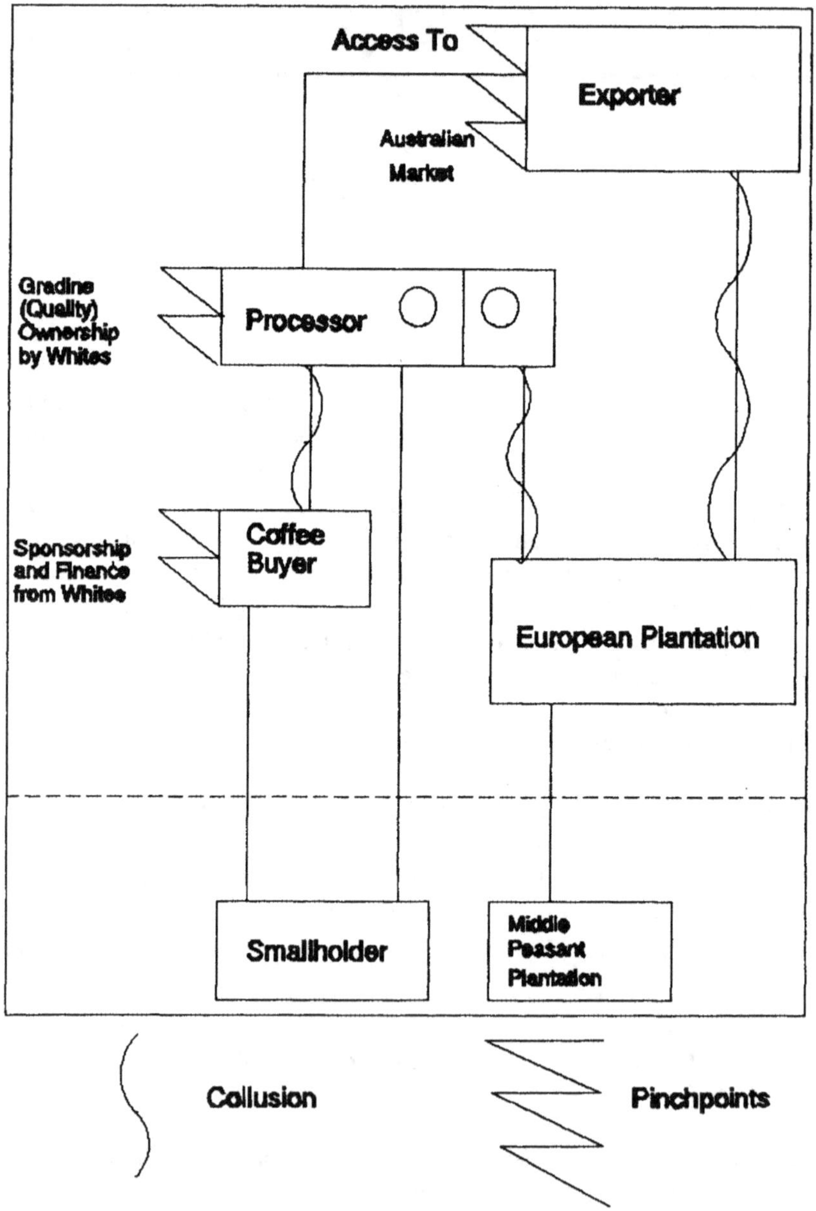

Jackett and Co. Pty Ltd. Some of these exporters were also roasters, while others were merely engaged in trade, providing cargo for their ships on the return journey to Sydney. The five exporters formed a voluntary organisation called the New Guinea Coffee Agents Association and maintained offices and agents in the main coffee export ports (Madang and Lae). The main destinations of New Guinea coffee were Brisbane, Sydney and Melbourne, and a small amount went to Europe. The purpose of the agents' cartel was to restrict competition at the export level as well as to lobby the metropolitan state for special tariff concessions for access to Papua New Guinea coffee. The cartel also enabled the exporters to present a united front in Papua New Guinea to the Administration.

How did the cartel operate to benefit its supporters? It charged different rates for agents' services so that uniform price setting appears 'not to be a feature of the cartel'. (Bureau of Agricultural Economics 1961:65) The New Guinea Coffee Agents Association was 'supported by most members of the Highlands Farmers and Settlers Association (HFSA) and native producers as well as the Administration'. (Bureau of Agricultural Economics 1961:63) Though there is no evidence of the New Guinea Coffee Agents Association using its cartel power artificially to raise the cost of transportation, it did benefit from its control over this pinch point. This can be shown in an analysis of the cost structure of exporting coffee from colonial Papua New Guinea. The cost of marketing coffee from plantation to the buyers' store in the country of destination (Sydney being the principal destination at this stage) was close to sixpence per pound. This was at a time when coffee was returning four shillings and two pence per pound in Sydney and smallholders were being paid between one-and-six and two-and-three pence per pound for parchment in Papua New Guinea. The sixpence per pound cost of marketing coffee from plantation to the buyers' store in the country of destination was made up of the following charges: (a) a penny per pound for internal air freight from the Highlands airports; (b) one-and-a-half pence per pound for port and shipping costs at territory ports; (c) one-and-a-half pence per pound for shipping freight on coffee from Lae and Madang to Brisbane, Sydney and Melbourne; (d) one-half penny per pound for bank exchange and insurance; and (e) one-and-a-half pence per pound for standard costs at the port in Sydney. (Bureau of Agricultural Economics 1961:68) In practice, the individual costs were by no means consistent for each shipment. The main factors affecting the charges were delays involving demurrage and storage, repacking, distances carted, the different rates charged for agents' services and freight rates for the different destinations. (Bureau of Agricultural Economics 1961:65)

This breakdown of the marketing costs gives some idea of the complexity of the marketing chain for coffee. Its complexity played a big part in the argument usually offered on behalf of the whites that they should dominate the marketing process (including the marketing of smallholder coffee) because the local marketing system was built up by the settlers and only they had the equipment and know-how to bring coffee to its port of destination. (Finney 1973:54) A significant aspect of this complexity was the extraordinary situation whereby all coffee produced in the Highlands was taken to the port at Lae or Madang by DC3 aircraft. This was a comparatively cheap system of internal marketing (a penny per pound for a fully loaded DC3 holding three tonnes). There was in any case no alternative because, until the construction of the Highlands Highway in the mid-1960s, the road from the Eastern Highlands to Lae was not trafficable for regular transport, especially between the Markham Valley and Kainantu. Even today there is no trafficable road between the Highlands and the port at Madang. But internal marketing by DC3 could only be kept relatively economical when very large cargoes were freighted. The BAE reports that the cost of internal marketing by DC3 doubled if the planes could not be filled (Bureau of Agricultural Economics 1961:66) This situation totally precluded smaller indigenous entrepreneurs from becoming involved in internal marketing in a way that marketing by road transport would not. The marketing structure from plantation to territory port ensured white planter dominance over this stage of the marketing chain. This dominance was enhanced by the fact that white planters often had financial linkages with exporters and vice versa and white planters entered into contracts with exporters to deliver to them a certain volume of coffee. Such an arrangement ensured for planters that their coffee would be exported and for exporters that they would have a supply for overseas buyers. At the same time, it discouraged both planters and exporters from deviating from contracts and established clients. In this way, competition in internal marketing was further discouraged. White planter dominance over this stage of the marketing chain was further enhanced by the fact that the grower had to bear the full cost of delivery from plantation to the buyers' store in the country of destination. (Bureau of Agricultural Economics 1961:63) This required considerable resources and access to credit as planters waited for payment from exporters. It was a cost that neither native growers nor entrepreneurs could bear.

Foreigners and white planters also retained control over processing factories and thereby dominated the market structure at this pinch point. Most of the processing plants in the Eastern Highlands were set up in colonial times initially to process plantation coffee, but also to hull smallholder coffee. In the Eastern Highlands, European plantations usually possessed their own coffee mills or had their coffee processed in mills with which they were financially associated. (Finney 1973:160)[1] Control of processing was important for it virtually guaranteed the processor control over the smallholder crop. Without access to a privately owned milling factory, smallholders were unable to get their coffee hulled. Smallholders were faced with the option of direct or indirect delivery of their cherry or parchment to the processing factory. Direct delivery was available to those who lived close to the processing factory.

Those smallholders who could deliver cherry to the factory had to live very close to it since the cherry had to be processed within 24 hours. Smallholders who were some distance from the factory and who were prepared to process parchment could store it and deliver it to the factory door when transport was available or when the price was right. The advantage of delivery to the factory door from the smallholders' point of view was that daily changes in coffee prices were posted on the factory wall and the smallholder could be sure that the price offered was the correct one.

The smallholder in Papua New Guinea also had the option of selling parchment or cherry indirectly to the processing factory through a possibly unique pinch point -- a system of roadside buying. Little is known about this in either the colonial or post-colonial period, for it is subject to immense variation. Simple observation of the process of roadside buying and selling suggests that the process is highly arbitrary. The system works fairly simply, being based on individual buyers with access to cash for buying coffee, a truck and a weighing machine. These buyers drive around the Highlands and offer to buy cherry or parchment from villagers waiting at the side of the road with their produce. The buyer will inspect the bag or bucketful of produce for quality, weigh it and offer the smallholder a price. The smallholder will sell or not sell, depending on whether the price is thought to be reasonable. There are many factors which affect the price that is offered to smallholders and one cannot generalise as to whether the price offered by a roadside buyer is fair or whether smallholders are justified in refusing, as they frequently do, to sell to the buyer. Among the factors that will cause the price to vary from one roadside transaction to another are the distance and difficulty of access of the site of the transaction from a major centre or processing plant, the degree of competition among buyers in the locality, the buyers' and smallholders' canniness and the variation from day to day, month to month, year to year of advertised prices and ultimately of the world price. (Howlett, Hide and Young 1976:232)

There are two structural features of the system of roadside buying which caused it to become a significant political issue in post-colonial Papua New Guinea. I will examine these in much greater depth. The first is that roadside buying offered one of the few commercial activities in the coffee industry that indigenous people could enter into apart from coffee growing itself. Thus it has always been a very sensitive issue among Papua New Guineans, and one which is politically controversial. The second feature is that coffee buying can require a fair amount of financial backing, cash to purchase smallholder coffee as well as finance for a truck, etc. It also requires a surety that the produce the buyer brings in will be processed at the factory -- if it is cherry it has to be done more or less immediately -- and that the buyer will not be turned away due to existing maximum utilisation of the factory. This feature has usually meant that the buyer has entered into a financial arrangement with the processor who will provide the financial backing and guarantee processing of the buyer's haul. 'Prior to 1974 most roadside buying of coffee was undertaken or controlled by overseas companies, most of whom also operated processing facilities'. (Densley n.d.:20) In this way, processors managed also to control the coffee-buying pinch point in the marketing structure.

Control of processing and coffee buyers enhanced the white planters' control over smallholder coffee for they were able to make substantial profits from processing smallholder coffee. Given the restriction on expansion of European plantations, this was an important source of extra income for white planters. It also advanced white planter accumulation through investment in processing plants. However, the fact that it was profitable to invest in processing reinforced the existence of two different forms of production in the coffee industry because white planters then invested in processing commodities produced by smallholders rather than undertaking the production of these commodities themselves. White planter control over processing allowed planters to engage in what Bernstein (1977) calls 'vertical concentration' of smallholders which "refers to the co-ordination, standardisation, and (greater or lesser) supervision of the production of numerous individual small producers through a central agency [in this case a central mechanism] . . . [which] represents productive capital directly". (Bernstein 1977:70)

In the colonial coffee industry of Papua New Guinea this mechanism was a grading system which was certainly introduced originally as a mechanism for quality control but which had the effect of further devalorising the labour of smallholder producers by further reducing the price paid for peasant coffee.

It is not an easy matter to show that processing the smallholder crop was a profitable venture in the absence of audits and taxation figures for colonial processing factories. However, it is clear that processors continued to process smallholder coffee so they certainly considered it an economical proposition, even if it was not a highly lucrative one. It can be shown that the returns to a processor of processing smallholder coffee were not greatly different from the returns accruing to a planter who produced and processed the crop.

Given that the processor of smallholder coffee did not have to pay the costs of production, it may even be that the rate of profit from processing smallholder coffee was higher than that realised by the planter-processor. We can use the figures presented from the BAE Report (1961) above to get some ideas of the return to the processor from processing smallholder coffee. At that time, one pound of coffee was returning four-and-twopence in Sydney, of which sixpence per pound was the cost of marketing coffee from the plantation or factory door to the buyer's store in the country of destination. Coffee was worth three-and-six per pound at the factory door. At the time, the smallholder was being paid between one-and-six and two-and-threepence per pound for parchment. The conservation rate for parchment to green bean (smallholder) is 1:0.7 so that one pound of parchment produces only 0.7 pound of green bean after processing. Thus 0.7 pound of green bean would be worth nearly two–and–tenpence at the factory door, at prevailing rates. The margin between what the smallholder is paid for parchment and the value of that coffee at the factory door is the return to the processor which includes profit margin as well as costs, interests on capital, etc. This margin is nearly one–and–fourpence to seven pence per pound.

What of the costs, interests on capital, etc. per pound borne by the processor? This would be a fairly low figure. For a start, the parchment has already been pulped, fermented and dried which are the most labour – – intensive parts of the processing operation. All the processor needs to do is sort, dry, hull, dry again and bag the coffee. The hulling and initial drying are done by machine, and are not labour intensive. Further, processing machines have a long life, so interest on capital and depreciation costs would not be high. A maximum figure for cost of processing would be one–and–one–half pence per pound. Thus the profit margin of the processor of smallholder coffee would probably be between fivepence and one–half pence per pound.

What of the profit realised by the planter–processor? The BAE provides an average breakdown for thirty colonial plantations covered in detail by the BAE survey. (Bureau of Agricultural Economics 1961:36) The average yield for the thirty plantations was 1150 pound of green bean. The average return to the operator after all operating costs had been extracted was £68. This is a return of approximately one–halfpence per pound. Thus, depending of course on the price paid for parchment, it was sometimes possible to have a return per pound on processing smallholder parchment equal to the return on the growing and processing of plantation coffee.

White planters managed in conjunction with the Administration to standardise and co–ordinate the production of the numerous smallholders by imposing upon them a system of grading. There is nothing unusual about such a system for agricultural produce. Almost all such produce has a system of differentiation in terms of quality so that a product of a desired standard should find its correct market. Grading systems are usually viewed as non–discriminatory, quality–control mechanisms which are especially important where the product is produced for an overseas market. In many cases, this is precisely how grading systems function. Quality control was stated as the reason grading was adopted in the colonial coffee industry of Papua New Guinea. Cartledge writes:

> as a principle, grading systems help to co–ordinate and to relate production with market demand. Aims of government trade policies include facilitating exports and in this connection a major component is the establishment and enforcement of export standards. Statutory export standards or grading, which are maintained on many agricultural commodities, contribute to a reputation for quality on overseas markets and assist marketing . . . A government function is to provide

> and maintain minimum standards, promoting the level and value of exports. (Cartledge 1978:157)

Grading systems are, however, also linked to internal price. This simple connection can give dominant classes a potential lever over subordinate classes and a means to maintain control of the system of production. Whether a grading system works mainly to enforce quality standards (as presumably the Administration intended) or to reinforce an industry structure which is unequal (as would suit planters) depends on whether quality controls are applied indiscriminately upon all coffee produced and whether they actually work to ensure better quality.

The grading system adopted in the coffee industry of colonial Papua New Guinea was based on a two-step process. A first step was the establishment of grades that applied at coffee auctions. The aim here was to differentiate coffee according to whether whole beans were required for roasting and thus were of suitable bean size and appearance or whether they were required for instant coffee manufacture, so that appearance was not so important. (Shand 1972:193) Plantation produced coffee was generally thought to be most suitable for roasting and was graded according to size and appearance as A, B or C (A being the highest quality). Smallholder coffee was thought to be suitable for sale to instant coffee manufacturers. This system was translated into one of internal quality control and price setting in the second step of the grading process. It is the internal grading system which plays a role in setting class boundaries inside Papua New Guinea, and it is this system on which I will concentrate.

The internal grading system divides into two sections, grades for green beans at the point of sale to the exporter and grades for the sale of parchment. There are three main grades for parchment: Grade X – – highest quality; Grade Y – – defective parchment that has been either over-fermented or has suffered from damp storage, has not been washed properly or has been ripped in the pulping process; and triage is the third level of parchment, of grossly inferior quality. (Department of Agriculture, Stock and Fisheries 1970:5–6) Quality control of the smallholder crop can be exercised through the grading for parchment (X, Y and triage) at the point of purchase either by the roadside buyer or at the processing factory door. The control of quality of green bean is exercised at the point of sale to exporter. The assumption in the colonial system of grading was that plantation green bean would leave the processing factory as A, B, C, etc. to be purchased by roasters while green bean derived from smallholder parchment would leave the processing factory to be purchased by instant coffee manufacturers.

Is this, in fact, how the system has operated? Perhaps, though, it is a loose system. It is the processor/planter who bags green bean and grades it. But is it always the case that smallholder coffee, once processed into green bean, must always be graded at an inferior level and therefore be of interest only to instant coffee manufacturers? Might it not be possible that, after processing, some X and Y parchment might be suitable for grading as A or B green bean? There would be economic incentives for the processor to grade coffee in this manner because the price paid for high quality coffee for roasting is higher than that paid for green bean sold for instant coffee. The exporter checks the coffee and ensures that green bean labelled A and B is of that standard but the exporter has no interest as to whether the origin of the coffee was a plantation or smallholder unit of production. There would seem to be few limitations to the processor/planter selling A, B graded green bean which is derived from X, Y parchment and from smallholders. If quality was the main criterion upon which a grading system operates then it should be the case that the assumption that plantation coffee was in all cases the most suitable coffee for sale to roasters and that smallholder coffee was suitable only for instant coffee production would be regularly overturned as the quality of the coffee from both plantations and smallholders rose and fell periodically. The actual organisation of the production unit where coffee was produced would be less significant in grading than a close inspection of the actual quality of the coffee revealed. The problem with the type of system operating at the level of processing is that if smallholder parchment of X, Y grade was actually processed into A, B green bean, there exists no mechanism to recompense the smallholder who sold the parchment at the X, Y parchment rate on the basis that it would produce the lower priced green bean. In other words, the processor could make a windfall profit if the quality control mechanism were to operate at this level only.

The point where smallholders could receive some recompense for high quality production is at the point of selling parchment at the factory door or to the roadside buyer. Here the choice is between the higher quality X grade parchment and the ill-sorted, perhaps over-fermented, Y grade parchment. The smallholder who sells parchment at the factory door can have it inspected for quality. Most evidence suggests, however, that this is not possible where parchment is sold to roadside buyer. Casual observation suggests that buyers know little about quality, test for it in a casual fashion or not at all and assume all roadside coffee is Y grade coffee and pay accordingly. This suggests that the main criterion for buying much of the smallholder crop, especially at the roadside, is the structure of the production unit rather than the actual quality of the parchment presented for sale. Smallholders are continually exhorted to improve the quality of their crop but if they are always to be paid at the Y grade level then where is the incentive to do anything about quality?

This study of grading at the level of processing and at the level of purchasing parchment cannot be taken to have shown conclusively that the grading system for coffee in the colonial coffee industry of Papua New Guinea was an artificial construct designed simply to profit the dominant planter class. But an examination of the relationship between quality and the production unit does show that arguments about quality control are very often not about quality at all, or even about profit, but about control of the industry marketing structure. The grading system ensures a concentration of smallholder coffee at a level of reduced prices compared with that of plantation coffee. It allows the dominant class to conflate unit structure with price structure whether or not the actual product deserves to be discriminated against on the grounds of quality. In this process, the dominant class has imposed a squeeze on household production beyond the simple reproduction squeeze because the quality argument allows peasant labour to be further devalorised through a price discrimination mechanism. The fact that it is done at the level of exchange, and presented simply as a question of quality control, makes the devalorisation of household labour less obvious, and therefore easier to accept.

White Planter Greed and the Failure to Sponsor a Prosperous, but Controlled, Black Élite

The white planters soon found, as a result of the expansion in the industry, that they had to devise a strategy for those who did not fit the neat division into planters and smallholders, and who could not be accommodated within the boundaries set by a market structure. This new group were advanced local coffee growers. The white planters attempted to establish a new class location in the industry by sponsoring the formation of a middle peasantry. The HFSA began sponsoring in the early 1960s certain local Papua New Guineans, a 'new élite' who were encouraged to go into coffee production on 'middle income' properties, small plantations of about 35–40 hectares. An editorial in the journal of the HFSA noted that:

> Unless the investment policy is pointed to a continuous plan to replace the dwindling group of expatriate owner-managers with a 'New Class' of substantial Papuan and New Guinean estate owners most of the middle income properties will disappear by being absorbed by bigger company organisations. We will then be left with an even wider gap -- between only huge expatriate estate owning groups and minuscule peasant farmers. This is the type of situation which has led to violent expropriation in newly self-governing countries, generally followed by mismanagement and damage to valuable properties because those who have taken over have not had the intermediate benefit of experience in managing anything larger than a peasant plot. (*New Guinea Highlands Bulletin*, July 1968:7)

The idea of sponsoring locals in this way was first suggested by Ian Downs in 1954–55 when he was District Commissioner in the Eastern Highlands district. Downs wrote:

> the idea of Partnership is not new but the means and circumstances of creating

> a genuine and sincere partnership between Europeans and natives seldom exists. This is probably the only place in the world at the present time where the circumstances actually exist for sincere partners to be created. (quoted in Finney 1973:49)

Europeans decided to assist selected 'natives' to produce coffee and, through the demonstration effect, ease them into advanced unit production.

Some observers of the development of the colonial coffee industry such as Finney (1973) took the language of partnership seriously, although he argued that its actual impact on black élite development was not great. Finney shows how partnership worked in some cases (Finney 1973:55), though in many cases he argues it was less European sponsorship which got indigenes started in business and more the fact that native entrepreneurs manipulated traditional structures and relations, which Finney argues were pre–adapted to capitalism. In fact, the attempt to sponsor a new black élite is reminiscent of many late colonial strategies in Africa and elsewhere, a strategy which suited the specific political needs of the white planters in the industry but which also appealed to the administration's dreams of gradual development – – the emergence of a 'yeomanry' – – in the context of increased talk about decolonisation.

The language of partnership misses the crucially important fact that few new black elites were sponsored into business ventures which would be endurable and hence most did not gain real power in the post–colonial period. In fact, there were at least two different paths which dominant class formation might take as a result of the expansion of the coffee industry in the late colonial period. One was sponsorship of small or medium sized plantations along the lines of the HFSA model and another was business activity – – private ownership of trade stores, trucking businesses, influential positions in co–operative societies or savings and loan societies – – all activities which were related to the fact that the Highlands money economy was dominated by coffee.

Each of these paths and the important difference between them can be illustrated by drawing upon the empirical material gathered by Finney on business leaders. The sponsorship of a Papua New Guinean into ownership and/or control of a medium sized plantation took many forms. Some, like Baito Heiro, were personal servants or foremen of white planters. (Finney 1973:55) They were established on land belonging to their own village and closely assisted and supervised in the care and operation of their own plantation by the planter for whom they worked. Others, like Bono Azinifa, were Big Men who had had contact with whites as personal servants during the war and were well placed to draw assistance both from the clan – – in the form of unpaid labour – – and from Europeans (Bono followed the advice of a European settler who had helped to gain land near his village on planting and establishment of a nursery. He owns the Kesa plantation of some 75 acres.)

Still others, like Sinake Giregire, left their clan areas as children. Such men usually began a series of European jobs, Sinake working as everything from a mechanic's helper, to operating a business based on a hand–operated pit–saw, to gold prospecting, before returning to the village with money to establish a coffee plantation. Sinake had shown he could be successful in European business, and this encouraged his clansmen to allocate him a large tract of land which he still operates. It is called Yan Owa plantation and it is of some 80 acres.

Another way to become established on a middle income property was through some connection with the colonial state. This could help in obtaining land, and gave many of the 'new élite' a start. Of Finney's ten big businessmen, for example, two had been *Luluais* (government–appointed officials in the village), two had been workers on the Aiyura agricultural station and one had been an agricultural assistant working with DASF extension patrols. Presumably knowledge of coffee growing plus an understanding of how the state operated and how the extension system worked, helped these businessmen into coffee. The colonial state connection was not, however, a guarantee of success in the Highlands because much of the production there was private and did not require DASF involvement. This was very different from other areas of Papua New Guinea where there was little private enterprise and where production, as well as marketing, had to be undertaken by the state. In the end, very few government officials such as *Luluais* or government employees actually got started in coffee. (Finney 1973:91) By the mid–1960s, when the Coffee Marketing Board had been established, DASF was virtually irrelevant as an economic mobiliser in the Eastern Highlands.

The experience of those who moved into middle income plantations to grow coffee in Eastern Highlands contrasts vividly with another group, a budding *petit bourgoeisie* which, in the 1960s, began to establish a base in the embryonic service industry around Goroka. The best known story of such a person is that of Hari Gotoha, as described by Finney. (1973:104–107) Hari established one of the most profitable and diverse Gorokan–owned commercial organisations in the colonial Eastern Highlands. Hari's business partner was his senior clansman, Soso Subi, who became associated with Cottle, a DASF officer. Soso learned to grow coffee and established a medium sized plantation. His plantation, which was really a plantation for the Asaroyufa people, provided the Gotoha–Subi partnership with its coffee base. However, most of their capital was invested in service industries such as a supermarket in Goroka town, a restaurant and two heavy–duty trucks used for local and long–haul work. (Finney 1973:105) Trucking businesses and trade stores were among the service businesses most favoured by Gorokans like Hari because they gave a quick return on capital which could be reinvested. Another businessman who began in the service industry rather than coffee – – and who later became a partner of Hari's – – was Auwo Ketauwo. Along with others such as the present premier of the Eastern Highlands, James Yanepa, Auwo got his start in the 1960s, not through coffee nor even through private commercial activity such as trade stores and trucking, but through the new institutions, co–operative movements and savings and loans societies. A base in these institutions gave these men access to credit which they used, sometimes in an extra–legal fashion, to acquire trucks or trade stores. It was only much later, in the late 1970s, that they began growing coffee on a commercial scale. Finney has been at pains to reveal that behind these budding *petit bourgeois* businessmen there was 'a strong clan element'. (Finney 1973:106) Of Hari's venture he writes:

> some money pooled from the Asaroyufa people had apparently been invested in one or more of the enterprises. In addition, the very location of Hari's store and restaurant on Asaroyufa land and the fact that money derived from the sale of Asaroyufa land and the sale of coffee from Soso's plantation (which, as we have seen, was partially built up by clan labour) had gone into financing the investments meant that in a sense the Asaroyufa people could regard the businesses as part of the general resources of the clan, rather than the strictly individual enterprise of one or two of their number. (Finney 1973:106)

The fact that the clan 'could regard' Hari's enterprise as their own is surely irrelevant if they have no power to expropriate his business or at least make plausible threats to do so. Unlike those moving into the production of coffee on middle income properties, the budding *petit bourgeois* businessmen were not only less tied to the clan and therefore freer to develop on the basis of profit, but also more independent of European planters.

The contrast between those who moved into middle income properties and those who moved into service activities is fundamental to understanding the process of class formation and much of the politics of the colonial and post–colonial Eastern Highlands. The key difference emerging out of these differences, i.e. coffee production and small business, is the degree of autonomy each had in colonial times from others in the colonial coffee industry, namely the dominant white planters and the subordinate smallholders. Whatever the future held for these two groups in the post–colonial period, dependence on white planters in the production of coffee proved a major barrier to further advancement in both the colonial and post–colonial economic order. The main reason for this, as the following shows, is that the new black élite in coffee production sponsored by the white planters had very little autonomy because, in the important areas of control of the productive forces (land and labour), access to investment capital and control of marketing, they were almost wholly dependent on the white planters themselves.

From the beginning, the new black élite were dependent upon white planters if their plantations were to be a commercial success. Their dependence was partly due to the fact that their plantations were very small in comparison with European holdings. This usually made it uneconomic for them to engage in processing beyond the parchment state. The black élite had greater overheads than smallholders. They could not afford the security that processing offered as a hedge against market prices if it also meant an economic loss. Thus the middle peasants proved even more vulnerable to control by white planters through the marketing structure than smallholders.

The dilemma of the black élite was that while their class location was similar to that of the smallholder in that land and labour were supplied from within the household, the class relations in which the black élite were enmeshed were more like those of a planter. The problem for the black élite was that the autonomy which should have flowed from household reproduction was undercut by the size of the production unit which limited their options and forced them into a dependent marketing structure. Their plantations were not large enough, however, to generate surpluses which would allow them to seize control and command the external network upon which they depended. Thus, for them, reproduction was more problematic than either smallholder or white planter reproduction. This, of course, suited white planters who were aiming to incorporate advanced Papua New Guineans into the existing system. The planters, in their paternalistic way, considered that the establishment of a small plantation by a black man was in itself a major achievement.

The black élite was also limited in the expansion of commercial activity due to the fact that, for most of the 1960s, credit was not available to them. This was because they could not present their land as collateral. The setting up of the Development Bank in 1967 hardly altered this situation, because over the decade 1968–77, the loans and advances of the Development Bank totalled K71.7 million, but of this amount only K1.1 million (or 1.53 percent) was allocated to the coffee industry, including both plantations and smallholders. (Lam 1984:181) Where credit was available to Papua New Guineans, this was rarely for non–agricultural purposes. Thus the middle peasants at the level of production remained locked into an unstable form of production. Production was unstable not because the scope of the production unit itself was inappropriate but because its survival depended on other strata (smallholders) and upon white planter processing of their crop.

Those in service activities suffered few of the difficulties of the black élite in coffee production. This was because the small, black businesspeople, through the nature of their enterprises, had broken the nexus between household control of the productive forces and production relations. They certainly used assistance from the clan when they could get it, but it had no call upon trucking businesses or restaurants as it did where production required the use of clan land and clan labour for coffee growing. They were also fairly free from white planter dominance. The marketing structures into which they were integrated were often particular to indigenes and not under expatriate control. They would of course have appreciated access to investment funds but this was difficult to achieve. Nevertheless, lending patterns show that after 1967 the Development Bank tended to lend more easily to small business activities such as trucking businesses than to black élites in coffee production. As a result of the much greater autonomy the small business stratum was not politically active in colonial Papua New Guinea. It had no need to be.

The colonial coffee market was structured in the interests of white planters. White planter class boundaries were conserved in the colonial coffee market mainly through their control of parts of the marketing chain, and as a result of their private enterprise and skill and knowledge of marketing procedures. The white planter class boundaries were also conserved *vis-à-vis* smallholders throughout the colonial period, not only because they controlled the marketing procedures but also because they managed to devalorise household labour at the level of circulation. This was done through a grading system which caused peasant coffee to be regarded as of inferior quality and to be paid for at a lower rate than plantation coffee. In effect this has doubled the squeeze on smallholders, as I have shown, for it advanced planter interests at the expense of smallholders. The colonial system of grading coffee has been retained in the post-colonial coffee industry.

A further aspect of white planter control of the marketing structure was the attempt by planters to manipulate race relations as a means of further conserving their control of the industry. Boundary manipulation on the basis of race should not surprise, for the colonial coffee industry was governed after all by a colonial state, one structured on racism. The racial problem for white planters in the coffee industry was how to allow the advancement of small numbers of 'natives' into ownership and control of advanced production units (i.e. plantations), but not at the same time to generate competition for themselves. This was attempted through the promotion of 'racial partnership'. Finney described this process as a system of patron-client relations, the aim being to diffuse plantation skills and knowledge, in the form of altruism or good citizenship. In fact, as I have shown, racial partnership was an ingenious attempt to co-opt leading 'natives' in the coffee industry, so that they would take the side of white planters. Racial partnership was doomed to fail because it was little more than an attempt to lock the black élite into a dependent economic and political relationship in the industry. As a result, the new black élite was inherently unstable as a social group. This was because it could reproduce itself only through specific relations with the dominant white planters (mainly because the state denied it access to financial capital for non-agricultural purposes), and through dependence on other strata, most particularly the smallholders. The smallholders were frequently mobilised by the black élites, through kinship ties, to perform labour on their plantations, labour often provided free, underlying the non-viability of the new black élite plantation.

Notes

1. The analysis is applied to the Eastern Highlands. In Chimbu, by contrast, the market structure at the processing pinch point was completely different, based on monopoly control of processing by the Chimbu Coffee Co-operative.

4

Administering the Coffee Industry in Colonial Papua New Guinea

Introduction

The manipulation of markets beyond normal commercial power became more and more important to white planters as the industry expanded. Only the use of the state to reduce competitiveness in the industry could enable the white planters to secure and extend their control. However, it is a paradox of white power dominance of the coffee industry that the colonial Administration never became an instrument in their hands. The previous chapter has shown how white planter power was established over exchange relations without any overt manipulation of the colonial state to establish that dominance. This is not to claim that the colonial state was non-interventionist. But its intervention was not at the behest of the white planters. Such a state may be described as a Bonapartist, in the sense that it was transcendent over all interested parties in the industry.

In this chapter, I show how the need to reduce competition by white planters caused them to lobby the colonial state's specialist branch, the Department of Agriculture, Stock and Fisheries (DASF) to attempt to outlaw, by force, the growth of the smallholder industry. This attempt was a failure and it is fairly clear that the Administration approached its task in a half-hearted way. More successful as a form of state intervention was the setting up, in 1964, of the Coffee Marketing Board (CMB). The CMB was not an instrument in white planter hands either, although it did ratify exchange arrangements already established by white planters. But it had no power to systematically advantage white planters and, in any case, its setting up was triggered by the establishment of the International Coffee Organisation (ICO) and the joining of that organisation by Australia on behalf of its Papua New

Guinea colony rather than as a response to pressure from domestic interests in Papua New Guinea.

The Establishment of an Agricultural Department to Police Rural Industry

Most observers who have analysed the establishment of the coffee industry in colonial Papua New Guinea give a good deal of credit to DASF for encouraging Gorokans through extension services to begin coffee production. Finney writes that:

> except for a few men who, like Baito Heiro, received direct assistance from European settlers, most would-be Gorokan coffee growers had to wait until the Department of Agriculture, Stock and Fisheries (DASF) began to offer extension services in 1953 before they could find out enough to grow it properly. (Finney 1973:57)

The BAE (1961) presented a more balanced picture. It stated that the expansion of the local coffee industry was mainly due to the help and encouragement of the Administration (DASF), supplemented to no small extent by the activities of the European planters and the religious missions. (quoted in Cartledge 1978:23) This view is endorsed by Cartledge himself. (Cartledge 1978:48) There can be little doubt that DASF did assist in the establishment of the coffee industry, because the setting up of extension services in 1953 coincided with an explosion of smallholder coffee growing. The success of the DASF extension effort in the 1950s was due in part to its monopoly control over certain of the productive forces essential for the establishment of coffee gardens. Good and Donaldson show how DASF:

> nurseries were planted close to the village post house and were left under the watchful eyes of the village Luluai and village constable. In July 1953 the extension officer from the Eastern Highlands district, R.W. Cottle, reported that nine nurseries had been established in the Goroka district. Of these nine, six were being looked after by Luluais and three by native men. (Good and Donaldson n.d.:22)

In the period of the establishment of the coffee industry, before smallholder gardens matured and thus generated their own seed, it is very likely that the only way in which seed could be obtained by smallholders was from DASF or from 'partnership' with Europeans. This gave DASF a power over a vital input in the establishment of the coffee industry. This was a power never equalled by DASF in the operational phase of the industry in the 1960s.

Influence in an industry is achieved only through the exercise of control at some point in the commodity chain (the production process and/or the marketing chain) and not by legislative right or executive fiat. It is often thought that those who operate and control DASF had the 'right' of influence in agriculture because it is the appropriate state department. But this view ignores the more concrete fact that in places and industries like coffee in the Eastern Highlands, where it does not control an essential input in production or a marketing pinch point, DASF could play only a marginal role in the development process. In most cases, technical expertise offered by DASF did not function as an essential input because it was ignored or not needed by smallholders. This point was conclusively demonstrated in the period after the withdrawal of extension services in 1961, because this had no effect on the continued expansion of coffee production and planting by smallholders. Also, it must be frankly acknowledged that the role of the *didiman* (extension officer) is limited, because he is rarely able to contact more than a handful of growers.

DASF failed to devise approaches to development in the coffee industry that were compatible with the structure-in-production of smallholders. Under its director, W. Cottrell Dormer, DASF adopted, in the late 1940s:

> a policy aimed at improving nutrition and living standards of the native people by mixed farming on individual smallholdings capable of producing adequate subsistence for a man and his family and in addition sufficient cash crops to obtain the money necessary to him for the satisfying of other wants and for the payment of taxes. (Good and Donaldson n.d.:12)

But there were some problems in this conception, especially insofar as it suggested a change to nuclear family-type farming and a reorganisation of households along individualist lines. I have shown how the success of smallholder coffee production was due in part to the fact that coffee production did not require a basic reorganisation internal to the household where the division of labour based on age and gender could be maintained and patterns of authority not be disrupted. However, the DASF approach appeared to be a policy aimed at reorganising the division of labour in the household. Could DASF seriously expect to initiate a change that capital itself could not achieve?

DASF staff were aware of the contradictions likely to be generated by sponsoring mixed farming on individual holdings, especially in coffee. Finney reports:

> in seeking to promote individually controlled coffee plots in Goroka the agricultural officers were actually following local precedents in land use, for the growing and exploitation of sweet potatoes and other subsistence crops was largely an individual matter for a man and his wife or wives. The agricultural officers did realise, however, that in traditional Gorokan society there was an important element of co- operation and pooling of resources, and they sought to tap this without violating the principle of individual coffee plots. The formula they hit upon was simple, effective and congenial to Gorokans: coffee nurseries where seedlings were grown for distribution to individual planters,

> became a group responsibility and the subsequent planting, caring for and exploitation of the coffee trees were an individual responsibility. (Finney 1973:62)

The only part of this 'synthesis' that alters internal household organisation is, paradoxically, the communal part. Having to work in village nurseries disrupts the time household members have to devote to internal household concerns. It is a mistake to assume that group organisation external to the household is somehow the same thing as internal household organisation. The form may be the same but the household is disrupted by these external duties. In any case, the abandoning of the village coffee nurseries in 1961, when the DASF put a ban on village smallholder coffee development, meant that the 'reorganisation' of the household was abandoned in favour of individual responsibility. The result was that the caring and maintenance of trees, etc. meant nothing more in terms of smallholder production of coffee than maintenance of existing internal household organisation. With the failure of the mixed farming strategy, DASF reverted to a tendency to present as a policy initiative a rationalisation of an existing situation. This meant saying little more about the structure of smallholder coffee production other than it should be on small plots containing 300–500 trees. (Densley n.d.:7) DASF even abandoned its attempts to get smallholders to line and space their gardens, and instead merely advised them how to care for and maintain coffee. In coffee, DASF also failed to make any impact on existing marketing arrangements. DASF accepted the 'private enterprise' approach of the Administration that government marketing was a necessary evil. In taking this approach, DASF undermined its support for coffee smallholdings as it failed to take the side of the smallholder where it mattered most, in marketing.

The failure of DASF was a political failure which expressed itself at a superficial level within the Administration, for DASF was regarded as a weak department in relation to others. DASF had no leader of the calibre of John Gunther at Health, for example, who continually achieved political and funding coups for his department. DASF officers were politically naïve. They did not see an industry structure as a system of resource distribution which created a field of struggle between contending groups. Instead, the DASF approach was one of facilitating technical innovation and diffusion (the Improvement Approach). This automatically weakened its support for the subordinate groups, the smallholders. The DASF never quite regained the authority it exercised in the establishment period of the coffee industry because it rarely sought it. Nor was it able to hold onto control over some valued input or market pinch point in coffee. It ended up by playing second fiddle to planters and then, in the 1960s, to the CMB.

Refining the Channels of Consultation and Control for White Planters: the Coffee Marketing Board (CMB)

White planters did not, however, have things all their own way in the coffee industry of colonial Papua New Guinea. Once the struggle began in 1962 to define the form and function of the special branch of the state in the coffee industry -- eventually set up in 1964 and called the Coffee Marketing Board (CMB) -- it became clear that though white planters were dominant in the internal marketing of coffee, they were merely one dominant class in one industry in one sector of the economy. It also became clear that the form and function of the CMB would be determined not only by the planters but also by the dominant classes throughout the social formation. In the setting up of the CMB, the other dominant class of influence was the metropolitan bourgeoisie and the Administration itself, a social category of great importance in a colonial situation.

The circumstances surrounding the birth of the CMB ensured that its early focus would be on the problem of exporting the crop. Among these circumstances were the existing Tariff Board arrangements. These provided for the marketing of a substantial portion of the Papua New Guinea coffee crop in Australia. A further circumstance was the establishment of the ICO, which it was correctly thought would soon require a branch of the colonial state to exercise certain controls relating to internal matters. There was in existence in Papua New Guinea, at the time the ICO was established, a coffee exporting committee which exercised controlling powers over the export of coffee from Papua New Guinea. The coffee exporting committee consisted of the Director of Agriculture and two coffee producer representatives, Downs and Hurrell. (Papua New Guinea Coffee Industry Board, April 1979)

Under the terms of the tariff arrangements Papua New Guinea was obliged to ensure that sufficient coffee was directed to Australia to satisfy this by-law arrangement. (Papua New Guinea Coffee Industry Board, May 1982:1) But the metropolitan bourgeoisie in Australia, like importers in the ICO, could not be sure that such an agreement would be honoured unless they had some policing power over the export of Papua New Guinea coffee or at least some say in the direction it took. It cannot be assumed that because Papua New Guinea was a colony of Australia that Australian commercial roasters could make demands and the metropolitan state would act automatically in the interests of its own bourgeoisie. In fact, political change had to be negotiated, arguments put, points of co-operation worked out, etc. This was especially the case in an industry like coffee with its complex internal and external dimensions. In decision-making in the industry it was not uncommon for the Administration in Port Moresby and the Department of External Territories (DOET) in Australia to disagree. In coffee, disagreement was made more likely by the fact that influential planters could extend their political reach to the metropole.

Under the existing arrangements, the export of the crop was solely in the hands of the Administration and the New Guinea Coffee Agents Association. This was an arrangement which usually satisfied the interests of Australian roasters but provided them with few guarantees of supply. The DOET, however, became concerned that the temporary by-law arrangements, and though offering assistance to producers, did not guarantee them a satisfactory sale and purchase price as had been the case in previously approved schemes. (Cartledge 1978:65–66) Concerning the earlier schemes it is important only to note that there were grounds for dissatisfaction from both importers (roasters) and exporters (or producers as DOET put it), and that this situation of dissatisfaction closely resembled the circumstances at the global level before the ICO was set up.

The outcome at the level of Australia-Papua New Guinea coffee trade was similar to that which occurred at the global level for it resulted in an attempt to devise a regulating authority to ensure both a supply of coffee to importers and a satisfactory price level for exporters. Thus the Tariff Board (1962) noted that further steps toward regulation might have to be taken if the by-law provisions failed. Among these steps, 'the establishment of a coffee marketing board was suggested [to the board] as a way of diminishing a number of problems facing the Territory's coffee industry'. (Cartledge 1978:64)

The HFSA had been calling for some time for a Coffee Marketing Board (Cartledge 1978:71) and seemed to assume quite naturally that such a board would be run by growers (meaning itself). This seemed to have been implicit in a statement by Hasluck in December 1962 when he said:

> The question of a coffee marketing board in Papua and New Guinea was discussed with the industry several times by the Tariff Board inquiry, in connection with arrangements for the marketing of the Territory coffee crop. The view taken by the government is that a marketing board should not be imposed on the producers and owners of a crop but should be organised at their request and in consultation with them. This consultation is close and continuous. (quoted in Cartledge 1978:74)

An initial problem the industry faced was in defining the form and function the CMB would take. This was not an easy matter because there were different problems, different state branches and different classes involved depending on whether the issue was control over exports or control over internal marketing. Grower control over marketing boards was the standard model for the majority of currently operating marketing boards in Australia. These operated under very tight regulating legislation and often gave the grower-dominated regulating board control over the internal market and export of the product. It was a system which the new Minister, Barnes, admitted in 1964 resulted in a view that "in Australia a marketing board for primary producers is a proven technique of significant advantage in improving marketing strength and obtaining a fair price for the producers themselves". (quoted in Cartledge 1978:301)

Part of the reason things were so difficult in the coffee industry was the complexity of the class structure as it related to the colonial industry. The HFSA represented the dominant class in the industry (the white planters), but the metropolitan bourgeoisie could exercise influence over the metropolitan state through the Department of Trade and Industry and in this way modify HFSA dominance, particularly over export of the crop. The fact that the state was split into Department of External Territories and the Papua New Guinea Administration also meant that the HFSA simply had neither the reach nor the resources to mount a lobbying campaign to get all branches on side. They mounted a campaign of this type over the tariff issue but it was costly and time consuming and not convincing. In any case, there were significant differences between the various state branches. The DOET and Administration were both anxious about revenue and conscious of the political power of the planters inside Papua New Guinea. They therefore aimed for export arrangements not altering the system of export restrictions into Australia which worked in favour of territory coffee. The Department of Trade and Industry, however, saw these restrictions as completely temporary and wished to have them removed as soon as possible. This complexity ensured that there was very little chance in the colonial coffee industry in Papua New Guinea of one class being singled out to dominate the industry through a marketing board in the way producer marketing co-operatives did for dominant classes in many Australian rural industries.

Each *dominant* class – – internal and external – – had a significant stake in the industry and therefore in the form and function of the CMB. Australian roasting firms and the representatives of exporters, the metropolitan bourgeoisie, were naturally interested in discussions about the form and function of the CMB. The former wished to be assured of supply and were concerned that existing tariff arrangements should not be altered in a way that would increase the cost of their raw material. The latter were apprehensive lest the CMB interfere with existing export marketing arrangements. Would the CMB act as an oligopolist on behalf of the territory's growers and sell to exporters through an auction system as occurred in most African colonies or would the system of private treaty continue?

The metropolitan state itself was also concerned about the form and function the CMB would take, for it would, through the Australian Department of Trade and Industry, conduct the affairs of the Papua New Guinea coffee industry when it represented Papua New Guinea at the ICO. The Department of Trade and Industry was concerned to defend the interests of Australian companies involved in coffee commerce and also to defend an ideological predisposition to minimise state control in industry and trade. The interests of the

Administration in the process of setting up the CMB were both internal and external. At the external level, the Administration was as determined as planters to ensure that the crop found an export market. This was particularly urgent at the time because, as a result of the establishment of the ICO, export restrictions would have to be faced for the first time. The Administration aimed to make sure that such restrictions had a minimum effect on Papua New Guinea. Internally, of course, the form and function of the CMB would affect the role of the Administration's specialist branch for rural development, the DASF. White planters were concerned lest the proposed marketing board undermine their control in the industry.

The complexity of the political struggle to define the role of the CMB in relation to exports meant that in the end the decision was made on the simplest of all criteria, that of cost. In 1963 when the establishment of the Board was under consideration, the Department of Trade and Industry prepared an analysis of the various functions the CMB could fulfil and in particular it presented 'hypothetical' budgets of CMB operations. (*New Guinea Highlands Bulletin*, April 1966) These budgets were based on a CMB which engaged in direct selling to exporters. The link between the function of the CMB and the cost of its operations was thus from the beginning very firmly established. Later in 1966 the wide range of possible CMB functions and the advantages and disadvantages of each of these were published by the HFSA. It added three further functions to the 'direct selling by the Board', functions outlined by the Department of Trade and Industry. These included (a) a public auction operated by the administration; (b) a proposal from an exporter (Harrisons and Crosfield [ANZ] Ltd) that a company be formed consisting of growers, buyers and the CMB to conduct auctions for the disposal of the Territory crop; and (c) a proposal for the Board to operate on the open market in competition with exporting agents.

All these proposals had advantages and disadvantages but the proposal that seemed least desirable was 'direct sales by the Board' as originally budgeted by the Department of Trade and Industry. It was a model of a CMB which would make the Board's functions very similar to those in many African countries. It operated through a system whereby the grower paid a levy -- usually through a reduction of the purchase price -- to a branch of the state which undertook to market the crop for the grower. The state branch incurs numerous expenses such as salaries, office equipment, remuneration and travelling, etc. in the process. This usually had to be paid for by the grower out of the levy. The argument for establishing such boards is 'organised marketing', which is supposed to reduce price slumps and equalise profits. The grower should become strengthened by having his own small stake in the marketing channels. The problem with the scheme is that it is expensive -- growers were told it would cost five pence per pound (*New Guinea Highlands Bulletin*, April 1966:9) to set up a 'direct selling board', and this was at time when the highest price for the best quality coffee was four shillings. In comparison, the entire marketing costs were only sixpence per pound at that time, as we have seen. Growers were simply not interested in the extra expense.

Another worrying feature of such schemes was that the board had to wait until the crop had been paid for before money was returned to the grower. The Department of Trade and Industry assumed:

> that the basis of sales will be the remittance of 75 percent of the agreed value after sampling, on receipt of shipping documents and the balance to come on receipt and acceptance of the consignment. This will mean that the entire proceeds of Australian sales should be received in the month following shipment. (*New Guinea Highlands Bulletin*, April 1966:9)

Anyone who knows how these arrangements operate in Africa would be wary of this statement. The white planters were powerful enough politically in Papua New Guinea to ensure that such a scheme would not be imposed upon them, so the proposal languished.

The result was that the existing arrangement was formalised and the CMB was relegated to a position where it played a very small role in the export of the coffee crop in colonial Papua New Guinea. Certain safety valves were built into the CMB legislation, but basically its function was mere regulation at the export level. The CMB regulated exports by means of licensing systems, exercising supervision over sales and distribution, standards and selling practices in respect of exports, and promoting trade, market research and developing new markets while ensuring continuity of supply. At the external level, the CMB was to function as a regulatory tool mainly for the purpose of administering ICO quotas. It did not operate in any particular dominant class interest at this level. The dominant class in the industry (the planters) had to share power with the metropolitan bourgeoisie, so the CMB's external role would be neutral in class terms. For the HFSA, a regulatory CMB meant precisely that, and while this was bearable at the export level, it was not conducive to HFSA dominance in the internal flow of coffee. White planters could survive the failure to fashion the CMB in their own class interest at the external level, for existing exporters were not threatened and the planters had close financial ties with them. In any case, the mere establishment of the CMB at the export level ensured that there was now a means of dealing with international quota restrictions on an industry scale. This was the planters' main concern.

However, the largest problem for the white planters with the eventual form and function of the CMB, was its internal role. The internal form of the CMB emerged as a direct result of struggles between dominant classes over its marketing role. The HFSA's initial proposals for internal marketing were made at the first Goroka Tariff Board conference in 1959. The HFSA suggested that the new marketing board undertake 'compulsory marketing'. (Cartledge 1978:32) The HFSA may have thought that 'compulsory marketing' would mean maximising the use of existing processing facilities at the direction of the Board (and therefore benefit the dominant class in the industry). However, this suggestion was not liked by the Administration, as should have been obvious to the HFSA, which had far greater political power than the planters in the social formation as a whole. The marketing role of the CMB which emerged was a classic class compromise. The Papua and New Guinea Coffee Marketing Board Ordinance No. 64 of 1963 contained a range of 'tough' control measures over internal marketing, but these have never been activated. The ordinance contained provisions for people to furnish returns which were to be verified by statutory declaration, giving details of all forward contracts, of all coffee trees planted or intended to be planted; of the estimated amount of coffee likely to become available for disposal during any period; of all sales in quantity and value; of provisions for registering coffee processing facilities; and the fixing of maximum or minimum prices or both at which any kind or grade or classification of coffee produced in the Territory may be bought or sold. There was also provision in the legislation for the Board to purchase the crop if necessary. (*New Guinea Highlands Bulletin*, April 1966:8) It is interesting to note, as we will see in the post-colonial section, that legislation to set up the Coffee Industry Board also contained control measures over marketing, but again these have never been activated.

The CMB had virtually no funds because, in the beginning, levies were collected only to cover the cost of the administration of the Board. In the Papua and New Guinea Coffee Marketing Board Ordinance, No. 64 of 1963, the permitted levy was 5 cents at this time and for most of the colonial period. The CMB did have written into its legislation the power to fix classification of coffee produced in the Territory "which may be bought and sold" and there was much talk in the beginning of the 'further valuable function' of setting a minimum price to be paid to 'native' growers for parchment coffee. (Cartledge 1978:73) But a viable price stabilisation scheme would have required the financing of a stabilisation fund and white planters were not prepared to contribute to its cost. (Cartledge 1978:233) The CMB expressed its position on planting policy but any power to enforce this was held by DASF, so again the CMB could exercise little social power in this area.

The low political penetration of the CMB in its actual market role came about because the HFSA realised that its political position was weak in the social formation as a whole and that 'compulsory marketing' by a board was likely to mean that the planters themselves would be the penetrated rather than the penetrators. 'Compulsory marketing' by the CMB would probably have triggered a demand from other classes (dominant and dominated classes, throughout the social formation), as well as the Administration, for market restructuring, so that benefits from coffee marketing could be spread more widely and equally. This is usually the fate of the dominant class in a competitive capital sector. The HFSA soon came to realise that its best interests were served by supporting the idea of a non-interventionist, purely regulatory board. As such, it could be one in which the planters themselves played a major role as personnel. The HFSA learned this lesson well, for their key political actors, President Ian Downs and Lloyd Hurrell (later long-serving Chairman) were responsible for the philosophical justification and systemisation of a regulatory, non-interventionist coffee board which retains its form as the Coffee Industry Board (CIB) in the present.

There were other advantages to the HFSA of a CMB with low political penetration. It provided a mechanism whereby middle peasants could be incorporated into an industry decision-making structure. Registration or licensing arrangements or processing changes which suit the large white planters may not suit the middle peasants, given their quite different class location in production. The HFSA overcame this problem, however, by claiming that the CMB represented all 'growers' in the coffee industry and by adding to the incorporation in production of middle peasants, their representation on the CMB. The first CMB had as members those from the new black élite such as Bono Azanaifa and Salaen Sakaen, along with white planters Downs and Hurrell. Later black élites including Soso Subi joined white planters such as Middleton. The CMB achieved a perfect synthesis of incorporation of black élites and the appearance of smallholder representation by labelling black élite representatives as smallholders, even though their properties were far in excess of the typical smallholder garden plot. This remained effective as late as 1982.

The polite fiction that the CMB represented the undifferentiated group 'grower' was also used by the white planters in an attempt to extend the power of the CMB. A.L. Hurrell, Chairman of the CMB from 1965 until the late 1970s, throughout the period of his chairmanship, systematised the idea that 'growers' were an undifferentiated category by constantly counterposing the interests of growers to those of government. In 1977 he wrote "One factor I regard as of utmost importance is that the Marketing or Industry Board cannot be regarded as a government institution. It has a direct and important responsibility to the growers." (*Post Courier*, 27 May 1977)

The planters were not very successful, however, in increasing the power of the CMB. In theory a statutory authority as it was should have had a direct line of authority to the Administration, and a degree of autonomy from other branches dealing with rural development, such as DASF. In practice, however, the CMB never achieved autonomous status within the state. Two reasons can be offered for this. First, the CMB simply did not have the resources to establish a strong measure of autonomy within the Administration: it did not, for example, have its own extension officers or inspectors. Second, though the CMB may have had a direct line of authority to the Administration, in a colonial situation this is not the same as a direct line of authority to the metropolitan government. In such a situation, these different levels of authority make the status of statutory authorities ambiguous.

Was the CMB to have a direct line of authority to the Minister and therefore achieve the autonomy Hurrell wanted, or was it to be incorporated into the Administration as simply another department? This was tested during the events of 1966–67, when the Chairman of the CMB went over the head of the Administrator in an endeavour to get approval from the Minister of Territories for the CMB to act as a buyer of last resort in a marketing crisis. In previous political struggles, the planters usually sided with the Administration against various branches of the metropolitan state such as Treasury or the Department of Trade and Industry. (Cartledge 1978:145) The Minister for Territories was not pleased by this departure and met with the Chairman of the Coffee Marketing Board at Port Moresby in September 1967 with the aim of setting out clearly the limited degree of functional autonomy the CMB was to be permitted. The Minister stressed that:

> Statutory Boards though independent are part of the governmental structure of the Territory and cannot operate in isolation from general governmental policies for the advancement of the Territory. Normally little need should arise for a Board to go beyond the Administration -- the Minister's representative -- in ironing out problems which may go beyond the scope of the Board to determine by itself. Where a question cannot be solved in the Territory it should go forward to the Minister with a complete statement on all relevant aspects and the Administration's recommendation. Effective liaison with the Administration should be noticeable through the official member of the CMB. Under legislation, CMB or its Chairman has the right of recourse to the Minister but at the stage of political development in 1967 the Minister would not normally expect to deal with a proposal until he had received the Administrator's recommendation. (Cartledge 1978:149–150)

The low level of autonomy in the CMB was not ideal from the viewpoint of the white planters for, although they had 'captured' the CMB, this did not enhance their political position inside the state to any great extent. They had attached their political future to a weak form of state. This realisation coincided with a general downturn in the economic fortune of the planters throughout the late 1960s despite their continued dominance of the internal marketing system. The cause of this downturn was largely due to the fact that international regulation meant that coffee prices stagnated in the late 1960s and early 1970s. After the 'netting' crisis in 1966–67 (see Chapter 6), many planters seemed to have definitely decided that the plantation coffee industry had no future because they could see no solution to the problem of exporting the crop on the world market other than coercing smallholders to stop producing.

At the internal level, the CMB took the form of a Bonapartist state. This reinforced the dominance of a particular class only in the most general way, because the class nature of its role was merely to represent a compromise between competing dominant classes, and to secure the reproduction of a class-divided society. A Bonapartist state emerges out of a series of skirmishes and class struggles which do not result in a complete victory for one class or fraction. In the colonial coffee industry, while white planters were dominant in market relations, they had to share political power in the coffee industry with the Administration and the metropolitan bourgeoisie. A Bonapartist state worked for planters because it offered them the possibility of managing conflicts between different segments of the class, particularly relations between planters in the Eastern and Western Highlands. It also offered white planters a mechanism which made it appear that decisions in the industry could be made by blacks. The appearance of decision-making ensured that the alliance established between white planters and the new black élite in production, would be maintained at the political level.

5

Crisis in the Colonial Coffee Industry

Introduction

It is not surprising to find that by 1966 many white planters were satisfied with what they had done in the colonial coffee industry of Papua New Guinea. On the surface, at least, the industry was stable and seemed to be evolving into a set of social and institutional arrangements that would preserve their dominance. They even believed, along with the colonial administration, that independence was twenty, possibly thirty, years away. However, as I have shown, the planters' position was far from secure. They had problems of accumulation masked by continued profits and cheap labour. They were dependent on the metropolis for their markets and for continued support for the CMB. The smallholders were neglected and exploited despite the rhetoric of 'partnership'. In the next few years, from 1966 to 1974, the whole colonial structure which underwrote the white planters' power collapsed like a house of cards. In this chapter and the next we will trace the crises which drove the white planters out. These began for the planters in 1966–67 but as the next chapter shows, merged with black nationalism and colonial administration fatigue, to sweep away the colonial officials, if not the colonial order, at Independence in 1975.

The Netting Crisis of 1966/67 as an Example of the Dependence of White Planters on Australian and International Goodwill

Australia/Papua New Guinea joined the 1962 ICA under the colonial clause (see Chapter 12 for details of these arrangements) as a net importer of coffee. This meant that Australia/Papua New Guinea was not given an export quota. Article 38 – – Shipments of Coffee from Dependent Territories – – 1962 International Coffee Agreement stated that:

> the shipment of coffee from any of the dependent territories of a Member to its metropolitan territory or to another of its dependent territories for domestic consumption therein or in any other of its dependent territories shall not be subject to any export quota limitations, provided that the Member concerned enters into arrangements satisfactory to the Council with respect to the control of re–exports. (International Coffee Agreement 1962)

The intention seemed to be that the colony was free to export any amount of coffee providing this went only to the metropolis or other dependencies. The idea of 'netting' went further than this, however. 'Netting' suggested:

> that if Aust/PNG joined as a single importing member, PNG exports to countries other than Australia would not technically become subject to quota limitations as long as Aust/PNG remained a net importer of coffee. The text specifically provided that each contracting party together with those of its dependent territories to which the agreement was extended shall constitute a single member. An importing member was defined as a member or country which was a net importer of coffee, that is whose imports exceeded its exports. In other words a legalistic interpretation was that while Aust/PNG was a single importing member, PNG exports were not subject to restriction. Prospects were thus that PNG could export up to the total of Australian imports of coffee (i.e. netting). (Cartledge 1978:104)

The idea of 'netting' was never formally agreed to by the ICO although it was the manner by which Papua New Guinea conducted its coffee exports for the life of the 1962 ICA.

The problem that arose in 1966–67 can be simply stated: whatever 'interpretation' was put on the colonial clauses of ICA, Papua New Guinea had reached the limits of its permitted exports, whether Papua New Guinea exports were based on 'netting' or on Article 39(2), which stated that:

> any Trust Territory administered under a trusteeship agreement with the United Nations whose annual exports to countries other than the Administering Authority do not exceed 100,000 bags shall not be subject to quota provisions of the Agreement, so long as its exports do not exceed that quantity. (International Coffee Agreement 1962)

Territory production in 1966–67 would exceed the maximum permissible exports by between 2,500 and 5,000 tons (*New Guinea Highlands Bulletin*, January 1967:12). A solution had to be found for the surplus production, and that proposed by the CMB was a fairly simple one. It was that a loan be obtained from the Rural Credits Department of the Reserve Bank of Australia, and advances made to growers and processors against unsold stocks. The amount of money involved for this loan was quite substantial. The CMB estimated that the cost of purchasing the surplus 5,000 tons in September 1967 would be about $2,000,000 on 1966 Board calculations (*New Guinea Highlands Bulletin*, January 1967:13). The Reserve Bank interest rate on such a loan would be 14.25 percent. The CMB proposed to minimise the cost of the loan to growers in a number of ways. It would restrict administrative charges for the advancement scheme to 0.25 percent per annum so that borrowers would pay a total of only 4.25 percent interest on the loan.

The CMB was determined to present the difficulties which arose in 1966–67 to both growers and the Reserve Bank of Australia as a temporary crisis which would shortly be solved. This was necessary in order not only to have the idea of a loan made acceptable to the Reserve Bank, but also to retain the loyalty of all planters. Some were unhappy both at the cost of the scheme and the implication for the industry of a high level of state involvement. Would it not be better to abandon 'netting' arrangements and go it alone in the ICO with a distinctive export quota for Papua New Guinea? The CMB seems hardly to have considered this prospect, preferring to cling to its colonial ties and dependence on the metropolis by retaining 'netting' and trying for a solution to the crisis which involved assistance from the metropolitan state. Both the Reserve Bank and some planters were sceptical at the claim that 'assisting' the industry through loans was a temporary measure at all, many wondering whether the industry would have to be 'bailed out' in this way in the future.

The proposed solution to the 'netting' crisis quickly exposed all the contradictions to which the colonial coffee industry was subject. It showed that even though the bulk of coffee was grown by smallholders, they played virtually no role in the politics of the industry, and were disadvantaged by 'deals' done by the dominant classes. Also exposed was the contradiction in the CMB's Bonapartist role. On the one hand, its low autonomy made it excessively poorly structured to advance or even defend the interests of white planters against other dominant classes in the social formation. On the other hand, it quickly became apparent to all concerned, including the CMB, that it would become interventionist if the plan went ahead, in fact becoming a buyer of surplus production. It would probably become the seller of this stock when a market was found.

Not all branches of the metropolitan state were opposed to the idea of a more interventionist CMB. The Department of External Territories appeared to support the CMB, for it felt that for example, a report by the Department of Primary Industry (DPI) failed to acknowledge that the Ordinance did give it the statutory power to market and control coffee exports (*New Guinea Highlands Bulletin*, January 1967:13). The Department felt that a structural surplus was not inevitable and that assistance of the type requested by the CMB was not unreasonable. However, the crucial weakness in the case put up by the CMB for assistance was that it did not have the full support of the Administration, which hesitated to support the proposal, perhaps because it feared the consequences that the marketing role of the CMB might have upon smallholders. It was not quite prepared to sell them short. It was convinced that they stood to benefit most from a fairly competitive privately operating marketing system. The Administration may also have been ambivalent towards the CMB proposals because of its action in going over the head of the Administration in October 1966, in an endeavour to get approval from the Minister of Territories for the CMB to act as a buyer of last resort (Cartledge 1978:145). The action failed, prompting the Minister for Territories to meet with the CMB chairman to tell him that the CMB was answerable to the Administration.

The breakdown of the alliance between the Administration and the planters, and the hostility of the metropolitan state to the CMB's proposed solution to the 'netting' crisis in 1966–67, resulted in the CMB's deciding not to pursue a loan from the Reserve Bank. The experience showed white planters that they would be very lucky to get even minimal assistance from the metropolitan state. The planters could not rely on subsidies or assistance from the metropolis in the event of a structural surplus, and it seemed they would be expected to bear the cost of overproduction in the industry. Even if the Reserve Bank were prepared to make available money to finance a stockholding scheme, it was clear this would be done only under extremely strict conditions: the loan would have to be repaid in a year. It would be difficult to get such a loan through Cabinet, and much opposition would be expressed if the proposal were to include a high-level interventionist role for the CMB. White planters in the colonial coffee industry were clearly not being underwritten by the colonial state. The CMB was not an adequate mechanism for the representation of their interests because of the severe limits imposed on its role, and the Administration was not prepared to back the planters in all cases in their disputes with the metropolis. The failure of their proposed solution to the netting crisis of 1966–67 clearly highlighted for all planters that their dominance of the colonial coffee industry of Papua New Guinea was being undermined as their alliances with other dominant classes in the social formation began to collapse. This alliance was strong enough to reassert class power against subordinate classes, and to engineer an agreement among the dominant classes that the solution to the problem of surplus production might be achieved by restricting the production of smallholders. But it was not strong enough to generate a solution to the problems of the industry which would involve some creative restructuring, or a rethinking of the role of the CMB.

The Suppressed Crisis of the Disadvantaged Smallholder: Coffee but no Consultation

At the same time that the alliance between white planters, the metropolis and the Administration was breaking apart, the planters became involved in a skirmish with the smallholders. It has become common to blame smallholders for most problems in the coffee industry, and those which began in 1966–67 can be explained as being the result of continued expansion of production rather than due to the inadequacy of 'netting' or the failure of the dominant classes to provide a suitable industry structure or proper role for the CMB. In the common explanation it was the smallholders who were blamed for most of the problems in the industry. This explanation was endorsed by all coffee 'authorities' including Densley of DASF who wrote that:

> The period prior to 1973–74 presented Papua New Guinea with marketing difficulties as coffee production, *particularly smallholder coffee production,* was outstripping Australia's consumption growth rate (around 10 percent to 11 percent) despite an almost complete withdrawal of coffee extension activity (Densley n.d.:17; my emphasis).

The solution, not surprisingly in a colonial regime, was an attempt to forcibly restrict native production or to adopt what the HFSA cleverly called 'planting restrictions of a non-racial type' (*New Guinea Highlands Bulletin*, July 1965:23). By this statement, the HFSA meant that controls over New Guinean planting should be imposed to equal the restriction on the European element of plantation expansion to the area granted in leases released for coffee before March 1962.

This was a 'silent' class struggle because, while the dominant classes were actively promoting coercive state measures to restrict smallholders' production, smallholders were resisting this dominance, albeit in an unorganised, non-conflictual manner. The 'silent' class struggle could be thought to have been won by smallholders because the continued might of the dominant classes and the state failed to halt their continued expansion. Their victory can be attributed to three main factors. First, the colonial state and its agency designated with the task of restricting smallholder production, the DASF, was simply not up to the task. Second, because the CMB was not a marketing authority and because marketing was in private hands, the smallholders were able to benefit from a good deal of flexibility in the system. Pinch points were not controlled by the state and smallholder provision of productive forces from within the household made them immune to attempts to control or restrict the use of productive forces. Third, the attempt to restrict smallholder production undermined the ideological hegemony of the white planters in the coffee industry. This caused the legitimate dominance of white planters to come under question. Their claim that growers were an undifferentiated category was made suspect by the extreme attempts of the HFSA to get smallholder production restricted. While the legitimacy of white planter dominance in the industry may have been undermined in the eyes of smallholders themselves (though this is difficult to demonstrate), it was certainly undermined in the eyes of the Administration, which was not totally convinced that restriction of smallholder production was a desirable or even plausible solution.

The initial enthusiasm of the Administration, chiefly through DASF, for smallholder coffee expansion and encouragement of local people to plant coffee was soon tempered by the very success of the growth of smallholder coffee production. Almost from the time of the first smallholder harvesting in the early 1950s, the smallholder stratum of the industry underwent a massive explosion of growth, both in terms of the number of coffee trees planted and in the amount of coffee produced. Between 1958–59 and 1968–69, production of coffee in Papua New Guinea increased from some 1,220 tonnes to nearly 20,000 tonnes, and much of this was due to an increase in smallholder production (Densley n.d.:3). Increased production was accompanied by a huge increase in the national stock of trees which increased in the 10 years from 1963 from less than 2,000,000 trees to more than 13,000,000. Quite clearly most of this expansion was the result of plantings by smallholders (Dick 1977:7).

The Administration was quite unprepared for this boom in smallholder coffee. It was concerned to ensure that the boom not turn into a decline in enthusiasm for cash crop development if smallholders experienced disappointment in coffee, as they had done with other cash crops. Disappointment might come through marketing difficulties, in getting the crop out, or a fall in price. Disappointment might also come through the inability of DASF to provide services and assistance to the new army of smallholders. As a result of these concerns a special conference was held in Goroka in 1959 to plan the DASF extension programme for coffee. The result of this was a decision to restrict extension activities in coffee (Finney 1973:66). This winding down of extension assistance was the first stage of restriction of smallholder coffee production. It became the established colonial coffee policy to discourage increases in smallholder coffee production by withdrawing active extension assistance for coffee.

The first stage of restriction of smallholder coffee production was well within the operational competence of DASF and its administration for it simply involved a redirection of resources already under its control. Instead of providing extension assistance for coffee, DASF could switch its assistance to helping smallholders develop other cash crops. Where advice was offered for coffee it would be mainly in the area of care and harvesting of the plant and not in processing technique or advice on establishment of new gardens. The DASF completely withdrew its assistance for the establishment of new smallholder gardens and closed its nurseries at Aiyura, which had provided much of the early seed for the establishment of both large and smallholdings in the industry. However, this first stage of restriction was not successful in slowing down either smallholder production or plantings.

In the period immediately after withdrawal, smallholder production increased at the fastest rate ever in the history of the Papua New Guinea coffee industry. It was:

> a period of self-generated smallholder production . . . in a situation where agricultural field staff had little influence on coffee plantings at this stage. In spite of minimal extension input from 1961, smallholder production increased in a seven year period to 1968–69 by about 28 percent per annum although the rate of increase dropped dramatically in the following five year period to about 9 percent per annum (Densley n.d.:3).

The explanation for the failure of the first stage of the restrictive policy of the Administration is to be found in an analysis of the structural features of smallholder production and the limitations of the colonial state in the industry. Both these aspects made it impossible for white planters to 'rule' over smallholders in a direct manner.

As we have seen, the main feature of smallholder coffee production is that the productive forces, land and labour are provided from within the household. This fact limits the role outside agencies such as the DASF play in smallholder production after the establishment phase. Smallholder gardens were established on customary land over which the DASF had no control and labour was unskilled and provided from within the household so its use could not be regulated by the state. Once the industry was established, it seems likely that smallholders had no need for seed or establishment advice from outside for the establishment of gardens because both were provided by other smallholders. This certainly seems to be the implication of Dick's survey:

> Coffee growing like many other agricultural enterprises involves certain key operations which must be performed satisfactorily if a marketable product is to be obtained. The successful planting and growing of the trees has posed little problem to people who are accomplished agriculturalists. The fact that nearly 80 percent of the growers surveyed learnt about coffee growing from other villagers is not surprising when it is remembered that extension services were withdrawn within two years of a policy of active encouragement being adopted. More critical -- and more notable -- has been the diffusion of knowledge of harvesting and processing. If these quite new skills had not been mastered the smallholder industry would not have developed. Most growers claimed that they learned processing from fellow villagers while a considerable number (14 percent) acknowledged plantation personnel or missionaries as having taught them. (Dick 1977:115)

Smallholders escaped DASF control over their production due to their location in a production system where essential inputs were provided from within the household. The state could have imposed restriction on smallholder coffee either by artificially tampering with the smallholder price or restricting the amount of smallholder coffee a processor could process, but this would interfere with the profit margins of the processors. In any case, the Administration was not quite prepared to argue that smallholders should be restricted in their sale of coffee due to poor quality. The marketing points were privately controlled and it would be difficult for the state to enforce any restrictions on the marketing of smallholder coffee. The degree of competition in the industry did at least ensure that restrictions on the internal marketing of smallholder coffee were not workable. The dominant classes and the state were thus unable to impose marketing restrictions on smallholder coffee largely because the dominant classes benefited from a state which was non-interventionist and thus not a marketing authority. In a supreme irony, the fact that the state was Bonapartist meant that it was not an adequate instrument to be used to roll back the boundaries of the subordinate class.

The failure of the first stage of restriction of smallholder plantings and production led Downs in the HFSA journal to accuse the Administration of 'incompetent and unimaginative' direction in relation to agriculture and lack of awareness of the gravity of the threat of overproduction in the country. He argued that:

> The New Guinea coffee industry is now confronted with essential international controls which establish a clear limit upon exports. The time has now been reached for firm restrictions to be placed upon further coffee plantings . . . our major crop now clearly faces a point of final limitation. Further development of indigenous coffee (expatriate production is clearly limited by existing leases) would be suicidal for the industry. (*New Guinea Highlands Bulletin*, April 1967:8–9)

and that:

> the Department of Agriculture may not have a mandate to stop the planting of coffee in the way in which it is being stopped in other countries who are our partners in the International Agreement, but it certainly should be directed to discourage forthwith the unrestrained planting which continues throughout the Territory. (*New Guinea Highlands Bulletin*, April 1967:11)

But, as the Administration asked, when it admitted it could not impose planting restrictions, how could the government prevent coffee planting on land it did not own when it did not have the authority to do so? And how was the government to solve the many problems of administration of any prohibitions on coffee planting by local people which were sure to arise (Cartledge 1978:275)? Downs did not accept the limitations imposed on the government due to either the structure of the industry or the structure of the state, and continued with his damaging broadside directed at the Administration.

In a sustained polemic, he used almost every spurious argument imaginable to get the Administration to adopt coercive measures against continued planting by smallholders. He claimed to be arguing, as is always the case with self-interested dominant classes, from a concern not based upon the interests of the European farmer but on those of the Highlands people as a whole (*New Guinea Highlands Bulletin*, April 1967:9). His tone was that 'we' -- meaning leading growers and the Administration -- must get together to protect the industry as a whole. He argued that the Administration was obliged to instigate planting restrictions on smallholders because Papua New Guinea had an inherent obligation to limit production under the terms of the ICA. He did not mention, however, that such production controls as existed in the ICA were not enforceable, nor did he warn that a country which did impose production controls disadvantaged itself against others which did not impose them. It later became evident that even the withdrawal of extension throughout the 1960s may have disadvantaged Papua New Guinea in later quota allocations compared with countries like Colombia which did not adopt domestic production controls.

Downs also rolled out the classic dominant class argument that smallholders who grew cash crops had to be protected from themselves to ensure they did not devote all their energies to earning cash, thus neglecting food production. He claimed that food garden areas had diminished, and that this was a good reason to restrict the expansion of cash crop production. As we have seen already, however, this issue is far more complicated than a simple trade-off between the area under cash crops compared with the area under food crops. Downs stood upon the record of the HFSA, claiming that it had led the way in introducing coffee in the Highlands despite solid opposition and obstruction from the Administration in the early stages. Similarly, he noted, the HFSA was again leading the way in warning the industry of the need to take more serious measures to restrict planting. He considered that the Administration was displaying a good deal of backwardness in not raising the alarm and informing the smallholders of the need to get out of coffee. Downs noted the excellent prospects offered to them through the development of alternative cash crops such as tea, locally grown staple foods, sweet potatoes, and rice, all of which could be developed, he claimed, by smallholders with proper Administration assistance. It could achieve all these changes, he argued, if only it was prepared to lead the way, and if those at the top did not get in the way of the individual agricultural officer who 'can lead the people of this country to economic salvation if his importance to this country were to be understood' (*New Guinea Highlands Bulletin*, April 1967:12). Downs's arguments did not, however, get far with the Administration, and may have succeeded merely in undermining the Administration view that the HFSA was the sole and legitimate representative of all growers. The Administration was in fact moving at this time towards a period of disengagement as self-government approached, and was not about to undertake coercive measures which might destabilise the main agricultural export crop in the Territory. Downs and other white planters may merely have further damaged the alliance between them and the metropolitan state in the run-up to Independence by voicing views that were obviously self-interested, emotional in tone and anti-Administration.

White planters in the coffee industry of colonial Papua New Guinea could not directly exploit smallholders, so they had to go outside the realm of production. They did achieve a degree of vertical integration in the market but, if they were to survive, they required state support for manipulation of marketing structures at both the external and internal level. But at both levels the colonial state in the Papua New Guinea coffee industry remained Bonapartist, and thus beyond the control of the white planters. At the external level, they failed to devise a form of state which would adequately defend their interests at a time of export quotas, and at the internal level they failed to have the state curtail expansion of their competitors, the smallholders. The planters also failed in their programme of incorporation, of leading national growers to adopt the interests of the planters through the middle peasant strategy. They felt bitter at what they saw as their betrayal by the Administration.

6

Transition to Post-Colonial Politics in Papua New Guinea

Introduction

The decade of the 1970s in the coffee industry of Papua New Guinea was one in which the participants' political and economic fortunes continued to be vitally affected by the flow of world coffee. The external marketing problems of the crop evident in the 'netting' crisis of 1966–67 finally demonstrated that these problems would remain insurmountable under existing colonial arrangements. In 1972, a new 'netting' crisis arose when PNG production again exceeded Australian consumption. The PNG surplus could not be sold overseas during a world surplus, and so had to be stockpiled, with funds made available to growers and to finance storage. The CMB managed to get approval for a loan from the Reserve Bank of Australia and this helped relieve pressure on some growers. However, plantations were having severe problems including a general increase in costs (especially labour), export taxes and low prices. When these were added to their worries about independence many white planters came to regard the 1972 coffee crisis, coupled with political defeat in the 1972 national elections, as the last straw. In the early 1970s most of them began winding down their plantations as a prelude to departure.

The 1972 Election and the Political Demise of the White Planters

The political power of the white planters was exercised, as described, through the Highlands Farmers and Settlers' Association (HFSA) and personal influence. Key individuals such as Downs used their personal contacts within the Administration and throughout white colonial society to promote the coffee industry and the interests of white planters. Downs at times could exercise extraordinary influence. Once he had the

Administration and the Australian government back him as a member of the delegation to the ICO, despite opposition from the ICO itself. The planters also maintained connections with formal political representatives. Wolfers notes that:

> The Highlands Farmers and Settlers' Association, and the various chambers of commerce, planters and graziers associations were more obviously organised to further specifically expatriate economic interests. Their secretaries and other officials tended to meet, and to politic, with men who spoke the same language as themselves in every sense of that expression. The expatriate members of the House of Assembly, and especially the Regional members among their number, therefore tended to act as brokers on behalf of these indigenous members from their Districts who did not openly resent their dominance or were not members of the Pangu Pati. They linked the increasingly important politics of and for Districts, even across party lines with the issues and interests of national politics.. (Wolfers 1976:11–12)

However, in the period before July 1970 formal representatives played a minor role in a political system where executive control was still tightly held by the Minister and the Administration. Representatives were to be available for consultation, provide advice and give their assent to executive policy proposals but they were not expected to compete for political influence in the open arena of the House of Assembly.

All this changed in the 1972 election when winning the electoral struggle became as important in gaining access to political power as did associational political activity and individual influence. After 1972, the crucial importance of the electoral struggle meant that from then on it was only when formal political representation, with associational and individual action, was conjoined to an economic interest that influence could be exercised. However, this more open, economic form of politics threw into sharp relief the role of the smallholders in the coffee industry. After 1972, all the interests in any particular industry or market could be openly represented. The change can be detected from 1968 to 1970 when political activity in the House of Assembly began to change. Before 1968:

> the majority of the elected members of the House of Assembly were not firm adherents to a particular party but by mid-1971 it was clear that Pangu Pati with eleven members in the House of Assembly and organised branches in some towns and villages would be a force to reckon with in the 1972 elections.. (Wolfers 1976:13)

Thus for the first time in PNG a competitive party struggle was likely to take place in the 1972 election, as other parties formed to neutralise Pangu. The main party to oppose it in the 1972 election was the Highlands-dominated United Party. The most prominent nationals behind the formation of the United Party were Tei Abal, then Ministerial Member for Agriculture, Stock and Fisheries, and Sinake Giregire, then Ministerial Member for Post and Telegraphs. Tei Abal became leader of the United Party. Sinake was a coffee plantation owner, one of the most prominent middle peasants and the member for Eastern Highlands Open. The General Secretary of the United Party was Anton Parao, from the Western Highlands, who later became one of the most influential coffee businessmen in that province. With the support in Abal's electorate of Wabag, which later became Enga Province, Sinake in the Eastern Highlands and Parao in the Western Highlands, the United Party covered much of the indigenous vote in the coffee producing areas. However, the party was in fact shaped almost entirely by expatriates such as Ron Neville (MHA for Southern Highlands, Regional) and Bill Fielding (member for Northern Regional). (Ballard n.d.:11, Stone 1976:53) The United Party was financed by supporters in Goroka and Lae which included almost total support from white coffee planters including the father of the industry, Jim Leahy. (Stone 1976:55)

The United Party did win the largest number of seats (37), but this was well short of an absolute majority. It lost some of its prominent expatriate members such as Leahy, reflecting the general political decline of the whites. Pangu won some 18 seats, People's Progress Party (PPP) 8 seats and the National Party 2 (later increased to 8 as the other Highlanders joined). (Ballard n.d.:12, Stone 1976:536) The United Party was out-manoeuvred by the Somare-led Pangu Pati, which joined with Chan (of PPP) and Okuk and Kavali (of the National Party) to form the first National Coalition government.

The failure of the United Party in 1972 and the continued decline of the United Party throughout the 1970s -- in the 1977 election the party won only 27 seats compared with 37 in 1972 -- created a disjunction between the successful exercise of class power in the coffee industry by the dominant class fractions, the big peasantry and the *petit bourgeoisie* and contributed to their lack of national political power.

The 1972 crisis in the coffee industry

It was the economic crisis in the industry, not political demise, that in 1972 was the last straw for many white planters. The 1972 crisis showed many of them that existing colonial structures and relations could not survive extended periods of international regulation. It was apparent well before the 1972 crisis began that Australian colonial control could no longer help the PNG industry in its international coffee relations. This was the case not only because the Australian connection tied PNG coffee to Australian imports, 'netting', but also because Australian representatives at the ICO were making decisions which were, from the PNG viewpoint, arbitrary and unsatisfactory.

The ongoing 'netting' problem of 1966–67 was exacerbated by the fact that in the renegotiation of the 1968 ICA, Australia failed – – despite high-level representations to Brazil – – to have its single importing membership status (and therefore PNG's export quota) increased by the 5000 tons that was in storage from the 1966–67 crisis. (Cartledge 1978:179) A feature of the changes in working out basic quotas in the 1968 agreement was a cut-back in the relative share of the total basic quota of big producers, and the promotion of increased production in small countries such as Tanzania and the Ivory Coast. That PNG should miss out on increased quotas when many other small countries were getting them, was inexplicable to many in the PNG industry and, coupled with the worries of the 1966–67 crisis, threw the PNG industry into a state of near-panic. There were exaggerated predictions of a surplus – – 5000 tons annually in 1972–73'. (Cartledge 1978:187) if Australia/PNG remained in the 1968 ICA. There was, however, little real consideration given to the idea that Australia and PNG might leave the ICA. This is not an option for most small producers and importers because the dominant bilateral oligopolists in the Agreement could ensure that much of the market was accessible only to those party to the Agreement.

In the first half of the coffee year 1971–72 (after September 1971), disaster struck the PNG coffee industry. Following the reduction in world export quotas by the ICO the amount of coffee export stamps allocated to PNG in the first half of the coffee year was reduced by 13 percent. These stamps were soon used up, with the result that none were left to cover coffee exports up to the end of March 1972 to category A countries; exports to Australia did not require stamps. (Reserve Bank of Australia 1971:5) This situation added at least 1000 tons to surplus stocks.

The possibility that the PNG coffee industry might have to store some 16,000 tons, when exports totalled only 27,000 tons, reflected badly on Australian administration. The Administration and the metropolitan state had been aware of the problem since 1966–67 but had taken virtually no steps to plan for the obvious difficulties the industry would face when it began to breach 'netting' every year. Stocks could not build up forever. But the Administration seems to have been unable to plan for the export of PNG coffee in a way that did not include 'netting'. Rather than acting boldly, to break the nexus between PNG production and Australian consumption, and presenting PNG with its own quota in the ICO, Australian representatives took the view that they ought to be careful not to attract attention that might lead to examination of the Australian/PNG single importing membership status. (Cartledge 1978:197) They thus acted to ensure the continuation of the very arrangement that was the cause of all PNG's difficulties.

White planters were in no position in the early 1970s to be able to finance the stockpiling of half PNG's total production. Prices were falling and costs were rising. The fall in international prices in 1970–71 and the virtual levelling–out of the international price until 1975 was accompanied in 1970 and 1971 by the actions of Australian importers who, taking advantage of the troubled conditions in the PNG coffee industry and assured of a guaranteed supply of coffee, if not from PNG at least from other sources, began paying prices of up to 5 cents below parity. (Reserve Bank of Australia, 1972) This was eventually stopped by the Administration and the metropolis in March 1972, but it did add to the difficulties of the PNG coffee industry.

The planters were also beset by increasing costs, particularly labour costs, which rose dramatically in the period 1970–75, with substantial jumps in the average earnings in 1971 and 1974 (Table 2.2). Both these increases occurred in years 'just after which the rural minimum wage had been increased'. (Jackson 1981:115) Of these two increases in average earnings, the 1971 increase was probably more difficult for planters to bear even though as Table 2.2 shows, the money value of the 1971 increase in average earnings was less than the 1974 increase. This is because the cash component of the minimum wage increased by one–half in 1971. (Jackson 1981:110) This tested planters' liquidity, and compares with the situation in 1972 when the switch to the all–cash wage was accompanied by a fall in real wages, until 1977. Price inflation taken into account and deflated by the 'product price' as measured by the export price index, excluding copper concentrate (Table 2.3):

> Also from 22 August 1974 the Minimum Wage Board No. 4 of 1974 introduced a two–tier rural minimum wage: a lower wage of K8 for the 'primary industry' of copra, cocoa, tea, coffee, rubber, oil–palm, fruit, vegetable and livestock raising industries, and K10 for all other employees. (Jackson 1981:109)

Thus planters received some relief from increases in the minimum wage due to both inflation and the two–tier system in the years 1974–77 which they did not receive in 1970–71.

In March 1972, discussions finally began between the CMB and the Australian government on how to deal with the PNG coffee crisis. The whole process of negotiation and decision making was marked by a crude assertion of colonial control and authority by the Australian government. It was agreed that there was only one possible way to deal with the over–supply problem. This was to adopt the solution proposed in 1966–67: for the Reserve Bank of Australia to provide a loan to the CMB to purchase and store the crop and to provide advances to growers. The plan that was proposed by a working group was that:

> a loan of $2.5 million would be obtained for CMB which would buy in 6,000 tons of the surplus stock at prices as close as possible to world parity. Purchases would be spread over the September and December quarters of 1972. The coffee purchased would be held for disposal as sales are arranged at discount prices in Annex B countries. (Cartledge 1978:207–8)

The loan was to be repaid by increasing the export levy from 0.5 to 2 cents per pound in July 1972. The 0.5 cents levy had been originally intended merely to provide for the operations and expenses of the CMB, but was now seen as a mechanism by which surplus stockholding and disposal schemes could be financed. (Reserve Bank of Australia 1972:6) This cost would be passed down the marketing chain and borne by growers through reduced prices paid for their produce at both the processing and export pinch points in the marketing chain. It was a condition of the loan that it be paid back as quickly as possible. Though the 2 cent per pound levy was a heavy cost to bear, this did mean that the loan could be repaid by July 1973.

While most of the stored coffee was subsequently sold in 1972 and 1973 to Annex B countries (Densley n.d.:17) and the loan was repaid, relations between the CMB and the colonial adminstration were soured by the crisis of 1972. Along with all the areas of dissatisfaction which the CMB had with the way the crisis was handled, the Australian government took a long time deciding whether to actually provide the loan. (Cartledge 1978:209) The loan and its short-term conditions put enormous pressure on the CMB to find markets for their surplus. This was not an easy task in a tight international market. At the same time the future of international regulation was uncertain. In December 1972 the 1968 ICA finally collapsed although the lifting of quotas did not relieve the problem of global marketing for individual countries. The coffee years 1973–74 and 1974–75 were extremely difficult for all producers, including those of PNG. Marketing difficulties were not relieved until the Brazilian 'Black Frost' of July 1975, which resulted in a loss of some 20 percent of world coffee supplies.

By the time the effects of the 'Black Frost' were felt, with the worldwide coffee boom of 1976–77, most of the white planters in the PNG coffee industry had left. Table 7.1 shows that a large number of coffee plantations changed hands in 1975, and a number of others were taken over at the height of the boom, which came in 1977. The change of ownership was caused by the white planters' response to the problems of the industry. Naturally their morale was affected by its disturbances, and the planters' difficult economic circumstances futher undermined their commitment to the industry. Their response was to make short-term plans to maximise their returns, and to sell their properties when the price was right.

Nationalism in Papua New Guinea

The failure of the United Party ended for many years the direct political representation in the national legislature of the dominant class fractions in the post–colonial coffee industry. This did not mean that coffee politics did not intrude upon national politics, that claims from within the coffee industry were not made for national resources. But it did mean that after 1972 these were again restricted to the political form of associational group action and individual representation and action. A disjunction grew between the economic power exercised by dominant class fractions in the Highlands coffee industry and the formal representation in the national legislature of parties and parliamentary coalitions. Even without formal political representation in the legislature by representatives of the dominant class fractions, the new government in Port Moresby was not able at any time to ignore the needs of the coffee industry as a whole, partly because coffee is such a large export revenue earner.

But there were also political reasons why the new government could not ignore the needs of the new dominant classes in the coffee industry. The new government was a parliamentary coalition made up of a mix of *petit bourgeois* representatives. These included Julius Chan, with his Islands trading interests, Barry Holloway and his Kainantu coffee interests and trade stores, Michael Somare, and others who later became interested in real estate and other service industries, with an assortment of teachers and clerks. They had no unified class location, and were elected at a time of the conjunctural crisis of decolonisation. This usually triggers an attempt by the dominant class in the social formation to achieve a degree of ideological integration. The purpose of this is to show that the interests of all dominant classes in all sectors are linked. Ideological integration of this type was attempted by the new government in its appeal to Papua New Guinea nationalism.

Most studies of nationalism in PNG have assumed that it is to be understood as an aggregate concept, usually described as a sense of national unity "and because the first task of the new state is to create a sense of national unity, the ideology will be a nationalist one of some kind." (Sundhaussen 1977:310)

Rowley takes essentially the same view. He considers nationalism to be the working out of unity. It commences, he argues, from the contrast of New Guineans' position with that of the white man in the country, and he feels that unity was being worked out on the basis of common opposition. (Rowley 1965:15) Such accounts usually see the absence of consistency or disaggregation within nationalist thought as evidence of the failure of nationalism as an ideology. But from a class perspective, inconsistency or disaggregation within nationalist thought is to be entirely expected.

Nationalism is a set of ideas aimed at linking the interests of diverse classes. It affects these differentially, for just as nationalism may organise some classes, it can disorganise others: it depends how success or failure is to be measured. In a country like Papua New Guinea, it may be that the success and failure of nationalism is not to be measured by its consistency of thought or by the success of individuals like Somare to 'kindle a sense of nationalism'. (Sundhaussen 1977:312), but by the extent to which its propositions and policy initiatives begin to accommodate the interests of a range of dominant classes.

The new *petit bourgeois* national coalition government set about developing a sense of nationalism more for the purpose of organising dominant classes and disorganising subordinate classes than for reasons of consistency of ideology. Ideological flourishes were not intended to encourage change in the production base. The government's major ideological statement was the Eight Aims, promulgated in December, 1972 and adapted from the Faber Report on PNG's development. (Overseas Development Group, 1973) Of these, the first and third have general relevance to rural industries. The first called for 'rapid increase in the proportion of the economy under the control of Papua New Guinean individuals and groups, and in the proportion of personal and property incomes that goes to Papua New Guineans'. The third was 'decentralisation of economic activity, planning and government spending, with emphasis on agricultural development, village industry, better internal trade and more spending channelled to local and area bodies'. (Somare 1975:108–9) These aims might appear to be so general as to be little more than rhetoric; they have often been labelled 'failures'. But Fitzpatrick (1982:6) argues it should be recognised that they were, after all, aims sponsored by a national *petit bourgeoisie*, and as such could hardly be expected to offer a comprehensive radical alternative. Instead they should be seen as a range of particular programmatic points. Seen this way, he argues, they have been implemented with enormous, if selective, success. (Fitzpatrick 1982:6)

The new government attempted to put the third aim into operation in the coffee industry by revitalising the Department of Primary Industry. (DPI; it was called the Department of Agriculture, Stock and Fisheries until 1976) In 1973 it announced a program to rejuvenate coffee extension activity and embark on a modest coffee expansion programme. (Densley n.d.:5) The government claimed to be interested in increasing the country's production so that PNG's bargaining position in any new ICA would be strengthened. The industry, however, was still having a difficult time finding export markets, so the expansion program was described by the CMB as involving '. . . not so much specific targets as approximate ranges of opportunity'. (Howlett, Hide and Young 1976:223)

Most of the expansion programme was aimed particularly at the lesser developed areas of Papua New Guinea, especially those areas such as the Southern Highlands which had not been encouraged to plant coffee by previous policy. (Densley n.d.:5) The total area to be expanded under coffee was 8000ha, with DPI playing a major role in terms of distribution of seed and extension advice. In 1975 the government appointed a national coffee coordinator. After the decentralisation of DPI in 1977 it also established Coffee Development Teams (CDT), to be headed by experienced coffee extension officers. They were based in the main coffee provinces and were expected to liaise with the national coffee coordinator. The effectiveness of these officers varied, but at least the government was being seen to devote resources to the industry. It also stepped up its provision of technical services, especially, after 1973 to the plantation sector. (McKillop, Williamson and Associates 1982:21) In the period between self-government and the decentralisation of DPI in 1977, the national government appeared to offer general support through it to the industry.

The main effect *petit bourgeois* nationalism had on the industry was through the Plantation Redistribution Scheme (PRS), an attempt to achieve the first of the Eight Aims in the coffee industry by facilitating the movement of Papua New Guineans into the control of coffee plantations and other cash crop industries. The PRS was set up to provide interest-free loans to clan groups to buy back European plantations in their areas. It was touted as showing the new government's commitment to the village, because it would assist clan members to benefit from land previously denied them by whites. It was also thought that the PRS would expand small-scale commercial activity along Papua New Guinean rather than Western lines, that it would promote egalitarianism, and that it would, according to Mr Somare, encourage self-reliance. (Papua New Guinea House of Assembly Debates, 1972–73:1494–95) The government's public statements on the PRS presented it as following closely the general policy on land adopted by the government from the recommendations of the Commission of Inquiry into Land Matters (1973). This stated that land policy should be evolved from a customary base, and not become a sweeping agrarian revolution; also 'individualistic extremes' should be avoided. (Papua New Guinea Government Strategies for Nationhood 1974:57) It was opposed to demands made by large indigenous coffee growers such as Sinake that land be convertible into permanent heritable estates. (Ward 1977:6–7) Such rhetoric presented the PRS as a progressive measure.

It is not difficult to show that the PRS was mainly effective in creating a climate whereby private purchases of plantations by commercial groups who were already potentially well-off would take place. (Munnull 1981:62) It certainly was not egalitarian in nature. The PRS did not alter the structure of land tenure in the Highlands. It opened up opportunities for nationals to gain access to land formerly privately held by whites and used as plantations, but did not expand the stock of privately held land at all. In this way it merely retained existing structures, and did not disadvantage big PNG growers, or upset the existing system of communal landholdings. It did not make any attempt to redistribute this privately held land to those locals most in need. In fact, quite the reverse happened. A group received assistance under the scheme provided they were local, not because they had special needs. In this way many established groups, such as those associated with Development Corporations, got assistance under the scheme. Indeed, the administration of the PRS virtually had to ensure that assistance went to already well-off commercial groups, for in this way plantation structures would be maintained and not broken up into small plots.

The PRS was also narrowly conceived. It had very little effect on plantations owned by foreign companies, such as Steamships Trading Co. as Table 7.1 shows. It also had very little effect on the coffee industry itself. In the industry, little government assistance was needed either in terms of finance or assistance in negotiations because, as we have already seen, white planters were eager to do deals with nationals and get out. In addition PRS funds were often not needed, because development corporations could draw on accumulated funds to pay deposits or marshal village savings, and some groups succeeded in paying off plantations in the boom of 1976–77.

The PRS – – or more properly the takeover of plantations by nationals – – did not have the negative economic consequences in coffee production that were thought possible. The takeover of plantations did not lead to their abandonment or drastic falls in production, as occurred in cocoa, copra and rubber. However, this was probably a result of the different circumstances in these industries. The Committee of Review into the Plantation Redistribution Scheme 1978, did emphasise that new owners lacked management skills, and considered this a cause for concern. The PRS was abandoned by the National-PPP government in 1980, but by then it had done its work in the coffee industry and could be said to have achieved its limited aims, albeit indirectly. It mainly succeeded in bringing pressure to bear on Europeans to sell at reasonable prices, encouraging a climate for national takeover. It was abandoned at a time when almost complete national ownership of plantations in the Eastern Highlands had been achieved.

The nationalism of the *petit bourgeoisie* was further limited by the role of the technocracy, the social category made-up of technical advisors (usually whites) who were influential in all policy arenas in the early independence period (see Ballard 1981 for their views). This technocracy is not a class, because it does not have a class location in production, and so cannot reproduce itself. But it can and did exercise a profound influence over the allocation of state revenue. The technocracy share the antipathy of the national *petit bourgeoisie* to state intervention in production, but unlike them afraid as they are of the class effects of intervention, the technocracy oppose intervention in production since their aim is to immunise policy decisions from class struggle. This is necessary if they are to achieve technical perfection in policy-making. The technocracy realises, correctly, that state intervention in marketing or production enhances the political penetration of dominant classes, and can give these influence inside the technical divisions and co-ordinating policy agencies of the state. The result can be a loss of power and policy perfection for the technocrats and an increase in political struggle inside the state.

In the transition period in Papua New Guinea, a remarkable alliance was established between the technocracy and the national *petit bourgeoisie*. The technocrats' continued refinement of policies and policy structures was carried through while the national *petit bourgeoisie* was politically dominant in the legislature. These technocratic changes affected industries and classes in all sectors of the economy. We will see in Chapter 9 the influence, through the setting up of the stabilisation fund, of the technocrats in the coffee industry. This involved the work of two consummate technocrats, Ross Garnaut and Mick Wheeler.

Garnaut, with others in the Ministry of Finance (including the long-serving secretary of the department, Mekere Morauta), designed a macro-economic plan known as the 'hard kina' strategy. It involved setting up stabilisation funds as a hedge against variable export commodity prices. (Garnaut 1981) Mick Wheeler, of the Department of Primary Industry, worked out many of the details governing the operation of the stabilisation fund in coffee. Other technocrats played a role which indirectly affected the industry. Land advisers such as Alan Ward and Jim Fingleton were influential in halting the drift toward individual land titles that had begun in the late colonial period. The absence of a private market in land has had an important influence on the class fortunes of many in the coffee industry, as we will see in Chapter 8. McKillop of DPI played a role in influencing it to focus its activities less on plantations and more on smallholdings. Less directly, technocrats like Tordoff and Watts, who influenced the design of the decentralisation process, and Hinchliffe, Allen and others in the National Planning Office (NPO), who designed the system of allocation, played a role in creating state structures which continue to affect class fortunes in the various regions and industries in post-colonial Papua New Guinea.

The technocrats were able to exercise extraordinary power over state allocations and influence the creation of state structures mainly because of the unusual manner in which the ruling national *petit bourgeoisie* exercised political power. The latter controlled the formal political institutions throughout the 1970s and the technocrats formed an alliance with them that gave them access to formal political power. However, the national *petit bourgeoisie* maintained formal political power during this period, mainly because they were hardly ever challenged. There was no other class in PNG which was organised at the political party level, so they could rule with a very loose political organisation. Also, the *petit bourgeoisie* did not at any point establish an organisational form which penetrated the state apparatus: they were at the helm of the ship of state, but they did not have control below decks. This is an important point, because it means that the bureaucracy in the post-colonial state did not form itself into a politically active social category as it would have done had an organised party of the dominated class penetrated the state apparatus. The bureaucracy was also disorganised by high functional autonomy in the post-colonial state. Decentralisation dispersed them through a range of institutions and removed many of them to remote regions. Bureaucracy also underwent rapid localisation in the early years of the post-colonial state, which added to its disorganisation as an influential social category. All this gave the technocracy a fairly free hand in the co-ordination and allocation branches of the state, especially at policy levels.

7

Who Owns the Coffee Industry in Independent Papua New Guinea?

The timing of the departure of the white planters in the early 1970s was opportune for the two class fractions, which emerged in the mid-1970s to dominate the industry: the *petit bourgeosie* and the big peasantry. Their formation coincided with the 'Black Frost' in Brazil in 1975, which created a worldwide shortage of coffee and boom conditions throughout the coffee-producing world in 1976 and 1977.

This boom provided an opportunity for a new group of national owners in the coffee industry and for a rapid expansion of the local economy. New groups and classes emerged and consolidated in a remarkably short time. This was partly a result of the changing nature of the local economy in the Eastern Highlands, particularly in the Goroka area, which from the late 1960s began to develop a service industry component to its mono-crop economy. Then, with the boom in prices of 1976–77, rapid accumulation took place.

Those nationals who opted for diversification out of coffee in response to the new opportunities opening up after 1970 are the local *petit bourgeoisie*. The coffee boom also opened up immense opportunities for those who chose the only other path – – expansion of coffee holdings and coffee production – – to accumulation in an industry where profits are limited by the production of absolute surplus value. Some new plantation owners followed the pattern set by white planters and vertically integrated the ownership of their plantations with processing factories and exporters. These new owners are the big peasants. Following Poulantzas (1978), fractions can be understood as competing segments of the dominant classes in circumstances where the subordinate classes remain politically unorganised. Competition between fractions is real for, as Poulantzas notes, to the extent that they become autonomous, fractions are capable of constituting themselves as social forces. (Poulantzas 1978:84) Class fractions have different structures in production, and can come into political competition, even though they may share a deeper antagonism to subordinate classes. This will be shown to be the case in the post-colonial Eastern Highlands.

The struggle between black élites and black technocrats to fill the vacuum left by white planters in the coffee industry

The Lowa Census Division (CD), which is also the Goroka Open electorate, is the centre of the coffee industry in PNG. Goroka had, at an early stage, a developing service industry exceeding in scope and sophistication that usually expected in PNG rural towns. In Lowa today, the local economy is still built on a base of coffee production and service functions. From the viewpoint of local Gorokans, the dual nature of the local economy offered a range of opportunities for entry into the cash economy. These opportunities were extended with completion, in the 1960s, of the all-weather Highlands Highway, for it now became cheaper to employ road transport to take coffee to the port of Lae. Many Gorokans got their start driving trucks or PMVs up and down the 'coffee highway'. Others, like Hari Gotaha, went into more sophisticated service ventures. Hari, who Finney (1973) interviewed in the late 1960s, had built a well equipped store and restaurant in Goroka worth $30,000. With his clansman, Soso Subi, who produced coffee, he had marshalled clan resources to finance business ventures. (Finney 1973:106)

The process of marshalling clan resources for business ventures has gone through various stages since the informal process described by Finney. Good and Donaldson have shown how the process was first formalised, with the establishment by the colonial state of cooperatives and savings and loans societies, and then intensely commercialised with the spontaneous emergence of indigenous Development Corporations. These are "the most advanced mechanism to date -- far more so than the earlier 'cooperatives' -- for mobilising key resources, labour, land and capital, behind the banner of rural capitalism." (Good and Donaldson 1980:24)

The Development Corporations were formed at the right time to take full advantage of two possibly unique occurrences: the Plantation Redistribution Scheme, and the 1976–77 coffee boom. As we have seen, the Plantation Redistribution Scheme did indirectly influence the change of ownership which resulted in the almost complete national ownership of plantations in Eastern Highlands. In 1976–77 the Highlands economy entered a period of frenetic expansion as world coffee prices rose six times higher than the level they had been two years earlier. (Wesley 1980 and see Figure 7.1) In this short period, the Coffee Industry Board Stabilisation Fund rose, by 1978, from K6.8m to K63.6m. (*Bank of Papua New Guinea, Quarterly Economic Bulletin*, March 1981:43) K28m was returned as disposable income to smallholders, local governments collected a record amount of head tax, new vehicle registrations in the Highlands far exceeded those in the rest of the country, K3.5m was deposited in personal savings accounts, and as much money was spent on beer (K8m) as was invested in formal savings such as vehicles and plantations. (Townsend 1977) Also, credit from the Papua New Guinea Development Bank (PNGDB) became available to nationals in the 1970s. It first became available to those engaged in commercial activities, but by the end of the decade also for agriculture. (*Papua New Guinea Development Bank Reports*)

The two main indigenous development corporations in the Goroka area are the Gouna Development Corporation and the Eastern Highlands Development Corporation. (formerly Bena Development Corporation) Akepa Miakwe founded Bena Development Corporation in 1973 because he realised that with Independence in 1975, Papua New Guineans would soon get control over their own resources. (*Post Courier*, March 29, 1977:17) Hari Gotaha and Auwo Ketauwo formed Gouna in 1977 for the same reason. (Good and Donaldson n.d.:34, *Post Courier*, November 7, 1980)

After 1973, the major Development Corporations did very nicely out of rising coffee prices, especially out of the boom. The Eastern Highlands Development Corporation, drawing on the resources of some 15,500 members, purchased 4 large plantations in 1975 and 4 more in 1977. Gouna (approx 2,000 members) bought 2 well-established plantations, Erinvale and Roka (Table 7.1). Gouna purchased its major plantations at the height of the boom and expanded its service activities to include a controlling interest in the Goroka Sports and Book Store, a Goroka soft drink company, Goroka Tyre and Battery, and to acquire major shareholding in Pacific Helicopters. This last enterprise, of which Hari Gotaha and Auwo Ketauwo are directors, is a particularly bold venture which began in 1975 with one helicopter, and had ten helicopters by 1980. (Anderson, *Post Courier*, November 7, 1980) The Eastern Highlands Development Corporation also benefited from the boom, spending some K200,000 on extending its processing capacity at its K.5m processing factory at Urona Plantation, and, by 1977, being in the extraordinary position of being able to repay in full loans taken out to buy its plantations -- total of K350,000. (*Post Courier*, March 29, 1977)

The differences between big peasant interests represented by the Eastern Highlands Development Corporation and the interests of those engaged in service or *petit bourgeoisie* activities, like Gouna, have always been apparent, though these have not until now been thought to constitute the existence of separate class fractions. This is because analyses by those such as Good and Donaldson (1980) have not dealt with the structure-in-production in the industry, nor with the appropriation of surplus value. To show how the existence of class power (doubly defined by role in production and by opposition at the point of production) explains the struggle for political power, it is necessary to enter the 'hidden abode of production'. (Marx 1954:172)

The deeper antagonisms between the big peasant class fraction (Eastern Highlands Development Corporation) based on a network of production relations centred mainly on the coffee industry, and the *petit bourgeois* class fractions (Gouna), based on a network of production relations, centred mainly on service-type industries, is most evident when it is realised that appropriation of surplus value by each takes different forms. We saw earlier that surplus value is the excess value created in the course of the capitalist production process. Marx showed theoretically that there are two possible ways to increase the rate of surplus value in capitalist production: the production of absolute surplus value and the production of relative surplus value. The production of the former is the most obvious, and historically the earliest form for increasing the rate of surplus value, for it occurs when the capitalist aims to extend the working day. But there are natural limits to the production of absolute surplus value. For example, there are limits to the lengthening of the working day due to the fact that labour power is also living labour. This sets natural limits on the amount of time a labourer can work, since the labourer must eat and sleep to renew his or her labour power. These natural limits have forced capitalists to attempt to increase the rate of surplus value by the production of relative surplus value: that is, by increasing the intensity (or productivity) of labour during whatever time it spends at work. The two main ways in which relative surplus value can be produced is by eliminating wasteful labour time through an increasingly sophisticated and complex division of labour (Taylorism), or by putting labour to work with new and more efficient techniques embodied in complex machinery or through the development of new skills which act to reduce labour time.

If we now apply this class analysis to the structure-in-production existing in Goroka it would appear that the big peasantry (Eastern Highlands Development Corporation) appropriate surplus value largely through the production of absolute surplus value, while the *petit bourgeoisie* (Gouna) appropriate surplus value largely through the production of relative surplus value. The big peasantry are limited to the production of absolute surplus value because, as we have seen, the care and harvesting of the coffee berry is a delicate process not susceptible to the introduction of new techniques in complex machinery or developed skill. Machinery is limited in the harvesting of coffee for the simple reason that not all coffee berries on a tree ripen at the same time, and a berry processed but not ripe develops a bitter taste. This reduces its value. Berries have to be processed within twenty-four hours of picking or they deteriorate. Thus 'pickers of quality coffee must return to the same tree time and time again to pick only the ripe cherries -- an inordinate amount of labour for the two pounds of cleaar

TABLE 7.1: Change in Ownership of Coffee Plantations

	Date of Take-over	*Acreage*	*January 1980 Current Owner/Manager*
Eastern Highlands Province			
Kami	1978	93	NPMA
Kiloparoka	1978	95	NPMA
Upegu	1979	135	NPMA
Aromet	1978	120	NPMA
Huvei	1979	232	NPMA
Lahamenegu	1977	50	Gouna Development Corporation
Erinvale	1977	170	Gouna Development Corporation
Roka	1978	110	NPMA
Aionora	1977	130	KKB Limited
Kawaita	1971	110	KKB Limited
Tuta	1979	80	KKB Limited
Numbia	1978	160	Highlands Henene Pty Ltd
Karangka	1978	80	Highlands Henene Pty Ltd
Hobe (including Muriho)	1976	100	Benbosi Pty Ltd
Asaro Coffee Estate		170	Asaro Coffee Estates
Obihaka		140	Asaro Coffee Estates
Clearance		250	Asaro Coffee Estates
Foinda	1974	80	Asaro/Watabung Rural Dev. Corp.
Kesa	1974	75	Mr. Bono Azanifa
Mountain Dale (Anego)	1975	125	Mr. Akapite Wamiri
Bena	1975	178	EH Development Corporation[a]
Sogopegu	1975	220	EH Development Corporation[a]
Matus	1977	120	EH Development Corporation[a]
Kapakamaliki	1975	112	EH Development Corporation[a]
Keya	1975	71	EH Development Corporation[a]
Duna	1977	80	EH Development Corporation[a]
Fano	1977	80	EH Development Corporation[a]
Kompafo	1977	70	EH Development Corporation[a]
Korona		200	Mr. J. W. Wan
Kasmaliki		60	Catholic Mission
Erimissoo		95	Mr. W. O'Brien
Tapo		65	KKB Limited
Akwitanu	1979	82	KKB Limited
Nori Kori	1979	247	KKB Limited
Ambaura	1979	70	KKB Limited
Bonta	1979	70	KKB Limited
Arau		106	Mrs. M. Larner
Abiera		30	Development Bank
Asafa		40	Mr. Arege Yamagu

continues

TABLE 7.1: *continued*

	Date of Take-over	*Acreage*	*January 1980 Current Owner/Manager*
Kama		77	Mr. G. Brough
Baro-Ida		200	Kainantu High School
Tudor		30	Kainantu High School
Arara	1979	110	KKB Limited
Korfena		160	Steamships Trading Co.
Gisumonoso		82	Steamships Trading Co.
Wantorifu		70	Steamships Trading Co.
Kenimaro		110	Steamships Trading Co.
Yanowa		80	Mr. S. Gire Gire
Bilati		100	Mr. J. Frame
Gurimba		60	Mr. P. A. Gurinawo

[a] Angco manages plantations owned by Eastern Highlands Development Corporation and Duna Coffee Estates Pty Ltd.
Source: R. Mitio in M.A.H.B. Walter (ed.) (1981)

green beans which is an average yearly yield for one tree'. (Roden 1977:49)

No machine has yet been invented which can tell the difference in ripeness of various berries, even if it could then get them off the tree without damage. In Brazil they use machines to strip everything off the tree at once, leaves, flowers, overripe berries, underripe berries -- but this can only be done with poor quality coffees at a time of booming prices, for it takes the mutilated tree two years to recover from such savage treatment. (Roden 1977:49) Thus, while human skill is needed to harvest the coffee berry, it is not a very high level of skill. Little investment is made in its application and little is devoted to developing it, for it is a simple procedure which cannot be made more efficient above a certain level.

The same point can be made as regards the care (weeding etc.) of the coffee tree. While some progress has been made in the use of new techniques such as herbicides, there are limits to which these can be used, especially when the plant is young. Shade trees can also be used to help cut weed growth, but excess shade reduces production, so there are also limits in the use of shade. The year-round care of the coffee tree is also labour intensive compared with crops such as cocoa, and there seem to be few ways in which the manual spading and weeding, by unskilled labourers, can be replaced by the development of new techniques.

It is difficult for labour to be coupled with machinery or developed in skill in harvesting (or weeding) to improve its productivity. Coffee producers must employ a sizeable labour force, but due to the agronomic features of the plant itself are limited in their ability to appropriate relative

Figure 7.1 Papua New Guinea Coffee Exports and Value

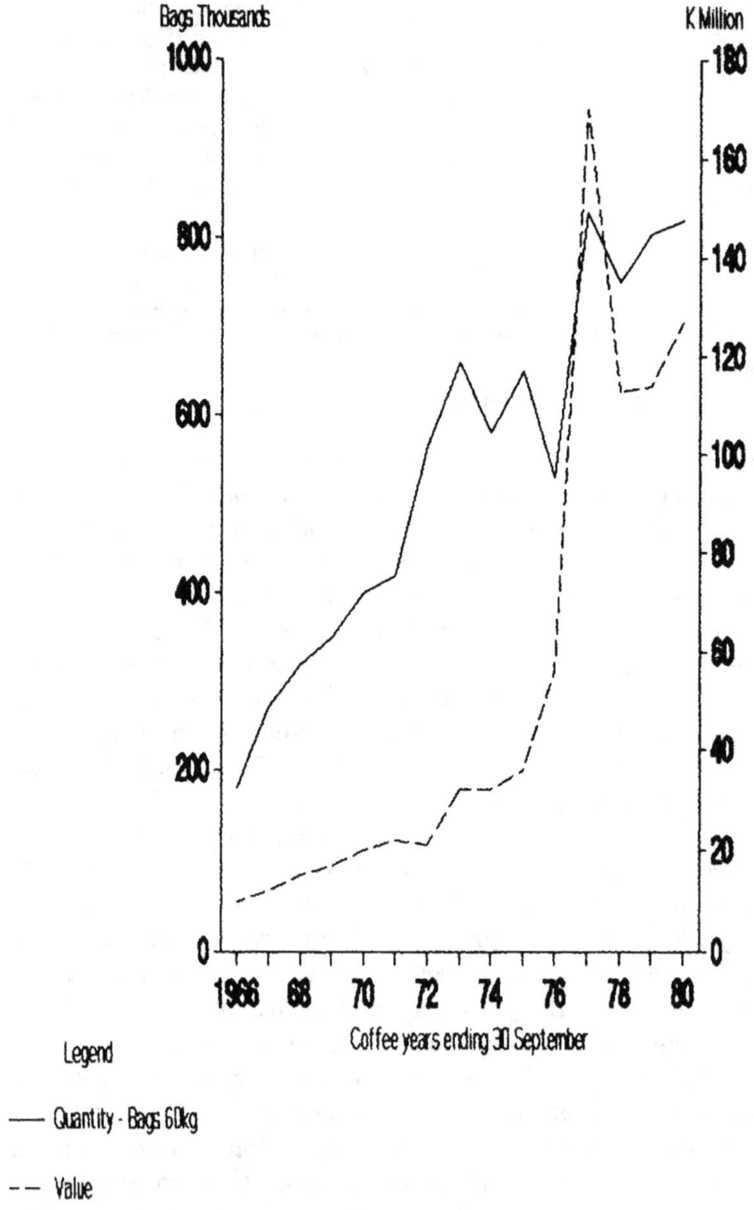

Source: Papua New Guinea Coffee Industry Board Report (1980)

Figure 7.2 Structure and Ownership of PNG Coffee Industry

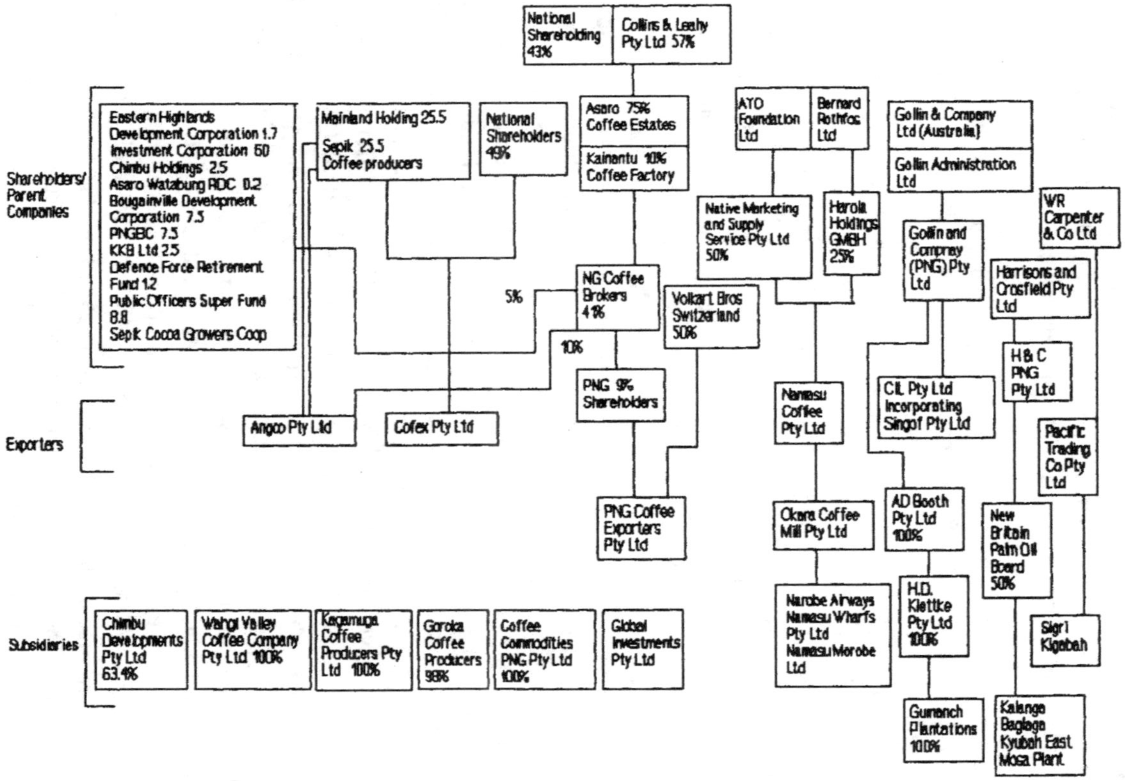

Source: Hassall and Associates (1982)

surplus value. It is through attempts to extend the surplus labour time via the lengthening of the working day -- through the production of absolute surplus value -- that coffee producers have attempted to increase the rate of surplus value and therefore profits. The length of the working day during harvesting has been extended by paying pickers piece rates. We saw earlier that this has been particularly successful in the Highlands, where pickers are generally local village women or wives of permanent labourers who see no need and have no desire to establish an agreement on what constitutes a 'fair' working day.

Planters can extend the working day by paying pickers piece rates, but they are still not as well off as those capitalists who can maximise profit in production by going beyond the production of absolute surplus value. In the service activities of the *petit bourgeoisie*, the only limits to the appropriation of surplus value is the present state of technological development and the cost of installing new machinery and developing new skills. In the Goroka Soft Drink factory, for example, there is a fairly sophisticated division of labour in which workers with different levels of skill operate different stages of the production process. Clearly also the intensity of labour can be increased with such things as faster, more efficient bottling machines. In the case of Pacific Helicopters, it is also true that a fairly complex division of labour exists among the various maintenance and service personnel employed by the company. The pilot is, of course, the ultimate specialist, whose productivity can be increased with the provision of new, faster, more specialised helicopters. The *petit bourgeois* class fraction has even attempted to produce relative surplus value on its coffee holdings. Gouna has trained teams of pruners and fertilisers who move around from plantation to plantation, and complete the job with greater efficiency.

So far I have argued that there are sufficient differences in the appropriation of surplus value at the level of class location (in production) to establish the existence of two class fractions, a *petit bourgeoisie* which produces mainly relative surplus value, and a big peasantry which produces mainly absolute surplus value. However, the analysis has also uncovered, though not yet highlighted, certain similarities that exist between the class fractions at the level of class location (in production). The major similarity is that both class fractions, despite their different forms of production of surplus value, are in the final analysis engaged in the appropriation of surplus value. They are both determined to alter the relationship between necessary labour time and surplus labour time, in favour of surplus labour time. It is this similarity which makes them antagonistic class fractions, but not antagonistic classes.

Production of a commodity for sale in a market with the object of realising profit is a process based on the appropriation of surplus value. By the 1980s, the possibility of increasing profits in the realm of production and in the process of exchange had reached certain limits for both the *petit bourgeoisie* and the big peasantry. The limits imposed in the production process by both the production of absolute and relative surplus value had been reached. The reorganisation of plantation labour into family work teams pushed the production of absolute surplus labour to its limits. Similarly, in industries based on the production of relative surplus value, limits had been reached with the purchase of the most up-to-date machinery in most of the service activities. At the level of exchange, limits had also been reached, because economic activity had slowed down nationally and locally, particularly as coffee prices had continued to fall despite international quotas. Goroka had fallen behind its Highlands rival, Mt Hagen, as a growth centre which brought a deterioration in its service industry to accompany its worries about coffee. Gouna turned in a very modest profit before tax of K17,672 for the year 1979. Its main investment since 1978 was the construction of a K800,000 shopping and office complex in the heart of Goroka town which is a major project, but Gouna was warned by its bank manager to slow down and consolidate in the three subsequent years. As far as is known, the Eastern Highlands Development Corporation made no major purchases in the late 1970s. When the limits are reached to appropriation of surplus value in the production process itself, capitalists must attempt to increase profits outside the realm of production, in the process of exchange at a time of economic growth and/or by receiving beneficial treatment from the state.

A result of the period of rapid accumulation by the Development Corporations and the decline in the economy was that the focus of their activities shifted from the marshalling of clan resources at the village level to protect their (by now) large-scale economic interests. This could only be achieved at the national level through access to the agencies of the state. It became economically imperative for the Development Corporations to gain access to financial resources, to seek protection from competitors and to forestall state encroachment on their profits through unnecessary taxation. Gouna appeared better able to adapt to these new political and economic circumstances. Its 2,000-plus members or shareholders were grouped into seven business groups,[1] each group structured more like a company than a clan-based business group, and tightly controlled by a Gouna director. Gouna's expatriate manager, Andes Berquist, could thus be sure that a decision passed by the directors would be acceptable to the shareholders.

Gouna benefited from the early nationalism of the *petit bourgeois* leaders, but by the early 1980s and especially since the formation of the PPP-National government in 1980, its national political influence had declined. Gouna's service or *petit bourgeois* activities had suffered from national government petrol tax, and Goroka Soft Drinks had not received the assistance an infant industry like this might have expected from a national government. However, the really sore point was Pacific Helicopters, whose plight had received little sympathy from the new PPP-National Party government. Although it had expanded its fleet, Hari and Auwo believed it would be even more successful if its operations could be protected by the national government from competition with overseas operators. They believed they were offering a valuable service to PNG, and that the national government should have acted to ensure that 'Pacific Helicopters must stay in PNG'. (*Post Courier*, January 29, 1981) Gouna was suffering from the antipathy its directors have always held for national political involvement, and from a commitment to the quaint liberal notion of a separation of business and politics, or as Auwo put it, 'Business is business, politics is politics'. (Auwo Ketauwo, Interview 23 June 1982) By 1982 with the recession deepening and a hostile government in Port Moresby for the first time, the *petit bourgeoisie* were forced to reconsider such beliefs about business and politics.

The Eastern Highlands Development Corporation's much looser chain of command, grouped its 15,500 members into 14 business groups, but these were of the more orthodox type, based on customary law and clan-based decision-making. This looseness in organisational structure affected the exercise of the management function so gravely that it soon became evident that it could not continue to be exercised from within the organisation itself. The Eastern Highlands Development Corporation contracted out the management of its coffee plantations to ANGCO Pty Ltd soon after they were purchased, in the mid-1970s. At that time ANGCO was a foreign-owned company, one of the oldest and largest companies in Papua New Guinea and the principal coffee export firm in the country. ANGCO is vertically integrated in the coffee industry, owning outright a number of coffee processing factories such as Wahgi Valley Coffee Company Pty Ltd, Kaga Muga Coffee Producers Pty Ltd and Goroka Coffee Producers (Figure 7.2 below).

In the beginning, the Eastern Highlands Development Corporation had an orthodox contractual arrangement with ANGCO. Their directors were denied influence on ANGCO management decisions in return for the efficient operation of their plantations, but as circumstances changed and realignments in class forces took place, so the nature of the relationship altered from a contractual to a symbiotic one. The major change which occurred in 1977, the purchase of a majority shareholding of ANGCO (60%) by the government's Investment Corporation (worth K3,214,281 in 1982) had an oblique effect on the relationship between ANGCO and the Eastern Highlands Development Corporation.

While ANGCO's top management remained unchanged and the government promised that it would continue to operate on profit or market criteria, the fact that it was now owned by a government statutory authority meant inevitably that more nationals would be recruited into the company, and that this recruitment was likely to bring in its wake an intrusion into the company of coffee politics. This trend became more evident with the appointment of Mr Benias Sabumei, former Deputy Secretary for Foreign Affairs and Trade and son of former House of Assembly member Mr Sabumei Kofikai, to a top executive position. Ben Sabumei takes a keen interest in politics and has often publicly mentioned his political ambitions. (*Papua New Guinea Times*, March 20, 1981) He is even an executive officer of the National Party. His appointment helped create the preconditions for coalescence of a big peasant class fraction which had a base in coffee through the Eastern Highlands Development Corporation, achieved a national reach by aligning with ANGCO, steered by Ben Sabumei, and achieved its political expression through the National Party, Sabumei's party and also that of Goroka's sitting national members Sailas Atopare and Akepa Miakwe, when they became ministers in the PPP–National Party Government.

The differences between the two class fractions has been most obvious in recent years in their relation to national level politics, and these have grown as declining economic circumstances have made it more and more necessary for fractions to consolidate their national reach. The defeat of the Somare government through a no–confidence vote in Parliament and its replacement by a PPP–National Party coalition in March 1980 was a crucial event, for it had the effect of polarising the fractions in the Eastern Highlands. The view from there was of a national government increasingly dominated by big peasant interests, leaving the national reach of the local *petit bourgeoisie* severely curtailed. The big peasant fraction used this opportunity to shore up the declining fortunes of the coffee industry. World prices determine the state of the industry, so big peasant successes could not be spectacular, but in this period the industry had the export tax withdrawn from coffee; dissuaded the Coffee Industry Board from establishing its own export company (a direct threat to ANGCO); saw Development Bank lending for coffee development double (by value) in 1980; and saw the return of a system of bounty payments to producers due to low world prices (*Post Courier*, February 4, 1981:13) and convince almost everyone that the industry had an overcapacity of dry processing plants so that no more should be licensed. More sensationally, the national government's sectoral funds for disbursement were captured by National Party (big peasant) ministers – – *inter alia*, Iambakey Okuk, Sailas Atopare – – rather than through provincial governments. As coffee producers, Gouna has benefited from assistance to the industry, but the value of this assistance is limited, given their level of diversification.

Thus by 1982 the Development Corporations were in a position where they were forced to compete for access to national resources. This was the effect of declining economic circumstances, but it was exacerbated by the defeat of the Somare government. The dominant class fractions had become so polarised that they were forced to enter national political struggle for the first time. We will look at the form this struggle took in the coffee industry in the following three chapters.

Notes

1. Gouna's share holders are Gagaso B/G 61,722, Joyu B/G 7627, Mimanlia B/G 18439, Yobamowaupi B/G 14190, Sitani B/G 24,662, Apiuha B/G 20,885, Gapo Guna Gaud B/G 7, 632, Nokondi Investment Corporation (Provincial Government Business Arm) 40,000, Auwo Ketauwo 1 share and Isembo Olekevea 1 share.

8

Dividing up the Coffee Industry Among Black Élites

Introduction

In Chapter 3, Exchanging Coffee, we saw that the power of the white planters in the domestic marketing of coffee was almost wholly determined by the functioning of a private market in coffee. The planters exercised commercial power to control key 'pinch points' in the marketing chain. They attempted to vertically integrate their activities in an effort to strengthen this control, but received little or no assistance from the colonial state to defend or further their power. They also attempted to 'co–opt' new black élites in an effort to broaden their power base and legitimacy claims.

In the post–colonial period, the tracking of power relationships in the coffee industry becomes more complex. One reason for this is the effect that state intervention has on the coffee marketing chain through its effect on key groups at the main pinch points. In the post–colonial period the state in the coffee industry takes the form of a strengthened, technocratic Coffee Industry Board (CIB), the form and function of which will be described in greater detail in Chapter 9. In this chapter, however, it is sufficient to note that the state, through the CIB, continues to intervene in the coffee market as a regulatory authority, but with the difference in the post–colonial period that it has the power to sanction (mainly through licensing) actors operating at various pinch points in the coffee market. This is not, as it appears to McKillop (McKillop, Williamson and Associates Pty Ltd 1982:7), an 'all pervading' state power because it stops short of state production. As Densley notes: "while there have been several major changes in the marketing of coffee within Papua New Guinea in recent years the basic structure of marketing has not altered significantly.". (Densley n.d.:19)

But the state's power is great at the pinch points. For example, at the exporter pinch point the CIB has control over local exporters through licensing and allocation of quota shares, a result of the joining of the ICA. Thus the CIB provides state support for large firms like ANGCO which are vertically integrated in the industry and in this way the state can have an impact throughout the coffee marketing chain.

A second reason for complexity in the post-colonial coffee industry is the class conflict that arises between the big peasantry and the *petit bourgeoisie* as a result of the split within the dominant class. It will be shown in this section that while dominant class fractions do control the crucial pinch points and use every means at their disposal to maintain this dominance, dominance in the post-colonial coffee market is not as clear cut as it was in the colonial coffee market. This is because in the post-colonial market the dominant class is fragmented, and because there exists regulation of the industry along technocratic lines, which often means that regulation does not always operate in the interests of the dominant class fractions. The market problem of the dominant class fractions in the post-colonial coffee market is to work out how to ensure that the market (and the accompanying regulations) stimulate the appropriation of smallholder surplus by dominant class fractions but at the same time does not drive these into competition with each other. The dominant classes must ensure that the market and its accompanying regulations provide sufficient incentive for smallholders to keep producing coffee, but also allow the cost of the inevitable stockholding and non-market sales to be borne in the main by smallholders. We will see how at the various pinch points different mechanisms have been tried to deal with this contradiction.

The system for rewarding exporters

There were seven licensed coffee exporters in Papua New Guinea in 1980-81 (Tables 8.1 and 8.2). These are (with their 1980-81 export quota allocations in brackets): ANGCO Pty Ltd (44.8 percent), Gollin-CIL (Coffee International Ltd) Pty Ltd (26.0 percent), PNG Coffee Exporters Pty Ltd (PNGCE - - 10.6 percent), Harrison and Crosfield Pty Ltd (7.6 percent), COFEX (5.3 percent), Namasu (4.7 percent), Pacific Trading Company Pty Ltd (1.0 percent). Two of these firms are wholly owned subsidiaries of Harrison and Crosfield Pty Ltd, the multinational trading and plantation company. The Pacific Trading Company Pty Ltd is the wholly owned subsidiary of W.R. Carpenter & Co. Estates Ltd. A third exporter, PNGCE is effectively controlled by foreigners. PNGCE is 50 percent owned by the Swiss-based multinational trader Volkart Bros and 41 percent by New Guinea Coffee Brokers. New Guinea Coffee Brokers is in turn 57 percent owned by the expatriate firm Collins and Leahy Pty Ltd. A fourth exporter, CIL Pty Ltd, PNG's second largest exporter, was until November 1982 a wholly owned subsidiary of the Australian parent Gollin & Co

TABLE 8.1 Export Quota Allocations, 1981–82

Company	*1980–81 percent Share*	*1981–82 percent Share*
Angco Pty Ltd	44.3	44.8
Gollin-CIL Pty Ltd	25.7	26.0
PNG Coffee Exporters Pty Ltd	11.0	10.6
Harrison & Crosfield Pty Ltd	8.0	7.6
Cofex Pty Ltd	5.5	5.3
Namasu Pty Ltd	4.5	4.7
Pacific Trading Company Pty. Ltd.	1.0	1.0
	100.0	100.0

Source: Hassall and Associates (1982)

TABLE 8.2 Export Shares, 1976–80

Exporter	*1976/77 Export (tons)*	*Market Share %*	*1977/78 Export (tons)*	*Market Share %*	*1978/79 Export (tons)*	*Market Share %*	*1979/80 Export (tons)*	*Market Share %*
Angco	24318.3	48	19026.3	41.6	22345.6	46.1	20785.3	41.4
CIL	10521.3	21	11978.7	26.2	12343.7	25.4	13320.4	26.6
PNGCE	3971.5	8	3973.0	8.7	6924.4	14.3	6237.0	12.4
H & C	3325.4	7	3870.3	8.4	4107.1	8.5	3823.6	7.6
Sincof[1]	5226.3	10.3	1241.9	2.7	–	–	–	–
Cofex	722.1	1	3080.3	6.7	1328.7	3.0	3498.0	7.0
Namasu	2143.9	4.0	1969.6	4.3.	1052.9	2.1	1579.7	3.1
Pacific Trading	568.6	2	514.7	1.1	352.3	0.7	511.5	1.0
Total Tons	50698.3	100.0	45655.7	100.0	48508.6	100.0	50142.1	100.0

Source: CIB data supplied by exporters

(1) Sincof acquired by Gollin-CIL in 1978

(2) Error due to rounding and CEM 0.8 tons exported in 1976/77

Source: Hassall and Associates (1982)

(Australia) Pty Ltd. In 1982 three Papua New Guinea business groups - - Piplika Development Corporation, the Bomai Development Corporation and Lapusa Investments Pty Ltd paid $10.5 million to buy a 75 percent majority holding in Australia's failed coffee and tea brokerage, the Gollin group. (*The Age*, November 24, 1982) CIL Pty Ltd now joins Namasu Coffee Pty Ltd, Cofex Pty Ltd and ANGCO Pty Ltd as wholly nationally owned exporters.

Foreign ownership remains at the exporter pinch point in the post-colonial coffee industry but this is not a crucial factor in the export of

Papua New Guinea coffee. This is so because the nationally-owned companies ANGCO and CIL dominate the export of coffee (72.8 percent of exports in 1981–82) and because the changing export patterns of PNG coffee has reduced Australian commercial influence over the marketing of coffee. Table 8.3 shows that the bulk of PNG coffee currently goes not to Australia, but to West Germany, and this probably means that advantages which once accrued to Australian owners of export companies are not now so great.

TABLE 8.3 Papua New Guinea: Export Destinations

	Australia	*U.S.A.*	*W.Germany* *(Tons approx.)*	*U.K.*	*Japan*	*Other*	*Total*
Financial Year							
(July to June)							
1959/60	1,422		9	1	4	52	1,488
1960/61	2,059		19		5	211	2,294
1961/62	2,388	32	110	84	5	824	3,443
1962/63	2,845	11	207	154	5	1,623	4,845
1963/64	3,665	20	889	271	129	1,857	6,831
1964/65	5,360	78	1,375	358	207	1,309	8,687
1965/66	4,780	1,211	1,370	1,221	265	1,957	10,804
1966/67	5,456	2,146	1,918	1,725	421	1,245	12,911
1967/68	5,500	5,000	3,400	3,200	92	1,075	18,267
International Coffee Year							
1968/69	6,831	5,694	3,794	3,482	75	683	20,559
1969/70	6,927	7,523	3,567	3,392	274	1,910	23,593
1970/71	7,552	9,505	2,136	3,614	nil	1,668	24,475
1971/72	8,322	6,872	4,652	3,428	464	3,999	27,737
1972/73	9,435	13,325	3,870	2,669	3,025	7,045	39,369
			(Bags)				
1973/74	160,763	180,383	90,717	53,512	34,118	68,603	588,096
1974/75	157,445	201,214	119,213	56,161	43,955	85,815	663,803
1976	188,829	245,692	195,842	64,830	33,458	70,569	799,220
1977	166,585	143,668	217,314	31,956	7,004	59,502	626,079
1978	152,279	165,755	297,316	59,838	15,759	79,425	769,372

For earlier years the destination was mainly Australia.

Source: Cartledge (1978) and Department of Foreign Affairs and Trade, Port Moresby.

Multinational exporters probably save on information costs due to their world-wide information networks, and therefore might experience some advantage on profitability. But this seems hardly to show up in comparison with nationally owned exporters. In any case, foreign ownership of exporting firms cannot give a firm an advantage in ICO member markets because quota shares are set by the CIB. Further, as Figure 7.2 shows, those firms which are foreign owned or controlled do not have a high level of backward integration into processing and production. Pacific Trading Co. exports coffee from Carpenters' two plantations. COFEX has no backward integration and indeed is the subject of forward integration by ASARO Coffee Estates and Kainantu Coffee Factory, which own 60 percent shareholding in New Guinea Coffee Brokers. Harrisons and Crosfields have four coffee plantations, but their main interest in production is not in coffee at all but in the colonial-sponsored New Britain Palm Oil Development. For all these reasons it is not necessary to consider foreign ownership as a major factor in the political economy of coffee exporters.

The allocation of quota entitlements by the ICO is done at present according to past market sales. In Papua New Guinea the immense power of determining quota allocations to exporting firms is held by the CIB. It must register a contract before coffee can be exported. It thus has the power to determine market shares in the highly valued member markets. This licensing system does mean, as the Hassall Report (1982) makes clear, that there is a complete barrier to entry at the exporter pinch points because it is the CIB which grants to the seven firms the privilege of permission to trade. (Hassall and Associates 1982:173) However, the privilege of entry into member markets does not solve the marketing problems of exporters. Regardless of the size of their present export allocations all exporters face circumstances where there are limits to the amount of coffee which can be exported to member markets -- limits set by the ICO. As a consequence, exporters have to export a good deal of their coffee to non-member markets, which is risky. These exports tend to be relatively large, forcing exporters to operate on a margin that is about one-third that for member markets. (Hassall and Associates 1982:72 and 173) Since 1980, with world coffee in over-supply and all market prices low, the marketing problem of exporting firms has been serious. Not only must they try to maintain profits and avoid competition, but must also subsidise their non-market sales in order to maintain margins at profitable levels.

In order to understand the export problem, the report by Hassall and Associates Pty Ltd prepared for the Papua New Guinea Coffee Industry Board in August 1982, examined, *inter alia* the market problem of coffee exporters, and recommended a restructuring of exporters in the industry. The report contains much useful information, but it is necessary to treat such a document cautiously. It will be used with the following caveats in mind.

In the first place, it is couched in technocratic language and presents a rather patchy analysis, of the type expected from consultants. It does not make any attempt to identify the social and political relations of exporters. Instead it focuses on a description of vertical integration and an examination of profitability levels of exporters. But in neglecting to show that behind these facts and figures there exist active social subjects -- mainly the dominant class fractions -- engaged in a struggle to further their own interests, the report makes some serious mistakes and ends up reinforcing the largely ideological and self interested claims of the dominant class fractions. A study of vertical integration in an industry should show, firstly, how the dominant class fractions are linked through various firms and levels in the industry, and then show how this vertical integration assists these class fractions to maintain their dominance over the industry.[1] The first task is difficult enough in the post-colonial coffee industry because there is a great deal of cross-class fractional ownership in the various export companies. In most companies there is not a neat correspondence between the class fractions which exist in the coffee industry and the majority owners of a company.

This non-correspondence is a result of the fact that the structure in production which generates classes is not as clear-cut in some provinces and areas as was described previously for the Goroka area.[2] In Chimbu, for example, where a plantation structure has never existed, the formation of class fractions must straddle production and distribution of surplus value. Thus the dominant classes there are not neatly divided into a big peasantry and a *petit bourgeoisie* as in Goroka, and various segments of the Chimbu dominant class fractions might look to coffee-buying or coffee-processing rather than ownership and control of coffee production as their means of objectively siting their class boundaries. (Standish 1981) This difference can translate into their relations with exporters, which may result in splits within the dominant classes, since they support different exporters.

In Kainantu, an equally unusual situation exists where the representatives of the local dominant class fractions, such as Barry Holloway, are *petit bourgeois*, but such men do not have a local *petit bourgeois* class base because of the limited development of the service industry in Kainantu. The representatives of dominant class fractions in Kainantu are also fragmented into supporting a range of export firms.

Similarly, in the Western Highlands the neat dominant class fractional split outlined for Goroka seems not to have been expressed in any phenomenal form such as Development Corporations. Thus when Western Highlands dominant local classes come to be integrated with exporters they, like Chimbu's, fragment into various class segments. In attempting to trace these patterns of dominant class fractional integration with exporters, we have no need to deal with Harrison and Crosfield Pty Ltd or Pacific Trading

Co Pty Ltd, because they are wholly owned by foreigners. Nor do we have to discuss Namasu, because this is an export company almost wholly engaged in the export of Robusta coffee.

Vertical integration is very pronounced in the case of the larger exporters such as ANGCO. This is despite public opposition to vertical integration from the CIB. (Papua New Guinea Coffee Industry Board Reports, September 30, 1980:42) Privately, many in the industry express the fear that ANGCO is attempting to take it over. ANGCO is certainly protected in its vertical integration by the fact that it is more profitable than other firms mentioned in the report. Hassall reports that ANGCO's operating profit earned some K250 per ton of green bean traded to 31 December. (Hassall and Associates 1982:68) ANGCO is also protected in the industry because it is 60 percent owned by the Papua New Guinea Investment Corporation, a government corporation. It would be misleading to see this ownership as evidence of public sector control, as the Hassall Report does. The Investment Corporation is a public holding company. It operates in exactly the same way as a private corporation would. Further, its purpose is to make its investments commercially viable so that its holdings can be sold off at the earliest possible time to national entrepreneurs. Investment Corporation ownership of ANGCO has probably had one important outcome, however, being that it has forestalled any moves to break up ANGCO. The view of the Investment Corporation is that ANGCO's operations have significant flow-on benefits for the whole PNG coffee industry. (Hassall and Associates 1982:68)

ANGCO is also protected in its vertical integration by the fact that it is the exporting base of the big peasant class fraction, and is thus supported by a politically powerful dominant class fraction. This is most clearly seen in the registered factories (and accompanying plantations) which have shares in it. Figure 7.2 shows that the major shareholders of ANGCO engaged in coffee production are big peasant development corporations of the Eastern Highlands, such as Eastern Highlands Development Corporation (1.7 percent), Asaro Watabung Rural Development Corporation (0.2 percent, the production base of the former big peasant member for Goroka Open Sailas Atopare of the National Party) Chimbu Holdings (2.5 percent) and KKB (3.5 percent). ANGCO is also owned by a string of financiers who play no part in production decisions, and by certain groups (Bougainville Development Corporation 7.5 percent and Sepik Cocoa Growers Coop) who support ANGCO's cocoa activities, but have no interest in the coffee side of its operations. ANGCO owns a range of big peasant factories and plantations extending throughout the Highlands (Figure 7.2).

In Eastern Highlands Province, ANGCO owns 98 percent of Goroka Coffee Producers Pty Ltd, in Chimbu it owns 63.4 percent of Chimbu Developments Pty Ltd, and in Western Highlands it owns 100 percent of

Wahgi Valley Coffee Company Pty Ltd. A further possible area of vertical integration in the coffee industry for ANGCO – – exporter financed processing factories – – is not formally undertaken by ANGCO. (Hassall and Associates 1982:89) The reason exporters finance processing factories is so that they have a tied supply at a guaranteed price. (Hassall and Associates 1982:88) The fact that ANGCO does not formally finance factories probably means little given the extent of its forward and backward integration. This integration through ownership achieves the same purpose that financing factories would have: it assures ANGCO of a supply. I will return to this aspect of vertical integration in due course.

Coffee International Ltd (CIL), the second largest exporter, is also vertically integrated in the industry. In 1982 three national groups purchased 75 percent of CIL from Collins. It then seemed to function as a base for disparate big peasant groups who were outside the Eastern Highlands big peasantry which dominated the industry nationally through ANGCO. This is suggested by the composition of the groups that purchased CIL: these include Bomai Development Corporation, led by Chimbu provincial member John Nilkare and his brother-in-law, Dominic Brae, ex-chairman of Chimbu Coffee. Bomai's interests straddle both coffee (mainly in the area of coffee-buying) and service activities in Kundiawa. Piplika Development Corporation is the production base of Michael Mel from the Western Highlands, whose interests in coffee include factories and plantations. The third partner is Lapusa Investments Pty Ltd, but little is known of this group. This purchase in 1982 meant that the factories of the various groups having a share in CIL, and CIL's ownership of the biggest coffee plantation in the Southern hemisphere, the 6000-hectare Gumanch plantation near Mount Hagen in the Western Highlands, further integrated CIL up and down the marketing chain. CIL, as reported by Hassall, did engage in tied financing of factories before the change of ownership, and it can be assumed that this activity continued after its sale. The factories were Busu Coffee, Timbug and Wahgi Mek. (Hassall and Associates 1982:70) Finally, PNGCE is also well integrated in the coffee industry. Collins and Leahy Pty Ltd registered factories and plantations virtually control PNGCE and one can presume there are also tied factories operated by PNGCE. PNGCE may function as a petty bourgeois exporter outlet although more details would have to be provided before much could be said about the class base of its patterns of integration. Little is known about COFEX except that it has only recently struggled out of receivership and may not have developed a class base as yet. It appears to be owned by small groups of nationals known as Mainland Holdings.

The main reason to study the patterns of integration in an industry is to show how these help classes and class fractions maintain their dominance. In this context three main questions arise: first, whether integration helps maintain dominant class control by enabling plantations to be paid more for their product than smallholders are paid by exporters; second, whether integration helps maintain class fractional control by increasing the price paid to tied factories compared to untied factories; and third, whether integration helps to overcome, through subsidy, the cost of exporting to non-member markets? The remainder of this chapter will provide answers to these questions.

TABLE 8.4 Exporters Trading Margins, 1981 (Y Grade)

	ANGCO	*CIL*	*PNGCE*	*H & C*	*COFEX*	*NAMASU*
Export Price (FOB) PNG [1, 2]	169.1	167.1	170.6	161.9	165.0	162.4
Exporters Margin	16.6	20.5	19.7	13.6	13.3	9.6
Storage, handling wharf charges	2.7	2.7	2.7	2.0	1.0	1.5
Insurance	0.5	0.5	0.5	0.5	0.5	0.5
Levy	1.0	0.5	1.0	0.5	0.5	0.5
Bank Interest	4.0	4.0	4.0	4.0	4.0	4.0
Administration/overheads	7.0	5.4	5.0	5.0	6.8	12.0
Export Tax		nil				
Export price-DIS Lae	133.5	133.5	137.1	134.8	138.9	134.3
Freight Highlands to Port	4.8	4.8	4.8	3.0	2.5	2.5
Prices Paid to Factories-DIS Highlands	130.4	128.4	132.3	131.8	136.4	131.8
Processing/Admin Costs	15.0	15.0	15.0	15.0	15.0	15.0
Processors Margin	10.0	10.0	10.0	10.0	10.0	10.0
Factory Door Price - Green Bean	107.6	103.8	108.0	109.9	113.8	107.9
Factory Door Price Parchment	80.7	77.8	81.0	82.4	85.4	80.9
Buyers Margin/Transport to Factory	12.0	12.0	12.0	12.0	12.0	12.0
Roadside Price	68.7	65.8	69.0	70.4	73.4	67.1
Bounty	0.10	0.10	0.10	0.10	0.10	0.10
Growers Price	78.7	75.8	79.0	80.4	83.4	77.1

[1] All prices in toea per kg

[2] FOB and prices paid to factories DIS Highlands based on registered contracts June, July, August, September, 1981.

Source: Hassall and Associates (1982)

Integration or at least control of a substantial proportion of the coffee exported, does appear to ensure that plantations are paid more for their products than smallholders are paid by exporters. This is largely a result of the differential grading system adopted since colonial times, but it can also be shown that the 'bigger' the exporter the greater their role in under-selling smallholder coffee. (Compare Table 8.4 and Table 8.5. Remember that Y Grade is mainly smallholder coffee and A Grade is plantation coffee.) We notice two things when we look at the price exporters pay to factories. In Table 8.4, as the Hassall Report notes, smaller exporters such as COFEX and Namusu pay higher average prices to factories for Y Grade than larger exporters pay to factories (except for PNGCE). (Hassall and Associates 1982:76) The reverse occurs in Table 8.5. Smaller exporters such as COFEX and Harrison and Crosfield pay lower average prices for A Grade to factories than the larger exporters pay to factories. Similarly, if we look at exporters' margins in Table 8.4 (Y Grade) and compare it with Table 8.5 (A Grade), we find that large exporters have higher margins compared with small exporters in Y Grade. But in A Grade (although the figures are less conclusive), larger exporters have smaller margins.

TABLE 8.5 Exporters Trading Margins, 1981 (A Grade)

	ANGCO	*CIL*	*PNGCE*	*H & C*	*COFEX*	*NAMASU*
Export Price (FOB, PNG)[1,2]	196.6	186.4	187.8	176.5	188.7	–
Exporters Margin	20.4	13.3	18.4	12.0	25.9	–
Storage, handling wharf charges	2.7	2.7	2.7	2.0	1.0	–
Insurance	0.5	0.5	0.5	0.5	0.5	–
Levy	1.0	1.0	1.0	1.0	1.0	–
Bank Interest	5.0	5.0	5.0	5.0	5.0	–
Administration/overheads	7.0	5.4	5.0	5.0	6.8	–
Export price – DIS Lae	158.9	158.4	155.1	151.0	148.5	–
Freight Highlands to Port	4.8	4.8	4.8	3.0	2.5	–
Prices Paid to Factories – DIS Highlands	154.1	153.6	150.3	148.0	146.0	–
Processing/Admin costs	15.0	15.0	15.0	15.0	15.0	–
Processors Margin	10.0	10.0	10.0	10.0	10.0	–
Factory Door – Green Bean	131.5	134.5	135.6	121.3	131.2	–

[1] All prices in toea per kg

[2] FOB and prices paid to factories DIS Highlands based on registered contracts June, July, August, September, 1981.

Source: Hassall and Associates (1982)

What can this mean? The Hassall Report notices it, but comments that the trend of smaller exporters paying higher prices to factories for Y grade is not a general one because larger exporters pay higher average prices to growers for A grade than do smaller exporters. (Hassall and Associates 1982:76) This merely confuses the issue, and in any case it is not useful to bring in the undifferentiated term 'grower' when the whole point in question is whether the size of the exporter allows them to pay growers differentially. In any case the Hassall Report concludes that while overall it appears that 'larger exporters generally trade on higher margins than the smaller exporters' this is not due to any single factor but rather a combination of prices received, prices paid and overhead costs. (Hassall and Associates 1982:86) But may not the higher margins overall of the large exporters be due precisely to the observed phenomenon in Tables 8.4 and 8.5. In other words, do large exporters' higher margins come from the fact that they have higher margins in Y smallholder coffee? Do they have higher margins because they are buying the bulk of their coffee - - Y grade coffee from smallholders - - at below its market value? Do the large exporters appropriate surplus from the smallholders and pass this on as a subsidy to 'tied' plantations producing A grade coffee?

The smaller exporter is in no position to do this because of less integration with A grade producing plantations. In any case, the smaller exporter is in a more competitive internal market situation. How can it be shown that this differential payment, which disadvantages smallholders, is the result of a big exporter appropriation and not merely due to more or less efficient operating procedures, as the Hassall Report claims? The answer could be found by comparing the ratio of factory door price Green Bean to Export price (FOB) for Y Grade and A Grade coffee. Whatever the efficiency of the exporter or the overhead costs, this ratio should not vary substantially from Y Grade to A Grade. The results are set out in Table 8.6. They show quite clearly that while the return to growers of A Grade coffee (green bean) hovers around 70 percent, the return to growers of Y Grade coffee is around 63 percent of FOB. This would suggest that Y Grade coffee growers are being unfairly discriminated against as regards the proportion of the FOB which returns to them. Most Y Grade is sold as parchment coffee, but when recovery rates are taken into account, an accurate price is obtained. A further interesting feature of Table 8.6 is that it is the larger exporters who have the greatest gap between the ratio paid to A Grade coffee growers and that paid to Y Grade growers. This further reinforces the idea that large exporters appropriate surplus from smallholders and return it to integrated plantations.

TABLE 8.6 Ratio of Factory Door Price (Green Bean) to Export Price (FOB, PNG)

	ANGCO	CIL	PNGCE	H & C	COFEX	NAMASU
Y Grade – 1981						
Factory Door Price (Green Bean)	107	103	108	109	113	107
	—	—	—	—	—	—
Export Price	169	167	170	161	165	162
Ratio	63%	62%	64%	68%	68%	—
A Grade – 1981						
Factory Door Price (Green Bean)	131	134	135	121	132	—
	—	—	—	—	—	
Export Price	196	186	187	176	188	—
Ratio	67%	72%	73%	69%	70%	—

Source: Hassall and Associates (1982)

Table 8.7 ANGCO & CIL – Tied and Untied and Owned Factories: Contract Analysis Y Grade, Contracts 1981–82 Price Series

		kina/kg					
		ANGCO			*CIL*		
Month	*Week*	*Owned*	*Tied*	*Untied*	*Owned*	*Tied*	*Untied*
March 1982	2	–	–	–	–	1.75	1.78
	3	1.67	–	1.76	1.80	1.68	1.73
	4	1.70	–	1.66			
	5	1.70	1.48	–	1.80	1.61	1.66
April 1982	1		–	–	–	1.68	1.65
	3	1.66	–	1.70	1.63	1.68	1.66
	4	1.68	1.40	1.65	1.70	1.65	1.64
June 1981	1	1.40	–	1.40	1.51	1.45	1.36
	2	1.32	–	1.35	1.00	1.40	1.30
	3	1.33	–	1.31	1.38	0.90	1.25
	4	1.27	–	1.35	–	–	–

continues

Table 8.7 *continued*

		kina/kg					
		ANGCO			CIL		
Month	*Week*	*Owned*	*Tied*	*Untied*	*Owned*	*Tied*	*Untied*
July 1981	1	1.25	-	1.26	1.30	1.26	1.21
	2	1.27	-	1.26	-	-	-
	3	-	-	-	-	1.28	1.25
	4	1.34		1.12	-	1.29	1.29
	5				1.40	1.32	1.36
August 1982	1	1.40		1.36	-	1.33	1.33
	2	1.37	1.38	1.36	1.40	1.30	1.31
	3	1.34	1.39	1.34	1.30	1.35	1.31
	4	1.34	1.34	1.34	1.15	1.30	1.23
	5	1.31	1.11	1.33			
September 1982	1	1.33	-	1.33			
	2	1.35	-	1.29			
	3	1.35	-	1.36			
	4	1.36		1.38			
	5	1.36		1.41			

Source: Hassall and Associates (1982)

The significance of the link between plantation holders and processing

If the big exporters are subsidising A Grade or plantation coffee by paying lower prices on Y Grade, they are subsidising only A Grade coffee which is processed in factories tied to them. This tying of factories to exporters is achieved mainly by financing the factory in return for all or part of the crop at a guaranteed price. It is this aspect of integration which the Hassall Report considers has the greatest influence on market behaviour, for factories which are tied through finance or directly owned by a large exporter receive more favourable treatment than untied factories. (Hassall and Associates 1982:173–74)

Table 8.7 contains the data used by Hassall, and while this is limited, it is enough for them to conclude that for both ANGCO and CIL: "indications are that directly owned subsidiary factories may receive more favourable prices than tied and untied." (Hassall and Associates 1982:91)

Hassall are of the view that the tied relationship only works one way. They argue that "factories wholly owned by exporters tend to sell to that exporter. Likewise, exporters financing factory operations generally do so on the understanding that they received amounts of coffee commensurate with the amount of finance involved." (Hassall and Associates 1982:174)

But Hassall claims that this does not mean factories with shareholders in exporting companies sell exclusively to that exporter. This may be the case. Such suppliers are free to shop around to get the best price from an exporter. But do they? Indications are that suppliers to ANGCO who have shares in it, such as the Eastern Highlands Development Corporation (EHDC) definitely do supply exclusively to ANGCO. This point was made obliquely by Tom Fox, Chairman of Directors of ANGCO. Fox said "some of our shareholders, such as the Eastern Highlands Development Corporation, Sepik Coffee Producers and Bougainville Development Corporation have a very direct relationship with the Company as suppliers." (*The Papua New Guinea Times*, Coffee Supplement, March 9, 1983:13)

If this is the case, then it further underlines the utility of vertical integration in the power struggle between contending class fractions. The integration of exporters and processors ensures that their power is maintained in all the areas where the fraction is active, and ensures that losses by the class fraction in one area of its market operations can be subsidised by profits from other areas of class fractional activity.

The Hassall Report correctly expresses concern at the extent to which the dominant class fractions are moving to close off the industry at the various pinch points, through integration and reduction in competition. The Report states:

> by owning and financing factories, exporters (mainly the two biggest exporters) have established claims on about 53 percent of the coffee crop. Thus, less than half of the coffee crop is available for purchase on a fully competitive basis. This degree of integration and control is probably not consistent with the concept of workable competition. (Hassall and Associates 1982:174)

However, it is not merely integration of factories with exporters which provides barriers to new entry to coffee processing. It is the CIB itself through its registration procedures and current policy against new negotiations which restricts entry to processing pinch points. In April 1978, the CIB issued 'savage' guidelines for the registration of coffee processing facilities, which included registration of facilities or plantations owned by nationals and established before 1978, and proclaimed that no new factories would be erected even on plantations. The CIB also issued strict building and equipment regulations, as well as tough requirements for management and finance of existing processing plants. (Papua New Guinea Coffee Industry Board Report 1979:4) In that same year court action was taken against "an organisation from Eastern Highlands Province for illegal processing of coffee in unregistered processing facilities and another person for hindering and obstructing board inspectors in the exercise of their duties." (Papua New Guinea Coffee Industry Board Report 1979:18)

Seventeen processors were convicted and given fines ranging from K27 to K120 because they failed to lodge their monthly coffee processing returns as required under the Act. (Papua New Guinea Coffee Industry Board Report 1979:18)

Given the existence of vertical integration in the industry, it could be asked whether the CIB is using the coercive power of the state to reinforce the power of dominant class fractions at the processing level. The CIB would claim to be acting in exactly the reverse fashion. It would argue that it is its registration of factories which has preserved the conditions for 'workable competition' in the factory sector, as Hassall puts it. (Hassall and Associates 1982:174) The structure of factory ownership and production 1980–81 (Table 8.8) does suggest there is a good deal of diversity in the processing industry. As the table shows, there are five different classes of owners – – national groups, government and semi government bodies, other citizens (including individuals and partnerships) coffee–exporting companies and exporters (both companies and individuals). There are processing factories in almost all coffee producing provinces although 60 percent are concentrated in Eastern and Western Highlands where, after all, most coffee is grown. There are nine independent factories (in the sense that they are not tied to plantations), six in the Western Highlands Province and three in Eastern Highlands. (Hassall and Associates 1982:44–47)

The CIB would argue that strict licensing procedures for processors are required because there is an overcapacity in processing in the industry and also as a means '. . . of safeguarding the quality and reputation of PNG coffee'. (*Post Courier*, March 30, 1978) It has been conventional wisdom for many years to argue that processing facilities are under–utilised in the coffee industry. Officers of the CMB were fond of saying that processing facilities were three times as great as supply. They argued that this was so because many plantations started small factories and were registered for purposes of processing their own coffee, but then moved into buying more widely. For many years this was an unquestioned assumption in the industry, and the standard justification for the strict restriction of the establishment of new factories. But this argument tended not to deal with two important factors which relate to the question of processing capacity. The first is that any assessment of such capacity must be related to the variation that occurs in the demand for processing throughout the year as a result of the coffee cycle. Overcapacity could be said to exist only if coffee factories were under–utilised during harvest time. Because of the coffee production cycle, most factories are quite naturally under–utilised for the 7–8 months of the off season. (Hassall and Associates 1982:49) Also, over–capacity could not be said to exist if there was under–utilisation in a flush year, which might in fact mean full utilisation in every other year.

TABLE 8.8 Factory Ownership and Production, 1980–81

Ownership Cateogry		National Groups	Govt and Councils	Other Citizens	Exporters	Expatriates[1]	Total
Operating Registered Factories	No.	12.5[2]	4	4	8	5.5[2]	34
	Prodn	8160	4880	7913	11334	7950	40245
	%	18	10	17	24	17	86
Registered Factories Operating but not buying	No.	3	2	–	1	2	8
	Prodn	1084	404	–	1170	769	3423
	%	2	1	–	3	2	7
Unregistered	No.	8	–	5	4	8	25
	Prodn	1075	–	154	1086	728	3043
	%	2	–	0.3	2	2	7
Total	No.	23.5[2]	6	9	16	15.5[2]	70
	Prodn	10319	5284	8067	13590	9447	46711
	%	22	11	17	29	20	100

[1] Three unregistered factories owned by missions and a special purpose institute are grouped with the expatriate category.
[2] One factory was owned by an expatriate company in partnership with a local group.
Source: Hassall and Associate (1982)

The second factor that the overcapacity argument barely recognised is that coffee processing is not an undifferentiated activity. There are, processing factories with the capacity to process cherry, 'wet' factories and those with drying capacity merely to process parchment, 'dry' factories. Was over–capacity a factor in both 'wet' and 'dry' processing? There was no clear statement of this aspect of processing in the debates that took place in the colonial period.

It would seem plausible to argue that this assumption of 'over–capacity' in the industry was never fully discussed, because it suited the dominant class in the colonial industry, the white planters, to restrict the expansion of processing factories. After all, the planters all had 'wet' processing factories on their plantations, and restriction of extra factories meant that smallholder coffee was channelled through their plants at a substantial profit, as I have shown. In the post–colonial period, however, the existence of dominant class fractions in the industry with different interests at various levels in the marketing chain means that any restriction of processing factories must be justified by more refined arguments. With the split in the dominant class into competitive class fractions the question of licensing of processing factories becomes a feature of their class fractional struggle. It is now argued by Hassall that, overall, 'wet' factories were more fully utilised than 'dry' ones, at 82 percent compared with 60 percent. (Hassall and Associates 1982:50) These figures would seem to cast doubt on the need to restrict 'wet' factories on the basis of 'over-capacity', and even 'dry' capacity may be more fully utilised than Hassall's survey allows. As the World Bank noted in its 1981 Report on PNG Agriculture '. . . it is not clear whether overcapacity exists in the 'dry' processing industry'. (The World Bank 1981:Annex E:2) The Hassall Report does not, however, take up any of these points. It certainly does not offer detailed information as to where overcapacity exists, so it does not disaggregate its argument in 'wet' and 'dry' factory capacity. Like the old colonial argument, it merely asserts that over-capacity of processing exists in the industry. The Hassall Report states that:

> In the Western Highlands, factories are only using an average of about two thirds of their capacity, and this despite the fact that two registered factories have closed down recently. This compares with average utilisation of over 80 percent in the Eastern Highlands. (Hassall and Associates 1982:49–50)

The Hassall Report thus remains mindful of the politics of the industry where competitive class fractions could be disadvantaged by a recommendation to expand 'wet' processing and not restrict 'dry' processing. The big peasantry, with their base in plantation agriculture, would be severely disadvantaged by such a recommendation. In the end, Hassall and Associates remain close to their technocratic leaning, recommending only that 'improved processing technology in drying' be adopted so that no restriction of existing dry processing facilities would be caused by inefficient equipment. (Hassall and Associates 1982:177)

It is also argued in the industry that strict restriction of processing factories is necessary if the quality of PNG coffee is to be maintained. (*Post Courier*, March 30, 1978) According to Hurrell '. . . the quality problem happened mainly with Y Grade coffee which represented most of the smallholder production and made up 55 percent of PNG exports'. (*Post Courier*, June 29, 1977) The general problem of quality is different depending on who is thought to be at fault. One 'quality' problem occurs at the dry processing stage in which parchment of different moisture content might be all dried together for the same amount of time. This can result in dry parchment being overdried and the wettest parchment being underdried. The processor would be considered responsible for this problem because insufficient care has been taken to separate out beans with different moisture content and give them different drying time. Another 'quality' problem occurs at the point of purchase of parchment either by a coffee buyer or at the factory door. Here the problem is that inadequate hand-sorting may have been done at the cherry to parchment stage by the smallholder. The buyer buys a bag of parchment which is of poor quality because it contains a good deal of rubbish. At this point the blame could be put either on the buyer - - either coffee buyer or the factory - - for accepting this inferior parchment or upon the grower for not hand sorting it. This is the argument of exporters and the CIB (sometimes) who tend to see the problem of 'quality' as mainly a problem for processors. (*Post Courier*, June 29, 1977) They argue that if they would only refuse to buy inferior parchment, then the quality of PNG coffee on the world market could be retained. The CIB has the power to appoint inspectors, "and such inspectors have wide powers to enter premises, vehicles etc., seize coffee, take samples, examine documents and books evidencing the purchase, sale, delivery ownership and place of production or destination of any coffee." (Papua New Guinea Coffee Industry Board 1979:2)

Inspectors have been placed at factory doors to check the quality of coffee coming into the factory from either coffee buyers or smallholders. The processors' reply by blaming the smallholders and coffee buyers themselves. An anonymous letter in the *Post Courier* (which sounds very much like the view of a prominent planter/processor) clearly showed that in most cases arguments about 'quality' are arguments about the objective siting of class boundaries, especially about dominant class attempts to roll back smallholder class boundaries. Time and again this seems to be the purpose behind 'quality' arguments which, from this perspective would not be ones about quality at all. For example, the anonymous letter writer stated clearly a 'commonsense' view held by many in the dominant classes:

> The whole issue must have its origin at the subsistence level where three quarters of this commodity comes from . . . what the buyer did [at a roadside transaction which the writer observed] was check if the beans were dried and not all the contents of the entire bag. Often one quarter of the bag is filled with malformed not well fermented beans along with other foreign matter. If you tell a villager to get rid of this he tells you, 'Larim Em Bilong Hapim Hevi'. In other words he means to leave them so his bags weight is increased and he gets the maximum for it . . . as long as the price stays at its highest peak this is one of the main ingredients contributing to the low quality of coffee exported. To combat this . . . DPI along with CMB should ensure that competition is reduced among buyers and only factory owner vehicles buy parchment from villagers. (*Post Courier*, June 21, 1978)

In many ways some of the points made by the Hassall Report in relation to factories and quality, support some of the points made in the above letter and in most cases they are just as ideologically loaded. The difference between the position taken by the writer of the above letter and the Hassall Report is that Hassall and Associates, like the CIB itself, have no class location. Their tendency is to be apolitical and technocratic, like the CIB is, on the 'quality' question. The CIB's usual approach is virtually to sanction all actors in the industry with responsibility for poor quality. (Papua New Guinea Coffee Industry Board 1980:40) The CIB has found that it is difficult to be technocratic on the 'quality' question because it is not essentially a technical problem but a class boundary one. To their credit, Hassall and Associates implicitly recognise this because they come out openly and argue that smallholders should bear the brunt of quality control. Their argument is a curious one. They write:

> In the mid-seventies when world coffee consumption exceeded supply, roasters had to lower their standards in order to maintain their market share. This had consequent effects on grower price received. In those countries where production had not fallen, high world prices meant high profits. To maintain market share and hence profits, factories fiercely competed for the available coffee lowering their quality requirements as to the moisture content of parchment coffee. To compensate for the longer drying time needed to prepare it for the market and to maintain through put additional drying capacity was installed. As a consequence costs rose and were covered by differentials paid for the wetter grades of coffee. *The return to the grower were proportionately diminished.* Additional expenditure was incurred in the purchase of fuel oil as with the wetter beans husk supply was insufficient. *Growers resorted to subterfuges, supported with in some cases, violent tactics to get maximum prices.* Section 2.7 has provided details of grower practices to disguise quality. (Hassall and Associates 1982:61; emphasis added)

Hassall and Associates are embarking here upon an entirely new principle of capitalism. We are asked to believe, contrary to hundreds of years of economic and historical evidence, that the adoption of new technology ('additional drying capacity was installed') increases the costs of production ('as a consequence costs rose'), rather than decreases them. We must remember that this argument is being applied to a section of the industry where there is supposed to be workable competition between capitals. Further, we are asked to accept that smallholders (for these are the growers who cannot engage in transfer pricing between plantations and tied factories and who are said to be responsible for the violent subterfuge) should accept that at a time of record high prices their returns should be diminished. The tone of this quote is that it was really mean-spirited of smallholders to resort to violence to get maximum prices when after all everybody in the industry is simply doing their best to maintain the quality of PNG coffee. It is finally time to recognise that arguments which appear to be about the quality of PNG coffee are rarely about quality at all but are in fact the cutting edge of class struggle in coffee market relations. The purpose of such arguments is not to improve the quality of coffee but to justify further appropriation of surplus from smallholders.

Finally we turn to the question of whether strict licensing of processing factories has contributed to a 'workable competition' at the processor pinch point. Competition is, as we have seen, severely reduced by the fact that many factories (53 percent) are tied in some way to exporters. Competition is further reduced by the fact that most coffee buyers are tied to processors. Competition seems to be on the decline if one regards the number of processing factories as a shorthand measure of competition. In 1976, according to Anderson, there were '81 processing facilities which process coffee from parchment to green bean'. (Anderson 1976:6) In 1980–81 there were 70 'wet' and 'dry' registered and unregistered factories. However, there is still competition at the processing level when judged by the large number of plants still existing, the fact that independent factories still exist, and also that 'margins and returns in Eastern and Western Highlands appear compatible with expectations of returns generally in the PNG economy, if a little high. (Hassall and Associates 1982:57) There is thus a real problem in working out the degree of competition that exists and what policy position the CIB should adopt toward the processing industry. Hassall reports,

> "There are therefore probably too many factories to permit the full realisation of potential economies of scale. On the other hand, it is the excess capacity which exists in the factory section which provides incentives to factories to compete with each other." (Hassall and Associates 1982:171)

It is probably the existence of this dilemma which encourages Hassall and Associates to use the adjective 'workable' when describing the level of competition. Hassall's recommendation to the CIB is basically that it should attempt to retain the level of competition in processing as it is. They write that 'steps should be taken to guard against further concentration within the processing sector through the takeover of existing operations either by other factory owners or by exporters'. (Hassall and Associates 1982:178)

However, there is an inevitable push from within the industry to realise economies of scale and a necessity for large operators to attempt to defend and extend their control of processing by driving competitors out. The same process that led big exporters to swallow up progress societies run by smallholders in the 1960s leads big exporters to swallow up small factories. While the CIB refuses to take an active role in production and marketing there is nothing it can do about it. Disruption to the present system comes not only from increased market concentration but also from other parts of the state such as provincial governments, who are eager to get into the coffee action in their own provinces. Chimbu has attempted to erect coffee borders around its province to stop buyers from others buying its coffee and processing it in their own. (Standish 1981)[3] Sailas Atopare, member for

Goroka Open (1977–82) put a motion before parliament to restrict coffee buyers entering other provinces to buy coffee. (*Post Courier*, June 4, 1978) Even though coffee borders are not supported by the CIB and are an infringement on its authority there may be little it can do short of a long legal challenge to provincial governments if the provincial government stands firm. In all this, there seems to be little the CIB can do to prevent further concentration and centralisation at the level of processing. Clearly the degree of diversity in the industry has slowed down this concentration but it seems likely that in the next few years the industry will come to be completely dominated by a few large, vertically integrated firms.

The CIB is attempting to forestall concentration of power in a small number of firms. This is being done in the best (technocratic) interests of the industry though such an action is only incidentally in the best class interests of smallholders. As the struggle is played out one can expect the dominant class fractions in the industry -- the big peasantry and the *petit bourgeoisie* -- to consolidate their hold over the processing sector. The dominant class fractions through ANGCO and CIL now virtually have a stranglehold on the processing section. *Petit bourgeois* interests are important because at least one-third of the registered factories are owned by organisations which own other factories, almost half of which are not directly connected with the coffee industry. "These links with other businesses could become extremely important during an extended period of depressed business conditions. Earnings from other businesses could be used to support coffee activities and enable them to survive." (Hassall and Associates 1982:48)

The CIB is not a tool of the dominant class fractions in the processing sector, but nor is it holding up their march to accumulate and exploit smallholders.

Nationalism or favouritism in coffee buying?

Coffee-buying is one of the few areas in the industry where, in colonial times, nationals could engage in substantial accumulation. It was thus an area in which the early independence period saw legislation which reserved coffee-buying for nationals and other citizens. In effect, the CIB gave unconditional authority to them to deal in the commodity. CIB drew back from licensing buyers, although there were attempts by provincial governments to license these in their province. Licensing buyers is politically risky because it threatens to uncover the various ties and secret contracts which tie buyers to factories. Many people in the industry still like to believe that coffee roadside buying from smallholders is a fiercely competitive business. But since buyers still remain tied to factories it seems unlikely that localisation of buyers has had any effect on the industry at all.

In the 1970s, there continued to be squabbles over whether smallholders should sell cherry or parchment, whether buyers should exercise better quality control, and even a suggestion from CIB that roadside buying be banned altogether. (Papua New Guinea Coffee Industry Board 1979:18) These were often self-interested arguments; they came to nothing and so need not detain us.

This section endorses the conclusion of Hassall and Associates that there is a considerable amount of integration in the industry. (Hassall and Associates 1982:173) This is particularly the case at the exporter pinch point in the marketing chain. At this pinch point, the strategy of the dominant class fractions has been vertical integration of exporters with processors. Exporters also have an assurance from the CIB of a guaranteed share of the export quota. This strategy has protected the market share of each exporter and forestalled competition between them, but it has not provided them with a subsidy for their non-market sales, except insofar as they can pass down their reduced profit margins to processors and then on to smallholders.

At the processor pinch point the strategy of the dominant class fraction has been vertical integration plus a strict restriction on the establishment of new processing factories. The restriction on the establishment of these factories is aimed at controlling smallholder coffee so that all parchment and cherry must be processed in existing factories. This restriction has succeeded in stopping new factories from being established, but it has not reduced competition between existing factory owners. It has in fact so heightened the competitive struggle between processors that moves have been afoot in Chimbu and Eastern Highlands to establish coffee borders and outlaw buyers and processors from outside from competing with their own. Such moves are evidence that processors are worried about their control over this pinch point. When this is added to the growing public doubt that there is any real case for believing that the number of processing plants should not be expanded, then the strong sugestion must be that dominant classes have not had a great deal of success in controlling the processor pinch point.

At the coffee buyer pinch point the strategy of the dominant classes is vertical integration plus pressure on smallholders to deliver cherry to buyers rather than parchment. It is claimed that the quality of smallholder parchment is inferior and that the whole industry would be better off if smallholders sold only cherry. Little progress has been made in this area as far as the dominant classes are concerned, for the outlawing of parchment would not be politically possible in post-colonial PNG. The dominant class fractions have had great success at the exporter pinch points but only limited success at both the processor and coffee buyer pinch points in their attempt to achieve class unity and appropriate smallholder surplus at the class relations (objective) or market level. The whole structure is presented graphically in Figure 8.1.

Figure 8.1 Structure of the Post-Colonial Coffee Market in Papua and New Guinea

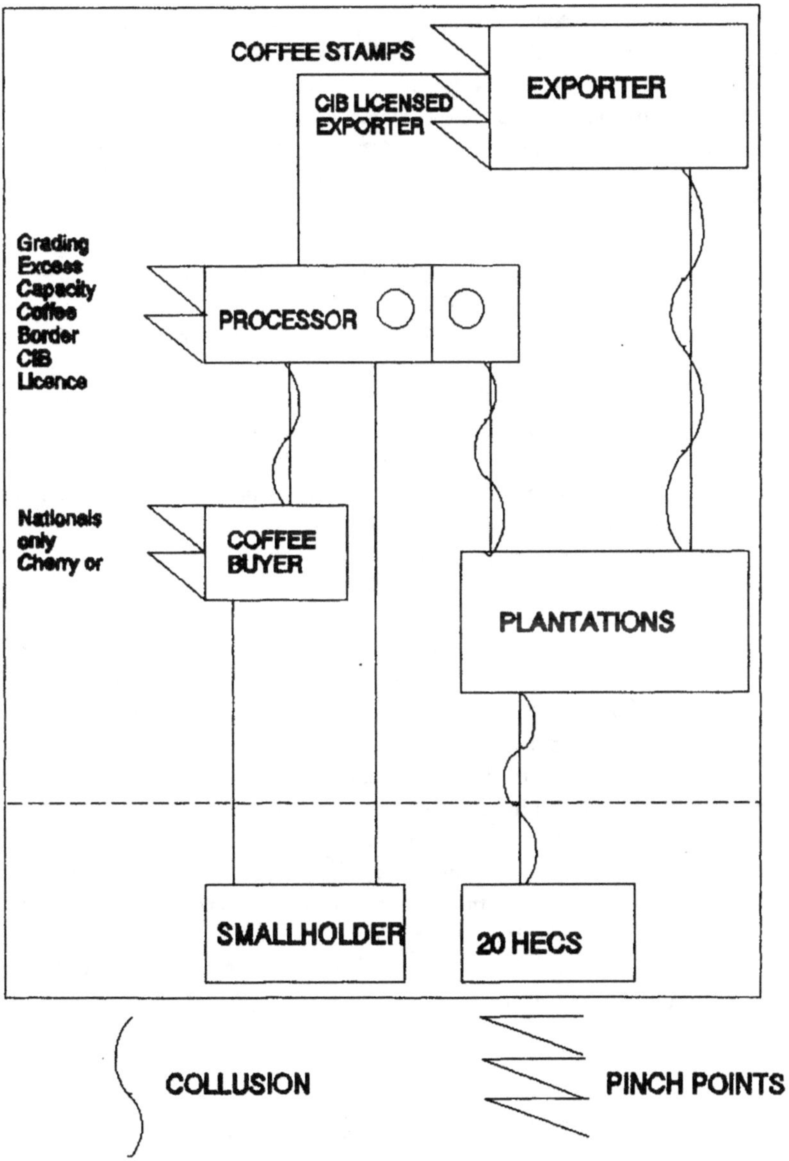

Notes

1. We have to accept that this is more easily said than done. The coffee industry in Papua New Guinea is politically volatile and as the *Post Courier* noted there is a certain secrecy about any new developments in the industry. (*Post Courier*, May 1, 1981) The information contained in the Hassall Report (1982), upon which this section is based, was available to the CIB, and to Hassall, only because it was gathered at a time when the CIB was paying bounties. This gave it the leverage to demand this information. One of the recommendations of the Hassall Report is that the CIB activities '. . . which should be strengthened and streamlined are contract scrutiny and analysis, policy and statistical/economic analysis and industry liaison'. (Hassall and Associates 1982:7)

2. We should not be disturbed at the sudden appearance of 'territoriality' in the analysis for as Harvey (1982) noted: "That class struggle and factional onflict assume a spatial, often territorial, aspect under capitalism is undeniable. Phenomena of this sort are often explained away as the product of deep-seated human sentiments - loyalties to place, 'the land', community and nation that spawn civic pride, regionalism, nationalism etc. But the preceding analysis allows us to explain the regionalisation of class and factional struggle independently of such sentiments. I do not mean to imply by this that human sentiments play no role in interregional conflict, or that conflicts cannot autonomously arise on such bases I simply want to assert that the material basis exists, within the circulation process of capital itself, for interregional manifestations of class and factional struggle." (Harvey 1982: 419)

3. The CIB view on the question of coffee borders is clear: "The Board is adamantly opposed to provincial Governments or any other authority being given power to introduce controls within the coffee industry which could in any way run counter to provisions introduced by the Board under its powers which are derived from a National Act. With the introduction of the Coffee (Mobile Buyers) Licensing Act, 1979 the National government has created a situation where the Coffee Industry Board under its Act can allow all coffee buyers to deal in coffee without any restrictions in the Chimbu province (and it has) while the Simbu Provincial Government says only those buyers whom it licenses may deal in coffee in the area. The Board has attempted to obtain a clear decision on which ACT prevails in this case, but advice indicates that it may be necessary to have the matter tested in a court of law to achieve a final solution." (Papua New Guinea Coffee Industry Board 1979:16)

9

The Role of Technocrats in the Post–Colonial Coffee Industry

Introduction

A new phase in Papua New Guinea politics began with the election of a national government in 1972. The promise of executive authority and decision–making by nationals for nationals was made to the nation as a whole and accepted by it. The promise was also made and largely accepted within the coffee industry. In the colonial industry, as we have seen, formal political activity was restricted to the role of the hapless DASF and the planter–dominated, severely curtailed, power of the Coffee Marketing Board. The informal politics – – the politics of the quiet meeting, the word in the right ear, the appointment of a colleague who was 'on side' – – was also planter dominated. The informal politics of the white planters went beyond 'quiet words', as we have seen, when it devised sophisticated strategies of co–optation, the middle peasant strategy.

From 1972, however, two main changes occurred in the state to change these colonial political patterns. The first was that the formal political institutions, the legislature and the public service, were opened up to national influence and control. The electoral struggle became the focus of political attention for legislative autonomy and ministerial responsibility, and rapid localisation of the public service seemed to many nationals to crack open the cold, colonial institutions, allowing nationals to enter and exercise their political and other skills in the best interest of the nation as a whole.

The second change to the state occurred almost as a by–product of the intensity of the electoral struggle. This was decentralisation. (Ballard 1981, Standish 1979, Conyers 1976) In Papua New Guinea, decentralisation has required the establishment of provincial governments in all nineteen of the nation's provinces. Each provincial government was intended to be a semi–autonomous second tier of government, and each was to have a provincial assembly, an executive and a secretariat, with a range of functions previously carried out at the centre. These changes to the state had the potential to determine the form politics would take in the post–colonial coffee industry.

In the 1970s, coffee politics did not dominate the electoral struggle in the Highlands. At the national level command of the executive was largely in the hands of a national *petit bourgeoisie* assisted by a very powerful social category, the technocracy. The defeat of the United Party in 1972 disorganised the dominant class fraction in the industry – – the big peasantry, and left them out of formal political representation for most of the decade. The local *petit bourgeoisie* and big peasantry settled in, as we saw earlier, for an extended period of class formation. Class politics in such circumstances became informal in a manner similar to that in which white planters had engaged.

By the 1982 election, however, circumstances had changed. The main catalyst for the emergence of an electoral struggle between local class fractions, the *petit bourgeoisie* and the big peasantry, was the replacement in 1980 of the national *petit bourgeois* government by the Okuk–Chan government. This was a government which increasingly came to bear the mark of being big–peasant–dominated. I have shown in a previous study (Stewart 1984b) how these circumstances drove the two class fractions into open electoral competition at the national level, for the first time. It is necessary to note here the more important empirical and theoretical findings of the study for a complete understanding of coffee politics in post–colonial Eastern Highlands to be achieved.

The focus of the study (Stewart 1984b) was the emergence of a competitive struggle between the local *petit bourgeoisie* and the big peasantry in Goroka Open electorate, heartland of the Papua New Guinea coffee industry. Smallholders played little or no part in the struggle for electoral representation. It was shown that the dominant class fractions were indeed the mobilising forces in the election of 1982. The parameters of this political struggle were established in the period before nominations closed, as fractions attempted to outmanouvre each other by standing candidates with competing characteristics. The class fractions selected candidates to represent their own in opposition to others. The selection process was unique: class fractions chose candidates not on the basis of their individual characteristics or background, but by their potential for winning and/or vote–splitting, which depends in turn on the candidates' strategic location in town and country. The apparent randomness of candidate nominees and voter choice could be traced back to spatial location and location in production, and shown to be logical when viewed in the context of an electoral struggle between two competing class fractions, the *petit bourgeoisie* and the big peasantry.

The theoretical contribution of this research was to demonstrate how class fractional competition in coffee can take place at the electoral level. It was shown that, in the course of the electoral struggle, the *petit bourgeoisie* had no alternative but to have the representative for Goroka Open labelled a Pangu candidate. It was emphasised, however, that this outcome was contingent upon the distinctive national and local circumstances that existed at the time. In 1982, in Goroka Open, these circumstances ensured there would be a correspondence between Pangu and the *petit bourgeoisie*, and between the National party and the big peasantry. The exigency of fighting an election can force a correspondence between a party and a class fraction. But it does not follow (nor was it claimed in the study) that a contingent correspondence of the type occurring in 1982 would prove durable. Instead, the analysis suggested that it is precisely because the party label is of so little importance in the struggle between class fractions that a correspondence between any single party and a class fraction is unusual and probably unimportant in periods between elections, and in most national and local circumstances. In any case, it is important to remember, as later sections show, that electoral struggle is only one arena for dominant class fractional representation and competition in the state.

The major structural change to the state in the post-colonial period is decentralisation. This represents an increase in state autonomy. It has allowed dominant class fractions to gain what Alavi (1982) has called representation in the state apparatus, including provincial governments and decentralised state branches. Increased functional autonomy in the state has also allowed dominant class fractions to press their demands inside the state through different modes of representation, either through parties, or by arguments for regulation and licensing and through formal and informal politics. Needless to say, in a new state with a good deal of functional autonomy between state branches and a state where there is great physical diversity anyway, class fractions have developed an impressive range of formal and informal ways of making demands in order to gain representation in the state.

Whether the establishment of provincial governments represents a major change in the class struggle, however, depends to a great extent on the resources available to provincial governments. The provinces appeared to have access to generous funding, and this led Good and Donaldson to believe that provincial government would become a class-contestable political arena. They predicted that provincial governments would inevitably be captured by the rich rural classes. (Good and Donaldson 1980:47) However, the executive powers of provincial governments are limited. The most substantial is the administration of primary schools, although such areas as the licensing of mobile traders could give them some leverage. Taxation powers of these governments are limited. Most of the important tax provisions (such as import and export duties, company tax, personal income tax) remain with the national government. The provincial governments do have the power to raise sales taxes but, as the Eastern Highlands government found (Stewart 1984b:19), these are politically risky. The resource base of the provinces varies greatly. Some provincial governments, like North Solomons, are rich on mineral royalties, but in other provinces, as Bob Adams of the Department of Decentralisation said in 1982,

> there still hasn't been an effective decentralisation in lots of provinces . . . Provinces don't really have much power. They are certainly involved in what is happening, they are held responsible for what happens but their capacity to control these happenings is very limited. (Bob Adams:Interview 17 May, 1982)

This is not to say decentralisation (as opposed to provincial governments themselves) has had no impact at all. Chapter 10, on the politics of coffee rust, will show that provincial premiers played a major role in determining political outcomes in the coffee industry. In this section on the form and function of the post-colonial state in the coffee industry, however, I first analyse the role of the Department of Primary Industry (DPI), and show that its decentralisation has completely emasculated its influence in the industry. I then turn to a study of the CIB which, through its stabilisation fund, achieved a measure of growth in functional autonomy in the post-colonial period. I show that beneath electoral factors such as the complexion of the national government and the declining economic fortunes which drove the dominant class fractions into electoral competition for the first time in 1982, is the restriction on development, imposed by quotas and the limitations of the world market in coffee. This fact has caused the dominant class fractions in the post-colonial coffee industry to turn to the state for assistance in squeezing more out of the industry. The cruel dilemma the dominant class fractions face, however, is that the growth of functional autonomy within the branches of the state, such as the CIB, has not given class fractions dominance within the CIB (and the payoff this should bring) because the CIB has been constituted on technocratic grounds. This realisation has only occurred very recently and it has given rise - - since the coffee depression of 1980-81 - - to feverish activity, and proposals for restructuring the industry at production and exchange levels, and to the CIB itself.

The Department of Primary Industry (DPI)

The third of the Eight Aims of 1972 aimed to put an emphasis on agricultural development in general and led in the coffee industry to a programme to regenerate coffee extension activity and to embark on a modest coffee expansion programme.

This programme, announced in 1973, was to focus on the less developed areas where it was envisaged that DPI would play a major role through distribution of seed and extension advice. In 198l, the World Bank review mission to Papua New Guinea warned that the agricultural sector was facing major difficulties. (World Bank 1981) In the same year, the new Prime Minister, Sir Julius Chan, a former Minister for Primary Industry, set up the National Agricultural Committee, a Cabinet committee described as an emergency committee because by then "the agriculture sector was already depressed, production and productivity had declined and commodity prices were well into a downward spiral. The plantation sector had virtually ceased to invest in property improvement." (Sir Julius Chan, *Draft Hansard*, September 7, 1981)

By 1981, agriculture, particularly the export commodity products sector, had entered a stage of static growth and was suffering from government budget constraints as well as public complaints about the effectiveness of government services. The assumption that somehow government was responsible for the decline of agriculture through the lack of provision of services (DPI in particular) and that it could do something about this led to a major review of manpower and training requirements in the Department of Primary Industry (DPI), undertaken by the consultants McKillop, Williamson & Associates Pty Ltd (MWA). Given the importance of downturns in international commodity prices and structural changes such as localisation and white planter exodus (in coffee), and the limits on the production of surplus value by dominant classes, DPI could not be assigned full responsibility. It is necessary to sort out the real extent of DPI's influence in industries like coffee, which are dominated by private actors. Is it a fantasy of technocrats to imagine that a study of manpower and training requirements in DPI could have anything at all to do with the revival of agriculture in PNG?

After independence the 'minor role' DASF played in the coffee industry in colonial times became even more minor in the post-colonial one. By 1982, DPI had lost all semblance of a policy role in coffee and was reduced to carrying out mechanical tasks. DPI's demise was caused by at least three factors internal to it. These included its adoption of the integrated rural development (IRD) approach, which was hopelessly ill-suited to a state in which state branches were extending their autonomy, and its continued, lamentable failure to settle upon a suitable extension method. Finally, the problem of decentralisation made co-ordination between national DPI (responsible for policy and planning) and provincial DPI (responsible for implementation) virtually impossible.

The approach adopted by DPI (DASF's successor) in the post-colonial period was known as Integrated Rural Development (IRD).

> In response to perceived failures of past strategies of rural development, particularly in alleviating poverty, planners in the seventies proposed a new strategy which goes beyond the agricultural sector to integrate other aspects of development to improve the life of rural people. Although integrated rural development (IRD) does not deny the need for economic growth and modern technology, it places greater emphasis on the mobilisation and development of human resource potential and on achieving a more equitable access to resources and a fairer distribution of income. (McKillop, Williamson and Associates 1982:11)

IRD is an approach as well as a project and it is mainly as an approach that it affected DPI's role in the coffee industry. It will be easier, however, to analyse IRD in its project form in order to explain its limitations.

IRD projects have been introduced in East Sepik and Southern Highlands Provinces and similar projects are planned for Enga, Milne Bay and Manus. They are resource-rich and usually internationally funded, though this does not prevent them from putting a strain on local state branches such as DPI for personnel and other non-monetary resources. The Southern Highlands project is based on cattle and coffee production so is relevant to our study. IRD projects present themselves as being in the interests of smallholders, and are usually based on some variant of smallholder block farming, but they are in fact the ultimate technocratic approach to rural development, because they reflect the technocracy's obsession with balanced growth. The strategy is basically a compromise which aims at slow transformation of traditional modes of production, a careful avoidance of discouraging rich farmers, and government adjustment in favour of the poor where gross inequalities do occur (*Papua New Guinea National Development Strategy*). As such it inhibits, or at least slows, class formation of local dominant classes. Its purpose, like Hasluck's 'gradual development', is to hold back the development of the local dominant classes until growth allows an equitable distribution of these resources. This is a recipe for much political strife in a capitalist society, as has occurred in the Southern Highlands, where conflict between the technocrats engaged in the project and local dominant classes whose base is the provincial government has been prevalent.

The basic problem with IRD projects is usually stated as being co-ordination. This is said to arise at the implementation stage, with the problem of co-ordinating the various state branches, consultants, households and so on which provide resource inputs to the project and at the project operation stage. These projects are often huge, the Southern Highlands project being virtually the development programme for the entire province. It therefore seems plausible to argue that co-ordination is the problem and that skilled management will provide the solution. (McKillop, Williamson and Associates 1982:11) To make the problem more difficult, the relevant agencies McKillop *et. al.* assert: "are technically oriented, and seldom do low level staff members have financial skills or experience to effectively administer and implement management and marketing programs." (McKillop, Williamson and Associates 1982:86)

Their conception of the management task is that of particular skills, such as financial ones, to be learnt - - even though they acknowledge at one point that "some employers in the plantation sector maintain(ing) the view that management skills can only be learnt on the job." (McKillop, Williamson and Associates 1982:179) They also warn in relation to the non-formal agricultural sector that "the issue of managerial expertise is a complex one due to the influence on cultural factors." (McKillop, Williamson and Associates 1982:122)

But what MWA really fail to emphasise is that management is essentially the process of applying labour to productive forces in the most efficient way possible. This process is pregnant with class political implications. It is a sense of the politics of the project and a perception of the class make-up of all those providing inputs and the trade-offs which can be made between them, that managers need. This is why on the job training and an awareness of 'cultural' complexities are needed.

The co-ordination of resource inputs is an intensely political task. The sense of politics required might involve the ability to set up meetings between the right state branches, the ability to motivate normally competitive state branches to cooperate in the project, and so on. No amount of expertise in financial skills or training can provide this sense of the politics of the project. Indeed, it may be that the political environment and relations between government agencies and the long history of inter-agency rivalry can make a project a failure purely for political reasons. This is more than likely to be the case for IRD projects in Papua New Guinea, where as we have seen there was growing functional autonomy in the state after Independence and where the whole basic organisation of Cabinet government is to encourage departments to bid against each other. At the project operation stage, 'political' management is also needed, especially in a volatile political environment like Papua New Guinea's. Here, classes or social categories are competing against each other and trade-offs have to be organised by a 'manager' who realises it is not the best technical argument which will generate cooperation but the best class political compromise. DPI is not an appropriate agency for this type of role, not only because it is technically oriented but also because, as the history of the DASF showed, it has never been politically minded. All this suggests that IRD was probably quite the wrong general approach for DPI to take in the first decade of Independence.

DPI continued in the post-colonial period to accept private enterprise dominance of the various agricultural industries in the areas of research, marketing and even extension. MWA found in their surveys that only about half the formal private sector (the plantation one) made much use of the services of DPI. (McKillop, Williamson and Associates 1982:121) The frequency of use was not only very low, but poorly regarded by the private sector Tables 9.1, 9.2, 9.3.

DPI research appeared to be relevant to plantations in the copra, cocoa and rubber industries, but was irrelevant to coffee plantations. (McKillop, Williamson & Associates 1982:101) All respondents felt that private organisations could better handle marketing activities and felt DPI should keep out of this area, which it did in coffee. In certain industries, it was felt that the private sector was more suited to the provision of extension services, and some private sector people even suggested that their sector provide all extension services for a fee, subsidised by government. (McKillop, Williamson and Associates 1982:104)

TABLE 9.1 Purpose for Use of DPI

	% of total users
Loan Assistance	10
Marketing/Commodity Data	12
Procurement of Materials	45
Technical Services	69
Field Trials	12
Solving Problems	24
Doing Research	14

Source: McKillop, Williamson and Associates Pty Ltd (1982)

TABLE 9.2 Use of Three Services (all DPI Users) by Agricultural Activity

	Market/Commodity	*Materials*	*Technical*
Coffee	12	50	38
Copra/Cocoa	6	53	40
Rubber	50	–	100
Extensive Livestock	–	12	75
Intensive Production	25	–	75
Management/Services	50	17	83

Source: McKillop, Williamson and Associates Pty Ltd (1982)

TABLE 9.3 Actual Tasks Undertaken by Extension Workers (% of time)

	Rural Devt. Officer	*Rural Devt. Technician*	*Rural Devt. Assistant*
Administration			
Supervising Staff	9.24	7.67	9.03
Writing Reports	6.42	6.12	4.77
Writing Letters	5.20	3.66	0.45
Staff Meetings	4.33	3.36	2.60
Training Staff	1.36	0.02	0.01
Other Administation Tasks	19.81	15.98	11.75
Sub Total	46.36	36.81	28.61
Farmer Services			
Advising Farmers	8.10	8.74	11.23
Training Farmers	2.79	1.92	2.25
Produce Inspection	0.46	1.82	2.66
Delivering Farm Materials	4.63	5.62	12.12
Buying Produce	1.51	2.68	1.09
Other Services for Farmers	3.30	10.17	9.60
Sub Total	20.79	30.95	38.95
Development Bank			
Interviewing Farmers for Loans	2.08	1.77	0.78
Budgeting	1.30	0.82	–
Bank Reports	1.60	0.82	–
Administration of Loans	2.28	1.69	0.54
Sub Total	7.26	5.10	1.32
Gaining Knowledge			
Reading Technical Material	1.98	3.03	0.68
Attending Training Courses	1.30	–	–
Data Collection	1.63	1.14	1.26
Sub Total	4.91	4.17	1.94
Production of Crops and Livestock			
Growing Crops	1.68	3.07	10.12
Raising Livestock	2.30	2.11	2.20
Fish Production	0.01	0.97	1.94
Sub Total	3.99	6.15	14.26
Travel			
Road Travel	13.86	11.32	9.63
Walking	1.16	2.55	2.20
Boat Travel	1.46	2.64	3.03
Air Travel	0.01	–	–
Sub Total	16.49	16.51	14.86
Total	99.98	99.64	99.94

Source: McKillop, Williamson and Associates Pty Ltd (1982)

Not too many years ago, the suggestion that DPI should virtually abandon agriculture apart from technical services and research, would have created a storm of protest claiming that the smallholder would be unable to carry on without assistance from the *didiman*. This myth has grown up and continues to be propagated by DPI itself: whatever happens in the agricultural sector, it runs, smallholders will always have DPI to look after their interests. But the fact is that since Independence, very few smallholders in most agricultural industries have been helped by DPI extension activities.

DPI is not an instrument of the dominant classes, because generally it is too incompetent to serve this purpose. Its incompetence has stemmed not from dominant classes capturing the extension service and then appropriating it for their own purposes, as is usually the case, but rather from the effect on DPI of structural alteration to the state in the form of decentralisation. It was decentralised along with a number of other departments with the establishment of provincial government, and this decentralisation created a national DPI located in Port Moresby, responsible for research, agricultural education and training, quarantine, economic services and regulatory functions, and a provincial DPI responsible for extension services. Decentralisation has opened up a gap between the planning of national DPI and its implementation in the provinces. This problem is not eased by the fact that national DPI has to go through provincial government administrators to communicate with provincial DPI. The result has been a lengthening of lines of communication. It was originally thought that the very different agricultural situations in the various provinces provided good reasons for decentralising DPI, but it was never clear how planning and policy coordination should be carried out. The World Bank has suggested a restructuring of national DPI to allow it to extend its planning functions so that a national plan can be co-ordinated with provincial ones, but this is still to be carried out. (McKillop Williamson and Associates 1982:44)

Technocrats Gain Control of the Coffee Industry Board (CIB) in the Name of Smallholders

In the earlier discussion of the form and function of the colonial state in the coffee industry, it was shown that the form the Coffee Marketing Board took was Bonapartist. It was Bonapartist for many reasons, but the fundamental one was that it could not function autonomously in the class interests of the dominant class in the industry, the white planters. The function of the CMB was regulatory and non-interventionist. It had low political penetration. It did not market the crop itself. This suited the planters (though they did not realise it at first) because their political position in the social formation as a whole was weak and 'compulsory marketing by a Board' was likely to mean that they would be the penetrated rather than the penetrators. The CMB also had limited autonomy. This did not suit the planters for, as its Chairman, Hurrell expressed it, the CMB should be independent from the colonial administration. (*Post Courier*, May 27, 1977) However, as we have seen, the Minister was of the view that the CMB was a part of the government hierarchy and under the control of the Administration. It was thus a Bonapartist state or a class-compromise one, through which white planter power was modified by the Administration, the Minister and ultimately the metropolitan bourgeoisie and the ICA.

In 1976, the Act governing the role of the CMB was altered and it was renamed the Coffee Industry Board (CIB). We have seen how the CIB functioned at the various pinch points, but so far its role has been presented in an unco-ordinated manner. It has been shown largely as suiting interests of the dominant class fractions, but its form and function have not been properly outlined. In this section I will examine the extension of power of the CIB that resulted from the establishment of the coffee stabilisation fund which, under the Coffee Industry Board Act, was the full responsibility of the CIB. The stabilisation fund in coffee was set up to even out the price received by 'growers' as a result of fluctuations in international commodity prices. The CIB collected a levy from coffee on a sliding scale to pay into the fund and was obliged to pay out when prices fell below certain levels. I will show that the functional autonomy of the CIB rose as dramatically as the level of the fund did in the 1970s, and that the fund gave the CIB a great deal of functional autonomy from other branches of the state. It could no longer be told it was just another part of the government hierarchy, and entered discussions with the Department of Finance and the Bank of Papua New Guinea with a good deal of weight behind it.

This rise in autonomy, however, was power in the abstract for the dominant classes, for there remained substantial barriers to the extent to which, in the industry, they could use the power of the CIB in their own interests. A major barrier was of course the division of the dominant class into fractions that were often competitive both at the level of production and in political arenas. But the main reason the dominant class fractions in coffee could not benefit from the increased autonomy of the CIB was that the stabilisation fund was constituted by technocrats, for technocratic ends. Thus even with the existence of a stabilisation fund, the CIB did not extend its function beyond the regulatory and non-interventionist function of its predecessor. The political penetration of the CIB remained low, and it remained a Bonapartist branch of the state after 1977, even though its autonomy was greatly increased by the existence of the stabilisation fund. The class power of the dominant class fraction in the state was modified by the existence of another dominant class fraction, by the intervention of the technocracy, and ultimately by the ICA.

The Coffee Industry Act 1976 (No. 67 of 1976) in outline did not vary a great deal from the previous Act governing the operation of the Coffee Marketing Board. In introducing legislation the Minister for Primary Industry, Boyamo Sali, noted that

> one change in this Bill from the existing Coffee Marketing Board Act is that it is proposed to rename the Board to be the Coffee Industry Board. It is considered that the new name describes more adequately the role of the Board, especially its role of representing coffee growers from all coffee growing areas. (National Parliament Debates, Coffee Industry Bill 1976, November 22, 1976:2042–43)

The Act set down in Section 4 the constitution of the Board. It should consist of 10 members. Section 12 detailed its functions, which were very broad and included controlling and regulating every stage in the commodity chain, price stabilisation, price equalisation and stockholding arrangements, buying and selling coffee. The Board was generally charged with the power '. . . to exercise its powers and perform its functions in such manner as the board considers to be in the best interests of the coffee producers of PNG'. (World Bank 1981) The CMB, of course, had a similar battery of formal powers but did not use them. Likewise, the CIB did not opt to use its extensive formal powers to take over production and marketing at any level in the industry. (Densley n.d.:19)

The main change to the Act was Section 25, concerning the Coffee Industry Fund. Its main purpose is to stabilise the industry by giving the Board the financial stability to implement schemes for first, stabilisation and equalisation of coffee prices, and second, stockholding of coffee. (The Independent State of Papua New Guinea, No. 67 of 1976 Coffee Industry Act of 1976) In his second reading speech the Minister said

> perhaps the most important change in this Bill compared with the provisions of the Coffee Marketing Board Act is the setting up of the Coffee Industry Fund. This will be a fund controlled and operated by the renamed Coffee Industry Board to help coffee growers in all parts of the country. (*National Parliament Debates*, 1976, November 22, 1976:2043)

As the Minister noted in his speech, there was already a fund in existence operated by the Coffee Marketing Board:

> The Coffee Marketing Board has in fact built over many years, from money received from an export levy, reserve funds which at the present time is slightly less than K6 million. The Board is to be congratulated on its foresight in having this amount of money put aside to help growers if we have marketing problems in the future. (*National Parliament Debates*, 1976, November 22, 1976:2043)

But this was not a stabilisation fund in the normal sense, for the CMB had no power to raise a levy solely for the purpose of an industry fund. The amount of money that could accumulate was limited, because the Coffee Marketing Board Act allowed only for a levy within a lower limit of 0.5 toea per kilogram and an upper limit of five toea per kilogram (Coffee Marketing Board (Levy) Bill (1976), *National Parliament Debates*, 30th August, 1976:1803) This was because it was thought that the CMB would impose a levy mainly for the purpose of covering its operating costs. It was only funds surplus to requirements that were expected to be invested and held for the purposes of assisting the industry in difficult times. Consequently the fund could never reach levels which could give the CMB real bargaining power within the state, as it was quickly wiped out when difficulties arose. This is what happened in 1972 when 'most levy funds and investments were required to pay a loan from the Reserve Bank of Australia which was used to purchase surplus coffee in PNG at ruling prices for resale to new markets at heavily discounted prices'. (Papua New Guinea Coffee Industry Board 1979:7)

The main purpose of the Coffee Industry Act 1976 was to overturn the upper limit of the levy so that it would be possible for the fund to maximise the amount of the levy it raised in a period of high international prices. Naturally, the Minister did not put the point so bluntly in his speech. He said changes to the Act were mainly due to

> a need to have clearly defined in legislation what these funds can be used for and how they should be controlled to ensure that growers, whose money it is, are fully protected by law. These aspects are covered in this Bill. (*National Parliament Debates*, 1976, November 22, 1976:2043)

The new levy schedule allowed the Coffee Industry Fund to take full advantage of the high prices in the mid-1970s and rapidly build up its funds, as Table 9.4 shows. The modest K6 million level of the Fund had, by 1980, reached a huge K94.6 million.

The rescheduling of teh levy shows the influence of the technocrats, for the timing of the Act was impeccable given the obvious fact that the 1975 'Black Frost' would lead to an international coffee boom in 1976 and 1977. The technocrats had sound macro-economic reasons for the establishment of stabilisation funds. In theory, it would provide a hedge against fluctuating international prices int he commodity itself, and by stabilising aggregate demand thereby reducing economic fluctuations in the country in general. The second purpose would be achieved if the fund was free, by removing the upper limit to the levy, to raise a sizeable investable surplus which could be held in the central bank and made available to finance general state

TABLE 9.4 The Coffee Industry Board and Stabilisation Fund Deposits and Investments (K Million)

Last Wednesday of Period	*Coffee*
1976	6.8
1977	46.4
1978	63.6
1979	83.8
1980	94.9
1981	90.3
1982	92.1
1983	85.3
1984	82.1
1985	83.5
1986	116.4
1987	79.0

Source: Bank of Papua New Guinea, Port Moresby, Quarterly Economic Bulletins

expenditure. The purpose of the Fund was not state revenue, like an export tax[1] would be, because these funds were held in trust for the industry as a whole and the levy was not particularly high. Nevertheless, there existed good technocratic reasons for the abolition of the upper limit to the levy at that point in time, and this was what the 1976 Act was all about. As the Minister put it: "this Bill will enable the Coffee Marketing Board to take advantage of the present high coffee prices and to fix rates of levy on all exports more in line with current export prices". (Coffee Marketing Board (Levy) Bill, 1976, *National Parliament Debates*, August 30, 1976:1803)

The abolition of the upper limit of the levy had advantages for the dominant class fractions in the industry, though this was not fully apparent until late 1977 and 1978, when guidelines for the use of the Coffee Industry Fund were discussed. On the basis of suggestions made by Mick Wheeler (National DPI), the purpose of the fund was more clearly defined. (Wheeler and Wyatt 1978) It is important to note, however, that while the abolition of the upper limit of the levy had advantages for the dominant class fractions, the abolition of the upper limit of the levy and the 1976 Act were not sponsored by the dominant class in their own self interest. We will see in the next section, in fact, that the Wheeler outline was more technocratic than class-based. Nevertheless, the abolition of the upper limit of the levy carried with it a *de facto* alteration to the use of the stabilisation part of the fund, and this was in the interests of the dominant class fractions.

This can be shown if we compare the operation of the fledgling stabilisation fund before 1976, and the changes that occurred under the CIB Industry Act. Prior to the 1976 Act the stabilisation role of the fund (as opposed to its stockholding role) was usually thought of as stabilising incomes. This was how the fund operated in 1972, when funds had to be returned to the industry as a subsidy (or a bounty as it is called in the industry) due to low prices. The size of the bounty to be returned was worked out on the basis of a defendable price, which itself was based on costs of production plus a small margin. If this approach was done equitably (and providing of course returns actually did flow down to producers) a standard or average cost of production would have to be calculated which would take into consideration the costs of production in both the planter and smallholder units of production. We can show in a hypothetical example that such an approach must always disadvantage the production unit, which has the higher money costs of production. Suppose A's cost of production is 10 and B's cost of production is 5. The standard or average costs of production would be 7.5, obviously lower than A's costs of production. Even if the margin to be added were graduated, it is unlikely that A could benefit as much as B from a stabilisation of incomes. As the costs of production in money terms in the Papua New Guinea coffee industry are higher for plantations' than smallholders' costs of production (because after all smallholders do provide most of the inputs from within the household), then it seems clear that this earlier system of stabilisation did not favour the dominant class fractions.

This of course was not the reason given for the 1976 changes to the stabilisation fund. Rather, the reasons given were technical. The system had to be changed, according to the World Bank, because '. . . production costs vary widely among producers and it is difficult to establish an average or representative level'. (World Bank 1981 Annex E:3) The concept of stabilisation in the fund was altered almost imperceptibly by the 1976 Act to one of price (not income) stabilisation. This meant that the bounty would return to the industry from the fund not according to the costs of production of producers large and small, but according to an agreed price to defend. The change broke the nexus between production costs and defendable price and therefore allowed levy appropriation and bounty payouts to range more broadly up and down the price scale. The result was that the more the price fell for coffee in PNG the greater the return to producers regardless of the varying costs of production. On the other hand, the higher prices rose the higher would be the levy extracted by the CIB to add into the fund. I will detail shortly how this levy schedule actually works but it is important to note that this redefinition of the stabilisation part of the fund, from stabilisation of incomes to price stabilisation, was dependent on the abolition of the ceiling on levies. In breaking the nexus between production costs and the return of the levy, these changes ensured that dominant classes would no longer be disadvantaged, due to their higher money costs of production, in the process of collecting a levy or being returned a bounty.

The rapid growth in the fund - - in the 1976–77 coffee year it grew by about K10 million, but then grew by over K50 million in the 1977–78 coffee year - - made it an urgent task to settle the purpose for which fund monies would be used. The legislation was too general to be of much assistance in this area. It simply stated that the purposes for which the fund can be used are laid down in the legislation. These specifically include the operation of price and income stabilisation schemes, price equalisation schemes, and stockholding operations. There was the possibility of the misuse of funds which so worried Hurrell, because various sections of the industry began to think of good purposes for which the money could be used. The Western Highlands Provincial Government made a number of requests for fund monies to assist with spraying fungus (*Post Courier*, March 10, 1980); there was talk of using fund money to improve the quality of PNG coffee for assisting smallholders to bring new areas into coffee, or for assistance with restructuring class and market relations at the various pinch points. The CIB was determined to retain as much money in the fund as possible, though at the same time it wished to show that the fund was operating in the best interests of the industry as a whole. The CIB badly needed a justification for following this course of action, especially as the Minister had speculated in his first reading speech of the 1976 Act that only K12 Million was required to overcome marketing difficulties. By early 1977 the fund was climbing to heights far beyond this figure, making it difficult for the CIB to resist the various industry-related requests that were flooding in. A crucial intervention was made by a technocrat with DPI, Mick Wheeler. This intervention, with its close support from the CIB, reflected on a smaller scale the way the technocracy had combined with the national *petit bourgeoisie*. In the case of the stabilisation fund operation, we can see very clearly how the class effects of such an alliance in the coffee industry limit the political penetration of the dominant class fractions.

Wheeler first put a working paper to a meeting of DPI and the CIB in December 1977. He argued that the switch away from costs of production and income stabilisation to price stabilisation was difficult to achieve while the CIB retained its dual function of stabilisation and stockholding. It was clear, he argued, that either the money in the fund could be used when needed for supporting prices and paying bounties which left the private sector in control of the actual surplus coffee, or the CIB could assist growers by purchasing and stockholding their coffee when there was a surplus. But which aim was to take priority? He argued in a later paper, in January 1978, that the stockholding function should take priority because, as the operation of the ICA was weighted against small producers, they would always get lower quotas than they should. Also, he added, quotas were the norm in the industry. He felt, therefore that the problem of surplus production was an almost permanent one, and was the industry's most urgent and enduring problem, which small producing countries would face while the ICA survived. But, while he felt the stockholding function must take precedence over the price stabilisation one, he said there was no need to limit the function of the fund to stockholding.

> Given this priority allocation, it was relatively straight forward to design guidelines which would ensure adequate funds for stockholding and also allow some measure of price support. A certain portion of the fund must be set aside for stockholding alone while the balance can be used for price stabilisation. (Wheeler and Wyatt 1978:8)

All that was needed was to settle upon a figure relating to how much of the fund should be set aside for stockholding. Wheeler's assessment of the amount required was conservative, but his logic was impeccable. He wrote:

> The actual amount set aside had to be calculated according to estimates of the amount of coffee that it would be necessary to store according to an estimate of how long quotas would remain in force . . . If quotas were to continue for any length of time PNG would certainly be storing large quantities of coffee. PNG would not be the only country forced to hold stocks, and it was estimated that after 2 years of quotas, storage capacity in the smaller producing countries will be fully utilised. Therefore if prices had not already recovered there probably would be pressure to break the agreement or remove the quotas. The present term of agreement is six years with the option to continue after the first three. It was therefore, felt that the reserve portion of the fund should be sufficient to cover 3 years of quotas. It was estimated that at a quota price (price at which quotas are brought into force) of K1300 per tonne FOB K65 million would be needed to cover all contingencies. Therefore the reserve portion of the fund should be sufficient to cover 3 years of quotas. (Wheeler and Wyatt 1978:8)

The K65 million seems to be based on the fact that 1976–77 exports of coffee totalled 49,797 tonnes (Table 9.5) which equals approximately K65 million when the price is K1300 per tonne. Wheeler is perhaps a little conservative in his estimate that the fund would have to finance 3 years of quotas. This seems to be based more on the fact that there would need to be a carry–over period from two years, when it is assumed the agreement would break. This seems to contain some questionable assumptions. Wheeler's proposal might also be considered conservative, as he seems to acknowledge, in proposing to fund stockholding of the total amount between the 62 percent quota level he thinks PNG usually gets, and the full amount exported in 1976–77 at ICA prices. Some of this coffee would in fact be exported to non–member countries at a lower price. Wheeler acknowledges this fact but does not consider it as requiring any reduction in the figure of K65 million.

TABLE 9.5 Papua New Guinea: Coffee Exports

	Tons	*£A*
1946–47	48	3,768
1947–48	7	1,402
1948–49	17	3,584
1949–50	21	4,101
1950–51	33	8,260
1951–52	35	11,000
1952–53	47	31,000
1953–54	87	60,000
1954–55	107	75,000
1955–56	171	93,800
1956–57	274	183,500
1957–58	385	225,100
1958–59	1,088	456,000
1959–60	1,488	717,100
1060–61	2,294	1,106,000
1061–62	3,443	1,557,000
1062–63	4,845	2,014,000
1963–64	6,831	2,683,000
1964–65	8,687	3,647,500
1965–66	10,804	4,393,500
		$A
1966–67	12,911	10,208,000
1967–68	18,267	14,320,000
1968–69	19,871	15,531,000
1969–70	25,376	20,182,000
1970–71	23,556	20,572,000
1971–72	27,748	20,457,000
1972–73	30,650	23,394,000
1973–74	32,196	28,847,000
1974–75	36,136	33,501,000
		K'000
1974–75	36,769	33,554
1975–76	35,952p	42,231
1976–77	49,797	132,619
1980	51,000	118,600
1981	47,100	74,200
1982	41,100	77,800
1983	52,500	94,700
1984	49,400	110,700
1985	40,600	117,500

continues

TABLE 9.5 *continued*

	Tons	K'000
1986	53,100	208,500
1987	64,800	134,700
1988	44,800	113,500
1989	85,000	140,400
1990	54,600	88,600

Source: Cartledge (1978) and Bank of Papua New Guinea Quarterly Economic Bulletins.

The main achievement of Wheeler's intervention was to reduce considerably the demands being made on the fund from within the industry, for it showed clearly that as much as K65 million of the fund could not be touched, except in the most dire circumstances. The fund gave the CIB a good deal of power in the industry and in the state as a whole, but beyond this Wheeler's arguments gave the CIB power without being forced to represent the interests of the dominant class fractions in the industry. It was a power that Hurrell had often longed for when he argued that the CIB must become independent of government, dominant class fractions and smallholders. It was the power to distance itself from large growers and exporters and from the state, and is the reason for the self–assertive claims to independence often heard from CIB representatives. Wheeler's intervention was a perfect example of the politics of a Bonapartist state or the exercise of power without class interest.

When a new levy schedule was announced in February 1978, incorporating the Wheeler proposals on the role of the stabilisation fund, the Executive Officer of the Coffee Industry Board, Barry Beil, and the Minister for Primary Industry, Julius Chan, both implied that the new schedule was in the growers' best interests. Beil was even quoted as saying that 'the new levy scale for coffee exports will mean growers will pay less on all prices', (*Post Courier*, February 9, 1978), and both he and Chan gave the example that under the new levy schedule, growers 'will be charged a levy of only 1.5 toea/kg instead of 13 toea a kg on K1.75 a kg prices'. (*Post Courier*, February 7, 1978) This sounds like a very big difference.

Did the new levy schedule generally offer growers a better deal? The key to the new schedule was the construction of an historical long term average FOB price for green coffee exported from Papua New Guinea. This was to be measured over the previous ten year period and expressed in terms of prices for the most recent calendar year.[2] The historical long term average changes each year, as the most recent year is included and the last year is dropped off. But in 1978, when it was introduced, it was around

165 toea/kg. This figure functions as a zero on the scale of levies as prices rise above it, and on the scale of bounties as prices fall below it. At this point a minimum normal levy of 0.5 toea/kg is collected. Levy, other than the normal one is collected when the FOB value of the coffee exceeds the long-term average price, and shall be at the rate of 50 percent of the difference between the actual FOB value and the long-term average FOB price, in accordance with the level published in the National Gazette. (Papua New Guinea Coffee Industry Board 1980, Appendix C) The minimum levy for the previous schedule applied only to exports below 95 toea/kg, a very low figure, so that it was certainly true that the new system corresponded favourably with the old at the lower end of the scale (i.e., on or below the 'new' historical long-term average). However, what Beil and Chan did not make clear is that the removal of the old numerical upper limit to the levy schedule and its replacement with an upper level 'at the rate of 50 percent of the difference between the actual FOB value and the long term average FOB price' meant that as the price got higher the new schedule made it possible for the CIB to extract a much higher levy than was possible before (in fact because there is no limit the levy can go as high as 50 percent, the highest price).

Does the rescheduled levy system affect all growers equally, as Chan and Beil and others seem to assume? This depends to some extent on how the levy is collected and whether the process is one which enables those with class power to avoid being levied or prevents them from transferring the cost of the levy to subordinate classes. The responsibility for paying the total levy is with the exporter of green coffee.

> The levy must be paid before the coffee is exported. The procedure for the payment of the levy is that the exporter completes a coffee levy payment certificate showing the details of the consignments and the amount of levy due. He then pays this amount to the account of the Board at the PNG Banking Corporation, where the certificate is stamped. This stamped certificate is then presented to customs with the other documents required to be lodged for customs clearance. (Papua New Guinea Coffee Industry Board 1979:7)

The exporter does not of course bear the full cost of the levy, even though he is more or less responsible for collecting it because its cost can be passed down the commodity chain for contributions from various actors at different levels. It is not known how the cost is distributed, but it can be assumed that it is simply passed down, because exporters have the social power through vertical integration -- as we have seen in the marketing sections -- to ensure this is so. However, the collection of the levy from down the line is not a self-interested class action by the exporter, since exporters do not extend their class power through this action, and it does not enhance their political penetration. It is simply a recovery operation.

The payment of a bounty is done in the same way: exporters are paid the bounty and they are expected to pass it down the line. But in the case of passing a bounty back, class and differentiation between actors in terms of their social power becomes an important factor. Perhaps it is even surprising that the bounty is passed back in the same way that the levy is collected, when in the case of the bounty those with the social power have an incentive *not* to pass it down. Various reasons are given for maintaining the same payment system for bounties as for levies. The CIB view is that:

> After considering various payment methods to directly benefit growers, the Board paid through the exporter, this being the central point in the marketing chain. Payment is based on a scale and delivery contract between the exporter and processors. The Board considered it feasible since export levy collection and payment is also done at this point. (Papua New Guinea Coffee Industry Board 1980:44)

It is also argued that the coffee marketing chain is complex and hence other systems of payment would not be feasible. In the copra industry, for example, prices are set administratively and so to pass down a bounty one must identify a point in the marketing chain where the dominant actors are identifiable. (World Bank 1981:33) The copra payment system would seem to make it a virtue for monopoly control to be exercised by some administratively sanctioned actor at a pinch point in the copra marketing chain. This is rightly rejected for coffee. It is also argued that if the coffee bounty was not being passed down the line then it would be evident that exporters or processors were making huge profits. But this seems to underestimate the degree of vertical integration in the industry and the potential for transfer pricing from one level to another.

In fact, what is probably being passed down the line is the same kind of hesitancy to hand over a bounty at all which the CIB itself displayed as prices began to fall. In 1980, prices began to plummet below the then bounty payment level of 202.5 toea/kg, but the CIB did not wish to pay.

> The bounty payable was in the Board's opinion so small that it was not worth paying. Mr Munnull said the board thought a very small bounty would make no significant change to the final price to growers and the cost of advertising its pay out would outweigh the benefits to growers. Mr Evara gave an assurance the Board would pay a bounty as soon as the weighted average price dropped to a level where a minimum 10 toea/kg was payable on green bean. (*Post Courier*, September 2, 1980)

In any case it was argued, somewhat ingeniously, that because growers had recently been paying a 22 toea levy and were now only paying the minimum levy of 0.5 toea, 'in effect they are already being protected by the fund'. (*Post Courier*, August 8, 1980) It is important to recognise that there are absolutely no mechanisms in existence to ensure that the bounty reaches the smallholder.

The argument that it does rests on a good deal of faith, and a belief in competition which we have already shown is limited. It is in fact extremely doubtful that the return of the bounty does anything more than present a free gift to the exporters and tied factories.

The study of the stabilisation fund shows the effect on the class conflict and class struggle of a Bonapartist state constructed along technocratic lines. The technocracy presents its handiwork of the stabilisation fund as a technical achievement in the best interests of society as a whole. Its arguments are simple and persuasive. The technocracy claim that the stabilisation fund will stabilise aggregate demand, thereby reducing economic fluctuations in the country as a whole and that the fund can also be used to protect growers when the price falls. But these two simple ideas are in conflict. The time when the price is falling is precisely that when the stabilisation of aggregate demand is needed. The technocrats inevitably find they must sacrifice one of their promises. Their response is to resist paying out bounties in order to protect the aggregate demand function of the fund. The result is that the fund operates in such a way that it becomes more difficult to pay out bounties but easier to collect higher levies. This is not in the interests of any of the classes in the industry. Even the dominant classes quickly find themselves running up against the fund as a barrier, and are found to resist 'sensible' technical arguments. In terms of class interest, technocratic structures represent the worst of all possible worlds for both dominant and subordinate classes in the industry. From the viewpoint of the dominant class, the stabilisation fund does reinforce and defend their class boundaries, but it does so without giving them political penetration: they can collect the levy but they cannot use it. In an industry where the production of absolute surplus value imposes limits on accumulation, the freezing of class boundaries at the level of class relations is not desirable. The smallholders suffer the most from the operation of the stabilisation fund, but receive the least. When the world price is high, they have a very high level of bounty extracted from them, but when the price is low, they probably do not receive this subsidy back as bounty, or they receive such a small proportion of their contribution when prices are high, that they make a significant net loss.

Notes

1. There is an export tax on the coffee industry which applies or does not apply depending on the international price. When the export tax is applied the rate is usually about 2½% FOB. (Densley n.d.:19) Export tax is not a major issue in the industry as it is in most other coffee-producing countries. The government gets little from the industry directly and gives little back. As Ian McChlerey, Executive Office of the Coffee Industry Board commented, "Finance department and the Government give nothing to the industry. They think it is self supporting and why not - - there are other more important agricultural areas. Last year (1981) they took the 2½% export tax off. We did not ask them to do it." (Ian McChlerey, Interview, June 21, 1982)

2. The average will be calculated according to the following formula. Each relevant years average price is to be multiplied by 100 and divided by the relevant figure from the index of Papua New Guinea import prices as published by the Bureau of Statistics if available or the World Banks index of international inflation. The result of these ten calculations are to be added up and divided by ten to give the average. The long-term average price should be recalculated in January of each year or as soon afterwards as the information required for recalculation is available. (Papua New Guinea Coffee Industry Board 1980:Appendix C)

10

Case Studies of Élite Exploitation of Smallholders

Part I

The 20–Hectare Coffee Development Programme

Introduction

If the dominant class fractions in the coffee industry -- the *petit bourgeoisie* and the big peasantry -- have not captured the technocratic Coffee Industry Board (CIB), this does not mean their social power is minor, or that they do not exercise domination over the industry in other ways. In fact, one area where the social power of the dominant classes is great is in the area of coffee development. This is an area in the coffee industry where agencies of the Bonapartist state such as the Department of Lands and the Papua New Guinea Development Bank (PNGDB) are more influential than the CIB. Paradoxically these state branches, though Bonapartist and therefore independent of the dominant classes, function to reinforce the social power of the dominant classes in the industry.

In this Part I of the Chapter, I analyse a new 20–hectare coffee development programme to show the patterns of class conflict and class struggle that currently exist in the Papua New Guinea industry. I argue that class struggle is indirect and truncated, but nonetheless real. It is indirect because the antagonistic classes are engaged in different forms of production. Householders are not directly exploited by capital, though the dominant classes would aim to extract land and labour from the household form, appropriate surplus in the form of monies or other household assets, monopolise the marketing outlets for the smallholder crop, or in other ways turn the domestic terms of trade against the smallholder producer. Class struggle is truncated principally by the land barrier. This is a result of the post-colonial government's endorsement of the Commission of Inquiry into Land Matters' (1973) view that land policy should be evolved from a customary base, and that there should not be agrarian revolution. It has ensured that customary land cannot be bought and sold in independent Papua New Guinea.

In the first section it is shown that the design of the 20-hectare development was flawed precisely because it was conceived in a class vacuum. The lease/leaseback mechanism it uses is an ingenious one, bringing land into plantation use without alienating it. Its flaw lay less in the mechanism itself and more in the 'business group' structure which accompanied it, for this gave little protection to smallholders in class struggle. The facilitation of credit was also flawed in the design stage, for though security of tenure was established and checks could be made of the supply of credit to the blocks by the PNGDB, it had no control over the demand side of funds requested for development of the project. Thus PNGDB had virtually no control over the components that made up the budget of the block. The administrators who designed the 20-hectare development assumed that the provision of management was a technical affair, but I show that even in the design stage of the projects it was possible to predict that technical control over the block by management would become social control over every aspect of its development.

The second section examines the implementation of the 20-hectare projects. It is shown that dominant classes -- whose phenomenal form is in this case the management agencies -- have managed to 'disenfranchise' the subordinate classes from their land. They have also appropriated the surplus monies of smallholders for a period of at least fifteen years -- until the loan is paid out -- and probably longer because the dominant classes are setting up control networks on the blocks. This suggests the projects may never be independent of management agencies. The 20-hectare coffee projects, then, I will argue, have been 'captured' by the dominant classes in the coffee industry.

The state, which promised so much to smallholders from this development, and which was so intimately involved in its design, has failed them in the implementation stage. How did this happen? I will show that the Papua New Guinea state, a Bonapartist one transcendent over the dominant class fractions, is not in the coffee industry an instrument in the hands of the dominant class fractions. As the analysis of the implementation of the 20-hectare projects shows, the Bonapartist state can function in the interests of the dominant class fractions.

Background to the 20-Hectare Coffee Development Programme

In August 1978 the Minister for Primary Industry Mr (now Sir) Julius Chan announced that the government would offer maximum support for the establishment of 20-hectare coffee development blocks. The idea behind these 'intermediate' plantations was that smallholders would pool land into a larger production unit and make free labour available in the early stages of the project for the purposes of clearing the land and planting the coffee seed. Finance in the form of a loan from PNGDB would be provided to the smallholders organised as a business group to operate the 'intermediate' plantation. Twenty hectares was thought to be large enough to support production based on current plantation practice (Wheeler 1979:4) and each 'intermediate' plantation was expected to produce plantation quality coffee at the high rates of yield expected from existing plantation units of production (average around 2 tonnes per hectare).

The idea was immediately popular with small peasants. By 1982, 74 projects had reached the minimal operation stage. In terms of the potential increase of production and increase in plantation acreage that the development of these 20-hectare projects represented, nothing less than a transformation of the entire Highlands coffee industry was set in motion by the establishment of the 20-hectare projects.[1] Many small peasants pooled their land, leased it to the government, formed a business group and leased the land back for 25 years to establish these 'intermediate' plantations. Much hard and dedicated work was put into the development by officials from the various government departments and agencies, and a good deal of money was invested in it by the World Bank and later by the Asian Development Bank.

Was all this effort worth it? Is the establishment of 20-hectare 'intermediate' coffee plantations in Papua New Guinea that rarest of all species of policy-making, a successful rural development programme?

The claims made in favour of the 20-hectare development projects were not simply that the development would increase coffee production but also that it would promote equality. Chan said in 1978 that it would 'ensure that the benefits of the industry spread among the people'. (Chan 1978a) In 1985, claims of involvement in and equity for, the 'people' as a result of 20-hectare development were still being made. In the recent review of the Economy of Papua New Guinea for example, it was claimed that 20-hectare coffee projects were 'usually run by the clan'. (Goodman, Lepani and Morawetz 1985:90) Equity was to be achieved by involving the clan or smallholders in the running of the block (or project) and also by modification to the existing structure in production -- plantation and smallholder production units -- in the Arabica coffee industry.

Land

The initial problem facing the development of 20-hectare projects was the land barrier. Customary land could not be alienated. To overcome this problem, officers of the Department of Lands began as early as 1977 to try to put together a Land/Credit/Management package which would break the nexus between the provision of credit and the maintenance of customary land. In attempting to devise a package, land transfer was the biggest hurdle. The land mechanism had to be flexible, it had to be able to be administered under the Land Act (1962) and clearly it had to fall in between the extreme positions of those on the one hand who wanted to maintain customary land at all costs, and those who wanted land to be freed for commodity production.

A new mechanism was required because existing ones such as the standard 99-year lease under the Torrens system were unacceptable to customary landowners. Attempts to introduce a registration system for customary land had not only failed but would not have solved the problem that disputes within a clan could not be settled in court, making customary title useless. Most other suggested mechanisms, such as freehold tenure, nationalisation of land, or tax measures to alienate waste and vacant land, all have high social and political costs. In 1977, the Department of Lands began experimenting with partial leases, short-term 'Special Purpose Leases' (25 years) and longer-term (40 year) leases, all of which were aimed at devising 'ways of utilising this land without ownership passing from the current owners'. (White 1977:1) The state -- through the Lands Department -- had to play a part in this process because the Land Act (1962) requires all land transfers to be authorised by the Lands Department, the state having an obligation to ensure that any transfer of customary land does not involve land that is under dispute and that all customary landowners are willing to transfer it.

The breakthrough in devising a new mechanism came when it was realised that the state might lease land as opposed to merely authorising transfers from customary owners (the lead lease). This allowed the state itself to provide title to the land, because the state held an estate in it. The customary landowners would be protected because in theory they could restrict the rights of the state to those secured in the lead lease. They would not have alienated their land because they would have merely leased the land to the state for an agreed period. The state, of course, did not aim to develop the land itself, so it would then endeavour to lease the land -- with title secured -- to a corporate body, which could be legally responsible for its development. The second part of the new mechanism was the leaseback arrangement, whereby the customary landowners formed themselves into a corporate body, a business group,[2] to lease the land back from the state (the sublease). 'Such a sublease may be to an incorporated group of essentially the same owners who lease the land to the government. This then becomes a lease/leaseback arrangement'. (Lands Department 1982)

Development finance and funding were to be forthcoming in the form of credit from PNGDB. Once title was secured, credit, in the order of K80,000, would be available for the development of 20–hectare coffee projects. In the Highlands of PNG where smallholders earn little more than K100 a year, this is a lot of money. It was a huge incentive for 20–hectare coffee development. Smallholders were also attracted to the lease/leaseback scheme partly because it could operate on a shorter leasehold agreement of 25 years (the lease is held by the financing authority – – in this case the PNGDB – – and should be handed back when the block is paid off, although it is valid for the full 25 years). Other attractions of the scheme for smallholders included the provision of credit as part of the scheme and the fact that incorporation as a business group promised to give customary landowners legal responsibilities, and probably greater autonomy and control over development on the project itself.

The fact that the land for these developments was put together through processes internal to the clan and not through coercive state or commercial pressure was seen as helping minimise the social costs of bringing it into commercial production. This meant that as far as possible land was pooled voluntarily into 20–hectare blocks. It is only when this happens that there is any chance at all of ensuring that land contributed is not required for 'use' value production. No–one can be sure if this was the case or not, but if Dick (1977) is right, land pooled for 20 hectares was not surplus land. He has argued that there are now few areas in the Highlands where people can establish new coffee gardens because 'with populations increasing many areas of the highlands are beginning to experience land pressures'. (*Post Courier*, 19 October 1976) If this is correct then customary landowners who put in land for 20–hectare development were probably making a quite rational calculation of the gains their household can make through a share in the 20–hectare projects, and naturally would have had high expectations that they would benefit financially from coffee production on such a block.

Credit

It is generally recognised that the provision of credit is vital to agricultural development, especially to a programme like the 20–hectare scheme which involves reorganisation of production. The World Bank provided lines of credit for development in the export tree crops of Papua New Guinea in the early 1980s, but it did not have a 'plan' for development in the coffee industry, much less a prescription for the social impact this credit would have in the industry. It is probably true to generalise that the World Bank sponsors reorganisation of production in order to standardise and rationalise peasant production of commodities, but it is also necessary to remember that the Bank will do this indirectly whenever possible. World Bank money is lent to governments and not to domestic credit agencies, and Bank loans are paid from government revenues and further borrowings, not from net returns on projects. (Williams 1981) It can be argued that the shared desire of the World Bank and PNGDB to reorganise coffee production represented a 'coincidence of general purpose'. (MacWilliam 1984) But there is no evidence at all that the World Bank played any role in the design or implementation of 20–hectare projects.

The PNGDB is a statutory authority which was set up in 1967 on the recommendation of a World Bank mission that had visited in 1964. In 1980, PNGDB made 33,127 loans – – K134.6 million – – to all sectors of the economy. In 1980, the capital of the Bank was K27.1 million, of which K24.2 million had been advanced by direct government grants. The PNGDB Act requires that it provides finance for primary production and for the establishment or development of industrial or commercial undertakings, particularly small undertakings, in cases where the provision of finance is considered desirable but would not otherwise be available on reasonable and suitable terms and conditions. The provision of credit to export crops, especially 20–hectare coffee development projects, altered PNGDB's pattern of lending, because this credit was for agriculture only.[3]

The design of the 20–hectare project development acceptable to the PNGDB was set out in two documents, Mick Wheeler's (National DPI) *Coffee Development Plan*, May 1979 which contained the original 20–hectare model budget, and Ian Oxenford's (PNGDB) *Guide to PNG Development Bank Policy on 20 ha. Arabica Coffee Development*, 6 June 1980, which set out the main policy guidelines for 20–hectare development. The documents assert that 20–hectare developments will be profitable,[4] that the casualty rate of 20–hectare projects will be lessened by the payment of skilled plantation–style management on the block, and that peasants will have responsibilities on their blocks. They must provide 'sweat equity' (free labour) in the early stages, but they will be rewarded for their labour contribution by the payment to them of a dividend in the early stages of coffee production, and by the establishment on the block of a 'wet' coffee processing factory giving them some control over the marketing of their coffee.

Wheeler's budget was based on the assumption that by year 7 the 20–hectare projects would be producing coffee at the plantation yields of 2,500 kg/hectare and that this would produce a cash return of K67,500, which works out as an average operating surplus (profit) of K20,050, from year 10. The budget anticipated that loan funds would be provided to the project in the establishment years (to year 5), but that these funds would only be a modest proportion (K63,750) of the total establishment costs (of K98,310). This is because Wheeler budgeted for a significant equity contribution from business group members. Wheeler costed the 'sweat equity', free labour, at K26,560 total contribution by year 5. It was anticipated that 'free labour' from business group members would be responsible for the entire clearing, draining, fencing and planting of the block in the first year. 'Sweat equity' would also be necessary to maintain the nursery for the first 15 to 18 months, and to contribute to the maintenance of the block (weeding and spadework) until production began in year 4. He budgeted only for an equity contribution from business group members in the form of 'free labour'. But Oxenford's 1980 policy statement extended equity contributions to include cash from various sources and the advance rental from the Lands Department for the 25-year agricultural lease, a sum of K8,000. It is important to understand that this K8,000 equity contribution was never budgeted for by Wheeler. The comparatively small size of the loan (K63,750) to be drawn in his budget is small only because of the major contribution made to the establishment of the project by 'sweat equity' contributions. If the business group could not be relied upon to contribute labour, then it is obvious that a larger loan would be required to pay labour costs in the establishment phase.

Wheeler also detailed how loan funds would be drawn to purchase necessary inputs and to finance management costs and capital outlays. Among the inputs the project would require in the establishment phase and throughout the life of the project were fertiliser and seedlings.[5] But the main outlay of loan funds in the establishment phase is to pay for management services and capital outlays. The cost of management services budgeted for was a substantial proportion of the total loan. Wheeler budgeted for a management fee of K5,000 from year 1. This represents a total outlay of K25,000 over the five years which, combined with the K12,500 assistant manager's salary, represents some 58 percent of total drawn loan funds to be spent on management services in Wheeler's original budget.

Both Wheeler and Oxenford emphasised the importance of skilled management to the success of the project. Wheeler recommended, and Oxenford made obligatory, that loan funds were conditional upon the signing of a management contract with a proven agency. The other major outlays were: in year 1 -- K3,750 for fencing and buildings; year 2 -- K5,000 for resident manager's house; and year 4 -- K6,000 for a wet factory and equipment. The final point to note about this basic outline of Wheeler's original budget is that the 20-hectare projects represent a long-term investment. Even with 'sweat equity' contributions, skilled management and few failings or hold-ups, the loan was not seen as being repaid until year 14. (Wheeler 1979) The essential feature of Wheeler's budget is that while it extracts a contribution from the business group members or clan landowners in terms of equity contribution in the establishment phase, it does balance this with a concern to provide some tangible and early benefits to business group members by budgeting for a dividend to be paid to them from year 7, when coffee is being produced at maximum yield, and by budgeting for a wet factory to be built on the block in year 4, so that business group members or clan landowners can store coffee.

The total repayment made by the project in Wheeler's budget, in year 7, is K16,000. Of this amount, some K8,075 represents interest on the loan, leaving a repayment of K7,925 on the principal. But the important point to note is that the surplus available for repayment in that year is K21,760 (slightly less in subsequent years), leaving some K5,760 to be divided up among the business group members as a dividend payment from the operation of the block. In Wheeler's budget a similar dividend is paid every year from year 7 to year 14, when the loan is paid off.

The provision of a wet factory in year 4 is also an important concession to smallholders, who generally prefer to process their coffee to the parchment stage. A 'wet' factory consists mainly of pulping machines to separate the hard outer casing from the bean itself, fermentation tubs so that the sticky mucilage substance can be removed from the bean, washing vats and outdoor drying arenas. The 'wet' factory's not a complex operation and the equipment is technically quite simple. It is often argued that processing to the parchment stage is not as economical for the smallholder as selling cherry. This may be true, but from the smallholder's viewpoint there are obviously other factors to consider. For one thing, processing coffee to the parchment stage allows it to be stored as a hedge against falling prices. Cherry, on the other hand, has to be sold at prevailing prices the moment it is picked. Smallholders do not and cannot control marketing chains, so that 'storing' coffee is the only means they have of regulating household incomes when prices are falling. It is important to recognise that the provision of a wet factory and the cost of labour required to operate it was considered to be an economic proposition by Wheeler, even using of pessimistic price projections.

The PNGDB saw itself in the early stages of the design and establishment of the 20–hectare projects as playing an active role in ensuring that projects followed policy guidelines and budget requirements. (Papua New Guinea Development Bank 1980) An important part of this active role was that the PNGDB be engaged in the defence of the interests of its clients - - the business group. The PNGDB, it could be expected, would strive to maintain what one PNGDB officer called the 'spirit' of the policy design which was, as Wheeler's budget emphasises, the idea that projects were being developed to benefit the small peasant and to further enhance the development prospects of ordinary people in PNG. But did it have the capacity to play this action role and to ensure the 'spirit' of equity in the programme would be maintained?

Management

In Papua New Guinea, the quality of managerial staff has come to be regarded as the greatest limitation to productivity/profitability in advanced forms of agriculture. (McKillop, Williamson and Associates Pty Ltd 1982:108) We have seen that, in the design of 20–hectare projects, the provision of plantation–style management was regarded as crucial to the success of the projects by most state agencies. We have also seen that a large proportion of the outlay of loan funds in the development stages was to go to management. But what does 'management' mean and how as it to be provided to 20–hectare coffee projects? In the agreement between the business group and the management agency in the 20–hectare development, management has a technical meaning.

Technical expertise does not come cheaply in Papua New Guinea. The original budget incorporated the view of the National Plantation Management Agency (NPMA) costings that a management fee of K250 per hectare or K5,000 per annum was appropriate. The fee has been criticised as very high by economists and politicians, though no official voice has been raised against the fees. So strong is the belief in Papua New Guinea that technical expertise is vital to success in agriculture that most have been willing to put up with this expense on the grounds expressed by Sir Julius Chan that 'If we want productive plantations we must pay management fees'. (Chan, *Draft Hansard*, September 7, 1981)

The exercise of these proper management techniques includes a co–ordinating function, one in which social actors (the production relations) and essential inputs (the productive forces) are brought together in certain combinations to produce coffee. It is at this point, where there exists some variation in the combination of forces and relations of production, that management operates as a system of social control. This is a position of power. The choice of management could determine the relative distribution of benefits from 20–hectare projects and ultimately of the whole development. In a situation where there appears to be a range of social actors with the requisite skills to perform the management task, the design of projects which require management might inadvertently favour those with existing advantages in the area of social control -- those with race, class or state authority -- to become managers.

The problem, then, is to determine the optimal package of technical skills and social controls managers should have. In terms of the state acting as a manager, the 20–hectare development was designed at a time when the limits of a direct state agency role as manager were very evident. DPI, the obvious state agency to perform such a role, had become incompetent. We have already examined reasons for this incompetence, such as the disruption to its services created by decentralisation, which effectively split DPI into a separate national DPI and a provincial one, to which we might add its growing tendency to concentrate its activities less on recurrent expenditure and more on NPEP projects or the limited opportunities that existed for DPI extension activities due to its small proportion of the budget (6 percent). Whatever the reason, 20–hectare projects had to be planned and designed without any expectation of management assistance from DPI. Without it, the only department of state with the technical skill to provide a direct management service, the agencies of the state could hardly expect to exercise control over the social actors who were chosen to be managers.

The design guidelines of the projects suggested that the PNGDB would exercise complete control over the development of the project through the management agency. The PNGDB, for example, appointed managers only from approved agencies, and the PNGDB could also initiate termination of the management agreement if it was not working out after three months. The problem with the assumption that the PNGDB could exercise control over the block was, as we will see, that the provision of technical expertise, as provided by management agencies, can lead to direct social control over a block.

The social actors who were to be chosen to perform the management task were never precisely identified in the design documents, but it was very clear from the beginning that this task was not to be performed by members of the subordinate classes. These people were eliminated on the grounds of technical incompetence, though it was thought they were able to be trained as managers. It was planned to, "allow gradual introduction of increased levels of management and technology under conditions that will lead eventually to a member of the group taking over the management." (Department of Eastern Highlands, Division of Agriculture) and Wheeler budgeted for the on–the–job training for assistant managers. We will see, however, that the actual extent to which management training takes place on the block is dependent upon the good graces of the management agency. McKillop eliminated subordinate classes from the management role on the basis of cultural limitations. He quoted Morris, who noted that in general terms people from other cultures could not be trained in Western managerial innovations. (McKillop, Williamson and Associates Pty Ltd 1982:53) McKillop argues this would make it difficult for traditional organisations in Papua New Guinea to manage complex commercial activities.

This meant that the main social actors to exercise the management function on 20–hectare projects would be those drawn from the dominant class. In the Eastern Highlands, the private management agencies, ANGCODEV and Gouna, are the phenomenal form of the dominant class fractions, the big peasantry and the *petit bourgeoisie*. The third agency, NPMA, is a branch of the state. NPMA is a government corporation set up to provide management to the former expatriate plantations. NPMA had three times the number of blocks in its management control in 1982 as the other two agencies. NPMA designed the fee schedule and went into 20–hectare development to make money. ANGCODEV and Gouna are NPMA's chief rivals in the Eastern Highlands. ANGCODEV is a subsidiary of ANGCO, the country's largest exporter. ANGCO is the base of big peasant interest in the Eastern Highlands, through its association with EHDC and people like Akepa Miakwe, Ben Sabumei and perhaps Iambakey Okuk. Gouna is the development corporation of the *petit bourgeoisie*.

Twenty-Hectare Project Implementation

The implementation of many 20-hectare projects began in late 1979, after Wheeler's 'model' budget was accepted by the PNGDB and funds began to be released. From the beginning, however, there were real problems in co-ordinating the state agencies and actors involved. In early 1981 this lack of co-ordination in the state was still a problem and on 9 April 1981, a meeting was held with the purpose of devising a series of 13 steps (Table 10.1) which would set down clearly the order through the state agencies a 20-hectare application would follow. Throughout 1980 and into 1981, the lack of co-ordination among the state agencies severely affected the development of the 20-hectare projects. During this period it was not possible for management agencies to get more than six or seven projects a year to the application stage. (McKillop, Williamson and Associates Pty Ltd 1982:105) It was also taking over a year for the management agencies to bring a project to the funding stage. On 3 June 1981, a coffee growers' meeting was held to try to sell the process established in the 13 steps to growers. These were based on the assumption that DPI would play a co-ordinating role. It is very instructive to note that these early meetings uncover the assumptions held by state bureaucrats as to how coffee development will proceed. They know the 'state' is the innovator in the development, but they assume this means that the state can control the process of development step by step. Their view is that the state may have to 'sell' the development to private actors, but essentially private actors exist at the margins of a coffee development scheme. (Department of the Eastern Highlands, Office of Agriculture, Goroka, Coffee Development Scheme n.d.:1)

TABLE 10.1 The Thirteen Steps Received from Kevin Murray June 17, 1982

Procedures to be followed when applying for a loan under the Coffee Development Scheme.

1. Blocks to be considered must be of area 15 hectares and over. It is possible to have two (or more) geographically separate blocks (each less than 15 ha, but totalling at least 15 ha).

2. All interested groups must approach the Department of Primary Industries in Goroka (Kevin Murray -- Coffee Development Section) and have them inspect the site for suitability (as to whether coffee can be grown) as well as have them carry out a preliminary survey to establish the likely size of the block.

3. DPI will advise the group of their requirements for business registration and then send them to the Office of Business Development where the process of registering their Business Group, or Company, will be started.

4. DPI will then forward their recommendation to District Services Goroka (showing Business Group, or Company, application fee receipt, group name, chairman's name, village, and copy of their preliminary survey plan). A copy will be sent to the Development Bank.

5. The applicant must then approach District Services Goroka (Daryl Woodward at Provincial Office, North Goroka) and fill out an application form (and pay a fee of K10).

6. District Services will then request that Lands Goroka conducts a Survey. If the applicant wishes to have a private survey carried out they should at this stage give a copy of it to Lands Goroka.

7. The Survey will be drawn up in Goroka and held. Periodically a draftsman from Lands Waigani will visit Goroka and check these Surveys for accuracy.

8. The Development Bank will be shown the application and approved Survey and will make their recommendations from these.

9. The Survey, application and Development Bank recommendation will be forwarded together to Lands Waigani where they will open a file on the Project.

10. District Services will have a preliminary Land Investigation Report compiled at this stage, while waiting for Lands Waigani to issue an Investigation Instruction. A copy of this Report will be released to the Development Bank if it shows there is no dispute over ownership of the land.

11. When the Development Bank has satisfied itself that all steps have been completed one of the Management Agencies will be asked to undertake the Project (if they haven't already become involved).

12. Once the Investigation Instruction has been received from Lands Waigani the other copies will be forwarded to the respective Departments and the process of preparing the lease will start.

13. The Development Bank will release funds according to their guidelines.

Drawn up or discussed in a meeting at Lands Department Office, Goroka, April 9, 1981.

The growers who attended the June 3 meeting were unimpressed with the 13 steps. They knew that DPI did not have the capacity to play a co-ordinating role as set down in them. At the time DPI was claiming they could co-ordinate the 20-hectare development, Murray was instructing DPI's Coffee Development Teams (CDTs) to concentrate on 5-hectare rather than 20-hectare plantations. In any case, by 1982 the CDT was in great funding difficulty, as the agricultural sectoral funds were syphoned off by national politicians.[6] In fact, by 1982 the development of 20-hectare projects was moving beyond the control of the state branches. Rather than playing an instrumental role in determining which social actors got what out of the scheme, state branches were being forced to respond to private social actors. The growers who attended the June 3 meeting knew that it was the management agencies which had co-opted the co-ordinating role from the state. They seemed to realise also that this made them very vulnerable to control by the management agencies. (Eastern Highlands Provincial Government. Rural Land Development Grant. File 6-8-6) The 13 steps were made irrelevant by the co-ordinating role of the management agencies (Figure 10.1).

The management agencies became involved in the blocks from the beginning, many seeking out clan groups and proposing that they consider establishing 20-hectare projects. The management agencies undertake no risk at any stage of this process and they stand to be rewarded for their efforts even in the pre-loan stage as a result of the award of government subsidies to them to encourage exploration of the possibility of establishing 20-hectare projects. Many management agencies carry out the project investigation stage in place of DPI and it is arguable that they are more suited to carry this out. The management agencies also oversee business group registration. The land investigation stage is still undertaken by *kiaps*, because this work is highly specialised and time consuming. Management agencies would begin to suffer financially if they were to undertake the endless interviews of customary landowners needed to ensure that those who claim to have use rights over the land really do have them. This is one stage where the management agency accedes control to the state. However, the agency usually supervised the 'sweat equity' stage of the development, the establishment of a nursery on the block (if the management agency approves of this), and the planting out of the block. It also drew up the budget for the block and made application for funds, which when received were channelled through it.

So successful were the management agencies at getting around the control of state agencies that it was frequently argued that the state should virtually withdraw from this and other areas of agricultural development. (World Bank 1981:10) Prime Minister Chan was known to favour this view (McKillop, Williamson and Associates Pty Ltd 1982:12), which certainly reflected his base of support in the big peasantry, and McKillop seems to agree with it too, because he recommended that the government should withdraw from providing

FIGURE 10.1 Procedural Chart

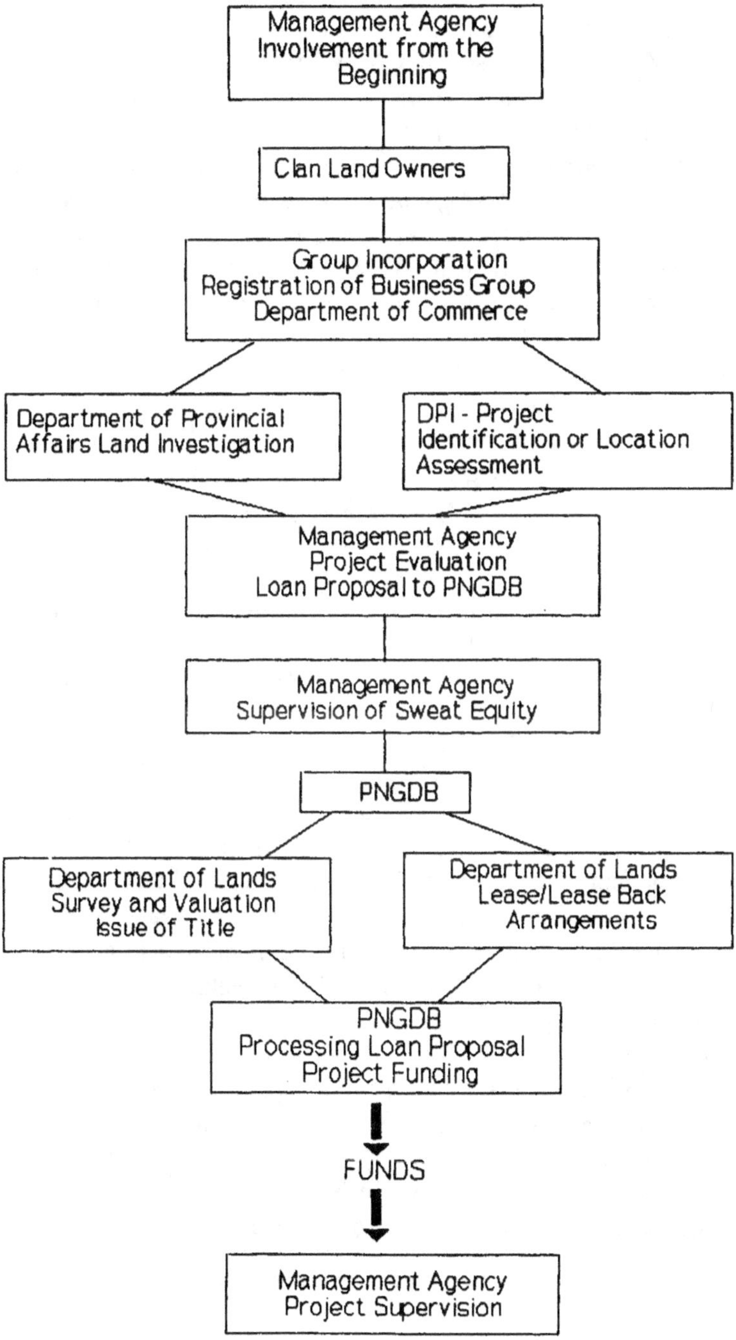

services and marketing in favour of the private sector. (McKillop, Williamson and Associates Pty Ltd 1982:121) MWA further and suggests that the proper role of the state (or the public sector as they call it) 'could well be that of arbitration and enforcement of commitments entered into by the various parties'. (McKillop, Williamson and Associates Pty Ltd 1982:103)

There is, however, a curious paradox in this type of thinking, especially as it relates to 20–hectare development. Had the state adopted the role of arbiter or enforcer of commitments in 20–hectare development, it is clear that the development would never have got off the ground. The state, as we have seen, had to be an innovator in the design stages, it had to initiate policies such as the lease/leaseback arrangement, it had to ensure that loan monies were available from international organisations and it had to create the loan facility for the disbursement of funds. The role of the state cannot be understood in these simple polarised public/private terms, because clearly there is so much overlap, so much complexity that the dichotomy is completely misleading. What we have seen in the policy design section is that the state has a good deal of autonomy at the design stage. By contrast, in the implementation stage, the management agencies' role becomes so dominant that the state almost appears to be an instrument in the hands of the dominant class. The state itself does not change as 20–hectare projects move from design to implementation, so there must be something in the form and function of the state at this level which allows dominant classes to be dependent on the state at a stage when state innovation is required, but which allows them to manipulate the state when the appropriation of surplus is a possibility.

How can this be explained? I argue in the following section that its Bonapartist form allows the state to be both autonomous and an instrument. It also allows it to function in a way that accommodates the interests of the dominant class fractions. This is because the PNG state at this level has high functional autonomy, i.e. it is very heterogeneous and divided into numerous unco–ordinated branches. This characteristic allowed innovation to occur in the design stage. It also allows, as we will see, management agencies to gain representation in parts of the state at the implementation stage and use that representation to make demands over and against other branches and institutions within the state apparatus. What all this means in practice, as I show in what follows, is that rather than the lack of co–ordination in the state undermining the development of projects (as bureaucrats presume it will), dominant classes know that this lack of co–ordination is in their best interests for it is an 'ideal' situation for them to be able to dominate and control the development and appropriate surplus from business group members.

Land

The procedure for bringing customary land into 20–hectare production was cumbersome, slow and fraught with administrative difficulties. This was partly caused by the fact that there were three quite separate state agencies involved in land matters: DPI (Office of Agriculture, Eastern Highlands Provincial Government), the Department of Community and Family Services, the *kiaps* (Eastern Highlands Provincial Government) and the Department of Lands, a national department. But more serious problems in the implementation of land policy on the projects were caused by problems relating to land itself, in particular to the difficulty of identifying customary owners. Part of the problem of land investigation undertaken by the *kiaps* is that the system of extending 'use rights' over land to influential people either inside or outside the clan immensely complicates the land ownership pattern. Land can be acceded to someone who may not own it but may have the use of it for long periods of time. This is a feature of the traditional use of land and one that has made all attempts to register customary land useless. This pattern of 'use rights' can undo modern attempts to settle the customary land situation because this system is very flexible. What it seems to allow is a sort of 'futures' dealing in land, whereby you might stake a gamble that someone will use the land in a way that might prove very successful. At the same time you insure yourself against losing the land, but if the 'use' it is put to really does prove successful, then the original owner can claim some benefits. This situation does cause problems and tends to undermine the trouble taken to establish a fixed settlement in the use of land even for the purposes of a lease/leaseback arrangement 20–hectare coffee development. The whole process is more malleable and flexible at the customary landowning level than more formal procedures such as land investigations can accommodate. The two tendencies noted by the District Officer were the tendency for control over the block to concentrate on business group leaders and the manipulation of customary landowners by powerful people in the area – – were both happening in 1982 on 20–hectare coffee blocks. The District Officer admitted that the whole process of land investigation is a sham.

On the two most advanced blocks I investigated, Arusafa and Molan (both managed by ANGCODEV), the business group leader was employed as Assistant Manager. This was, however, the only evidence of a business group presence on the blocks. Both Tom Neke of Molan and Makeyu Lekesavi of Arusafa claimed that the group had recognised that they had done all the work on the block during the development stages and therefore they were considered by the others to have earned rights over all the benefits coming from the block. (Tom Neke, Interview June 9 1982, Makeyu Lekesavi, Interview June 9, 1982) This dropping away of support from ordinary business group members occurs not because their expectations are 'unrealistic' (May in McKillop, Williamson and Associates Pty Ltd 1982:114), but because group leaders and later management agencies are at work to 'disenfranchise' group members so that 'no' or 'few' expectations are realised. Initially the social actor engaged in this process of 'disenfranchisement' is the leader of the business group. He lays claim to control over the group and the land, on the basis of 'use rights' rather than on that of claims made as group leader. The Business Group Act itself facilitates concentration of power on the leader in the group. However, the leaders' claims to 'control' do not extend to control over the operation of the block. In the process of 'disenfranchising' business group members from their land, leaders play directly into the hands of management agencies. This is where the real concentration of power is greater than others. Equity considerations aside, the land procedures seemed not at all to be 'sorting out the land problems'. In fact, given the way in which customary landowners and business group members were being manipulated and outmanoeuvred, bringing land into 20–hectare coffee development projects might be seen at the same time to be establishing preconditions for a whole new wave of land disputes.

The appropriation of land from smallholders by the powerful is a form of 'silent' class struggle. It is class struggle when manipulation systematically favours a certain class with a certain location in a system of production. In this case, the managers are appropriating surplus from the smallholders (or customary landowners and ordinary business group members). The class struggle is 'silent' because the structure–in–production is such that exploitation by the management agencies over the smallholders is indirect. It must take the form of appropriation of surplus (money) and land. Even when the block is producing coffee it can only be said that management agencies are exploiting labour employed on the block. To add to these complex relations of exploitation is the fact that management agencies have relied heavily on the state to set the preconditions for appropriation and exploitation. In the case of the 20–hectare projects, we have seen how the state played a vital and innovative role in the design stages, but this is true also in the implementation stage. The appropriation of land and surplus from a block by management agencies relies heavily on the facilitating role of the state, which plays this role indirectly. The state is not an instrument in the hands of the management agencies, but rather the form and function of the state facilitate their dominance. In relation to the land procedures on 20–hectare projects, a number of aspects of the form and function of the state at this level facilitate the appropriation of land. For a start, management agencies are advantaged by the fact that in Papua New Guinea land procedures are exercised by different branches of the state at different national and local levels. These different levels which deal with the land procedures have allowed some management agencies to subvert the lower levels of the state (DPI and *kiaps*), and proceed directly to the centre (the Department of Lands). I was often told that it was because many management agencies were pushing their blocks ahead in the queue that hold-ups were occurring at the Department of Lands in Waigani. Some even said that block applications were going to the Department of Lands regardless of the fact that the land investigation processes had either not been completed or had failed.

The management agencies could use their national reach, mainly through politicians, to get a block application to the Department of Lands. The low political penetration in the state as it relates to the coffee industry also enhances the appropriation of land and surplus by the management agencies. The state's low penetration, not only from the centre to the local area, but also into the block itself, meant that no part of it could monitor every aspect of the land procedures to ensure the integrity of the customary landowners was protected and maintained. To achieve this it would have been necessary for a branch of the state to have an extension role on the block itself, as well as a monitoring role at the centre on land procedures. The functional division of the state precludes this. The centralisation of some branches and the decentralisation of others also precludes such a monitoring role (i.e. the Department of Lands is centralised, as is DPI). DPI would be the most suitable agency to exercise this extension function but, as we have already seen, it never played this role on the 20-hectare blocks, and its influence at the national level was probably even less than that a management agency could exercise over influential national politicians.

In addition, and related to all of the above, the management agencies' appropriation of land from smallholders was helped by the high functional autonomy in the state. The state's role in land procedures was divided according to functions and processes; there was virtually no communication between the *kiaps* and the Department of Lands, for example. The high functional autonomy and low political penetration seem to allow development to take off with a rush in the design stage, but the loss of communication and lack of a monitoring function means that such development is always vulnerable to manipulation by dominant classes. A final very important example will emphasise this point. There was no clear responsibility inside any state branch for informing ordinary business group members and customary landowners that the lease was for 25 years. Which branch should take this responsibility, Department of Lands, *kiaps* or DPI? It was never decided because it was probably not considered very important. By default, the task fell upon business group leaders and management agencies. But one cannot be confident that the full impact of this situation was made clear to the smallholders. In fact, it is very difficult indeed to explain to illiterate and innumerate people this type of long-term concept. One cannot be confident a great deal of care is taken on this point. Nevertheless, all business group leaders and management agencies assured me that the people had been properly informed; in any case, they usually added, the lease will be surrendered to the people after the block is paid off. Even so, the lease remains valid for

25 years, and it would seem proper for a state agency to take responsibility for informing people of this.

Credit

At the same time that land procedures are occurring on a 20–hectare project, a budget proposal and a loan request resulting in the eventual release of funds for development will have begun. There are three main stages in this process. First, a proposed budget is submitted to PNGDB by the management agency. Second, PNGDB process a loan request from the management agency and PNGDB extension staff visit the block to assess the adequacy of preparatory work. Third, project funds are released after land title is secured. The budget, drawn up by the management agency on behalf of the business group, is the single most important document of the 20–hectare project, because it locks all the actors -- state agencies, management agencies, business group members -- into a programme of future development.

An examination of three budgets, Arusafa business group, Safakofi Pty Ltd and Nipiamoka business group, shows that while each project draws a similar amount of funds (around K77,000), there is great variation in the way these are used. For example, while Wheeler anticipated a payout period of some 14 years, Safakofi and Nipiamoka are budgeted to take less than 10 years to pay out the loan. How realistic are these budgets and what is the difference between them and Arusafa? Both Arusafa and Safakofi are ANGCO–managed, so the cost structure of inputs is similar. This is the case with the cost of labour inputs (K20,708 in year 5 of Safakofi and K18,297 in year 5 of Arusafa). There are, however, large differences in the cost of fertiliser for both blocks. In year 5 Arusafa is paying some K17,296 for fertiliser whereas Safakofi is paying out K11,154 for fertiliser in the same year. This could of course be the result of agronomic differences on the two blocks. Further differences in the cost structure of these are in the areas of management fees and capital costs. Arusafa is paying a very high proportion of its total costs in management fees. The usual K5,000 management fee is budgeted for, but so too is what is called 'supervision' in the budget. Wheeler budgeted for an assistant manager salary of some K4,000 in year 7, whereas Arusafa are paying some K6,800 in year 7 for 'supervision' as well as the K5,000 management fee. Safakofi, on the other hand, are paying K4,000 as Assistant Manager salary in year 7, and no management fee after year 5. Safakofi seem to be getting special treatment from their management agency while Arusafa seem to be paying quite a bit extra to retain the services of management.[7] ANGCO justifies the extra management expense on Arusafa by claiming the Assistant Manager is actually the Field Manager, and that this position will disappear when an Assistant Manager from the business group is trained.

The other big difference in the budget between Arusafa and Safakofi are the different capital costs incurred by each project. Neither project incurs the cost of a wet processing plant which was budgeted for by Wheeler but both incur a capital cost which Wheeler did not predict, namely the cost of seedlings. On Arusafa, seedlings up to 20 months old were provided by the management agency at a cost of 20 toea each delivered by the management agency, at a grand capital cost of some K14,000. Safakofi paid K6,000 for its seedlings. Wheeler envisaged that seed would be provided free by DPI and that seedlings could be obtained from nurseries funded by the CIB or from nurseries on the block or, if purchased at 5 toea each. ANGCO have forbidden their block-holders from establishing a nursery and has insisted on providing its own seedlings.

There may be very good reasons for the variations in these budgets compared with Wheeler's original budget, but the main point to note is that there is tremendous latitude for the management agencies in putting budgets together, and that few questions are raised by PNGDB on variations. This latitude is also evident in the Nipiamoka budget, where NPMA calculates an income at K1,600 per tonne (which is far too high), while it seems to underestimate the cost of labour required (K3,323 in year 5). There is a good deal of room for manoeuvre on the part of the management agency. The difference between the apparent perpetual dependence of Arusafa on the management agency and the quick release of Safakofi is best understood in class terms, because Safakofi is owned by the Sabumeis, a dominant big peasant family. Ben Sabumei explained the terms of the loan to Jeff and Beijo Sabumei. Sabumei has used the full resources of his position to ensure that Safakofi has access to various state services, and that it will not remain too dependent on ANGCO.

The management agencies are not only systematically appropriating surplus monies from blockholders, but are also engaged in 'silent' class struggle against the smallholders whose interests they are paid to defend. The appropriation of monies by management agencies is quite sizeable. They have control over the original K8,000 paid by the government for the lease from the customary owners. They also control the K3,000 government subsidy for the pre-loan period, during which time they supervise clearing, lining and holing, and planting out of the block. As soon as the loan is made available, they have access to K6,000 per year for a 20-hectare block in management fees, plus at least K2,500 per year in Assistant Manager's fees. We have already seen how the manipulation of these fees occurs, but much worse cases were discovered in the course of investigation. On many blocks, the Assistant Manager's fee was not paid. In others, a business group leader acts as 'field supervisor' on rural minimum wages or a management agency field supervisor is hired on the rural minimum wage.

There are other less direct ways in which management agencies can benefit financially from control over 20–hectare blocks. They are normally large organisations which are active in all areas of the coffee marketing chain. As we have seen, they may choose to charge blocks for inputs which only they can supply. The price of such inputs is checked by the PNGDB, so it is rare for this price to be inflated, but this is nevertheless good business for other aspects of a management agency operation. The agencies also benefit from the charge of liquid funds which are made available to them every quarter for the 20–hectare blocks. It is not known quite how the agencies manipulate their complex operations to take advantage of this charge of liquid funds, but so unpredictable are their requests for funding every quarter – – sometimes late, sometimes early – – that one can only assume these funds are being moved around within the organisation to finance other short–term projects. One management agency (Gouna) complained about the slowness of getting quarterly advances from PNGDB:

> Our blocks then have to get bridging finance which is expensive. GOUNA does this by giving them an advance on coffee sales if we have trouble with our advances. We never stop work. That would cost more in the end. (Andes Berquist, Interview June 10, 1982)

But on the other hand, Gouna could benefit from the interest received on bridging finance if this was supplied by the agency itself, and by the delay to the loan payout which results from the mortgaging of coffee sales. This was the same agency whose actions puzzled a PNGDB officer because they were always so late in their requests for quarterly advances. It should be clear that there are numerous ways in which the agencies can benefit financially from control of the loan funds.

The agencies also act as a dominant class to disorganise and subordinate the 'budding' middle peasant business group members and customary landowners. The principal instrument of management agency control over a 20–hectare project is the budget. Wheeler's original budget, it will be recalled, contained two provisions which showed consideration of the interests of the smallholders, measures which would have given them a base in accumulation and the potential for middle peasant class formation. The first of these provisions was a dividend to business group members which would be awarded in year 7, when the block reached maximum coffee production. The second was the provision of a 'wet' processing factory on the block. Both these disappeared in the implementation of 20–hectare projects. There is no dividend budgeted for on any 20–hectare project in the Eastern Highlands Province. The management agencies are unanimous in their belief that money should not return to 'clansmen' until the loan has been paid out, and this has also become the firm policy of the PNGDB.[8] This is a particularly short–sighted and unnecessary policy. Is it possible to imagine smallholders watching passively as coffee is produced on their land without their getting a share in it for a period of over ten years? This decision shows how acquisitive the management agencies have become, and also shows the lengths to which they will go to mobilise against the subordinate classes.

The failure to budget for a 'wet' processing factory on the block applies mainly to the private management agencies, ANGCO and Gouna. NPMA will allow a part of the crop to be processed on the block if business group members insist upon it (Tom Leydon, Interview June 23 1982) The absence of a 'wet' factory on Gouna and ANGCO blocks means that cherry must be taken off the block the moment it is harvested. When smallholders sell cherry they usually take it to the roadside and sell it to a passing buyer, but the 20-hectare development is a far too professional an operation for cherry to be sold in this way. Rather, on Gouna and ANGCO managed blocks, cherry will be taken off the block the moment it is harvested by management company trucks, and transported to a processing plant. Coffee from 20-hectare projects managed by ANGCO is sold to Goroka Coffee Pty Ltd for processing, an ANGCO owned company (Tom Neke, Interview June 9, 1982, Makeyo Lekesavi, Interview June 9 1982) It is hard to justify the tying of the processing of a crop to a processor owned by the management agency, but McKillop's arguments come closest, for he argues that a private system of marketing is 'efficient' because DPI could never have provided a marketing structure equivalent to that provided by the management agencies. He argues that the failure of DPI or the government to offer a critically important, adequate and efficient marketing service suggests that marketing 'is a function demanding innovative management skills' (McKillop, Williamson and Associates Pty Ltd 1982:50) But even if this is accurate it does not justify marketing tied to the provision of management services on a block. In most of EHP, the marketing of coffee has never depended on government. Private marketing is available. It would seem to be in the greatest interests of the block that processors bid competitively for the right to process coffee from it.

It has been shown that the 'credit' or budget stage of the implementation of the 20-hectare projects has been almost entirely 'captured' by management agencies who have used their control over the budgets to appropriate surplus from the blocks and to forestall middle peasant class formation. How has the PNGDB allowed this to happen, especially in view of its intention to play an active role in the implementation of the projects? Also, how can one explain statements by people who work in management agencies that 'as far as 20-hectare blocks go, policy is dictated by the Development Bank. They are the ones who call the shots' (Bill Lloyd, Interview June 7, 1982) Part of the answer to this question is that the PNGDB has not been able to overcome its low political penetration. It has not managed to achieve penetration of the block itself by maintaining a keen extension presence. This would be necessary if it were to properly control demands made at the level of production. It has not overcome the difficulty that while it can control the supply side of budgeting -- through the release of funds -- it has no control over the demand side of budgeting on the block. Despite the fact that PNGDB was employing two very able field officers at the Goroka branch in 1982, their on-the-block checking function was very limited. The management agencies' use of labour was checked on the block from time to time, but most checks on expenditure were done in the PNGDB office.

On-the-block checking by the PNGDB became less frequent as the block developed, even though it was at this stage that this function was most needed, because by then large amounts of money were involved. For example, the PNGDB extension officer I travelled with constantly expressed surprise when we found out people were not being paid the Assistant Manager's salary when that salary was being drawn by the management agency. He said, 'I will check it out back at the office,' but it was clear there was no possibility of ongoing checks of this kind while the PNGDB was checking only the supply side of the budget, and while the management agency had complete control over the demand of funds on the block itself.

The other reason the PNGDB failed to control the activities of the management agency and insist upon the 'spirit' of the original conception of 20-hectare development, is because the state has high functional autonomy in the coffee industry. This in the state as a whole means that the function of checking budgets and loan requests from management agencies falls to the PNGDB and to it alone. No other state agency could intrude on this functional responsibility, and those who do take an interest in such matters, such as DPI, are treated with intense hostility by the PNGDB. In a Bonapartist state with high functional autonomy, state agencies will jealously guard their autonomy vis-à-vis other state agencies. This hostility and competitiveness between branches of a Bonapartist state with high functional autonomy have only one possible outcome. The branches are driven into collusion not with others, but with other social actors. In the implementation of 20-hectare projects, collusion is most evident between management agencies and the PNGDB in circumstances where they perceive a threat from the subordinate classes to the development itself.

Management

In the design section on management it was shown that it could be defined as both technical expertise and as a system of social control. It was suggested in that section that technical expertise as provided by management agencies can lead directly to social control. So far we have seen how the strategic location of the management agency gave it social control vis-à-vis state agencies over land procedures and controls of 20-hectare development budgets. In this section I turn to the question of how the management agencies operated on the block itself. Did they use their technical expertise to provide a demonstration effect for business group members so that they could eventually take over management of the block, or did they turn their technical expertise into a system of social control of business group members so that their involvement on the block was suppressed? I show in this section that management agencies properly performed the technical role on the projects. They did not short-change projects either in terms of management time spent on the blocks, or in the management services provided. There is no evidence of any block failing because a management agency did not fulfil its responsibilities. However, I also show that agencies had a limited view of the extent of business group involvement on the block. The three management agencies in Eastern Highlands Province - - Gouna, ANGCO and NPMA - - tended to view business group members more as minority shareholders than as partners in the operation of the project. Some agencies (Gouna) were more extreme than others (NPMA) in forbidding business groups a role on the block. All agencies, however, tended to be hostile towards business group members, more in the manner of 'silent' class struggle, than as demonstrators of management techniques to business group members. Such members rarely directly challenge the exercise of social control by the management agencies over their block.

The amount of time managers spend on the actual projects depends on the stage of development of the project and the internal structure of the management agency itself. My survey revealed that management agencies tended to spend a good deal of time on blocks in the pre-loan stages, on the original blocks they established. This work is very rudimentary, and the management agencies soon realised they did not need to provide highly-trained personnel to the block until the loan came through. On later blocks, ANGCO provides a full-time female Agricultural Assistant to help with the pre-loan work, but it is a very low key operation at this stage. Sometimes this 'sweat equity' work is carried on by business group members, as in Wheeler's original budget, but as we will see in the next section, this depends very much upon the agency's philosophy toward business group involvement.

The agencies have different philosophies to managing a block. This philosophy in turn stems directly from their different locations within the dominant classes of the private management agencies, Gouna and ANGCO. In their attitude to business group members and their approach to management, Gouna, a *petit bourgeois* company, displays precisely the emphasis on 'business practice' and 'sound management' one would expect from the *petit bourgeoisie*. ANGCO, a big peasant company, on the other hand, displays the big peasant tendency of using any and every avenue, including clan connections, to increase its flow of profit. In other words, the *petit bourgeoisie*, used to realising relative surplus value in its commercial enterprises, manages the blocks purely on factory agricultural lines. ANGCO, which profits from the production of absolute surplus value, manages blocks in a way that allows them room to fiddle and deal to extend the working day in order to increase profits. It is this 'class' orientation in management that is much more important in terms of its impact upon business group members in the 'silent' class struggle than the formal public or private ownership of the management agencies. NPMA, ostensibly a public company, operates in a way similar to ANGCO in terms of its impact upon business group members.

The different class orientations of the private management agencies and NPMA's indeterminate class position can be shown if we look at the three agencies' attitudes to the role of business group members on the blocks. In particular we can examine the agencies' view of the contribution of 'free labour' -- the 'sweat equity' stage -- and their approach to training a business group member to eventually take over management of the block. It will be recalled that both these forms of business group involvement were allowed for in Wheeler's original budget and Oxenford's PNGDB policy statement. Gouna will not allow business group member involvement on the block at all. John Leahy, Gouna's Papua New Guinean coffee projects manager, said:

> Our policy is to run blocks on a business basis. We believe they must not slip back to a village level. There is no way of disciplining people if they work for half price. The Wantok system is antipathetic to good business practice. (John Leahy, Interview June 10, 1982)

Gouna will not allow business group members to contribute 'sweat equity' to the block. This policy must add considerably to the size of the loan on Gouna blocks and to the length of time it will take to pay it out. This could not be confirmed without access to Gouna's budgets, but it is known that, in some cases -- and this probably applies to some Gouna blocks some well-off men were prepared to finance pre-loan work out of their own pockets rather than be obligated to other business group members. Gouna will not allow business group members to work as paid labour on the block, either. Andes Berquist, Gouna's expatriate Financial Adviser, explained that:

> We have a policy of avoiding employing people from this area. The reasons for this are because *Wantoks* want to have a big *mau mau* all the time and because we are trying to teach people to run their blocks as a business. We insist that blocks take on outsiders both as managers and labourers. The group should be the owners and they should get other people to run it. Not one of the assistant managers is from a business group. (Andes Berquist, Interview June 10, 1982)

Gouna believes it would be harder to discipline Assistant Managers if they were subject to claims from the clan. For this reason it will not train business group members to become Managers or Assistant Managers. As it is, Gouna has established very tight discipline over its managers by encouraging competition between them and by keeping them circulating throughout the Gouna organisation. This 'business' approach is applied to all stages of the implementation of the 20–hectare development where specialist skills can be exercised.

Gouna's refusal to allow business group members a role on the block is justified on an ethnocentric basis. It argues that if business group members were given any role on the block at all they would be swayed by clan pressure to ignore proper business practices. This is, however, a selective argument, because Gouna does not, and cannot, take this approach to all business group members. Auwo Ketauwo and Isembo Olekevea are business group members with blocks that are managed by Gouna, but because they are Gouna Directors they have extensive involvement in their own, and others', blocks. The argument put forward by Gouna is in fact an argument for class domination, because its real position is not that all business group members are unable to practise proper business behaviour, but rather that some powerful people should be able to dominate development on the projects. Gouna's role in a system of dominance, in a 'silent' class struggle is to use an ideological screen based on talk of 'proper business practice' and 'clan interference' to justify exclusion of ordinary business group members from any involvement on their block. They claim proudly that: "Business group members must come into head office if they want to know anything about their block. The business group knows they cannot interfere." (Andes Berquist, Interview June 10, 1982) Gouna is also engaged in ensuring the maintenance of its dominance in the 'silent' class struggle by establishing networks of dependence – – through specialised pruning, company transport, tied processing, restricted knowledge of management practices – – for every block. These patterns of dependence will be hard to break even when the loan is paid out.

ANGCO's policy on business group involvement is almost the exact opposite Gouna's. ANGCO's aim is to reduce costs and to squeeze the maximum amount of free labour it can out of business group members. ANGCO has learned through its operation of larger plantations, where it produces absolute surplus value, that profits can be substantially increased not only by developing a sophisticated division of labour on a plantation as Gouna does, but also by having labour work harder (greater labour productivity) and longer (extending the working day) for delayed payment if possible. This is the kind of labour practice that occurred under the old agreement system in colonial times. Today, the big–peasant–controlled ANGCO corporation is trying to encourage business group members to work on their own land as 'agreement' labour. Bill Lloyd, expatriate manager of ANGCODEV, explained ANGCO's philosophy as being to reduce labour costs by encouraging members of business groups to work free (Bill Lloyd, Interview June 7, 1982)

ANGCO seems to rely very heavily on business group members to labour free during the pre-loan phase, for if they do not, the block will not go ahead. But ANGCO's real innovation is to attempt to encourage the business group members to labour 'free' on the project *after* the loan money has been approved. They have attempted to put this into practice by developing a roster system, whereby business group members are rostered to labour free on a certain day on their ANGCO-managed block. As Bill Lloyd explained:

> We try to get business group members to continue to work well after the project is planted up. We give them a shareholding equivalent to what their wages would be. This shareholding or 'work mark' is registered in a work book. This time is converted into shareholdings which is the proportion by which they will receive a share of any dividends. This [free labour] cuts down on labour so the less they eventually have to pay back. (Bill Lloyd, Interview June 7, 1982)

It is this system that I am calling 'agreement labour'. The system is dubious to say the least. This is so not only because of the possibility that 'work books' can be lost, as happened on Molan (Tom Newke, Interview 9 June 1982); not only because, as on Safakofi, so few business group members turned up to labour free anyway (Jeff Sabumei, Interview June 10, 1982); but also because there is no dividend in sight for most business group members for about ten years:

> ANGCO is not prepared to appoint business group members as managers because: we think it best if we don't have any interference from the people we are developing the block for. Such interference just confuses the whole issue. (Bill Lloyd, Interview June 7, 1982)

The typical ANGCO Manager is a national, agriculturally trained, responsible for one to five blocks and living on site on one of them. ANGCO is, however, prepared to appoint business group members as Assistant Managers, providing they follow instructions. It is not clear whether such an appointment is a position from which the Assistant Manager will be trained to be a Manager, or not. ANGCO's standard reply to the question is that it is too early to begin management training. Some Assistant Managers such as Jeff Sabumei of Safakofi assume they will be trained as Managers to take over their block as soon as possible. Others are convinced that they are being trained as Managers already, because they exercise a good deal of control over their labourers. They do not, however, have an agreement from ANGCO as to when they would take over. It was impossible to tell in 1982 what ANGCO's position on training business group members as Managers really was, although it was clear, at that stage, that it had not undertaken any training of business group members to take over their blocks.

NPMA's management philosophy lies somewhat mid-way between that of Gouna and ANGCO. Rex Naug, Manager of NPMA, emphasised that business group members contribute 'sweat equity' on NPMA-managed blocks if the project is to go ahead. This work involves planting seeds in a nursery, clearing and fencing. NPMA's policy is, however, that no business group members will work free on the project after the 'sweat equity' stage. NPMA does allow business group members to labour for a wage on their project but, as Tom Leydon, Senior Manager for NPMA, says, their interest wanes (Tom Leydon, Interview June 23, 1982) NPMA seems to allow for the greatest involvement of business group members on the block and to be closer to the spirit of the original agreement than the private management agencies. However, lest it be thought that a state agency is a progressive force in PNG, we must add that there were severe limits to the extent to which NPMA was prepared to tolerate interference from business group members. Such members could be involved if they accepted that NPMA would continue into the foreseeable future to co-ordinate the project and exercise the management function, and if they left all decision-making to NPMA.

Conclusion

In this section I have examined the design and implementation of the 20-hectare projects in the areas of land, credit and provision of management. The conclusion of the section based on 1982 data is that the land and surplus monies of smallholders were 'captured' by the big peasants and the *petit bourgeoisie* and that smallholders were 'disenfranchised' on their own blocks. I have specifically cited the flaws in the design of land, credit and management, all of which ended up allowing management agencies to initiate and control the pooling of land, to neutralise business group involvement, to control budgets, to decide that the business group would not receive a dividend until the loan was paid out, and prohibited processing on the block (except for NPMA blocks). The management agencies also managed to tie the coffee produced on a block to their own marketing network, so that blocks may never be freed from dependence on management agencies. In addition, I have shown that management agencies are making good profits for minimal risks out of 20-hectare development projects.

Part II

The Coffee Rust Outbreak of 1986

Introduction

The analysis so far has concentrated on the Eastern Highlands Province, and the coffee town of Goroka, since by focusing on local economic and political developments, the basic structure of the political economy of the coffee industry in Papua New Guinea is revealed. However, Eastern Highlands coffee is only one segment of a national industry. The political and economic patterns which have been identified there are repeated in all the coffee-growing regions of Papua New Guinea, albeit with important local variations. In order to understand the political economy of coffee beyond Eastern Highlands it is necessary to shift the focus to an issue - - the coffee rust outbreak of May 1986 - - which cut across local political economies and drew all coffee interests into an industry-wide problem to be dealt with at national level.

Papua New Guinea coffee production grew so spectacularly in a mere thirty years partly because the industy was disease-free. Many other coffee-producing nations had periodic production cuts through outbreaks of disease, whose treatment was time-consuming and expensive. The most serious disease to affect the coffee tree is a fungus known as Hemileia Vastatrix, commonly known as coffee rust disease. Coffee rust appears on the lower surface of coffee leaves as yellowish-orange coloured spots or pustules. It causes the plant to lose leaves and thereby weakens it. On susceptible plants, all the leaves drop down and this results in the dropping of cherries (berries or fruits) and the death of twigs. The absence of leaves on the plant causes coffee not to ripen well, twigs to die back, and no new or very limited vegetation to appear. Poor vegetative growth results in poor or no crop in succeeding years. The disease can be controlled if it is detected at an early stage on a few plants. Eradication means destroying the disease-causing organism at the site of observation. If the disease gets established in many areas, however, then spraying coffee plants with fungicides will control the disease. If it is not eradicated and spreads quickly, it has a devastating effect on coffee production, reducing it by as much as 70 percent to 80 percent.

Coffee rust disease is not unknown in Papua New Guinea. In 1965, a small outbreak occurred in the Robusta crop grown in the Port Moresby hinterland, but this was some distance from the main Arabica crop and did not threaten it. An eradication campaign was quickly put in place and was very effective in preventing the spread of the disease. Nevertheless, even this small-scope campaign, conducted with colonial authority and some efficiency, cost $70,000 (Shaw, Bourke, Bell and Shaw 1986:34), a large sum at the time.

Coffee-growers in Papua New Guinea had always been nervous about the possible outbreak of coffee rust disease in the main Arabica areas probably because they felt their good luck could not last, knowing full well that Papua New Guinea, like most other coffee-producing countries, would one day have to face the cost of disease prevention eating away at coffee profits. Dr A. Kabaara, Director of the Coffee Research Institute at Airuya, warned as early as July 1985 that an immediate need was to 'breed coffee resistant to the dreaded Leaf Rust' (*Kofi Tok*, July 1985:4) and in July of that year, the then Minister of Primary Industry, Mr Rabbie Namaliu (later Prime Minister) received urgent communications from the industry that the PNG crop should be protected from the danger of coffee rust entering the country from across the Indonesian border. The Minister stressed that the Quarantine Service was being expanded (*Kofi Tok*, July 1985:6) The outbreak of coffee rust was widely feared but various assurances notwithstanding, it seemed to some people in the industry that not enough was being done. Nor were adequate safety provisions in place.

The Problem

The first sighting of rust seems to have occurred on April 30 or May 1, 1986. It was discovered in a patch of coffee near the turn-off to Tigi on the main Hagen-Baiyer Road in Western Highlands province. The Wahgi Valley itself seemed free, as did the Eastern Highlands province. The new Prime Minister, Mr Paias Wingti, a Western Highlander and the first Highlands Prime Minister, was immediately informed. The government moved quickly to institute emergency measures. On May 1, the Minister for Primary Industry, Mr Iambakey Okuk, also a Highlander from Chimbu province, declared the five Highlands provinces a disease area. The Minister imposed restriction on coffee plant movement from this area (*Papua New Guinea National Gazette*, Port Moresby, May 1, 1986) Plantations and smallholders in the Baiyer area were immediately quarantined and their coffee sprayed or destroyed. By May 7, however, coffee rust had been identified in the Wahgi Valley itself in the North West Wahgi at Tremearne, in the mid-Wahgi at Kimel, Nebilya Valley and at Alimp plantation. Occurrences of coffee rust disease were being reported throughout the five provinces, including the Eastern Highlands. It was clear that the disease was spreading fast and that a co-ordinated effort of control was required. But how, when and where was co-ordination to take place?

A National Centre for Development Studies, Canberra, Report by Shaw, Bourke, Bell and Shaw on coffee rust in Papua New Guinea was released within ten days of the outbreak, showing admirable speed in making the agronomic and economic implications of coffee rust outbreak clear. The report emphasised that because eradication was not feasible and because a new strain of rust-persistent Catimor selections would not be fully tested to replace existing strains for some years, the only alternative form of control in Papua New Guinea was to institute a control programme based on the spray application of fungicides. The Report's salutary warning was that:

> even if chemical control measures were immediately undertaken (as is happening), this would only slow the spread of the fungus and reduce the *incubation* and perhaps save a lot of next year's crop of cherries. The ultimate spread of the cherries to all the coffee-growing areas is probably inevitable. This means that if coffee bushes are to be protected in the future, chemical control in all infected areas will be necessary (Shaw, Bourke, Bell and Shaw, 1986:38)

The favoured chemical is sold as Bayleton 125, and is marketed by the Bayer company. It should be applied at 2 litres/ha after pruning in September, and again at 2 litres/ha, within four weeks of the first application. One month after spraying with Bayleton 125, copper spray should also be applied. Bayleton is mixed with water and sprayed from knapsacks. It is expensive -- increasing total cost of production in the plantation sector by at least 10 percent (K120 per litre for the chemical alone) (Shaw, Bourke, Bell and Shaw, 1986:55) -- and it is dangerous. The manufacturer warns of the need to wear waterproof gloves and rubber boots when mixing, and a mask when spraying.

It is clear that while the plantation sector would be badly affected by the increased cost of production caused by spraying, the problem and cost were not insurmountable for plantations. Plantations have always operated only a portion of their productive capacity and can, if necessary, step up labour productivity to cover increased costs. As well, spraying is more manageable on a plantation where coffee is arranged in neat 9 x 9 rows. The plantation could expect to pass on some costs to the consumer, for there exists more price flexibility in the quality market. However, as Shaw, Bourke, Bell and Shaw pointed out, it was the 20-hectare blocks and the smallholders who were likely to be most badly hit by increased production costs.

We have already seen that coffee growers on 20-hectare plots are disillusioned by the high cost of management and the long lead time before they receive profits. They would not have been amused by the increased production costs associated with spraying which would further delay their receipt of cash. Smallholders too, would find the cost of spraying excessive. They have not replanted, nor have they practised good management techniques. They are unlikely to want to either pay for, or undertake, spraying. As the disease is contagious and as the smallholder sector is the largest in the PNG coffee industry, it is clear that specific policies towards smallholders needed to be adopted. But would these be adopted in the smallholder interest, or would the smallholders again find themselves being manipulated by powerful interests, this time on the pretext of disease prevention? The history of the industry, as presented in this book, does not give optimistic ground for decent treatment of smallholders in a crisis. In the context of a history of smallholder control and manipulation, the conclusion by Shaw, Bourke, Bell and Shaw that "An adequate smallholder response to coffee rusts demands an improvement in management and understanding of coffee" (Shaw, Bourke, Bell and Shaw 1986:94) has an ominous ring to it.

There is no doubt, however, that the coffee rust outbreak was a national crisis which could have had an impact on the national economy severe enough to require a nationally organised response. Shaw, Bourke, Bell and Shaw show that, all things considered and allowing for buoyant mineral prices, 'the effects of coffee rust are not likely to be very dramatic on Papua New Guinea's balance of payments position'. However, coffee rust could be expected to have a significant effect on private consumption by coffee producers with a multiplier effect much larger than the initial reduction in coffee producers' income and consumption. It would also have a marked impact on government revenue, both as a result of loss of excise revenue and because chemicals had to be purchased. Employment would be affected and so too might law and order, especially when smallholder households begin to feel the impact of loss of coffee income. As we have seen, there are numerous coffee bodies in PNG such as DPI, CIB and regional organisations of growers and exporters, but it was clear from the start of the coffee rust problem that none of these was especially competent to mount a rust control programme on the scale needed. Shaw, Bourke, Bell and Shaw did not, as usual, in the work of the Centre, consider the political and organisational implications of their analysis. However, their report leads to the inescapable conclusion that a new national organisation might be needed to mount the rust control programme.

The Actors

At the time of the coffee rust outbreak in May 1986, both national and coffee politics in Papua New Guinea were in a state of flux. The country had a new and enthusiastic Highlands Prime Minister, Mr Paias Wingti, whose charter was to increase spending in agriculture and help the smallholder. Wingti was especially closely linked with coffee interests in the Western Highlands, his home province. But he was backed by many old politicians of the Independence period, such as his Minister for Primary Industry, Sir Iambakey Okuk, and the Deputy Prime Minister, Sir Julius Chan. These politicians had scores to settle, particularly against the ousted Somare regime and in some cases against certain provincial leaders.

By 1986, provincial government was well established, albeit with many provinces short of cash and with weak policies, partly as a result of budget constraints. Still, most of them had held successful elections at least once, and provincial premiers had begun to come together to represent regional interests at national level, either through the annual Premiers' Conference or through its informal secretariats of Highlands Premiers, Islands Premiers, etc. If national government still retained control of the purse strings, provincial Premiers were often in the political limelight, and had begun to influence the national political agenda.

Coffee politics was also in a state of flux at the time, partly due to several good seasons of high prices (1983–84, 1984–85), making coffee politics virtually unnecessary. There was however, a 'changing of the guard' in coffee politics. The previous government of Mr Somare, with Denis Young as Minister of Primary Industry, had blundered badly in the industry (see Chapter 12), and it was waiting to see what the Wingti government -- perceived as more sympathetic and with its roots in the Highlands -- had in store for it.

One major change which had occurred in coffee politics was the emergence of a new association, the Coffee Industry Association (CIA) Inc. The CIA was formally established at a meeting in Goroka on 12 November 1984, where a draft constitution was adopted and an interim executive elected. The objectives of the Association are broadly defined under the constitution, but may be best summarised by quoting the first: 'to serve, protect and promote the interests of all members of the coffee industry, whether growers, producers, marketers or exporters'. (*Kofi Tok*, January 1986:3) Membership includes most of the important Arabica growers (Eastern Highlands Development Corporation Pty Ltd, Gouna, Asaro Coffee Estates Ltd, Wahgi Mek Plantations Pty Ltd), and processors and exporters (ANGCO Pty Ltd, Coffee International Pty Ltd, Kundu Coffee Exports Ltd). A significant development was the appointment of a full-time executive officer, Mr Craig McConagahy, ex-*kiap* and Eastern Highlands provincial planner, who has done much to establish and maintain a good working relationship with the Minister for Primary Industry, government departments, the Coffee Industry Board and the members of the CIA.

The emergence of the CIA is no surprise because the rapid development and economic expansion of the coffee industry made it inevitable that an interest group would be formed to put the industry case to the government. What is remarkable, however, is that, despite all the changes which had occurred in the industry, the CIA not only claimed a direct lineage with the old white planters' HFSA, but also contained some key white activists who were actually instrumental in the operation of the HFSA. How did this arise, considering most white planters had been driven out of the industry in the early 1970s?

The return of some white planters was caused by an extremely odd set of circumstances in the Papua New Guinea coffee industry. Even though the plantations were now owned by black élites, who as we have seen consolidated their holdings in the 1970s, the white planters who once owned these properties were waiting in the wings, usually on the Gold Coast in Queensland in Australia, where they quickly spent their accumulated fortunes. By 1986, they were ready to return to Papua New Guinea and, remarkably, the black élites were ready to welcome them back. The old white planters often came back to their old plantations, as white managers employed by the new black owners.

The history of one of the larger Arabica coffee plantation groups in Papua New Guinea, Wahgi Mek Plantations Pty Ltd (WMP) in Western Highlands illustrates the process. WMP is the investment arm of the North and South Wahgi Local Government Councils, with head office and factory near Banz. WMP was not run by either a big peasant or *petit bourgeois*–oriented entrepreneur, but fell between the two, both in management practice and purchasing strategy. From 1974, it expanded rapidly, adding ten plantations to the two it purchased in 1974, as well as developing trading activities, such as a Shell fuel distribution agency, a trucking operation and other non–coffee enterprises. However, by the end of 1982, WMP had lost K5,700,000 through bad financial control and poor plantation management.

A rescue package was put together by a local firm in February 1983: Agricultural and Resources Management Services Pty Ltd (ARMS). This signed a management agreement with the owners to cut costs and exercise tight control. The process was not dissimilar from agreements made by owners on 20–hectare blocks. They agreed not to interfere with management prerogative, to accept no dividends until creditors were paid out, and to support the management company. ARMS was in the process of turning WMP from a group enterprise into a big peasant operation headed by ARMS principal, Michael Mel.

Mel himself, an aspiring politician and strong supporter of Iambakey Okuk's National Party was not expected to be involved in the day–to–day operation of WMP. For this process, he needed a coffee Manager, and employed the former white planter owner of a number of Wahgi Mek plantations, Dick Hagon. Hagon had been a very active member of the HFSA, and was one of the founding members of the Coffee Marketing Board (CMB). Neither Mel's nor Hagon's services came cheap, as we can anticipate from the 20–hectare projects. Among the conditions of the agreement is that the Manager must buy 25 percent of the shares of the company. Thus the management agreement allowed Dick Hagon to return not only in person but also as an owner in property, of at least a part of his old plantation. The government guaranteed the agreement and underwrote new loans for the company. ARMS claims to have turned the 1982 loss of K5,700,000 into a profit of K665,620. It claims to be planting an extra 600 acres, engaging in a vigorous replanting programme, has sold off *petit bourgeois* assets and prevented theft and stealing on the plantations. These are worthy achievements but it will take many years for all creditors to be paid off, during which time it will be essential to retain the services of ARMS management.

The return of Hagon, in partnership with Mel, represents a process of tighter management control on large plantations, similar to what we have seen in the 20–hectare agreements. In the case of companies like ARMS, there can be no doubt that some form of management was required. But should the price of good management be an absolute loss of control of the plantation by the owners? As in 20–hectare management agreements, so too in this case there is no–one to manage the managers or control the controllers. Almost inevitably, it seems, groups like ARMS will attempt to consolidate their position over time. The inevitable price falls in the industry are used as justification for further delaying management withdrawal. In the case of WMP, Hagon's 25 percent share ensures that he may not be forced to leave even when, and if, debts are cleared and profitability ensured.

Hagon is a powerful figure in Western Highlands coffee because of his deep roots in the region. He knows Prime Minister Wingti well and exercises influence over Mel and others. The return of other white planters like him, has the potential to recreate old patterns of colonial coffee politics, with 'growers' (i.e. planters) taking the lead, supposedly on behalf of smallholders, to twist and bend government to their will. The technocrats who became influential after Independence would be in for a surprise if these old colonial patterns of coffee politics began to re–emerge. They do not have experience in handling Hagon and other white planters like him. It was with no irony that founding Chairman of the CIA, Barry Corin, could say in his first address that:

> To my mind this Association is an extension of the now defunct Highlands Farmers and Settlers Association (HFSA) which held similar aims and objectives but lost membership during the lead–up to and post–independence period. (*Kofi Tok* January 1986:2)

It can be seen that by the time of the outbreak of coffee rust in mid–1986 the political economy of coffee in Papua New Guinea had increased in complexity and unpredictability. The history of colonial coffee suggested an economy based on a minimalist state where a unified dominant class represented by a tightly organised association controlled the industry through the market. The establishment of the CIA and the return of white planters prefigured a political economy of this type. But was such a throw–back to the past possible? Had not a great deal changed since the lead–up to, and post–Independence period?

As we have seen, the political economy of coffee in the post–Independence period could no longer be based on a unified, dominant class. Or could it? Perhaps the sense of crisis in the industry would unify the petty bourgeoisie and big peasant class fractions around the objective of assisting the industry to survive? Changes, however, had also occurred in the role of the state. Structural changes were significant, particularly decentralisation which created a new set of actors in coffee politics, the provincial premiers and provincial agricultural departments. While not necessarily competent, they were capable of tying up resources and causing blockages in decision–making.

The state had changed in other ways as well. It was no longer a minimalist one, although nor was it consistently interventionist. Rather, as we have seen, the public authority represented at least in part, the power base of the technocrats. Unlike the colonial administrators, they had their own policy charter, usually derived from technical and organisational prerogatives. They had great political power and could often over-ride class and interest group politics. The technocrats had not managed to turn the independent state of Papua New Guinea into an African-style command economy, and had not themselves formed into a bureaucratic bourgeoisie, but they were influential and could be expected to play a major role in coffee politics. When the coffee rust crisis broke in May 1986, the stage was set for an exciting and possibly chaotic policy-making process.

May 1986: Initial Reaction to the Coffee Rust Crisis

There was by no means unanimity for the establishment of a new coffee institution to manage the coffee rust crisis. In particular, Sir Iambakey Okuk, the Minister for Primary Industry, and a number of (National Party) Highlands Premiers were opposed from the outset. They were, worried (justifiably?) that, in a new institution, they and their big peasant supporters would be outmanoeuvred by a combination of white planters, technocrats and the *petit bourgeoisie*. In the view of the big peasants, the whole idea of a new coffee institution was closely associated with a technocratic, organisational and managerialist solution to the problem. Okuk was hostile from the beginning, because the first concrete proposal for the new institution, the Coffee Development Authority (CDA) as it came to be known, emerged from a sub-committee meeting of the technocratic CIB, on May 14. The need for the institution was obvious to some people but, to others like Okuk, it represented a risk, involving potential power losses and gains in the ever-volatile environment of Papua New Guinea coffee. The fact that the establishment of the institution was bitterly disputed -- let alone questions of its structure and function -- suggested that the coffee industry was about to be plunged into long and bitter political and economic disputes.

By early May 1986, however, it was clear that the industry had a serious crisis on its hands, and that emergency procedures for spraying and quarantine would have to be co-ordinated -- with or without a new institution. Wingti visited coffee growers, processors and exporters in Mount Hagen on 10 May and, as a result, the Department of Primary Industry, along with provincial departments, rapidly set up monitoring, quarantining and spraying procedures. The new Coffee Industry Association (CIA) found itself well placed to influence events. Its most active and forceful member, Dick Hagon from WMP, was at the site of the outbreak. He was able to issue an avalanche of telexes to the Minister for Primary Industry and the Prime Minister, which not only reported the latest developments to Port Moresby but also put the idea of the CDA on the agenda. Naturally, Hagon proposed a CDA which would be dominated by the CIA. He went so far later to propose that the three CIA members on the CDA would choose the Chairman, who would have a casting vote. (Hagon Telex July 4, 1986)

The brutal facts of the crisis were, however, that exporters did not stand to suffer in the short term. This was because coffee rust had no impact on green bean, so, no specific quarantine treatment needed to be adopted by importing countries like Australia. At the time, export prices were high. The CIA estimated that over 30 percent of the crop would have to be wiped out in one year for exporters to feel an impact on their overall profit levels. Such a result was very unlikely, given the procedures that had been put in place.

But coffee rust had a direct impact on cherry and parchment. Thus its impact would fall disproportionately in the industry and would bear especially severely on smallholders, those who relied on the sale of small quantities of cherry or parchment. As well, spraying costs would fall disproportionately on smallholders because they were most vunerable to the spread of coffee rust from one area to another. The emergency measures put in place targeted the small grower because, in most provinces, the sale of all cherry and parchment at the roadside was completely, and immediately, banned. Coffee borders were closed at the province to all coffee except green bean which was, also sprayed at the borders. Among the new measures that would be needed in a restructured coffee industry, the DPI and CIA agreed, was the centralisation of buying depots, and to 'rationalise the smallholder sector and encourage communal projects of catimor coffee using proper husbandry techniques'. (CIA executive minute n.d.).

The emergency procedures put in place in early May had largely been an informal affair partly supervised by Noreo Beangke, Secretary of DPI and Chief Inspector of Plants, the CIA, the CIB and provincial DPI officers. New Inspectors of Plants had been appointed and gazetted but apart from these powers, the Provincial Disaster Committees, as these informal groupings were called, were operating without legislative authorisation. They had taken dramatic steps to ban the sale of parchment and cherry, but they had perhaps overstepped their legal authority. Such was the fear and alarm at the extent of the emergency that it was thought that legislative support was a mere formality. At this point, the Minister for Primary Industry Sir Iambakey Okuk stepped in. In his inimitable way, he issued a telex on May 15, which read:

> Please note that experts have confirmed that coffee rust has been present in Papua New Guinea for at least one year. Restrictions on the movements of people, vehicles and coffee not likely to prevent spread of disease at this stage. This, the disruption to the industry and inconvenience caused to many people have convinced me that controls need to be reviewed. I have decided therefore that all restrictions

on the movements of people, vehicles and coffee are to be removed. Cherry, coffee parchment and green bean buying and selling within and outside of provinces must resume immediately. (Okuk, Telex, May 15)

It was a bombshell. The big peasants, hurt by losses to their processing works, were striking back on the side of the smallholder.

The immediate reaction by most other interests in the coffee industry was that Okuk was unbalanced and was trying to destroy the coffee industry. Hagon, in a (for him) moderate telex, told the Minister that Western Highlands was the province worst hit by the disaster and that 'it is very important that you and I work together'. (Hagon, Telex to Wingti n.d.) The Western Highlands Provincial Disaster Committee met the day after Okuk's telex, and did not mention it in their report, but reiterated that the ban on roadside buying of cherry would continue, although roadside buying of parchment was permitted. But the ban on the movement of parchment into or out of the province would continue. (Susy Bommell, Coffee Rust Co-ordinator Office, Telex, May 16, 1986) The CIB, however, was more cautious. It realised the limits of its power because it could only use existing legislation to uphold banning. Under this, the CIB was able to ban roadside buying of cherry but not parchment; nor was it able to prevent parchment being moved across provincial borders, although it could, and did, advise that the movement of such parchment should proceed in container trucks only. (CIB, Telex, May 16, 1986)

The CIB could not ignore the wishes of its own Minister, even if it was Iambakey Okuk. It moved to redress the burden of sacrifice borne by smallholders and big peasants by imposing a 10 toea/kg levy on exporters to pay for coffee rust controls. In the short term, at least, this spread the burden and promised to take the heat out of coffee politics.

Meanwhile, ideas for the organisation of a CDA were proceeding. They were promoted by Craig McConaghy, in a CIA paper which proposed to use a 10 toea/kg levy in the first year to fund the CDA. McConaghy had in mind a private authority which would nevertheless have the other key institutions -- DPI, CIB, CRI and CIA -- as directors. McConaghy wrote that 'A General Manager to the Authority would be empowered to hire and fire and operate a separate accounting system as in any other private corporation'. (McConaghy, CIA May 15, 1986) Reaction was noticeably cool in some quarters, the Western Highlands Premier, Mr Philip Kapal, promised to discuss the matter at the annual 1986 Premiers' Conference, but expressed no direct enthusiasm for the CDA.

June 1986: A Hiatus as the Combatants Regroup

June 1986 was a phony war period in the conflict over how to manage the coffee rust problem. The various actors began to grapple with the technical complexities of combating rust. Coffee politics was not abandoned, but overt conflict was suppressed while arguments were mustered and troops were briefed. In such encounters, the technocrats always have an advantage, because of their mastery of expertise, and the opportunities this offers for promotion of their own position. The Department of Primary Industry and the Coffee Industry Board commissioned a study from Waller and Turner, plant pathologists, to report on June 3, on control measures for coffee rust. Surprisingly, their report seemed to support Okuk in its analysis of the problem, but not in its implications for reorganisation of the industry.

Waller and Turner found that coffee rust had indeed been in the Highlands for over a year, that if eradication is 'impossible, it is also unnecessary'. (Waller and Turner 1986) They believed that most of the containment measures undertaken thus far were unnecessary, though restriction of cherry must be retained. (Waller and Turner 1986) Instead of trying to eradicate infected areas, attention should be turned to 'reducing spore production' using curative sprays. These would be effective only where good agronomic standards were maintained. Thus the report argued, as the technocrats had already pointed out, that sprays could be used to save the plantations but would not work on smallholdings 'unless this is preceded by an extensive rehabilitation programme, followed by good maintenance standards'. (Waller and Turner 1986)

Waller and Turner were not unaware of the social and political power implications of their recommendations, although they probably did not see rust control from a political perspective, as an exercise of political power, as smallholders and big peasants were likely to do. Nevertheless, they showed that if their approach was to work, an immense resource base had to be established. They noted that, in the short-term, a force of 200 would be needed:

> Such a force could be organised into 10 teams of 20 men, each with 12 sprayers and requiring 5 trucks for transport, 2 water trucks and a jeep or (preferably) pickup, with a central maintenance depot. At 400 1/ha of 0.05 percent triadimefon (a.i.) about 10,000 litres of Bayleton 250 EC will be needed at this level of assured activity. (Waller and Turner 1986)

For longer-term disease management, smallholders must have:

> hydraulic knapsack sprayers with ULV nozzles are recommended for routine activity, and should be adequate for rehabilitated coffee. Spraying should be carried out by local farmers or youth groups, initially trained and under the supervision of

> DPI and CIB staff, considerable training/ extension work will be needed. Fungicides and sprayers will need to be provided, at least initially. Suppliers of these, spraying times for different villages and other aspects, will need to be arranged and organised from local administration centres. (Waller and Turner 1986)

For the CIA, the implications of these logistics requirements led to one inescapable conclusion: that a Coffee Development Authority (CDA) be established as a separate organisation established along similar lines as the Coffee Research Institute. (McConaghy, Letter to CIB, June 30 1986)

Those opposed to the CDA also began to firm up their position through June. The overwhelming technical evidence of the spread of coffee rust made it senseless to oppose spraying *per se*, as the Okuk telex hinted. However, the big peasants could not see why the need to spray coffee rust caused the industry to be turned upside down. At a specialist meeting of the Highlands Regional Premiers' Council in early June it was resolved to:

> (a) Support the Coffee Industry Board's decision to levy 10 toea per kilo of coffee exported.
>
> (b) Disagree, however, with the Coffee Industry Association's proposal to set up another organisation to manage the funds collected from the levy.

The premiers believed instead that the levy fund collected should be managed through the existing system. (Kapal to Mitio, June 3, 1986) The big peasant fear that rust control might develop into political and economic control was not unreasonable, given the history of the industry. This fear was not offset by the many reports from *didimen*, coffee rust survey teams and disaster assistance teams, which continually attempted to widen the agenda by justifying bans on cherry in broad terms such as 'stopping children and other people from stealing cherry' or 'encouraging families to co-operate with each other' and 'educating the people to sell their parchment through central selling areas'.

July 1986

The historical pattern of development in the coffee industry of Papua New Guinea as presented in this book has been of élite exploitation of smallholders through the exercise of market power, either with the connivance or indifference of the authorities. In July 1986 this same pattern began to appear with respect to the coffee rust problem. The alliance of technocrats in the CIB, and the powerful exporters and plantation owners in the CIA, overwhelmed big peasant and smallholder interests. DPI played its customary role of bowing to powerful interests on the one hand and appearing irrelevant on the other. The alliance in favour of the CDA was able to bring Prime Minister Wingti on side by a combination of superb political timing and the threat of loss of political support if he was seen to be opposed to the coffee industry. Iambakey Okuk was silent throughout the month, losing precious time to influence the agenda.

Any proposal to establish a Coffee Development Authority (CDA) was obliged to demonstrate that a new institution was necessary and show how it should function. One could not, however, expect interested parties to explain how such proposals would affect the distribution of power in the industry. It is possible to examine proposals for the structuring and funding of the CDA and assess who would be advantaged and disadvantaged by the proposed institution.

The Belfield Report, released on July 30, and commissioned by the CIB as its blueprint, contains proposals which are very political, which clearly display a desire to discipline and exploit the smallholder. It is a measure of the one-sidedness of the industry's politics that such a crude power grab as presented in this Report could be sponsored by a responsible agency like the CIB. Belfield was later chosen to form the CDA's interim management board. But first, an examination of the background to the Report will put is findings into perspective.

Early interventions with proposals for the CDA came not from the CIB but from various DPI coffee officers. Joe Harvey-Jones, DPI Goroka, wrote a paper entitled the 'Coffee Rust and Rehabilitation Plan'. Harvey-Jones assumed that DPI would play a major management role in the coffee rust and rehabilitation plan. He assessed the responses required, which he considered to be modest, and discussed how resources might be deployed. A principal feature of his proposal was that village communities should liaise as a group with specialist officers, that these village clusters organise 'sweat equity'; and communal pressure to have growers undertake rehabilitation. Village clusters would pay for the service by depositing a 'bond' for the whole village and would discipline miscreants or non-co-operators through the village system. These proposals are 'classic' DPI strategy based on paternalistic assumptions about village togetherness and a fear of disrupting traditional rural life. Harvey-Jones hoped that the village clusters might emerge into group activities for a range of coffee growing tasks, such as village nurseries and even provision of 'wet' processing plants. John Wilkinson, another former DPI officer, also wrote a report placing DPI at the centre of management, although his proposal recognised the need for an overarching authority to direct these DDOs (dedicated DPI officers). These proposals, which put DPI and the village community at the centre of rust and rehabilitation control, were not acceptable to the technocrats and the CIA. As Craig McConaghy wrote on July 10:

> As the coffee rust cess is growers' money and has a potential of raising between K4-5 million p.a. (subject to seasonal fluctuations and possible production losses

as a result of rust destruction) the Coffee Industry Board *must* play the major role in management of these funds.

The coffee industry met with the Prime Minister, Paias Wingti in Goroka on July 16, 1986. The agenda reflected the alliance of interests now favouring a CDA. That old 'Uncle Tom' Sinake Gire Gire spoke for the 'smallholders'. Hagon and McConaghy outlined well-worked-out plans. Most submissions to the meeting supported their views. Hagon proposed that the Coffee Development Authority be completely independent of government - - not a quango, and that it be run on private enterprise lines with a board of 8 made up of 3 CIA, 2 DPI, 2 CIB and 1 CRI. There were still many details to be worked out but clearly those present were satisfied with the Prime Minister's 'positive' approach. McConaghy wrote a letter thanking the Prime Minister for 'giving the go-ahead to form a specialist coffee unit within the Coffee Industry Board'. (McConaghy, July 18, 1986) Obviously, he felt that government approval was a mere formality at this stage. This perception seemed to be reinforced by a report from National DPI economist Paul Baker who, perhaps sensing which way the wind was blowing, reported in favour of 'industry' ideas but failed to mention DPI proposals of communal organisation and DPI management.

Barker's intervention was crucial because DPI, was at this stage the only agency that had the information to challenge the CIB/CIA proposal. Wingti was persuaded by the unanimity demonstrated at the July 16 meeting, but did he really have any idea of what the CIB/CIA had in mind for the industry? Between the meeting with the Prime Minister and the handing down of the Belfield Report, the cynical observer could have picked up some disturbing signs of what was in store for the smallholder if the CIB/CIA were allowed to restructure the industry. In particular, some of the costing implications now began to be discussed. Hagon said at a meeting on July 22 in Banz that the CDA should receive funds direct 'and not through any other statutory body or Government agency'. Despite the brave talk of the CIA of 'no say, no pay', it became clear that the government was expected to pay the salaries of seconded DPI officers, not the CDA. Hagon dropped a bombshell on the July 22: 'Any plantation wishing to carry out its own [spraying] should get a rebate minus the administrative facilities of the controlling authority'. In effect, this opened up the possibility that the government might subsidise plantation spraying. Naturally, this would not apply to smallholders, who were expected to pay for their own chemicals and use 'sweat equity' to do the spraying. However, but it was still not clear how they would be 'encouraged' to spray if they did not choose to.

A DPI document on July 25 by Paul Sai'l, Secretary for Primary Industry, showed that at this stage, not only had the DPI lined up on the CIB/CIA side and were assuming that the CDA would go ahead, but also that DPI was taking the rapacious demands of the CIB/CIA into the inner organs of executive government. Sai'l's document stated that the National Department of Primary Industry would have to contribute K12.7 million over 1987–90 to the CDA, the CIB would provide K22.5 million over 1987–90, and the Highlands 'coffee' provinces would have to contribute over 30 seconded staff and 3–4 vehicles each.

But it was the Belfield Report of July 30 which showed how far the CIB/CIA planned to go in order to realise the historic mission of the technocrats and white planter/*petit bourgeoisie* to discipline and control Papua New Guinea's smallholders. Despite the fact that coffee rust had been in the country for over a year before it was reported and despite the agronomic evidence that it would spread slowly through the dispersed, heavily shaded gardens of the smallholder, Belfield provided a blueprint for CDA control of every garden coffee plot in Papua New Guinea. It was the most audacious proposal yet to control the smallholder grower.

Belfield (1986) was asked to report on the proposal to establish a CDA and, in this sense, his report goes far beyond the agronomic detail provided by Waller and Turner. In fact, the Belfield Report is a political document. He accepted, without challenge, the previously stated views of Hagon and McConaghy from the CIA, quoting 'industry people' who 'have emphasised that [these] resources be under the exclusive control of the Coffee Development Authority and that this authority be non-government and fully autonomous'. (Belfield 1986:2.2) He repeated the claim that 'as the Coffee Rehabilitation and Rust Control Program is financed mainly by the coffee growers, it is logical that their representatives have control over the Board of the Coffee Development Authority'. (Belfield 1986:2.6) Clearly, he had no qualms about the use of the undifferentiated term 'grower'. He made explicit what had been clouded before: that the CIA aimed to run the CDA.

Belfield assumed that the CDA's activities would be directed at smallholders and did not even bother to justify this assumption. By July, it was widely agreed that the coffee rust problem was principally one of finding a means whereby smallholders would be forced to cut out and burn infected coffee, undertake curative spraying and engage in a process of rehabilitation. Belfield noted that new legislation would be needed to police and carry out these activities. (Belfield 1986:3.3) He did not shirk from the implications of his position, but wrote that 'DPI Minister should change the Coffee Act to give the CDA the right to register and control smallholder coffee plots'. (Belfield 1986:3.6)

For Belfield, the organisation of the CDA was a comparatively simple matter. The CIA should run it and it should be completely autonomous. The provincial governments would not be allowed to handle funds (3.5) and the national government should keep its hands off (3.20), despite the recognition that both levels of government would continue to provide financial and resource assistance.

Belfield, whose list of 73 people interviewed contains only 3 listed as 'smallholders', nevertheless focused all his important recommendations on the reorganisation of the smallholder sector. Special legislation would 'be aimed specifically at the coffee plots' (3.22). The smallholder must pay for the chemical and man the spray 'so that he is fully involved' (3.22). Belfield entertained no wimpish ideas about communal bonds or village organisation. If the smallholder did not pay, let the full power of the state descend on him or her! As is common in the most coercive regimes in Africa, he wanted the state to cut out and burn out gardens where growers would not co-operate, such gardens would be 'declared noxious' (3.22). Belfield envisaged the CDA as teams, with the local Kopi Garden bosses acting as policemen over garden coffee, registering plots and monitoring growers.

Belfield knew he was in a political situation, for he mentioned a number of times that politicians might interfere with the CDA in the run-up to the 1987 election. He also noted Western Highlands provincial government opposition -- because intellectuals and politicians were channelling coffee money away from the province (4.19) -- and was afraid that national, local and field level interference might occur to upset the CDA chain of command. But he seemed to consider all these problems as simply the irascibility and mischief-making of individuals like Okuk. This was also the CIA's analysis. Belfield did not look at the broader political implications of what he was recommending or, if he did, he did so with the contemptuous attitude of the *kiap* who believed he knew what was best for ignorant people.

The Belfield Report release was timed for the July 30, the day before the self-appointed interim steering committee of the CDA met and agreed in principle to the CDA concept. There was, however, still a lot of political water to go under the bridge before the necessary legislation would be passed.

August and September 1986

Those who favoured the CDA had been playing a gigantic game of bluff for some time. They bluffed their way through the July 31 meeting. Hagon said in a letter to Barker, National DPI, 'that we were lucky on Thursday with the meeting in getting general endorsement for the establishment of the CDA'. (Hagon to Barker, August 4, 1986) They were also bluffing when they pretended that 'government approval' had been given in principal to the establishment of the CDA on July 16, when they had met the Prime Minister. They were bluffing because they knew very well that Okuk and the Highlands Premiers did not agree. They were bluffing when they proposed three CIA members should be on the executive board, but most of all they were bluffing when they asserted that smallholders needed to be strictly controlled.

Iambakey Okuk was also playing a similar game. Instead of attacking the CDA directly, he switched to the offensive in another area, calling for a re-evaluation of export quotas. This could have been a good strategy, but it frightened his own supporters as much as it did his opponents, giving substance to the analysis that Okuk's position was meandering rather than thought-out. It was not Okuk but the Highlands Premiers, however, who stood firmly opposed to the CIB/CIA proposals. Without them the CDA would not become operational, so that most of August and September were spent trying to persuade them to accept Belfield's report.

Okuk began August by trying to neutralise Hagon, threatening to withdraw the export licence of Wahgi Mek Plantation Pty Ltd. Hagon mobilised support, claiming that Wahgi Mek would be finished unless its export status was clarified. Okuk's arbitrary action alienated the CIB and other exporters, but more importantly enraged *petty bourgeois* interests. No one wanted a Minister who could change the existing rules with a telex. Auwo Ketauwo of Gouna was enraged, claiming Okuk must be stopped before 'he betrays PNG's "lifeline", the coffee industry for good'. (Ketauwo, Press Statement, u.d.) Okuk, none too subtly, replied that he did not support 'certain ambitious elements' among local growers in Eastern Highlands. He directed them to: "look after Papua New Guinea growers' interests and prevent the opportunists who are again trying to use our own people for their own interests and ends." (Okuk, Telex to Premier, Eastern Highlands August 6, 1986)

Meanwhile, Hagon had enlisted the support of Paul Barker, National DPI, to draft a Memoranda of Understanding (MOU) for the CDA, to be presented to the Highlands Premiers' Council on August 9. The scheduled meeting did not eventuate. Informal discussions were held, however, and the CIA was convinced that James Yanepa, Eastern Highlands Premier, appeared in favour of the CDA concept. The CIA tried to believe that the premiers were men of good sense who would support the concept, but who were afraid to cross Okuk, who had a stranglehold over other powerful men, such as the Highlands premiers.

On July 16, the Prime Minister was asked questions in Parliament about the coffee rehabilitation and rust control programme, but at no stage was the term CDA mentioned. Wingti's reply demonstrated just how extensive the CIB/CIA bluff had been up until this point. He did not openly endorse the establishment of a special authority, nor did he openly criticise the Highlands Premiers, although he did damn some of their staff: [who] 'just drive around and say they are using it [the vehicle] to control coffee rust' (*Hansard*, Fourth day, August 15 1986:6) Wingti, however, left much of the decision-making in the hands of the responsible Minister, Okuk and the premiers.

Conclusion

All attempts to shift the Highlands premiers failed through August and September. Neither CIB heavyweights visiting Port Moresby, Hagon's threats, nor Highlands premiers' briefing meetings had any effect. The premiers were not about to see their resources diverted for the benefit of the private coffee industry, and in this stubbornness they proved the unexpected ally of the smallholder. Iambakey Okuk died tragically in September. He had been making continuous announcements in that month to the effect that the CDA concept would be scrapped. No doubt those who favoured the CDA had hoped the opposition to it would die with him.

However, and as always, they underestimated the breadth of the social forces they had unleashed with their sweeping CDA proposal to restructure the industry. The premiers eventually agreed to the establishment of a CDA in November 1986, although they demanded significant changes to its charter, particularly on the executive board, where five provincial secretaries would take their place with one from DPI, one from CRI, one from CIB and one from CIA. For the CIA, the establishment of the CDA was a pyrrhic victory, though the organisation had been 'blooded', and would be more powerful in future. Its future, if successful, had the potential to cause significant alteration to the coffee industry. The CDA may well be the mechanism to allow the powerful to discipline and control the smallholders through coercion rather than through the market, as historically has been the case.

Notes

1. Some idea of the scale of the potential increase in coffee acreage which the 20-hectare plantation development represented can be gained from figures provided by Densley, which show there were approximately 32,000 hectares nationally under coffee in both Highlands Arabica and coastal Robusta coffee. If the 94 projected 20-hectare intermediate plantations in the Eastern Highlands went ahead then this would have added about 6 percent to the stock of national coffee land from this one province alone. The share of increased acreage under coffee which 20-hectares would provide, again from this one province, can be judged from the fact that in 1978 Chan anticipated an increase of 2,900 hectares nationally for 'intermediate' coffee plantations out of a total national increase of coffee acreage of 13,500 hectares for all production units in Eastern Highlands Province. (Ameri 1982) By 1982, if the 74 blocks in Eastern Highlands went ahead, the increase in area under coffee (some 1,480 hectares) would have exceeded the Eastern Highlands target for intermediate plantations in its first years of operation. The national government's coffee policy guidelines of 1978 also targeted a coffee production figure of 60,000 tonnes by 1986. (Wheeler 1979) This was an increase of some 10,200 tonnes over the 1976–77 export figure from PNG (almost all PNG coffee is exported) of 49,798 tonnes. (Densley n.d.: 26) If by 1986 the

74 'intermediate holdings in the Eastern Highlands were producing at maximum plantation yield, they have would produced 2,960 tonnes, 30 percent the targeted national increase in coffee production -- from this one province.

2. A business group is a corporate-like entity which can sue and be sued, buy and sell, etc. but with the difference that the internal functioning of such a group is based on the customary law of its members. (Independent State of Papua New Guinea, Chapter No. 133. Business Groups Incorporation Act)

3. From July 1967 to December 1977, 130 Loans were approved for coffee development, a total of K1,138,600. By 1980, however, 76 loans had been approved for coffee development (almost half the number in one year of the previous ten-year total) worth K3,398,600 (almost three times the ten-year total of loans given to the industry in one year). (Papua New Guinea Development Bank, *Annual Reports and Financial Statements*.)

4. Wheeler's budget does establish that 20-hectare projects will be profitable but this is not enough to make the projects attractive to commercial banks. Commercial banks assess projects not only in terms of their profitability but also in terms of the length of time it takes to recoup capital outlay. Ian Afflick noted that commercial bank lending to 20-hectare projects is untenable because: "of the obvious risks involved [and] . . . because the time for getting the banks' money back is so long it reduces our cash flow from which we are obliged to lend." (Afflick in M.A.H.B. Walter, 'What do we do about plantations?' 1981: 89) But for the PNGDB, whose cash flow is assured by international agencies, this is not such a problem.

5. Fertiliser is required as soon as coffee is planted, in year 2, at a cost of K3,640 which averages out to K6,760 by year 8. Seedlings are also a cost to the project in the establishment phase though Wheeler assumed these would be provided free by the CIB-funded nurseries at the government research station at Aiyura or that nurseries would be established on the projects themselves for the provisions of seedlings. Wheeler costed seedlings at 5 toea each in the event that they had to be purchased. Fertiliser application rates are based upon Aiyura recommendations:

Year 2 - 0.7 tonne per hectare
Year 3 - 0.8 tonne per hectare
Year 4 - 1.1 tonne per hectare
Year 5 and thereafter - 1.3 tonne per hectare.

6. Briefly, the background to the sectoral funds programme is that large amounts of money (total for 1980 was K10 million and for 1981 almost K13 million) where to be allocated through a formula designed and to be implemented by the NPO (National Planning Office). The money was intended to be used to redress the inequalities between provinces on national functions such as education, agriculture and transport.

Behind the design of the sectoral programmes was the realisation in Port Moresby that new and poor provinces were not able to put together adequate submissions for funds allocated through the NPEP process and hence were failing to compete for funds with the rich provinces and the national departments. Rather than change the rules of the NPEP, the NPO designed the sectoral programme. The sectoral funds in transport and agriculture were redirected however by the Deputy Prime Minister, Mr Okuk, who, contrary to the plans of the NPO, gained Cabinet approval for the funds to be disbursed personally through the offices of national parliamentarians.

7. Indeed, it is very difficult to work out from the Arusafa budget how the project will ever pay out its loan. My calculations show the following:

	Arusafa (ANGCO–managed) (on production figures)	
Year (calculated at K1,350 per tonne green bean equivalent)	Income	Costs
1	–	31,433
2	4,860	26,806
3	24,705	38,149
4	61,695	49,776
5	61,695	62,165
6	61,695	61,885
7	61,695	65,996
8	61,965	66,000

8. 'It is Development Bank policy not to give money back to the clansmen. The Bank is not keen to let money go back to the people. If they want more money then the Agency and the Bank will say no.' (Keith Schirmer, Interview 8 June 1982)

11

The International Coffee Agreement

Introduction

In the next three chapters, I focus on the international distribution of power in the world coffee industry. The main question here is how power is distributed. Does this distribution favour or disadvantage small coffee-producing countries such as Papua New Guinea? To answer this question we must direct our focus to a study of the International Coffee Agreement (ICA), the world's longest surviving commodity agreement. The aim of the ICA is to regulate the world's second largest trade commodity, coffee, a task it has been undertaking since 1962, on and off, in an agreement that, on the face of it, appears spectacularly successful. But how does the ICA work and who really benefits from its operation? In this chapter, we examine the economists' explanation for the existence and survival of the ICA. They argue that commodity agreements are cartels established by producers for their benefit. This analysis, the dominant one in the industry, predicts that commodity agreements will be unstable because there is an incentive for producers to go it alone, but that they will favour all producers ahead of consumers while they are in operation. Contrary to this analysis, the ICA has survived and, as will be shown below, may have benefited big consumers ahead of small coffee-producing countries like Papua New Guinea.

This chapter aims to explain why economists are wrong in the case of coffee, and proposes an alternative explanation for the operation of the ICA. This is based on the simple observation that taste is important in world trade for coffee. The taste factor makes coffee unusual as a trade commodity, because one variety of coffee is not easily substitutable for another. Thus, unlike many primary commodities, the importance of taste and consumer reluctance to experiment with different tastes create quite inflexible import/export relations in world coffee trade. International regulation of coffee through the International Coffee Organisation (ICO) not only complements but reinforces the already tightly structured circulation of coffee. This is achieved, it is argued, by the informal establishment under the ICA of sets of bilateral alliances made up of importers and exporters. These alliances can be ranked hierarchically according to the magnitude of world coffee which they control. The influence of the big importer/big exporter alliance of the United States and Brazil is greater in the ICO than lesser strata such as European importers and African exporters of Robusta coffee.

World Coffee and the International Coffee Agreement

Coffee has always been dependent on world trade for a market, and over the years certain countries have come to dominate this. The largest market for any type of coffee - - green bean or soluble (instant) - - is in the United States. In 1979–80, with total world imports of green bean at 60.9 million bags ('bag' = 60 kilograms or 132.276 pounds of green coffee), the United States imported 20.1 million bags, with West Germany next at 7.9 million and France following with 5.6 million bags (Table 11.1).

The United States was also the largest importer of soluble coffee. In 1976, for example, it imported 1.5 million bags (green bean equivalent), followed by Britain's 698,000 bags, out of a world export total of 4.5 million bags in 1976. In the United States alone it was estimated in 1973 that coffee trade (dealing) and production (roasting and instant coffee manufacture) are worth $2 billion and provide some 200,000 people with employment (Galloway 1973:355). Just as world trade in coffee imports is dominated by the United States, so world trade in coffee exports is dominated by Brazil and Colombia (Table 11.2).

Table 11.3 shows that Brazil and Colombia are the world's principal exporters, not only because they are the world's largest producers, but also because they dominate supply to the United States market. Together, Brazil and Colombia provide 38% of coffee imported into the United States. Indonesia, Mexico and El Salvador follow, each with a 7% share of the United States market.

Coffee, then, is a commodity whose circulation in the world economy affects the lives of a great many people in both developed countries (DCs) and less developed ones (LDCs). Almost since its inception, however, the world coffee industry has been prone to the most severe fluctuations of price and supply. In recent decades, supply and demand have been so out of phase as to cause at least three great crises in the world coffee market. In the 1930s, a combination of bumper crops and world Depression resulted in huge supplies on the market, with a corresponding fall in prices. In the early 1950s,

TABLE 11.1 Imports By Importing Members From All Sources, September-October 1975–76 to 1979–80 (000 bags)

Importing Member	1976–76	1976–77	1977–78	1978–79	1979–80
Total	60,321	54,502	49,876	63,906	60,808
U.S.A.	21,833	18,400	17,228	21,890	20,128
E.E.C.	24,125	22,444	21,495	26,664	25,417
Belgium/Luxembourg	1,472	1,396	1,317	1,739	1,663
Denmark	1,119	974	869	1,029	1,038
France	5,438	5,029	5,064	5,885	5,626
Germany, F.R. of	6,620	6,754	6,560	7,960	7,994
Greece	343	268	259	382	372
Ireland	63	46	42	68	61
Italy	3,528	3,256	3,116	3,668	3,794
Netherlands	2,984	2,538	2,489	2,938	2,585
United Kingdom	2,558	2,183	1,779	2,995	2,284
Other Members	**14,363**	**13,658**	**11,153**	**15,352**	**15,263**
Australia	504	533	371	582	640
Austria	645	580	560	721	845
Canada	1,746	1,492	1,581	1,863	1,685
Cyprus	24	29	23	35	28
Finland	1,135	974	743	1,121	1,195
Hong Kong	197	313	48	73	122
Hungary	625	658	455	507	634
Israel	288	179	175	205	168
Japan	2,678	2,765	1,497	3,266	3,231
New Zealand	91	79	79	101	134
Norway	734	585	582	715	678
Portugal	328	240	142	203	193
Singapore	378	393	588	477	426
Spain	1,518	1,454	1,414	1,855	1,707
Sweden	2,004	1,487	1,382	1,687	1,734
Switzerland	998	1,019	812	1,009	1,037
Yugoslavia	470	878	701	932	806
Green	55,288	49,196	45,764	57,414	55,057
(Processed)	(5,033)	(5,306)	(4,112)	(6,492)	(5,751)
Roasted	1,080	1,226	1,133	1,422	1,352
Soluble	3,917	4,029	2,905	4,951	4,300
From					
- Exporting Members	56,163	50,588	46,687	59,647	56,732
- Importing Members	3,567	3,504	2,788	3,883	3,741
- Non-members	552	396	388	353	316
- Unspecified Origins and Designated Territories	39	14	13	23	19

Source: Mwandha, Nicholls and Sargent (1985). *Estimated.

TABLE 11.2 Estimated Exportable Production October–September 1975–76 to 1981–82

Exporting Member	(000 Bags)						
	75–76	*76–77*	*77–78*	*78–79*	*79–80*	*80–81*	*81–82*
Total	**47,391**	**46,502**	**54,571**	**62,964**	**58,703**	**70,434**	**72,692**
A. Sub-total: Members entitled to a Basic Quota	**45,247**	**44,405**	**52,447**	**60,586**	**56,335**	**67,707**	**69,497**
Colombian Milds	**9,458**	**10,596**	**11,774**	**13,081**	**12,805**	**14,275**	**14,816**
Colombia	7,335	8,134	9,643	11,062	10,431	11,590	12,150
Kenya	1,204	1,679	1,313	1,192	1,601	1,647	1,643
Tanzania	919	783	818	827	773	1,038	1,023
Other Milds	**12,632**	**12,897**	**15,324**	**16,862**	**15,802**	**16,866**	**17,754**
Costa Rica	1,104	1,156	1,303	1,566	1,229	1,936	1,669
Dominican Republic	748	482	755	462	676	746	600
Ecuador	1,519	1,137	1,596	1,370	1,177	1,383	1,416
El Salvador	1,614	2,445	2,675	3,228	2,832	2,976	2,700
Guatemala	1,761	2,170	2,263	2,501	2,175	2,412	2,453
Honduras	543	576	931	1,024	1,020	1,120	1,264
India	760	1,004	1,295	1,022	1,684	1,115	1,800
Mexico	2,514	1,734	2,019	2,966	2,304	2,370	2,600
Nicaragua	714	774	881	897	936	833	1,170
Papua New Guinea	675	699	760	808	835	887	982
Peru	680	720	846	1,018	934	1,088	1,100
Unwashed Arabicas	**9,104**	**5,856**	**12,968**	**15,941**	**13,783**	**18,937**	**17,833**
Brazil	7,826	4,507	11,633	14,474	12,230	17,233	16,000
Ethiopia	1,278	1,349	1,335	1,467	1,553	1,704	1,833
Robustas	**14,053**	**15,056**	**12,381**	**14,702**	**13,945**	**17,629**	**19,094**
Angola	1,029	930	926	548	264	696	451
Indonesia	2,037	2,505	3,430	3,653	3,757	4,210	4,112
OAMCAF	(7,734)	(7,592)	(5,392)	(7,658)	(6,934)	(9,521)	(9,916)
Benin	18	16	2	2	1	3	48
Cameroon	1,455	1,281	1,344	1,604	1,624	1,930	2,250
Central African Republic	140	155	153	88	185	196	225
Congo	28	36	60	90	40	41	61
Gabon	3	4	2	5	9	13	12
Ivory Coast	5,107	4,782	3,087	4,677	3,908	5,958	5,783
Madagascar	833	1,142	663	1,088	996	1,203	1,302
Togo	150	176	81	104	171	177	217
Uganda	2,288	2,630	1,799	1,814	1,912	1,850	3,265
Zaire	965	1,399	834	1,029	1,078	1,352	1,350

continued

TABLE 11.2 *(continued)*

Exporting Member	*(000 Bags)*						
	75–76	*76–77*	*77–78*	*78–79*	*79–80*	*80–81*	*81–82*
B. Sub-total: Members exempt from basic quotas	**2,144**	**2,097**	**2,124**	**2,378**	**2,368**	**2,727**	**3,195**
Arabicas	**1,653**	**1,427**	**1,533**	**1,533**	**1,581**	**1,648**	**2,021**
Bolivia	74	114	60	111	101	139	144
Burundi	323	320	339	453	345	590	471
Haiti	364	264	317	236	412	245	367
Jamaica	22	15	14	14	17	13	16
Malawi	2	3	3	4	6	7	9
Panama	3	13	60	35	50	80	76
Paraguay	88	25	71	80	29	140	246
Rwanda	507	401	320	452	494	498	489
Venezuela	222	189	271	75	59	114	110
Zimbabwe	48	83	78	73	68	86	93
Robustas	**491**	**670**	**591**	**845**	**787**	**1,043**	**1,174**
Ghana	41	55	22	9	38	26	42
Guinea	17	33	10	54	28	55	100
Liberia	62	156	146	157	150	150	175
Nigeria	109	31	37	31	12	0	40
Philippines	172	196	225	268	325	502	463
Sierra Leone	52	144	100	221	169	155	178
Sri Lanka	–	–	–	–	–	8	50
Trinidad and Tobago	38	44	29	37	25	35	19
SUMMARY							
Total	**47,391**	**46,502**	**54,571**	**62,964**	**58,703**	**70,434**	**72,692**
Members Entitled to a Basic Quota	45,247	44,405	52,447	60,586	56,335	67,707	69,497
Members Exempt from Basic Quotas	2,144	2,097	2,124	2,378	2,368	2,727	3,195
Brazil	7,826	4,507	11,633	14,474	12,230	17,230	16,000
Colombia	7,335	8,134	9,643	11,062	10,431	11,590	12,150
OAMCAF	7,734	7,592	5,392	7,658	6,934	9,521	9,916
Other Arabicas	17,686	18,135	20,323	21,881	21,310	22,939	24,274
Other Robustas	6,810	8,134	7,580	7,889	7,798	9,151	10,352
Brazil	7,862	4,507	11,633	14,474	12,230	17,233	16,000
Others	39,565	41,995	42,938	48,490	46,473	53,201	56,692
Arabicas	32,847	30,776	41,559	47,417	43,971	51,762	52,424
Robustas	14,544	15,726	12,972	15,547	14,732	18,672	20,268

Source: Mwandha, Nicholls and Sargent (1985)

TABLE 11.3 Shares of United States Green Bean Imports, 1977–80 (Column Percentages)

Source	*Calendar Year* 1977	1978	1979	1980
Brazil	16.6	14.9	9.8	19.3
Colombia	13.2	15.5	20.1	18.8
Indonesia	5.8	6.5	6.6	7.2
Mexico	9.5	7.7	10.1	7.4
Uganda	6.5	2.4	1.9	3.5
El Salvador	7.0	3.5	5.8	7.6
Ecuador	3.4	5.8	3.3	3.0
Guatemala	5.6	5.2	6.5	5.1
Ethiopia	1.9	2.5	2.8	2.2
Peru	3.1	3.6	4.9	3.1
Ivory Coast	4.5	4.3	4.3	2.4
India	1.1	1.5	1.5	1.2
Dominican Republic	3.9	2.5	2.8	1.9
Honduras	1.5	3.0	2.8	1.8
Philippine Republic	–	0.3	0.5	1.0
Rwanda	0.8	1.2	0.9	1.6
Madagascar	1.4	2.2	1.4	1.7
Cameroon	0.7	1.2	0.9	1.1
Zaire	2.0	3.3	0.4	0.8
Costa Rica	1.8	1.8	2.7	1.6
Burundi	0.8	1.0	1.0	1.0
Paraguay	0.1	1.1	3.9	1.0
Nicaragua	0.8	0.8	1.0	0.8
West Germany	–	–	–	0.9
Haiti	0.6	0.3	0.1	0.3
Liberia	0.4	0.3	0.2	0.3
Venezuela	1.0	1.3	0.6	0.2
Angola	1.4	2.2	0.2	0.7
Tanzania	1.5	1.8	0.9	0.3
Sub-total	96.9	97.7	97.9	97.8
Others	3.1	2.3	2.1	2.2
Total	100.0	100.0	100.0	100.0

Source: Mwandha, Nicholls and Sargent (1985).

world coffee prices were high as coffee shortages and supply problems were affected by the Korean War, but by 1957–58, new areas of coffee were producing and thus large amounts of it were coming onto the world market. This caused a fall in world prices to the pre–1954 level and the industry again faced a crisis. In 1962, the International Coffee Organisation (ICO) was set up to manage world supply and demand through a system of export quotas, and for nine years, price and supply stability were maintained. However, towards the end of the 1960s, problems of overproduction again occurred, leading producer nations to attempt to restrict supply outside the International Coffee Agreement (ICA). The agreement collapsed, the producers failed to control supply, and by 1972 the world coffee industry was again facing a crisis of overproduction. In 1975, the Black Frost of Brazil wiped out one–third of the world coffee crop. As a result coffee was in short supply for most of the late 1970s. Exceedingly high prices resulted, such that by 1977 world coffee prices were six times what they had been four years earlier. A new ICA was negotiated in 1976, but it came into effect only in 1982 when the old problem of overproduction was again beginning to affect the international market. The dominant trend in supply and demand throughout the century has been that of overproduction, with supply far exceeding world demand. Certainly in 1962, when the ICA was first negotiated, constant overproduction was the single most important feature of the world coffee market and the cause of the periodic crises that affected the industry.

Thus, not only are coffee export sales important as a source of export earnings to producer countries, but the form of international regulation adopted by the ICO determines the contribution that coffee makes to these export earnings. Table 11.4 demonstrates how important the basic quota in exports of coffee is to total export earnings in many small countries. In many cases, the basic quota represents more than 20% of total export earnings.

I discuss in greater detail in Chapter 12 the form of the ICA, but at this stage it is sufficient to note that there was a problem of disequilibrium (overproduction/underproduction) in the international coffee market before it came into existence; that its establishment was bound to have a marked impact on coffee producers, especially small country producers; and that the market was structured around bilateral trading relations between consumers and producers. The turning point in international coffee regulation occurred in 1962 when the United States, the world's largest importer, joined the ICA. This produced a fundamental alteration to world coffee relations, one which not only extended the scope of regulation to include almost all international coffee actors but which provided for the first time a formal political authority structure through which international coffee flows could be policed and international coffee relations managed.

TABLE 11.4 Value of Exports of Coffee by Exporting Members Entitled to a Basic Quota as a Percentage of Their Total Export Earnings, January–December, 1975–80

Exporting Member	1975	1976	1977	1978	1979	1980
Members Entitled to a Basic Quota						
Colombian Milds						
Colombia	44.9	55.6	64.6	66.3	58.1	61.9
Kenya	15.0	27.0	41.3[a]	31.5[a]	26.8[a]	21.1[a]
Tanzania	18.6	33.0	41.0	36.5	27.1[a]	26.9[a]
Other Milds						
Costa Rica	19.7	26.9	41.2	36.2	33.8[a]	24.2[a]
Dominican Republic[a]	4.8	14.1	23.7	14.3	18.2	8.0
Ecuador	7.2	18.2	13.1	18.8	13.4	5.3[a]
El Salvador[a]	35.9	54.7	63.0	51.9	63.6	53.8
Guatemala	25.6	32.0	44.6[a]	42.8[a]	34.1[a]	30.1[a]
Honduras	19.3	25.2	33.0	34.9	26.9[a]	25.3[a]
India	1.7	2.6	4.6	3.1	2.7[b]	4.0[b]
Mexico	6.6	12.4	11.5	7.3	6.1[a]	2.9[a]
Nicaragua	14.8	20.4	30.5	31.4	28.0[a]	36.8[a]
Papua New Guinea	10.0	23.0	26.6	21.4	18.1[a]	15.7[a]
Peru[a]	3.9	8.5	11.7	8.9	7.3	
Unwashed Arabicas						
Brazil	10.8	23.7	21.6	18.1	15.3	12.4[a]
Ethiopia	34.0	57.3	75.9	80.9	68.6[a]	64.1[a]
Robustas						
Angola						
Indonesia	1.4	2.8	4.9[b]	4.5[b]	4.0[b]	2.7[b]
Cameroon	23.8	24.0	31.9[a]	29.7[a]	25.3[a]	21.8[a]
Ivory Coast	25.1	34.3	37.5[a]	25.0[a]	31.1[a]	
Madagascar[a]	21.8	42.9	48.8	41.9	45.4	
Uganda	73.5	85.4	93.4	90.2	98.0[a]	98.7[a]
Zaire[a]	6.3	13.8	19.5	17.8	10.4	10.1

Note: If no source is indicated, the figures are those provided by Member.
A blank denotes that the information was not available.
- Less than 0.05
[a] International Financial Statistics of the IMF, February 1982
[b] Monthly returns and UN Statistical Yearbook, 1979/80.

Source: Mwandah, Nicholls and Sargent (1985)

Explaining the establishment of the ICA

Economists begin their investigations of the causes of disequilibrium in world coffee with the assumption that, because the type of international capital in world coffee is commercial capital, it must be price-responsive. They ask why it is that the price mechanism does not operate in the world coffee market as it is supposed to in all markets, to cause producers to stop producing when prices are very low, i.e. before the market has reached a crisis of overproduction. This is a market failure-type question which naturally generates a market failure-type answer. Bilder (1963) argues that the main reason for market failure is the coffee cycle, the coffee price or production cycle or the cobweb cycle. The coffee cycle refers to the biological lag of four to five years between planting and production. Bilder argues that the coffee cycle affects decisions about planting and uprooting which are in many ways unrelated to current price levels. Geer (1971) argues that smallholders cannot respond to international price levels because state marketing branches intervene to distort the international price. Both writers assume that smallholder producers of coffee are in a position where response to price is socially possible.

In this section I survey the market failure arguments of Bilder (1963) and Geer (1971) and show that their explanation for coffee disequilibrium is only partially correct. I argue that it must also be noted that much trade in international coffee is not responsive to price, for the international coffee trade is structured as much around taste and historical factors as it is around market ones. It is precisely these other factors, when added to the coffee cycle argument, which explain why international coffee trade with or without regulation does not function as a competitive international market.

Bilder (1963) tackles the question of disequilibrium in world coffee in the familiar way by arguing that the world coffee market is an exception due to certain inelasticities in supply and demand. Bilder regards the short-run inelasticities on the supply side as caused when circumstances such as the Korean conflict bring rapid upward movements in demand and price, but rapid adjustment to meet this demand is precluded by the fact that coffee trees cannot be brought into production for a period of several years. Conversely, if demand and price fall because of such factors as an economic recession in a principal-consuming country, producers cannot reduce production. Similarly, on the demand side, consumption of coffee is relatively stable, expanding or contracting only gradually in response to sharp changes in supply and price brought about by short-run factors such as variation in crops due to changes in weather (Bilder 1963:333). The inelasticities on the supply side that Bilder alludes to are said to be caused by the coffee cycle. Coffee cycle arguments suggest that a rise in the world coffee price:

> results in the planting of new (and possibly improved) coffee trees. However, the new trees do not mature rapidly: new plantings begin to bear in 2 to 4 years if seedlings are used, and in 4 to 5 years if plantings are from seeds. Substantial crops cannot be expected until, say, 5 to 8 years after a new plantation is

> if seedlings are used, and in 4 to 5 years if plantings are from seeds. Substantial crops cannot be expected until, say, 5 to 8 years after a new plantation is established, with yields rising a maximum after 10 to 15 years. So for at least 4 to 5 years after new planting has begun, prices are likely to continue high, thus inducing continuing new planting. Once a substantial number of young trees begin to bear fruit, supply for the market will greatly increase, and prices will begin to weaken. This discourages new planting and eventually brings it to an end. However, the market does not reach a new equilibrium there, at that point where net investment has ceased. Production goes on rising for some years as trees of a later vintage bear fruit and this forces the price down further. Unfortunately, however, this fall in price has little immediate effect in choking off supply. (Streeten and Elsen 1971:15–16)

In the long term, Bilder argues, inelasticities in supply and demand are caused by more general features. These include, on the supply side, the fact of comparative ease of entry into coffee cultivation because many areas are suited to its production and because high yield and returns possible for the successful grower per unit area of cultivation compare favourably with other tropical crops (Bilder 1963:334). On the demand side, Bilder sees long-term problems of inelasticity caused by the fact that 'consumption has grown quite slowly (about 3–3½ percent per annum) principally as a function of normal population growth and the gradual development of new markets' (Bilder 1963:334).

There are some problems with this explanation. On the demand side, evidence was building up by the late 1970s to show that consumption was perhaps more responsive to price than had first been thought. In almost all consuming countries, the consumer response to price increases was significant. In European countries the decline in consumption varied from a 5 percent fall in West European countries to a 20 percent fall in the USSR and a 30 percent fall in Portugal. In the United States, the world's largest market, due to what coffee men called the emotional response of the American housewife, consumption plummeted. Furthermore, it was apparent, even before dips in consumption caused by high prices in 1977 were known, that consumption of coffee had been declining over the long term since 1962 (Calvert 1974:18). This is not to say that consumption trends refute Bilder's argument, for there is no consensus on the significance of these trends. But they do perhaps suggest the need for modifying his assertion that consumption is not responsive to price.

On the supply side, Bilder's argument has been challenged in an important work by Geer (1971). He agrees that coffee is an exception because of the lag in the production cycle, but makes the point that this argument still depends, after the lag is taken into account, on the further condition that the market is in a state of pure competition (Geer 1971:43). Geer's starting point is that domestic markets in almost all coffee-producing nations are not, and never

> the output of domestic farmers in more or less every coffee-producing country . . . need not be a function of the world market price, but may depend on the domestic price policy of the single national marketing board, that is, the principles and methods of the single seller in deciding what output shall be produced in any one country. (Geer 1971:75)

To make this argument, Geer turns to an analysis of coffee in two areas of Brazil, Sao Paulo and Parana. Clearly if he can prove that these farmers were responding to the prices set by the Brazil marketing board, then because Brazilian coffee is so crucial to the world market, he can generalise that world production is crucially influenced by the action of Brazil's domestic marketing board.

The problem Geer has in generalising about the international impact of the internal domestic policy of one oligopolist, Brazil, is that much of Brazil's domestic production was held in stocks throughout the 1950s and 1960s, and much of it did not enter the world market at all. But Geer argues that this is precisely why overproduction at world level did occur, because Robustas, which are generally interchangeable with Brazil's, continued to be produced in order to take up the markets left vacant by Brazil's withholding of stocks. The fact that prices were low did not stop Robusta production because such production was subsidised and regulated by marketing boards in the African countries just as coffee was in Brazil (Geer 1971:135).

Geer has argued a plausible case for the fact that governmental marketing boards contribute to overproduction and that it is mainly due to these 'oligopolies' that the world price is unable to bring supply and demand into equilibrium. However, we need to be aware of the limits of his analysis. In the first place, not all coffee-producing countries have state marketing boards which set internal prices. In Papua New Guinea, for example, the coffee board is merely a regulatory one, so it could not be seen to have contributed to the fact that, at current low world prices, Papua New Guinea production continues to increase. In the second place, Geer's argument is established by way of the relatively sophisticated structure-in-production in Sao Paulo, his major case study. He does not have to enter the hidden abode of production in Sao Paulo in his analysis, for all he needs to show for the purposes of his argument is that Sao Paulo farmers actually do respond positively to changes in domestic price, but not world price, by switching to competitive crops and uprooting their coffee trees. However, it should be obvious that the mere fact that they react in this way means not only that they are wholly engaged in commodity production but also that the option of switching to a competitive cash crop is not dependent on state assistance or outlawed by the state.

Bilder's analysis, like Geer's, is also built on simplistic assumptions about the range of choice open to Third World peasants. This analysis, with its emphasis on the rationality of peasant farmers, is a great advance on the notorious backward sloping supply curve argued by some economists, (the argument that peasant producers respond irrationally to low prices by continuing to produce). But the rational peasant farmer argument fails to situate the peasant in his/her social location. The responses to price by peasant producers, as was demonstrated in Chapter 2, must be assessed in terms of the reality of the need to reproduce the household, where the cash crop is merely one aspect of a complex interdependent cycle of household production. In such circumstances alternative cash crops may not be available or viable if they displace labour from food growing activities, for example. Another important aspect of simple commodity production at household level is the dependence of the household on the state for the assistance to switch cash crops which is necessary in Papua New Guinea. Also to be considered in an analysis of the 'rational' calculations a household might make is its vulnerability to the state. The household is vulnerable not only to attempts to appropriate surplus from the peasants by state tampering with price, as Geer would argue, but it is also by a series of regulations which, in some countries such as Tanzania, restrict peasant options, including even the prohibition of uprooting coffee trees.

Both orthodox economists' and radical accounts tend to assume that the existence of commercial capital in world coffee means by definition that a pure competitive market for world coffee exists, buried beneath the mire of international coffee relations. They see their task as an archaeological one, uncovering and refurbishing the market by exposing distortions in world coffee which keep the market buried. This is essentially what Geer did in his analysis of the role state marketing boards play in distorting the world price in developing countries. The main difference between orthodox and radical accounts based on the type of international capital (commercial and therefore market structure) is that the former see the market as ultimately mutually beneficial if distortions are removed, whereas the latter see it competitive or not, as shifting the terms of trade between centre and periphery in favour of the centre.

A recent document from UNCTAD entitled *Marketing and Processing of Coffee: Areas for International Co-operation* (1983) takes the same approach. It assumes a competitive (commercial) market and proceeds by exposing the obstacles that exist for producing countries, particularly the small ones, in entering the markets of major consumer countries:

> These obstacles are duc, first, to the degree of concentration of international traders, processing companies and distribution networks and, second, to the existence of trade barriers such as tariffs, quotas, discriminatory trade controls and consumption taxes. (UNCTAD 1983:47)

The report then goes on to mention areas in which producers and importers might co-operate to reduce anti-competitive behaviour and to co-operate and share in the provision of more information about coffee flows, to reduce discrimination on freight rates, to co-operate to improve the existing capacity of stockholding facilities, to make joint requests of international financing agencies that they provide for expansion of coffee processing facilities in small countries, and so on.

The archaeological 'dig' for the market proceeds on the assumption that it is economic concentration, in the form of monopoly capital, that is causing the market to be non-competitive. Dinham and Hines (1983), for example, note that two giant transnationals (General Foods and Nestlé) dominate both trade and processing in the West, and go on to make a very convincing case that the major transnationals have made it very difficult for peripheral countries to build up their own coffee processing industry. Such analyses rest on the very real facts of market concentration in world coffee flow as noted by UNCTAD which:

> estimated that 50 per cent of international trade is traded through international trading houses. Transnational corporations account for the greatest part of the remaining 50 per cent of world coffee trade. The international trade companies are also concentrated. In the United States, some 50 per cent of coffee imports is traded by ten trading houses. In connection with the concentration of the roasting industry, it is estimated that, in the major coffee-consuming countries, the four-firm roasted coffee sales concentration ratio was between 55 and 90 per cent in the late 1970s. In the same period, and for the same group of consuming countries, the four-firm soluble coffee sales concentration ratio was between 80 and 94 per cent. In the last two decades, the food distribution industry has also become increasingly large-scale and concentrated. In the 1970s, for example, the four largest food distribution (grocery) firms' market share was in the neighbourhood of 50 per cent in the United States. It is estimated that the over-all gross margins of trading, processing and distributing companies represent approximately a quarter of the retail price of coffee. It is also estimated that approximately 50 per cent of the retail price of coffee is due to manufacturing and distribution value added. Developing countries could thus substantially increase their share of coffee retail price by processing coffee and marketing it internationally. (UNCTAD 1983:47)

Monopolies certainly exist and undoubtedly play a significant role in certain aspects of world coffee flows. However, if monopoly or market concentration is to be considered the key form international coffee capital takes, it would seem necessary to argue that large corporations can exercise their monopoly power in areas other than mere processing. In particular, monopoly power is generally taken to mean that multinational corporations can act to influence green bean prices and that they can exercise influence over where, how and in what quantities the commodity is produced. Further, it would seem logical that, if market concentration by large corporations is as significant as the aggregate figures of UNCTAD imply, then large corporations would be opposed to any interference with a market which they dominate. In other words, it would seem to follow from this analysis that large corporations with monopoly power would mobilise to oppose state intervention in the form of an international coffee agreement into the world flow of coffee.

In fact, none of these activities is engaged in by coffee transnational corporations. Far from being able to influence green bean prices, transnational coffee corporations probably suffer as badly from price fluctuations of green beans as do any other coffee actors. Transnational trading and processing companies find it necessary to stockhold in large quantities the whole range of green bean that might be required for a particular blend. This of course is due to the importance of taste in world coffee flows. The diversity of stockholdings makes it almost impossible for transnational corporations to focus their activity upon the manipulation of the price of any particular coffee variety. Should the price fall in any variety then transnational corporations stand to make large losses on their stockpiles. Their inability to control raw material price is very evident in their increasing turn to futures markets and in their general support for international regulation. Further, transnational corporations engaged in trading and processing cannot influence production decisions inside producing countries. Considering their market concentration in the importing countries, the major roasters, Nestlé, General Foods, Proctor and Gamble and Consolidated Foods, have a very low level of vertical integration. Although the situation varies from company to company, UNCTAD found '[w]ithin the roasted coffee industry the . . . industry concentration measure increased from 28 per cent in 1960 to more than 32 per cent in 1978' (UNCTAD 1983:17). Transnational corporations could of course affect production decisions in developing countries without necessarily controlling production but the peculiarities of coffee trade, which include settled trading patterns and continuous overproduction, make it unlikely that they can exercise their power to restrict purchases and hence influence production decisions made in the periphery. Finally, very few transnational corporations opposed the establishment of the ICA. This would suggest there are significant limits to the dominance of transnational coffee corporations in world coffee flows and that regulation may have offered them benefits which did not flow automatically from market concentration.

While certainly the monopoly form of international coffee capital is effective in capturing a large slice of the value added to coffee through processing, the inability of large coffee corporations to influence price and production decisions suggests monopoly capital is not the major form which international capital takes in the industry. While co-operation of the type suggested by UNCTAD is clearly desirable and while the empirically correct fact of declining coffee terms of trade as emphasised in unequal exchange theory is a cause for concern, my argument is that none of these accounts, based on the type of international capital which assume a competitive market, goes far enough.

How taste and history have been structured into the agreement to advantage big producers and big consumers

Both the orthodox economists' accounts and radical ones fail to explain the success of international regulation in coffee because they do not focus on what is distinctive about coffee itself, namely that it is not an undifferentiated commodity in world trade, that it circulates according to taste and a history of preferred blends and taste preferences. The main commodity that circulates in international coffee trade is the green bean. There are four different varieties of this. It can be blended with different beans to produce an immense array of different tasting formulae and it can be processed in one of two main ways, into roasted or soluble coffee for consumption. The green bean which circulates in international trade is thus not an undifferentiated commodity. There are the milds or washed Arabicas which are either Colombian Milds (from Colombia, Kenya and Tanzania) or Other Milds (from other South American countries, Caribbean and Papua New Guinea). There are also the unwashed Arabicas which are mainly from Brazil and the Robustas which are grown mainly in Africa.

The difference between the unwashed Arabicas, principally from Brazil, and the washed Arabicas is in the manner of processing. In Brazil, ripe coffee cherries are initially processed to the parchment stage by spreading them in the sun so the outer flesh is dried to a crisp husk. This contrasts with the manner of processing almost everywhere else, as with the washed Arabicas, which is processed by pulping and fermenting the cherry in vats of water so that the bulk of the outer flesh is removed before the beans are spread in the sun to dry to reach the parchment stage. Each method of processing the ripe cherry results in dried coffee beans that ultimately produce coffee beverages of different qualities. Brazilian beans processed in this way generally produce a bean which is neutral in taste and is used as the base bean when various other types are being blended. Brazils are used in both roasted and soluble coffee (Stuckart 1977:571). Brazil is thus important in the world coffee industry, not only because it is the world's biggest producer, but also because its beans can be used in most blends. The fact that Brazils are neutral in taste also means they have traditionally been lower priced than the fuller flavours of the Milds, especially of the rich Colombian Milds.

Robustas, on the other hand, are grown from a different variety of coffee trees from Milds and Brazils. Robusta is a much more vigorous tree which can grow in tropical areas of Africa, as opposed to the sub-tropical conditions that suit the Arabica variety. Robusta coffee trees bear more heavily than Arabica though their bean has a much higher acid content, creating their typical bitter taste (Geer 1971:49). Robustas have traditionally been the cheapest of the world's coffees.

Thus green beans are in demand for reasons other than price. In particular, different varieties of green bean are in demand for taste reasons. These taste patterns may well have been established as a result of political rather than trading relations between coffee-producing and coffee-importing countries. It is a well known fact that consumers in the United States and several western European countries regard the mild flavour attributed to blends containing Milds as superior to the blends of bitter taste in their choice of roasted (not soluble) coffee. In southern and northern Europe, however, consumers prefer the stronger taste of the more bitter types of coffee. The establishment of such contrary tastes might seem to suggest fairly distinctive trading patterns with Robustas going mainly to Europe and Arabicas going mainly to the United States. This is generally the case. Brazils have found their biggest market to be in the United States (Haarer 1962:457), the world's largest consumer, because traditionally American consumers have favoured the less distinctive, mass-produced blends. This trade relationship has been the principal one influencing prices of coffee in world markets and it is the dominant one in trade in Arabicas. The New York Coffee and Sugar Exchange continues to be the focal point in Arabica coffee trading. Robustas from Africa, on the other hand, are traded through the London terminal market for European consumption (Munnull and Densley n.d.:15).

Most Brazils still go to the United States, most Robustas to Europe and a large proportion of Papua New Guinea coffee to Australia, but the taste factor creates even more complex and more rigid patterns of trade than sketched so far. This complexity stems from the simple reason that very few coffees have a suitable taste, or indeed are cheap enough, to be drunk by themselves:

> here lies the reason for blending which seeks to create, by blending various coffees, a single one with a combination of delightful traits -- a balanced composition of the best attributes of each. With the changing components which are the beans, the blender must maintain a standard of quality and consistency. Here lies the art of blending, for it is an art as much in the mass market as is the specialist trade, and the results are a closely guarded secret. Seven or eight coffees with complementary characteristics are generally chosen. Acidy, syrupy, and neutral varieties are combined in such a way that flavour, aroma, appearance and price are properly related to produce a smooth drink combining all the better qualities. (Roden 1977:53)

Hence the dominant trading patterns are cross-cut by even more subtle patterns created by the taste factor. Once a blend is established then it has an individual market to cater for and it must be assured of a continuous supply of all component beans which are required.

It is difficult to isolate causative factors in these dominant taste patterns, though probably the geographical closeness of the United States and Brazil played a part in at least reinforcing them. The colonial relationship based on tariff and exchange concessions probably reinforces taste patterns between African producers and European consumers. Geer has shown how the European market in coffee has been hampered by the fact that France, England and Portugal assured their former dependent colonial countries market access through preferential tariffs (Geer 1971:67) which were often established in colonial times. A most-favoured-nation trading relationship in coffee was established between the Territory of Papua New Guinea and Australia in 1961, principally because the Territory was a colony of Australia.

Some buyers and sellers are locked into trading relations which have their origins more in political factors such as the colonial relationships than in market determinants. Thus factors other than simply economic ones, such as colonial history and politically mediated state action, intrude to create dominant trading patterns.

Why is the International Coffee Agreement the World's longest surviving commodity agreement?

The success of the ICA, as we will see in detail in the next chapter, relies on the fact that, in its organisation, both formal and informal, it operates on the basis of patterns of taste and historically established trading patterns. Thus, while the type of international capital in the coffee industry is commercial, trading relations are highly structured by the particular nature of the commodity itself and by established patterns of taste. Market analysis of world coffee may be less useful than political analysis which recognises that patterns of trade respond less to changes in price and more to processes of political negotiation, coalition formation and exercise of authority by actors in the world coffee industry. Partly as a result of problems in the coffee industry such as disequilibrium between supply and demand, but also as a result of the need to formalise political relations in world coffee, coffee traders have adopted a distinctive institution, the International Coffee Agreement (ICA) established in 1962, to attempt through negotiation and the exercise of authority to regulate the flow of coffee.

International regulation of coffee not only complements but also reinforces its already tightly structured circulation. This is achieved by the informal establishment under the ICA of sets of bilateral alliances made up of importers and exporters. These alliances can be ranked hierarchically according to the magnitude of world coffee which they control. The greater the magnitude, the greater the influence exercised by one bilateral alliance, e.g. the big importer/big exporter alliance of the United States and Brazil, over lesser strata in the ICA such European importers and African exporters of Robusta coffee.

Such a network of alliances cuts directly across the myth of the dominance of the importer/exporter cleavage, which is formally embodied in the ICA.

The analysis of bilateral alliances in the ICA reveals a much more subtle form of exploitation at the international level than has yet been posited. The analysis which will follow shows that the effect of a regulated international coffee market upon small producing nations -- those countries outside the major alliances such as Papua New Guinea -- is the underdevelopment of their industries. Underdevelopment of small peripheral coffee industries occurs because the dominant alliances within the ICA aim to stabilise existing patterns of trade and thereby to maintain the influence of large importers and big exporters over world coffee trade, particularly over the small producing nations.

12

The Politics of International Coffee Regulation

Introduction

The failure of the market to bring world supply and demand into line meant that world coffee relations had to be managed through direct intervention in the market by an authorised international body. The 1962 International Coffee Agreement came provisionally into force on July 1 1963. It endorsed a list of objectives which set down the various interests which it hoped to accommodate. The signatories to the agreement were the major importers and almost all producers for '. . . it obtained the acceptance of countries accounting for 97.4 per cent of world coffee exporters and 96 per cent of importers'. (Streeten and Elson 1971:20) The objectives stated in the agreement were:

(1) to achieve a reasonable balance between supply and demand which will assure adequate supplies of coffee to consumers and markets for coffee producers at equitable prices

(2) to alleviate the serious hardship of burdensome surpluses and excessive fluctuations in the prices of coffee to the detriment of the interests of both producers and consumers;

(3) to contribute to the development of production resources and to the promotion and maintenance of employment and income in the member countries;

(4) to assist in increasing the purchasing power of coffee exporting countries by keeping prices at equitable level and to encourage the consumption of coffee by every possible means, and;

(5) in general recognition of the relationship of the trade in coffee to the economic stability of markets for industrial products to further international co-operation in connection with world coffee problems. (International Coffee Agreement, 1962 Objectives)

The formal mechanisms of the various agreements appear, on the surface at least, to translate the stated commitment to objectives of neutrality and fairness into the form of the actual mechanisms. Those adopted appear to be non-discriminatory because they are based on objective criteria which seem to favour the producer countries:

(1) the key regulatory tool is based on export quotas operating on supply and not on direct price manipulation. This is a paradox in the Agreement, for while stabilisation of price was perceived as the means by which supply and demand could be brought into line and equity achieved in the world coffee industry, the agreements themselves make no attempt to stabilise prices directly. They rely instead upon a comprehensive system of export quotas which would limit supplies put on the market by exporting members to estimated levels of demand. To administer the agreement, a new international institution -- the International Coffee Organisation (ICO) -- was created;

(2) fairness is evident in the manner by which the ratio between the absolute (global) quota and the individual (country) quotas was worked out and adjusted, though not perhaps in the manner by which producer country quotas were allocated in the first place;

(3) the effect on price of quotas in the 1962 and 1968 Agreements was to put a floor on price (Pincus 1967:274) rather than a ceiling on it, suggesting a good deal of favouritism toward the producer countries;

(4) and the lack of controls on production in the producer countries, except for diversification policies and the related lack of guarantees of supply for importers also appeared favourable to producer countries.

The purpose of this section is to analyse the quota, price, production control mechanisms in the 1962 and 1968 ICAs, and to compare the same mechanisms in the 1976 ICA. When these mechanisms are analysed in isolation they appear fair and neutral, even biased in favour of producers, but when they are analysed over time and the changes made to the mechanisms in the 1976 ICA are related to the problem of undersupply in the 1970s, it is evident that they are altered at the behest of, and in the interest of, the dominant bilateral oligopolists. In the last section of this chapter, coffee regulation in the 1980s will be examined.

The Role of Quotas

The main problem faced by the signatories to the 1962 Agreement was global overproduction. In the mid-1950s, for example, total coffee production averaged over 72 million bags. (Galloway 1973:362) Though production was beginning to fall by the late 1950s, due (it was thought) to lack of incentive for producers to maintain trees when prices were low, the gap between the supply of coffee and importers' requirements was, by 1961, still very great. In that year, total world imports were a mere 43.4m bags. The remainder had to be stored in the producer countries. The signatories to the 1962 ICA had a choice between two primary mechanisms around which to structure the Agreement: either direct price control, or regulation of the physical quantities of coffee (the supply of coffee) as it passed from producers to importers. They chose an export restriction scheme and hoped that the regulation of supply would lead indirectly to price control.

There are good theoretical as well as practical reasons for eschewing direct price control. Theoretically it can be shown that the effects of direct price intervention are uncertain and might in fact add to, rather than relieve the instability of world coffee flows. Practically, adherence to price control is almost impossible to police. It is not a difficult procedure for parties to a transaction to strike special deals and thereby hide the real price paid, as transfer pricing shows. On the other hand, control of physical quantities of coffee across state boundaries can be policed. While in practice the Agreement has not been totally successful in overcoming the problem of special deals struck either on a price or a supply basis, it has been successful in creating a degree of certainty and stability in world coffee flows.

The export restriction scheme for coffee was largely inherited from the earlier Coffee Study Group and this has remained the normal method of intervention which economists have favoured. (Bilder 1963:333)[1] Economists argue that more direct methods of price stabilisation seem not to work. In theory it is argued that the stabilisation of money prices will not occur, but will instead destabilise money income if the main source of instability is unpredictable fluctuations in production. (Johnson 1967:141) If direct stabilisation of money income to producers were adopted it would probably take the form of multilateral contracts which would specify a maximum price at which consuming countries were obligated to purchase from producing ones. The particular problem for coffee in such an arrangement is that its general price level is constantly changing, because the general price is made up of four separately moving price levels, those of the four varieties. Contracts which attempt to stabilise money income in this way may not actually stabilise purchasing power or real income when there is a degree of movement in the general price. (Johnson 1967:141) Direct price intervention would also be inequitable for it would benefit coffee importers more than coffee producers, because in the case of coffee, he asserts, price fluctuations are primarily the result of supply changes rather than changes in demand. (Johnson 1967:147)

The major practical reason for eschewing direct price intervention is that its effects on both long-term price levels and established trade patterns are very uncertain. Uncertainty of effect which might result from direct price intervention was a major concern which was expressed by both importing countries and producers at the setting up of the Agreement. Importing countries were politically unable to agree to a price level which might indicate to their domestic consumers that their own state was endorsing sharp increases in prices. Moreover, it was becoming gradually clear that negotiation of specific figures on price-spreads for the various types and grades of coffee was an impossible task in the time available if, in fact, it could be done at all. (Bilder 1963:358) Exporting countries were concerned that the uncertain effects which might result from direct price intervention could have the effect of altering trading patterns. This could occur as price intervention altered the price levels of different varieties. In such circumstances Other Milds, for example, might begin to be substituted for Brazils or vice versa, or Robustas might begin to be substituted for Brazils. Significant shifts in established patterns through substitution would have a direct impact on particular geographical regions and might lead directly to serious political problems between producing countries. Such risks could not be taken, but in direct price intervention they are always present.

With quotas, on the other hand, established trade patterns can be serviced and even reinforced. Quotas ensure that changing trade patterns evolve slowly over time, monitored by a world coffee authority. It is probably this political reality, rather than economic argument, that made export quotas acceptable to importers and exporters as the primary mechanism for intervention in the flow of world coffee. It is political rather than economic logic which supports the case for the establishment of an International Commodity Agreement. (Gerhard 1963:292) Stabilisation of price and supply contributes to the efficient use of capital for crops such as coffee. It is also thought to allow producing states to plan their economic programmes in a more rational manner and avoid the disruption that occurs when prices fluctuate violently. (Galloway 1973:360-61) Certainty of price and supply also allows importing processors to manage their stockholdings more efficiently.

Another major practical reason for opting for control of supply and not direct price control is that control and regulation, if they are to be adhered to, must be backed up by sufficient authority to uncover misdeeds and if necessary impose sanctions. This requires a policing agent. The International Coffee Organisation functions through its main organs, the International Coffee Council (consisting of all the members of the Organisation) and its executive Board (consisting of eight exporting members and eight importing ones, elected for each coffee year). It is important to realise, however, that the Executive Director and his staff of the ICO have very limited power or authority. This is due to the fact that the members of the ICO are sovereign states. While the International Coffee Council and the Executive Board can sanction a member in relation to that member's role in the ICO, within coffee countries the ICO can only advise on production programmes. Limited powers, coupled with the lack of reliable information concerning prices actually paid by importing firms to producer-based exporting agencies, means that direct price control cannot be exercised by the ICO.[2]

With export quotas, information is more easily obtained because physical supplies are more easily checked. It is not the ICO that does this checking but the importer state through its customs officials at the border entry point. The importing state is the de facto policing agent of the Agreement, providing information to the ICO which the organisation itself could not provide. Quota control as opposed to direct price control is the only mechanism that could have been adopted in the Agreement because it was only by recognising the sovereignty of the state and having it exercise control over its own domestic industry that the authority of the International agreement could be maintained. The centrality of the state as a policing agent also gives the Agreement some control over flows of coffee to and from non-member countries. For example, importer state control allows the International Coffee Organisation de facto control over importer firms of member states who may wish to buy coffee in large quantities at lower-than-agreement prices from exporting non-members, undermining the established shares of world coffee member exporting countries. In addition, because it is states which are the policing agents, the ICO can in fact exercise control over the quantities of coffee which enter importer states. This also allows the ICO control over the sale of coffee from member exporters, so that members cannot hide shortfalls and must hold to the quota allotted. On the other hand, such control leaves producer members with great control over domestic price, for they can withhold coffee under a quota system, if their domesitic production is greater than their quota, just as they could in a competitive market system.

The choice of quotas as the primary formal mechanism raised the question as to what exceptions to quotas the Agreement would allow. It is significant that the United States and the large Latin American producers argued that there should be no exemptions from quota restrictions for member exporters. (Cartledge 1978:95, Bilder 1963:357, Marshall 1979:5) This was an example of the collusion existing between dominant bilateral oligopolists and the crudeness of their attempts to retain dominance. However, their position was difficult to maintain because the amount of coffee circulating outside member countries was only 5m bags, at a time when regulated coffee flow was about 45-55m bags. There were also possible benefits for world coffee as a whole in nurturing the growth of coffee consumption in new areas. The solution proposed in the agreement was to exempt exports to Annexe B countries, those 'certain areas of the world having a low per capita consumption and considerable potential for expansion'. (Article 40, 1962 Agreement) Annexe B countries include the Soviet Union, South Africa and Japan. The ICO requested that members 'supply such statistics and other information as the Council may require to assist it in controlling the flow of coffee to countries listed in Annexe B and its consumption therein' (Article 40, 1962 Agreement) but in the absence of importer state control there is no mechanism to enforce these provisions. Thus the flow of member coffee to non-member importers is virtually a competitive market.

The allocation of quotas and the price mechanism in the 1962 and 1968 ICAs are closely intertwined, but we can take these in two separate stages by looking at the determination of quota levels in the first instance, and then at the adjustment procedures. The adjustment of quotas involves the question of what price levels the Agreement is aiming to defend and by what means the quota adjustment is made as a response to movements in price above or below the defendable level. Clearly when the price falls below the defendable level less coffee must be exported and quotas must therefore be reduced.

The quotas in the 1962 Agreement were expressed by the specific number of bags which was a country's basic quota. The total of these made up the aggregate number of bags to be exported from all member countries, which was the total basic quota. The total basic quota in the 1962 Agreement was based upon a projection of the future consumption patterns for world coffee, minus the expected exports from non-member countries, minus expected shipments from dependent territories to the governing country, minus expected member exports to non-quota markets and plus or minus expected inventory changes. (Msuya 1979:131) Having established an estimate of the total amount of member coffee to be released onto the member market, it then became necessary for the ICO to divide up this total into basic country quotas. Countries were given a choice of opting for their quota being based on their average exportable production of either the two coffee years 1961–62 and 1962–63, or the four coffee years 1959– –60 through 1962–63. The figure for each country's exports was established and applied to the estimated total basic quota for the coming year to give the pro rata allocation.

The importer country members are interested solely in the total basic quota. The United States came to the 1962 Agreement determined to ensure that there would be no exemptions to basic quotas and determined also to see that the sum total of coffee circulating internationally should equal the total basic quota. (Bilder 1963:343) The big Latin American producers, Brazil and Colombia, held a similar position. For these, their dominance of both old and new markets would be frozen into place if the total basic quota were fixed. However, such a position was unacceptable to small producers, who demanded that if quotas to member countries were to be determined on the basis of historical patterns of trade and not on projected production, then at least they be allowed possibilities for expansion in new unregulated markets.[3] Accordingly, the Agreement endorsed quota exemptions for new markets as well as exemptions from quotas for small exporters whose coffee exports were less than 100,000 bags. The Agreement also contained a special clause to deal with the situation of dependencies exporting to their metropolitan power (as discussed in Chapter 5). The big exporters and big importers lost out in their campaign to refuse exemptions. Had they won, it would have jeopardised the entire agreement, and in any case, it is in everyone's interests to expand consumption, and the opportunities offered in new markets may be better realised where market competition opens these up. Also, it was obvious to the big producers and exporters that these exemptions did not involve large amounts of coffee.

Once the total basic quota is settled much of the coffee politics in the ICO takes place between exporting members. Such members concern themselves initially with the desire to see the total basic quota rise and also to see their own absolute basic quota figure rise, but they must also be concerned to see that their proportion of the total basic quota stays the same or rises vis-à-vis other exporters. This is their relative quota. As the absolute quota is based on an estimated figure for the future year's consumption, quotas are often adjusted upwards or downwards each quarter as new information about consumption, supply, etc., becomes available, and as the price changes. It is the adjustment of these quarterly quotas which have the potential to affect not only a country's absolute quotas but also its relative ones, and which has over the years caused the most acrimony among exporting countries.

As Bilder shows, this is where real coffee politics inside the Agreement takes place. Of the original negotiations in 1962 he writes:

> The real negotiations, therefore, centred about the question of the 'division of the pie' - - the share which each country was to have in any global quota, and the general basis on which such shares were to be calculated. Of course, each country argued for a system of allocation which would tend to increase its relative share; and many countries suggested that their case was unique and their needs greater, and that they should therefore be entitled to special treatment and a higher quota than other countries. Thus, the large established producers wished quotas to be based primarily upon supply and historical shares of the market. Moreover, in order to further protect their existing market positions they wished the respective shares of the various exporting countries to be firmly established in the agreement and not to be subject to later negotiation. The newer African producers, on the other hand, while developing productive capacity and a belief that the trend in consumer preferences would continue to favour their coffees, wished quotas to be established on the basis of potential production, with relative shares to be subject to flexible adjustment based upon the demand for different types of coffees as indicated by price or the degree to which quotas were actually utilised. (Bilder 1963:356)

The 1962 Agreement did not provide an adequate mechanism for the adjustment of quotas:

> Under this agreement every price and quota change was to be negotiated separately by the Council. This meant that during the years of erratic prices the Council had to be convened frequently to negotiate price or quota adjustments, and since the agreement did not provide any substantial price or quota adjustment guidelines, the negotiations were very time consuming. Furthermore, in the absence of specific guidelines, differing guesses as to the probable outcome of the negotiations often tended to create considerable uncertainty. (Myusa 1979:132)

The situation was even more serious than Msuya says. It was especially serious for small producers. Adjustments were made in relation to the Agreement's stated aim of defending the general level of 1962 prices. (Article 27, 1962 Agreement) This did not take into account the fact that coffee circulates in four different varieties and that a price which averages out these takes no account of the separate price levels and supply needs of individual varieties. The manner of adjusting quotas on the basis of a pro rata adjustment, which was based on a price that treated all coffee as though it was a uniform product, severely disadvantaged small countries both in terms of their absolute quotas as well as their relative ones. Under this system the absolute quotas of small producers might be reduced solely as a result of unilateral action by a big producer. Brazil or Colombia could risk quota cuts in their own absolute quota and flood the market, engage in special arrangements, or send out tourist coffee, all of which would affect the overall price of coffee leading to absolute quota adjustment. Small producers could also see their relativities change against them, even though they might merely be responding to the requirements of the circulation of coffee in their own particular variety. For example, Tanzania might sell all its mild Arabicas in member markets while at the same time Brazils and Robustas were in oversupply. The result would be that, if the price fell below the 1962 level, all countries, Tanzania included, had to take a pro rata cut in quota.

During the period of the 1962 Agreement, some changes were made to the mechanism for setting and adjusting quotas which appeared in the 1968 Agreement and which to some extent made quota allocation fairer. The main change initiated, in March 1965, was a shift to an indicator price which allowed for automatic adjustment of quotas. Under this system, the prices of different varieties of coffee were monitored and when the average of these over fifteen days fell below or rose above a price ceiling, then automatic quota adjustments were made. In December 1965 this system was refined even further so that floors and ceilings were put on the main varieties of coffee. The system was fairer because absolute quota setting would be linked more closely to supply and demand of a particular variety of coffee, meaning that relativities might alter in accordance with the type of coffee, not simply the quantity, a country was exporting. The result was that some major changes did occur in relativities between the 1962 and 1968 basic quotas. For example, in the 1962 Agreement, the total basic quota was 45,587,183m (60kg) bags. Of this, Brazil was allocated 18,000,000 bags (Unwashed Arabics), Colombia 6,011,280 bags (Colombia Milds), Tanganyika (Other Milds) 435,458 bags, Ivory Coast (Robustas) 2,324,278 bags. In the 1968 Agreement, the total basic quota was 55,041,000m bags – – an increase of 10,000,000 bags – – of which Brazil's quota was 20,926,000, Colombia 7,000,000, Tanzania 700,000, Ivory Coast 3,073,000. Thus the relative quotas shifted in favour of the Other Milds in which market demand was strongest, and against unwashed Arabicas where it was weakest. The new system still, however, used basic quotas determined in relation to historical patterns, even though these now included a study of the variety of coffee exported and the total basic quota for that variety. The objection was still made by small producers that setting absolute quotas in relation to historical patterns and not projected production put unfair limits upon the development of their coffee industries. (Stuckart 1977:574)

The changes made to the allocation of basic quotas in 1968, taken in isolation, favoured the small producers. But these were minor compared with those made to quota allocation in the 1976 ICA. The United States entered negotiations for a new agreement in July 1975. Its aim was to have the agreement embody measures which would promote production, and to ensure that supply problems would be overcome. With falling prices in

1974 and early 1975 and the 'Black Frost' an unknown event, the United States was in a strong position to dictate to the gathering the form the agreement should take. It succeeded in restructuring the 1976 ICA so that quota allocation ensured a continuous supply of coffee and that Brazil's historic share of coffee exports was protected.

The main change made in 1976 was in the manner of allocation of quotas. The purpose was to provide incentives to producer countries to maintain extensive stockholdings inside their country. This change is mentioned in Article 35(1) under the heading Allocation of Annual Quotas. It read:

> In the light of the decision taken under the provisions of Article 34 and after deducting the amount of coffee required to comply with the provisions of Article 31, annual quotas shall be allocated in fixed and variable parts of exporting Members entitled to a basic quota. The fixed part shall correspond to 70 percent of the global annual quota, as adjusted to comply with the provisions of Article 31, and shall be distributed among exporting Members in accordance with the provisions of Article 30.
>
> The variable part shall correspond to 30 percent of the global annual quota as adjusted to comply with the provisions of Article 31. These proportions may be changed by the Council but the fixed part shall never be less than 70 percent. Subject to the provisions of paragraph (2) of this Article, the variable part shall be distributed among exporting Members in the proportion which the verified stocks of each exporting Member bear to the total verified stocks of all exporting Members having basic quotas, provided that, unless the Council establishes a different limit, no Member shall receive a share of the variable part of the quota in excess of 40 percent of the total volume of such variable part. (The International Coffee Agreement 1976:24)

Producer countries, in order to maximise their quotas in subsequent years, are thus encouraged to maximise their production, whether it can be sold or not. But as much as 30 percent of their quota must be held back from the market and stored at their own expense within their own country. At a time of coffee shortage, due to a frost in Brazil, for example, these accumulated stocks are available to flood onto the market. Stocks were brought into the Agreement for the first time because the coffee problem was now under-supply rather than over-production. Far from being a simple technical device, however, the arrangements concerning stockholdings allowed importers to structure the Agreement in the way they wished, one which put the cost of overcoming under-supply onto the small producers. Though the 1976 Agreement did not begin to operate until 1980, when the problem was again over-production, the innovation of fixed and variable quotas ensured that, in the long run, over-production would always remain a feature of world coffee and that under-supply caused by some natural catastrophe could not happen again.

It should not be thought that importers such as the United States devised the 1976 ICA entirely in their own interest for, in altering the manner of allocating quotas they took into account the interest of their bilateral oligopolist, Brazil. Brazil's problem in signing the 1976 ICA was indeed a serious one. The reason for global undersupply in the early 1970s was the frost in Parana in 1972. Brazil could support its bilateral oligopolist and sign an agreement which provided supply and stockholding incentives. However it did not want to sign an agreement by which its quotas under the new Agreement would be based on its reduced production during the years of frost. In other words, the Agreement had to first, encourage production and reward expansion by adjusting quotas upward when this was done, but second, should not reduce Brazil's relative share of world coffee. The first requirement was achieved through the stockholding provision. Small countries would be encouraged to produce and store. The more they did of both the higher their quotas would be. The second part was achieved by having two base years upon which the allocation of quotas were based: one a recent base year suiting expanding producers and one that suited Brazil.

If the Agreement had been introduced later than 1976, producers could choose the higher of the two years. Sections 2 and 3 of Article 30, headed Basic Quotas, outlined this provision:

> (2) If, under the provisions of Article 33, quotas come into effect during coffee year 1976–77, the basic quota to be used for the distribution of the fixed part of the quotas shall be calculated on the basis of the average volume of the annual exports of each exporting Member to importing Members in coffee years 1968–69 to 1971–72. The distribution of the fixed part shall remain in effect until the quotas are suspended for the first time under the provisions of Article 33.
>
> (3) If quotas are not introduced in coffee year 1976–77 but come into effect during coffee year 1977–78, the basic quota to be used for the distribution of the fixed part of the quotas shall be calculated by selecting for each Member the higher of the following:
>
> > a) the volume of its exports to importing Members during coffee year 1976–77 calculated on the basis of information obtained from Certificates of Origin; or
> >
> > b) the figure resulting from the application of the procedure established in paragraph (2) of this Article. (International Coffee Agreement 1976:20)

The requirement that producers withhold 30 percent or more of the production in stocks thus protected Brazil's market share at times of crisis in Brazilian production, and Article 30 allowed Brazil to calculate its quota on the basis of a year of known higher production, 1968–69.

Another device built into the agreement to protect Brazil and to ensure continued supply was the new provision on shortfalls. Msuya explains technically how this works though any explanation must consider, as he notes, that the major country to experience problems of shortfall which have any significant effect on world coffee is Brazil. (Msuya 1979:146) Thus to a significant degree shortfall provisions in an International Coffee Agreement are provisions designed to deal with frosts in Brazil. Msuya notes:

> the agreement requires members to fill their quotas or declare any expected shortfalls as early during the coffee years as possible so that these shortfalls may be redistributed amongst member countries with extra capacity to export. Seventy per cent of any declared shortfall is first offered to members exporting the same type of coffee as the declaring members, and the rest is offered to other members. These redistributions are made amongst members offering to accept them in proportion to their respective basic quotas. An inducement for early declaration of shortfalls, shortfall declared within the first six months of a coffee year are rewarded with a bonus equivalent to 30 percent of the declared shortfall added to the declaring country's export quota during the following coffee year. The bonus is charged against the quotas of the beneficiaries pro rata to their participation in the redistribution. (Msuya 1979:146)

This provision designed to deal with frosts in Brazil, encourages countries to declare shortfalls and is a way of enlarging the annual quotas of the beneficiaries of the redistribution. But it is also a way of protecting the interests of the dominant bilateral oligopoly. Brazil knew it would have shortfalls but did not wish these to affect its quota in subsequent years. The provisions protected the United States which came to the meeting, according to the leader of the American delegation 'determined to secure protection against undershipment'. (Coffee International 1976:21)

Price and Production Controls: Who Benefits?

Throughout the 1960s, when over-production was the major problem, the aim of the 1962 and 1968 ICAs was to defend a minimum or floor price, which was defined as the general price level of 1962. The Agreement contained no corresponding price ceiling. (Geer 1971:23) As Geer notes: 'Contrary to other international Agreements no provision was made in the International Coffee Agreement regarding a corresponding price ceiling and subsequent obligations of member countries if the price ceiling is reached' . (Geer 1971:23) Doubtless the long period of overproduction seemed to preclude the need for building a price ceiling into the Agreement. Of course, the indicator price scheme did mention an upper price to defend but in the absence of production goals or stockholding schemes this mention of an upper price was fairly meaningless.

The minimum price was defended, as has been noted, by instituting an export restriction scheme which aimed to regulate prices indirectly. The total basic quota from member exporters was reduced when in a set period prices fell below the 1962 levels. The withdrawal of supply would raise the price and bring it back to an acceptable level. The Agreement worked very well throughout the 1960s, not only to hold prices above the floor price, but also to reduce the variation in price levels above it. (Geer 1971:183) The success of the Agreement should not be overstated, however, because the fact that the problem was over-production was a very important part of its success. In the 1970s, when the problem was under-supply, the Agreement worked less well. Also, it should be noted that the very success of the Agreement on the price front in the 1960s contributed to growing ambiguity and confusion on the question of the role of prices under a regulated Agreement.

Under an ICA, the selection of a price to defend is arbitrary, determined not by supply and demand but by negotiation. The 1962 ICA took 1962 prices as a floor price to defend, mainly because it was recent and mid-way between what the producers wanted and what the price was likely to fall to, given the prevailing conditions of over-supply. But no-one could be certain that this was an actual midway point. This uncertainty also arose in relation to the setting of a price to defend for the 1968 Agreement. The existence of indicators in the 1968 Agreement did not alter the fact that an agreement had to be made upon a range of prices instead of a single price. These would then be the basis upon which indicators would operate. It was often argued that, by 1968, the 1962 price was too low, though some economists argued it was too high. Once the Agreement had been operating for some time, it was impossible to say what the 'real' market price might be. In many ways the price to defend is only that, because all those party to the Agreement agree to defend it. In market terms it is virtually, as Haarer (1962:452) notes, a fictitious price. Geer (1971) also makes this point. He notes that there is an assumption among those party to the Agreement that the ICO should not interfere at the level of prices in a way that causes long-term prices to differ from what they would have been in the absence of an Agreement. Since the future is unknown, a neutral price can be ascertained only ex post, whereas the technical solution presupposes that it is known ex ante.

This dilemma has led some economists to attack the whole concept of commodity agreements. Kindleberger and Machlup argue that:

> We lack techniques for determining and applying the equilibrium price in commodity markets. Intervention in the price formation process leads directly to the disequilibrium system in which incentives are created to undermine the pegged price, stocks pile up (or shortages develop) and ultimately the price collapses or explodes. (Kindleberger and Machlup, quoted in Geer 1971:41)

Kindleberger and Machlup are arguing that the fictitious price created by ICAs exaggerates trends in the price and supply areas rather than correcting them. This exaggeration may not be apparent in long periods of stability but it is this very gap between the market price and the defended one that can ultimately lead to a collapse of agreement. In the case of coffee the problem surrounding price levels that Kindleberger and Machlup allude to is exacerbated because, as prices are not tackled directly by the agreement in the ICO, a time lag develops between action taken on quotas and effects on price. This can be a serious problem for all coffee actors. Importers find their inventories being altered in value some time after new quotas have been established. Both importers and exporters attempt to cover the lag by selling on the futures markets, but this is only possible for corporations and large firms. Inside producer countries, scaled-down prices are charged immediately for coffee delivered by small growers, even though this new price may not yet be reflected in export prices. A very significant surplus can be transferred from small producers to big coffee processors and exporters inside coffee-growing countries in this way. Further, the gap between quota and price creates the precondition for a great deal of manipulation of pegged price levels, not only through special deals but in the political struggle that takes place within the ICO. The ambiguity over prices and the gap between prices and quotas means that under conditions of regulation, the management of international coffee flows and prices is an intensely political process in which price and quota merely reinforce existing power relations which have their base in taste patterns and past colonial linkages.

There is a further issue, not mentioned by Kindleberger and Machlup, to be found in the fact that price adjustment is an effect of quota adjustment. This concerns the impact of price upon production in the coffee producing countries. The dominant view of the economists is that price provides the incentive to farmers to plant, or refrain from planting, coffee. But can one assume such a connection, or does one have to demonstrate it? What is evident from the way international prices emerge out of the agreement process is that they bear little or no relation to what is going on at the level of production. The amount and direction of the flow of coffee in the world market, which is being restricted or expanded by negotiation and which eventually should affect price levels, is obviously not a reflection of the amount of coffee that is being grown, processed, and either exported or stockpiled in producer countries. There is thus an asymmetry between the stock of producing coffee trees and the amount of coffee flowing internationally. The surplus coffee is kept off the regulated market by the quota system and is either sold in non-member markets or held in stocks. There is an even more important asymmetry between the stock of mature coffee trees and the negotiated price, the difference being very much a question of production policy. In other words, the negotiated price which is set indirectly by the quota system is not linked -- under conditions of the Agreement -- directly to the amount of coffee being produced in a country. When the asymmetry between the stock of producing trees and the international price is added to the biological fact that coffee takes between 2–4 years to mature, and therefore is only distantly related to price, it becomes very clear that the whole assumed analysis that prices provide the incentive/disincentive for farmers to plant or not plant coffee can be maintained only if the international price mechanism were accompanied by internationally or nationally devised production policies.

There are essentially two main ways, under conditions of the Agreement, in which production policies can be pursued. The first and the most logical is that such policies are designed at the international level.[4] A policy of this sort would close the gap between the negotiated international price and the incentives/disincentives for farmers to expand or contract their stock of mature coffee trees. Production control devised on an international basis would be in the interests of all coffee actors under conditions of both overproduction and underproduction. If disincentives could be built into the Agreement at the international level during times of over-production, then gradually the need for international intervention would diminish. Exporters would also stand to benefit because they would be freed from the expense that is involved in stockholding and might also be able to get subsidies from the international body to sponsor diversification programmes and to relocate former coffee farmers. This is in fact precisely what was laid out in the first Agreements. As Geer explains:

> the agreement had stipulated that 'not later than one year after the agreement enters into force, the council shall . . . recommend production goals for each member country and for the world as a whole' . . . intertwined with the issue of production targets has been the question of assisting the surplus-ridden countries in diversifying out of coffee into other economic pursuits. It was felt that the availability of financial and technical assistance would facilitate the implementation of production controls. In 1966, the Council approved

> therefore, in principle, the establishment of a coffee diversification fund but left the scale of contributions to the fund open. In 1966 and 1967, discussions on the establishment and arrangement of this fund were continued. Finally, new guidelines for the diversification fund were embodied in the renegotiated agreement of 1968. (Geer 1971:27)

But, as Geer and many others note,

> the problem of controlling production on an internationally co-ordinated basis proved to be such a difficult and involved task that it has remained unresolved for the life of the 1962 and the present [1968] agreement. (Geer 1971:27)

This failure reflects not merely a lack of political will on the part of the authorities. Rather, because production control must take place within the boundaries of sovereign states, implementation cannot be policed by the ICO or any other coffee actor apart from the sovereign state itself. While some exporting countries took up the challenge of diversification in the 1960s others did not (such as Colombia). The result was that Colombia was in a stronger position for expanded quotas in the future.

The lesson of the Agreement during the years 1962 and 1968 was thus that production policy at an international level was doomed to failure if its implementation could not be policed in some way. Under conditions of over-production there was little incentive for importers to engage themselves in debate on production control, because their essential concern, supply, was not a problem. Further, they were very hesitant to become involved for fear that they might be asked to contribute to the cost of diversification. The importers took a very casual approach to production policy in the first two Agreements because the problem for coffee relations at that time was over-production. When in the 1970s the coffee problem was under-production, the importers became sufficiently interested in production policy to press for a linkage of production growth with allocation of quotas in the 1976 Agreement.

Another and more frequently adopted form of production control is that instituted inside developing countries by state planners and state authorities. Because of its politically sensitive nature control usually takes the form of manipulation of prices inside the country. This is then spuriously justified on the basis that prices for coffee are set internationally. Politically this method is feasible because the assumption is often held within a country that because prices are set globally, the internal price merely reflecting this, and there is little government can do. Governments can also be selective in the distribution of necessary inputs such as fertiliser or pesticides and, coupled with price manipulation, this selectivity can become a de facto production control. Selectivity is often used to favour one area or one group of producers over another. Thus even when production control is internal, the existence of an international price plays a role.

The 1976 Agreement is fairly unremarkable on the question of price and production control. The Agreement institutionalises the concept of indicator prices which were again touted as taking defendable price levels out of the realm of negotiation and into the orbit of the market. Kirschen claimed that 'by allowing "market"' forces to determine the famous trigger price level which sparks off export quotas the negotiations have . . . for the first time, given the coffee trade a say in the running of the Agreement'. (Kirschen 1978:51) There is some truth in this claim, for the indicator prices were further refined in the 1976 Agreement. In this, the indicator price determined not only the adjustment of quotas but also when quotas would actually begin to operate. The formula agreed upon to have indicator prices trigger the quota system was to take:

> the average of the last 20 marketing days of the 1977–78 coffee year plus the average of the first 20 marketing days of the 1978–79 year in turn, and their average would spell out the trigger price for the current coffee year. If, during the year, the ICO composite indicator were to fall to or below 15 percent under the trigger price level and stay there for 20 consecutive market days, the Executive Director of the ICO shall, within 14 days, call the Executive Board which will meet to set export quotas. (Kirschen 1978:51)

The Agreement was also the first to mention an upper price to defend. (Stuckart 1977:570) But these refinements did not alter the fact that the formula for the indicator price was a negotiated one which allowed room, as with earlier Agreements, for argument to take place as to whether the agreed price to defend was too high or too low. On production control and diversification, the 1976 Agreement recognised at last that there is very little that can be done globally to force countries to adopt production controls. However, it could be said that the requirement under the Agreement to hold stocks represents a de facto control.

The comparison of the formal mechanisms in the early agreements with the changes made in the 1976 ICA contradicts predictions based on the analysis of economists such as MacBean (1966) and Johnson (1977). If they had been correct, under the 1976 Agreement, importers would have been discriminated against by the changes that were made to the Agreement. But I have shown that they did very well out of the changes. In fact the changes were directly in the interests of importers, for they aimed to ensure supply in circumstances where it was short due to frosts in Brazil. I have also shown that a comparison of the formal mechanisms in the 1976 Agreement with those of the earlier Agreements discloses discrimination. Big producers and importers are free to initiate change of the type that suits them, when they need to. In the 1962 and 1968 ICA, clauses to ensure supply were not urgently needed, but the 1976 Agreement made it mandatory for small countries to hold large stocks. They also had to bear the cost of a quota allocation mechanism that largely benefited importers and larger producers. In this section I have shown that it is only when we study the formal mechanisms comparatively across agreements and in varying circumstances that it becomes evident that the flow of international coffee under conditions of regulation benefits bilateral oligopolies, and discriminates against small producers.

The 1976 Agreement came into operation on October 1, 1980. The effect of the 1975 Brazilian frost was a distant memory, and by this time, the world coffee industry had begun to be plagued by the old problem of overproduction. 1980 was seen as a crisis year. Stocks were rising at an alarming rate amid suggestions that gross overstocking could be expected by the mid-1980s. At Goroka in Papua New Guinea the coffee industry was spending millions of dollars on the building of huge sheds in which to store coffee. This pattern was repeated throughout the producing countries. When the Agreement came into operation, it failed to stem the fall in prices. Producers were told by coffee authorities in producing countries that the future looked very grim. These problems are usually cast as the impersonal effect of market forces. However, as is now obvious, it is the 1976 Agreement itself and its provisions for allocating quotas which is pushing the world toward over-production. When an agreement like the 1976 Agreement is structured with the main aim of putting world coffee back onto a footing of over-production, it hardly matters what is happening to global demand.

The extraordinary aspect of this process is that the technocrats who work for governments in the coffee industry, such as Msuya of Tanzania and Densley of Papua New Guinea, display naïveté in ignoring the effects of the Agreement in structuring outcomes. Both adopt the technocratic logic on which the Agreement pretends to be based. Msuya's advice to Tanzania is precisely of this type. He concludes his study by writing that:

> Our empirical results and discussions thus far lead one to believe that Tanzania could improve the size and predictably of her earnings from trade in coffee by adopting a production and export expansion policy. But before one can recommend such a strategy it is necessary to evaluate the trends and prospects of consumption and production in the major consuming and purchasing areas. (Msuya 1979:148)

This should be regarded as a naive conclusion given the powerful hierarchical and structured interests which dominate the Agreement. Densley advises Papua New Guinea to expand forthwith, noting that if quotas do come into operation then it is in Papua New Guinea's interests '. . . to maximise coffee exports to member countries in the period prior to 1978–80'. (Densley 1977:18)

When quotas did return, in the 1980–81 season, it was obvious that in broad terms the world coffee industry had changed little since the 1960s. Overall quotas were put at 57.37m bags, a figure slightly more than that of the first year of operation of the 1968 Agreement, though in 1980–81, basic quotas were immediately cut as the indicator fell below 135 cents. (Marshall 1981:4) The amount of coffee going to non-members had barely changed from the 5m of the early 1960s. In 1980–81, non-member sales were as high as 7.7m, but soon settled down to the expected 6m figure. (Marshall 1982:3) Overall then, it would appear, the period of international regulation followed by a period of restructuring which did not substantially alter coffee relations, merely reinforced the previous pattern of flow of world coffee.

Coffee Regulation in the 1980s

The agreements of the 1960s have been closely compared with the 1976 agreement to show how details in them are refined and changed, and to demonstrate that these changes generally occur as determined by the political powers in the ICO, particularly the dominant bilateral alliances of the United States and, Brazil and Western Europe and African Robustia producers. These informal political alliances make a mockery of the myth of the importer/exporter cleavage formalised in the Agreement, and held so important by economists. The 1976 Agreement shows how strong the power of bilateral alliances is to invent and have accepted biased clauses in their own interests and against those of small producers. The 1983 Agreement continued the tradition, building on the 1976 Agreement through maintaining the historical market share of big producers in collusion with importing countries. By the end of the 1980s, however, collusion between the United States and Brazil began to collapse.

The 1983 Agreement refined the indicator trigger and also aimed to focus as much on quality as quantity, by encouraging improvement at production level. Quotas, however, remained the major control instrument embodied in the 1983 agreement and this directly affected exchange rather than production of coffee. In the 1980s, quotas remained in effect for most of the decade except for a brief period from early 1986 to October 1987. Thus for most of the 1980s, the world coffee market was controlled, to a greater or lesser extent, by the operation of ICA quotas. The story of world coffee trade in that decade, can be told by examining the role of the ICO. However, by 1989, when a new agreement was required, negotiation and collusion proved more difficult than ever before to engineer. By October 1, 1989, with no new agreement in sight, the world's bilateral alliances had no alternative but to agree to an extension of the 1983 ICA, though without economic clauses, until September 30, 1991.

The reactivated quotas of 1980 stabilised the world price within the agreed price range of US 125 cents to 140 cents per pound, with very buoyant prices in 1982–83 and 1983–84. Prices were buoyed by the Brazilian frost in 1982–83 which reduced world coffee production to 4.9m tons, to a level 17 per cent below the previous years. A worrying development also began to occur in the world market: the quite sharp increase in the non-quota, and therefore cheaper markets, from an estimated 6.9 million bags in 1980–81 to 9.6 million bags in 1982–83. The non-quota market, considered irrelevant in the 1960s and 1970s was becoming, by the end of the decade, a 'parallel market' of serious concern to those participating in the regulated one.

Each importer and exporter country had their own interest to consider when assessing the importance of the growth of the non-quota market. Importers in particular were put in a difficult position. Membership of the ICA prevented coffee drinkers not only from getting coffee at a cheaper price, but also restricting their access to coffee of high quality. This was because Brazil, which dominates the quota market with a 30 percent share, also produces the poorest quality beans. As a result, the high quality Other Milds (India, Indonesia, Nicaragua, Tanzania, Kenya, Costa Rica, El Salvador, Papua New Guinea *et. al*) were restricted. Further, as we have seen, the 1976 and 1983 Agreements encouraged the Other Milds to hold stocks as part of their quota allocation. But stockholding was becoming increasingly expensive by the mid-1980s, and some producers began to offload what they had to non-member consumers in large quantities, in order to recoup some of their costs. It could be foreseen, from the 1976 Agreement, that the stockholding scheme designed for Brazil, in its interest, would rebound on the membership of the ICA because not only was it pushing them toward over-production, but also because it was building up unacceptable stockholding costs for small producers.

The problems first became evident in 1986. In that year, quotas were suspended as a result of continuing high prices. There was a flood of coffee into the market as stocks were released and Brazilian production recovered such that the ICO anticipated quotas could be reintroduced by December 1986. But suspension of quotas creates the even more difficult problem of their reintroduction. For, while there is very little argument about the price level at which they should come into existence, there is furious political controversy about relative shares at the global level and inside each producing country. Globally there is controversy over the quota awarded to each producing country relative to others. Inside producer countries, fights arise between export companies regarding the relative share each exporter gets of the quota.

In Papua New Guinea, political conflict during 1986 between exporting companies and the CIB was vicious. By 1986, the profile of exporters had changed, largely as a result of unwarranted intervention by the Minister of Primary Industry, Mr Denis Young, in 1984. Young upset the established control of the industry by supporting the establishment of a new coffee company, Kumul Kopi, ostensibly to give smallholders a greater share in the lucrative export industry. He also encouraged the CIB, in the 1983–84 season, to drastically reduce the quota share of the small exporters -- such as Volkart and PNG Coffee Exports Ltd. -- and to redistribute their share to Kumul Kopi and Wahgi Mek Plantation, a huge Western Highlands plantation group owned by Michael Mel and other villagers and managed by its former 'white' boss Dick Hagon.

The Minister's actions injected a new element into the political competition between Papua New Guinea exporters. The fear was that not only might the state take a more active role in allocating shares inside the country than hitherto acceptable -- more along the lines of African coffee politics -- but also that, inevitably, this intervention would go beyond a Bonapartist role to actually intervene in favour of some black élites against others. This threat required vigorous political mobilisation. The immediate result was the formation of the new industry representative group, the Coffee Industry Association (CIA). CIA traced its origins back to the colonial HFSA, but this was independent Papua New Guinea, and coffee politics had become more complex. Initially, the CIA found it difficult to make any political moves at all, for Young was setting the agenda and dividing its members. The CIA found itself hamstrung because Young was making war on some of its export members and favouring others. (See Chapter 10 for the story of the CIA during the coffee rust period).

By 1986, the meddling by Minsters in the coffee industry and the appearance of 'bias' and favouritism by the CIB had undermined consensus on quota allocation, had politicised the process and weakened the CIB's claim to be merely administering coffee quota allocations in a technical way. The demise in the credibility of the CIB was a boost for the Coffee Industry Association (CIA), which was poised to play a major role. The CIA had appointed a very capable executive officer, Craig McConaghy, who began to influence the agenda, aiming to position the CIA between competing exporter members and to devise a CIA position which would be in the interests of the membership as a whole. However, as he soon found out, getting agreement from member exporters was difficult. The smaller exporters wanted quotas to be allocated on the basis of exports in the 'free market' period from February 1986 to December 1986, rather than on market share prior to this period, that under quotas, because they correctly believed that the quota period favoured the big exporters. The big exporters in Papua New Guinea were, of course, unprepared to give away quota share, and therefore market share when quotas were reapplied. Initially, the CIB seemed to be persuaded by the small exporters' argument. Even the suggestion that the CIB *might* allocate quotas on the basis of performance in 1986 caused big exporters to pay growers between K300 to K400 per tonne, *above the world price*. The CIB responded that they approved of the 'increased competition amongst exporters'.

The CIB and, in particular, its Executive Officer, Mr Ricky Mitio, were seriously disturbed at Ministerial intervention from Young and, later in 1986, from new Minister Iambakey Okuk. The latter offered Wally Perdacher an export licence for no apparent reason, simply through the exercise of ministerial fiat. But the CIB was determined to get coffee politics out of national politics. The strategy adopted was to set up the Coffee Industry Review Committee made up of growers, exporters, buyers and representatives from CIA and DPI. The task of this committee was to establish guidelines for quota allocation which accommodated the interests of big and small exporters and which, once established, could operate in a technical fashion. On May 14, 1986, the committee agreed to a draft compromise:

> In the event of the reintroduction of the ICO global quota the allocation of a PNG quota must take into account the following criteria:
>
> (a) historical performance
> (b) non-member market performance
> (c) free market performance

It seemed like a good compromise - - but would it be acceptable?

In the event, the compromise failed to appeal to the technocrats. They are still very powerful in the industry and able to exercise political weight far beyond their numbers. The main intervention was by CIB economist Paul Barker, seconded from DPI, who is very experienced in coffee industry economics and politics. Barker released a CIB discussion paper which proposed once again that the mechanism for determining quota allocation will be that:

> Each exporter would gain market share according to the proportion of total coffee export earnings earned by his company in the previous coffee year, October 1st - - September 30th. The quota allocation will be determined in two parts, member and non-member, in the event that non-member sales have occurred. (Barker n.d.)

This is nothing like the proposal adopted by the Coffee Industry Review Committee. Nevertheless, it had the political advantage of expanding the quota share of the very large exporters and the very small ones. Under

Barker's scheme, ANGCO would get 43.47 percent of the quota, PNGCE 13.7 percent, Gollin/CIL 12.8 percent, Kumul 9.3 percent, Namasu 6.3 percent, Kundu 5.5 percent, Waghi Mek 3.2 percent, Cofex 3.2 percent, PTC 1.6 percent and Panga 1.07 percent. This distribution compares with the proposal of Kundu (formerly Harrison and Crossfield), a medium sized exporter, that ANGCO should get 35 percent, Gollins/CIL 15 percent, PNGCE 8.5 percent, Kumul 8.5 percent, Kundu 8.5 percent, Cofex 7.5 percent, Namasu 7.5 percent, Waghi Mek 2.5 percent - - which would have represented significant flattening out of quota share.

There were strong protests to Barker's proposal. Kundu claimed that 'the CIB would be taking a step backwards if the system were implemented in its original state' and protested that the CIB was 'dictating to private enterprise companies'. Gollin/CIL were more moderate, agreeing with the concept of value as the basis for determining quota, and supporting an annual review. PNGCE supported the Barker proposal, not surprisingly, as they would do well out of it. Kumul, Prime Minister Wingti's 'baby', and Cofex were not satisfied. The response of the CIA was interesting. McConaghy took the initiative and returned the debate to the 'historic' clause proposed by the Coffee Industry Review Committee, which Barker seems to have forgotten. McConaghy suggested a 36-month moving average be adopted. He proposed that this include a period up to October 1, 1987 (not October 1, 1986) which meant that both quota and free market performance would be taken into account. This seemed broadly acceptable. Barker redrafted his memo to this effect, undoubtedly grateful that 'value' had been accepted as the basis of quota allocation and that this ". . . mechanism recognises the efforts made in 1983-84 by exporters to attain substantial non-member sales and the implication by the CIB that this would be considered in future quota allocations." (Barker n.d.)

An acceptable formula could not, however, be found at the global level. In 1989, ICO delegates met to devise a new ICA. It had taken almost two years - - from early 1986 to December 1987 - - to agree on the reintroduction of quotas, but the problem they faced in 1989, the negotiation of a completely new Agreement, was even more divisive. Perversely, it was precisely because countries like PNG had made such efforts to build up its non-market sales, that the dominant bilateral alliance of the United States and Brazil - - the informal 'political' alliance which held the agreement together - - began to fall apart. The seriousness of the breakdown in this bilateral alliance was not widely understood until April 1989. At that time, the end of the 1983 agreement was only five months away, but neither Brazil nor the United States had altered their antagonistic positions.

The antagonism was deep and strongly held on both sides. The United States administration had finally decided that its coffee drinkers needed a better deal, particularly better quality coffee at a cheaper price. It was rumoured also, that the United States trade was not getting a reasonable share of non-quota markets. This also made coffee merchants in the country hostile to the agreement. The United States believed there were two ways to overcome the problem: first, to abandon the ICO and have a free market, which would lower price but also allow American coffee drinkers unlimited access to a higher quality, such as the Other Milds or second, to adopt a universal quota (UQ) which would combine quota and non-quota markets into a single, universal one.

Brazil, Colombia and most other large producers opposed both suggestions. A feature of the international coffee politics of the period was that Brazil did not take its customary lead in putting the producer case. This may be partly because coffee is now much less important to Brazil's export income than it was twenty years ago, worth-only 7 percent of Brazil's export earnings. Brazil is able to be much more relaxed about international coffee politics than was possible when the Agreements were first established. Consequently, it was Colombia which played the leading role in representing the position of large producers and it was she who had the most to lose from a collapse in the Agreement, and thus the collapse of the bilateral alliances.

The reasons for Brazil and Colombia's hostility to incorporating non-market coffee into the ICO was simply that it would reduce their relative share of world coffee. Further, both claim to have protected -- by supporting the agreements -- the market share of Other Milds since 1963. Brazil and Colombia argue that Other Milds who have sold too much coffee on the cheap non-quota markets, should not now be rewarded for their dumping actions by having non-market coffee taken into account in a new quota system. Brazil and Colombia, in making such statements, are opposing their interests to those of other producers, particularly the Other Milds. This is a necessity at this point in time, from their point of view, but it is an unwise strategy in the long run, because, as has been shown, the success of the ICA rests not only on the maintenance of the informal bilateral alliances but also on formalising the myth of the importer/exporter cleavage.

The Brazilian delegates to the ICO in 1989 were constrained by conflicts within the Brazilian administration, and by the impending presidential elections. This was another reason for Colombia taking the lead in pushing for a new agreement. Colombia proposed that the ICO establish quotas in both markets, quota and non-quota, and that these be added to stockholding provisions so that a figure could be arrived at which would eventually give a percentage share of world coffee to each country. This percentage would then be applied to both markets. Of course, monitoring such sales in non-quota markets is very difficult because importer states in such markets are not prepared to police ICO resolutions. However, both Brazil and

Colombia believed a system of controls and penalties could be applied to countries which oversold in the non–quota market – – something which was of course essential if their proposal were to succeed. They aimed to re–establish the bilateral alliance because it would preserve their market share. It was touted by them as an interim measure. But there was understandable cynicism that it might last a very long time. Much depended on the reaction of the United States. In the past, it would have accepted big producer arguments. However, in 1989, the United States stated that it would only support the proposal if it was an interim measure pending the adoption of a universal quota system – – not what Brazil and Colombia had in mind. The Other Milds would not support it at all, because it made no attempt to respond to their desire to continue to increase market share. The proposal would have had the effect of limiting their non–member sales.

The seriousness of the collapse of the bilateral alliance, and the intransigence of the United States, was revealed on June 13, 1989 when motions before the ICO called for its extension. The danger of such a forthright motion was that if it was not carried, the ICO would have to terminate, there and then, and not simply suspend quotas. The extraordinary feature of the political manoeuvering in relation to this motion was that it, and a counter–motion, showed how serious the split in bilateral alliances had become by 1989. In the past, the issue would have been resolved by a formal discussion of importers and exporters on the issue, followed by voting along the lines of the informal bilateral alliance. But by 1989, the two 'sides' now composed an 'unholy alliance' (for the ICO) of the United States joined with Other Milds producers, opposed by *inter alia*, Brazil, Colombia, IACO (African Robusta producers), the Philippines and the EC consuming countries. The vote was not taken, but the ICO was thrown into chaos by these alliances. The temporary solution reached was to have quotas suspended.

Within the producer group, divisions run deep. These are ironically caused by the Agreement itself. In particular, they are a result of the massive over–production and stockholding encouraged by the 1976 and 1983 ICAs. Compromise between the Other Milds and Brazil seems impossible to reach because if the latter insists on retaining its 30 percent world share, *and* increased production of Other Milds since the 1970s is recognised, then only some 13 percent of global quota will remain to share out among the world's Robusta producers. In effect, the producer countries have reached a stalemate that cannot be resolved on the basis of the old bilateral alliances.

The suspension of quotas on June 13, 1989 caused an immediate and spectacular plunge in the world coffee price. In May 1989, the composite indicator price (1979=100) was at 115.89 US cents per pound and by July it had plunged to 76.67 US cents per pound. This was the lowest price for many years, and it shocked the industry. In the past, a collapse in price has stiffened the resolve of bilateral alliances to negotiate a new agreement. However, this time there are too many interests who feel they can do better in a 'free market' than in an ICA based on quotas. By the end of the 1980s, United States coffee drinkers wanted to take advantage of cheap prices. As well, the United States coffee trade wants to compete freely with Western European traders in non–quota markets. On the producer side, Brazil, now less dependent on coffee, wants to abandon what it sees as 'help' for other producers offered through the ICA, ensuring their market share; she now wished to compete with Other Milds in all markets. These latter are convinced their higher quality coffee will gain market share in non–regulated markets.

The abandonment of quotas and the failure to negotiate a new Agreement led all coffee interests to search for someone to blame. It is true, as was repeatedly said, that over–production was to blame for the problems. But it was rarely pointed out that the ICA itself, and the process of reaching an Agreement based on bilateral alliances, was a principle cause of over–production. It was also rarely acknowledged that bilateral alliances emerged because production cannot be controlled. Bilateral alliance is the only way coffee flow can be controlled, and with its breakdown international coffee regulation also ceases to exist. Coffee politics, however, seemed to turn on false assumptions about price and importer/exporter behaviour. Ultimately, all coffee producers and importers are dependent on the hope that everyone will eventually see sense. This is a poor outcome after almost thirty years of international coffee regulation, a result, it seems, of the failure to submit the ICO to critical analysis – – as this study has attempted to do.

Yet world coffee may still be saved by a completely unpredictable development. Colombia, which has seen most of its technical proposals defeated by political intransigence from Brazil and the United States finally resorted, on August 31, 1989 to a dirty, but effective trick. Rodrigo Llonedo, a presidential candidate, blamed the United States for a loss of coffee income because of its withdrawal from the ICA, and claimed that Colombia could not be expected to lose coffee income *and* spend money fighting drugs. Surprisingly, this argument seems to have made an impact on the United States, 'the world's largest consumer of coffee and illicit drugs'. In response to this issue–linkage, United States coffee negotiators seem to have developed renewed interest in at least discussing coffee quotas.

Recent developments in world coffee organisation show how important informal bilateral alliances have been to the world's longest surviving commodity agreement. It is obvious that the myth of the importer/exporter cleavage formalised into the ICA can no longer be maintained. If a new ICA is to emerge from the ashes of the 1983 Agreement, it will be an organisation structured very differently from the ICO of the past. There is no sign at present that far-sighted thinking has been applied to the organisational structure of the ICO. Rather, *ad hoc* political negotiation still dominates. There is still minimal consideration of future implications of deals done in the present.[5]

Notes

1. There are other mechanisms which can be used for stabilisation such as:

(1) trade quotas,
(2) long run purchase contracts, and
(3) buffer stock schemes.

Buffer stock schemes have been favoured by various developing countries in general though economists have argued that for at least two reasons they are less suitable for coffee. The first reason has been outlined by Edwards who notes that, "An examination of the relative merits of buffer stocks and quota policies reveals that there is very little to choose between them on practical grounds. Policy simulations suggest that while both have reasonable success in dampening out short-term fluctuations, only quota policies are likely to have any effect on the long term cycle owing to their freedom from resource constraints. (Edwards 1977:193)

The second reason has been outlined by Gerhard who notes that: "The choice of methods associated with buffer stocks is extremely limited and the criteria for negotiability is far from sufficient to ensure economically positive effects -- at least as long as renegotiations are hampered by incomplete foresight. Thus buffer stock schemes require a degree of agreement between countries not likely and a commitment over a longer time than the coffee cycle would seem to allow. " (Gerhard 1963:277)

2. A major problem that arises in relation to production is due to the fact that members of the ICO are sovereign entities is that the ICO can only advise countries on production programs. The ICO cannot force sovereign states to adopt production policies it would favour. We will see later however, that the ICO through the 1976 ICA did manage to more or less dictate production policies through forcing countries to hold certain stocks.

3. Some economists, upon noticing this interproducer rivalry, have even argued that the main purpose of the ICA is not to regulate prices at all but to manage a conflict between producers, one which is structural because some are producers of Robusta and some of Arabica. Kabir-Ur-Rahman Khan notes that the Agreement: "Though coy about giving open recognition to the differences between the [producer] groups has been moving slowly toward resolving them. The stated objectives of the Coffee

Agreement do not refer specifically to these conflicts nor to the existence of any machinery to deal with them." (Kabir-Ur-Rahman Khan 1979:181)

4. Geer regards the linkage of production control with price as the most desirable form of international regulation. However, it is implicit in his views that price control (direct or indirect) which is separate from production control virtually ensures that production control will be unsuccessful. "If such a change [production control] in the national policy of a producer country cannot yet be attained through an international commodity agreement it follows that no long-run equilibrium price, as defined under price competition, can be arrived at. This, then, leaves room only for bargaining between both sides of the market determined through an identity of interest. the bargaining solution prevents the two results stated above (surplus as a weapon in price war and oligopolistic indeterminate prices). Given the structure of the world coffee industry, the ICA seems thus to be the only possible second-best solution that could be aimed at. The further regulation of production goals is thus not relevant if we analyse the International Coffee Agreement as a form of exemption, since the production policy does not influence the price determination on the world market so long as the agreement stays in operation." (Geer 1971:176)

5. This section has been compiled by reference to trade journals such as F.O. Lichts and Reuters *Coffee Newsletter*. I was also assisted by a visit to the library of the International Coffee Organisation, London, on 10 May 1990.

13

The Use of Liberal, Negotiated, Institutionalised Global Commodity Agreements to Cause the Underdevelopment of Papua New Guinea's Coffee Industry

Introduction

The exploitation of small coffee-producing nations by dominant alliances is achieved partly through the formal mechanisms of the ICA, such as the quota system, and also through what could be called informal mechanisms. These include the meaning attached to formal mechanisms such as the myth of the dominance of the importer/exporter cleavage, and the fiction of formal equivalence between ICA members because they are all states. Informal mechanisms leave a political space in the workings of the agreement that is filled by the influence exercised by the dominant alliances acting in their own interests.

In the case of world coffee, its regulation imposes limits and costs upon production in small countries. These occur in at least two ways. First, the virtual freezing of trading relations in the interests of dominant bilateral strata ensures that the production possibilities, especially of small producers like Papua New Guinea, are severely curtailed. Second, most of the indirect costs of operating an ICA, which have increased in the 1976 ICA since stocks must be held in producer countries, accrue to them. Thus in the case of small coffee-producing nations which are dependent on foreign exchange earnings from the crop, these limits are severe enough to contribute to their overall underdevelopment.

The state in small producing countries plays a crucially important role in the operation of the ICA and therefore in the maintenance of dominant bilateral alliances over the flow of world coffee. Two important qualities of the state make the ICA work. The first is the fact that a state is a territorial entity which has a monopoly over the means of coercion within a social formation. This is used in the regulation of world coffee to police the quota system. The second quality of the state vital to the operation of the ICA is the fiction that all states have a degree of formal equality. This fiction plays a very important role in the process of negotiation which takes place within the ICA, so as to mask the reality that negotiation is dominated by alliances of big importers and big exporters.

How Does the ICA Justify its Underdevelopment of Coffee Industries in Small Producer Countries?

The main cost to small producers of international regulation is encapsulated in the figures which show that the Agreement largely worked to freeze the distribution of market shares as they existed between 12–20 years ago. The principal mechanism of the Agreement is export quotas, and as late as 1981, when they were operating under the 1976 Agreement, the allocation of quotas could be determined on export figures from 1968–69. Small countries like Papua New Guinea, whose independence came only after the beginnings of the ICA, have had little chance to sponsor their industries and expand without the limitations of regulation. The vent for surplus existing in the non-member market is hardly viable because of its small size and slow growth. In any case, prices in non-member markets are always much lower than that in member ones. The very existence of price stabilisation probably means that traditional market shares and division of labour among exporters is reinforced by the Agreement. (Payer 1975:183) This reinforcement of traditional market shares may be the main cost to small producers of international regulation, but it is one which is intangible, and rests on the counterfactual and unproven assumption that, without regulation, small producers would have done better in world coffee than they have done under regulation. I will not attempt such a proof, but will show in this section that small producers have experienced tangible economic costs under the Agreement as well as political costs, in that the ICA has been institutionalised within producer countries by having the producer state perform a midwife role for it.

The economic costs experienced by small producers include the fact that under the workings of the Agreement the cost of any significant global readjustment which has been required has been borne by the producing countries. This was the case with the diversification programme of the 1960s and is the case with stockholding schemes in the 1980s. The idea behind the Diversification Fund was that at a time of overproduction, producers in exporting countries ought to be encouraged to diversify out of coffee and into other economic activities. Some countries took the diversification suggestions from the ICO very seriously, though there is no easy way diversification could have been enforced, and in any case the producer countries were paying the total cost of the programme. It could well be argued that the dilemma of over-production was caused by the producer countries and therefore it is fitting they should pay the cost of diversification. It must be remembered, however, that the problems were exacerbated by the imposition of quotas in the Agreement. These benefited both importers and exporters and in this sense it seems unfair that producers alone should pay for long-term programmes designed to alleviate over-production.

In the case of the variable quota provisions in the 1976 ICA, producer countries paid the full cost of ensuring continuous supplies to importing firms. The producer countries cannot be blamed for under-supply, for they continue to grow and trade coffee in circumstances of coffee shortage. Importing firms must, however, have supplies and have managed, through the 1976 Agreement, to have developing countries take responsibility for ensuring long-term supplies. Importers have also managed, through the Agreement, to pass on to producer countries the very high risk involved in holding stocks when prices are falling. (*Business Week*, July 6, 1981)

It would be wrong, however, to consider the costs of the Agreement to producers solely in economic terms. More important are its political costs. In general, these include the fact that the ICA imposes itself upon small developing countries in a way that causes their internal choices to be structured by external factors. The ICA embodies a series of structures which are imposed upon the coffee industries of small producers. These achieve the institutionalisation of the ICA within producer countries. They generate the legitimation necessary to have it accepted inside a producer country that the ICO is the governing body of world coffee. These structures also create the concrete institutional channels by which actors inside producer countries can participate in the ICO. It was set up under the auspices of the United Nations, which meant that its internal structure, including voting rights, membership, etc., had to conform with UN requirements under the standard set forth in the Havana Charter. Among the important provisions of this charter was the requirement 'that participation by all countries be permitted on equal terms and that the exporting countries as a group have equal representation in any agreement'. (Bilder 1963:341) Also of significance was the point that 'the interests concerned are represented not by the industry or consumers but by the government of countries which declare themselves to be exporting or importing members'. (Geer 1971:28) To give legitimacy to the deal finally struck at the first of such agreements, it was declared that an international commodity agreement had to be signed in a conference held under the auspices of the United Nations, and that only the UN Secretary-General could commence the first session of the administering council. (Geer 1971:28)

In line with the Havana Charter, the agreement shared out votes within the ICO to importers and exporters on an even basis. The 1968 ICA, for example, stated in Article 12: (1) The exporting members shall together hold 1,000 votes and the importing members shall together hold 1,000 distributed within each category of members - - that is exporting and importing Members respectively - - as provided in the paragraphs of this article; (4) . . . votes of exporting members shall be divided among those Members in proportion to the average volume of their respective coffee imports in the preceding three-year period . . . (7) No member shall hold more than 400 votes. Thus in the 1968 agreement votes among importers were distributed as follows: USA - 400 votes, Federal Republic of Germany - 101, France - 84, Italy - 47, Sweden - 38, Netherlands - 35, Canada - 32, etc. Among exporters, votes were distributed as follows: Brazil - 332, Colombia - 114, Ivory Coast - 47, Portugal - 48, Uganda - 41, El Salvador - 34, Mexico - 32, Tanzania - 15.

It is obvious that such a structure of voting, while balancing importer/exporter interests, also nicely accommodates the interests of dominant bilateral oligopolies. The Agreement allows for the possibility of collusion between Brazil and the United States, giving them the capacity virtually to force through a position, as well as veto power over their importing or exporting group. (Marshall 1972:133) The structure of voting, and in particular the dominance of Brazil over exporters, is functional for regulation. On the one hand it manages to contain the inherent conflict among exporters and on the other the belief that Brazil is an exporter no different from others generates legitimacy for its dominance. The issues that have divided the exporters are legendary and broke out from the very first meeting, setting quotas when many exporting countries claimed special circumstances in their demands for higher ones. (Bilder 1963:333) Exporter countries have fought bitterly over the issue of quota allocation at almost every session of the ICO. Naturally, all want higher quotas but obviously the agreement cannot work if all get them. In addition, big exporters such as Brazil may have a greater interest in restricting export country quotas than working to extend them. It has been well known for some years that a key role of Brazil has been to keep other exporters in line. (Cartledge 1978:180)

The decision making process within the ICO is further structured to allow for collusion between big importers and big exporters, and to distance small producers from big exporters and from decisions taken in the interests of dominant bilateral oligopolies. Big exporters have little need to attend to

ICO directives -- Colombia, for example, used diversification funds to switch to a new fast-maturing coffee plant. They can raise prices at will by withholding their own coffee. (Geer 1971:186), or they can threaten small producers with price falls by promising to release their accumulated stocks. Small producers have very little power within the Agreement to challenge the dominance of the big exporters. Not only do they have a very small number of votes, but much of the decision making within the ICO takes place at the executive level within a board of eight exporters and eight importers. The board is democratically elected by a ballot of exporting and importing members. On the exporter side, board members are usually representatives of the major producer organisations. These change regularly, though the oldest, Oamcafe, was established in 1960. It is made up of eight French-speaking African coffee producers. The two other main producer groups in existence in 1981 were the Inter-African Coffee Organisation, also set up in 1960, which contains 19 member countries producing about 28 percent of world supply, and an international organisation, World Coffee, created in 1973 by 5 leading producers (Brazil, Colombia, Costa Rica, Angola and Ivory Coast) and controlling 80 percent of world production. (United Nations 1981:137) These organisations exist to co-ordinate the interests of their member countries' demands for quotas, etc., within the ICO, and attend meetings with set demands negotiated within their groups. (Kirschen 1980:40)

The problem with the role of these organisations in the executive and their role in co-ordinating a position on quotas, is that through this process small producers become further and further removed from the ICO centres of power. The producer organisations and the existence of the executive create multiple layers of authority, each dominated by a large exporter, which merely legitimates bilateral oligopoly dominance. Through the power of the executive the small producer can continually be presented with a *fait accompli* when it comes to decision-making. This was done in 1976 when the negotiations to set up the new Agreement took place within a small group of eight. (*Coffee International* 1976)

The single most important barrier to understanding the political cost to small producers of ICO membership is the dominant view that big exporter interests and small exporter ones can be conflated. The reason this view is so pervasive is that almost all analysts consider the importer/exporter cleavage to be the primary structure in which international coffee trade and political relations take place. The importer/exporter cleavage is relevant, for the ICA works through a quota system which is policed at the import/export point. But it would be fundamentally misleading to consider this the primary cleavage in world coffee. Taken in isolation, this cleavage does not explain why coffee actors behave in the way they do, and its persistence as the primary mechanism in the minds of analysts of world coffee can only be explained by the failure of economic analysts to fit bilateral oligopolies into their market models. Further, some analysts are linked to the bilateral oligopolies themselves, and thus have a vested interest in reinforcing a view of the world that assures the legitimacy of the dominance of world coffee by the United States and Brazil.

Why Do Coffee Technocrats Collude in the Underdevelopment of Their Domestic Industry?

It is a paradox in the structure of the ICA that though most international coffee trade - - processing, roasting, soluble manufacture and retailing - - is in private hands, the delegates who attend ICO meetings are representatives of governments. The role of government officials in these negotiations is a direct result of the sections in the Havana Charter which state that parties to the Agreement must be governments. But what role does the state play in ICAs? How do the distinctive features of the state affect the success or otherwise of the Agreement, both when it is actually operating and when it fails to adapt to changing circumstances? How exactly does the state legitimate the power of the dominant bilateral oligopolies? Finally, what is the effect of the state's role in the agreement on the domestic role of the small producer state?

Economists have attempted to explain the role of the state as though it were itself a market actor aiming only to maximise its own returns. Waters writes: "The implementation of the ICA constitutes an attenuation of the property rights of various parties in order that others, usually those in authority, can appropriate to themselves in either pecuniary or non-pecuniary form a share of the existing rewards." (Waters 1974:789) Another view of the role of the state is expressed by Rangarajan. He writes, "The charitable explanation [for governments joining ICAs] is that they are legislating for a visionary world - again, for what ought to be rather than for what will be. The cynical explanation is that it is a political act for the benefit of the . . . main participants." (Rangarajan 1978:161)

In the economists' writings on the state, we are presented with two main explanations for state involvement in ICAs. The state is either a rational actor, and therefore the equivalent of a market actor maximising its own interest, or it is an irrational actor pursuing idealist or political aims.

It is the custom of economists to assume that political goals are by definition irrational. The image presented in both views is of the state bumbling into a market place, replacing the more rational market forces and leaving long-lasting distortionary effects in its wake. All of these arguments, in the usual manner of economists, tend to turn the real world upside down. As we have already seen, the international market in coffee has failed of its own accord numerous times and without the help of the state. No agreement, whether it be based on exporters alone or in combination with some importers, has been thought to have the remotest chance of success if the members were not states. Waters' explanation fails because even at the level of appearances the state has functions quite different from those of market actors. The unique qualities of the sovereign state cannot be reduced to buying, selling or producing. Among these qualities is the spatial function of boundary maintenance through internal/external differentiation, and the political role of monopoly of coercion. It is precisely these properties at the level of appearances which make state membership indispensable for any international agreement. Beneath the procedural advantages that the state offers for the achievement of an international agreement is the substantive one that state participation in ICAs is functional for international capital. This functionality, however, must not be thought of as the state being an instrument for such capital, for underneath its international role is a domestic one, whereby it must ensure the conditions of national accumulation. To do this, the state at the international level must retain a degree of relative autonomy. It must aid international capital as thoroughly as possible at the level of circulation, but it must be able to distance itself from it whenever this threatens domestic accumulation. The clearest label one can put on the state's role at the international level is therefore that of midwife for international capital.

A key feature of the modern state is its control over definite spatial boundaries. It is a feature of it which gives it both an internal and external role. This spatial characteristic was first elaborated as a legal aspect of the state, as sovereignty. Sovereignty asserts the idea that there is a final and absolute authority in the political community -- the state -- and that no final and absolute authority exists elsewhere. (Hinsley 1966:26) Sovereignty theorists acknowledge that the exercise of this final authority was coterminous with physical boundaries, but in their thinking the spatial factor was downgraded in favour of its legal implications. The study of sovereignty suggested that there was a differentiation between two levels of state activity, but sovereignty theorists cast this differentiation solely in terms of the patterns of authority at different levels rather than the internal/external differentiation which a spatial analysis would emphasis. Sovereignty theorists admitted that sovereignty was Janus-headed:

> Applied to the community in the context of the internal structure of a political society, the concept of sovereignty has involved the belief that there is an absolute political power within the community. Applied to the problems which arise in the relations between political communities, its function has been to express the antithesis of this argument -- the principle that internationally over and above the collection of communities, no supreme authority exists. (Hinsley 1966:158)

But sovereignty theorists have failed to bring these two levels together in their analysis. The sovereignty thesis has had to be modified by students of politics because it suggested a rigid relationship between a pattern of authority and the domestic or international community with which it was related. Or, to put it another way, it was only by seeking refuge in legalism that the analyst could possibly pretend that some states were not more powerful than others at the international level or that there might be actors in the domestic society and economy as powerful as the domestic state. Such a conception of separate spheres of state power also did not attend to the important political changes that can lead to an alteration of either relationship.

For this reason, Weber's notion of territoriality is now favoured in place of sovereignty. This notion does suggest spatial differentiation between domestic and international levels but it does not prejudge political outcomes in the way the sovereignty thesis does. Territoriality can deal with a 'separation between internal and external, regardless of the form of the internal order or that of the external relations. This separation is inherent in the concept of territory'. (Freund 1968:220) Territoriality emphasises the spatial dimension of the modern state, for it assumes that politics takes place within a circumscribed territory. The frontiers of the state do not have to be strictly established in this analysis; they may be variable, but without the existence of a territory individuating the group, there can be no external politics.

It is safe to say that without this notion of a territory individuating the group, without the participation of the state and its spatial differentiation into internal and external levels, an ICA based on export restriction quotas would not be possible. The export restriction quota scheme works on the basis of regulation through interruption of the flow of the green coffee bean. The break must be made at a point in the marketing chain which is uniform for both producer and importer. If such a uniform break point did not exist, attempts to flout the regulation scheme could never be brought under control. Further, there must be a significant degree of control by an agency at the point of break because quotas must be easily adjustable to changes of supply and demand.

The quota scheme thus relies on another feature of the modern state identified by Weber, that the state has a monopoly of the means of legitimate coercion. The obvious point at which control can be achieved is that at which the commodity crosses national frontiers, a point where the state exercises almost total control. The involvement of the state as a member of the ICO ensures that the Agreement can use this special power of the state to regulate the movement of coffee. The Agreement makes use of the state's monopoly over the legitimate means of violence, for the state's agents of coercion, customs officers, are the real policemen of the ICA.

The main point of control in policing the Agreement which has been used thus far is the point of import. In the first 1962 ICA, coffee entering an importing country was accompanied by a certificate of origin. Once a country's total quota of exports had been imported that country was simply not able to release more coffee onto the world market. By 1965 this method of policing was being evaded by producers who were exporting coffee first to a third country and then on to an importer. This coffee, known as tourist coffee – – coffee shipped from signatory producing nations to either new markets or non–signatory importing countries and then reshipped to signatory importing countries without the original certificates of origin or export stamps – – was halted by measures taken in 1966 when the ICO issued stamps to producers equivalent to the amount of coffee each country was allowed to export. The number of stamps issued to each country was the same as the quota and these were held in a country's central bank to be dispensed by an ICO–approved domestic agency to exporting firms. This made the job of policing quotas easier for importers because any coffee accompanied by ICO stamps must be legitimately within the global quota. The issue of stamps merely formalised the power of the ICO but did not extend it, and it did not alter the crucial policing role performed by the importing states.

The notion of internal/external differentiation which is structurally present in the modern state served further purposes for the establishment of an ICO, given that its members were states and not market actors. Making a uniform break in the flow of green bean at the point of export meant that coffee relations could be treated quite separately at the internal and the external level. The internal and external levels of coffee flows are like two separate policy fields. Each has a distinct pattern of coffee relations and within each the exercise of ICO authority takes a different form. At the external level, the midwife role of the state ensures that importers and big exporters are favoured in the operation of those ICO clauses which are designed to prevent price manipulation. At the internal level importers are favoured because they do not contribute to production control or diversification programmes inside the producer state. At the internal level, however, the main beneficiary is the domestic state (both importer and exporter states), because the ICO respects the internal sovereignty of the state and does not predetermine the structure of internal coffee relations.

At the external level, the Agreement contains two articles, 32 and 33, which impose sanctions on any coffee actors who attempt to manipulate the world coffee price (though, for obvious reasons, the articles are relevant only to the very large exporters and importers who have this capacity). Both articles operate on the assumption that there is a direct connection between price and supply. The basis on which an attempt is made to sanction price manipulators is of course the primary formal mechanism in the Agreement, the quota restriction scheme. But there are at least three limitations to this structure, which cause it to fail to sanction big exporters and big importers. The first limitation is that the Agreement can do nothing if the larger exporter decides to obey the quota system but sells at a secret price which is higher or lower than the current price. The second limitation is that Article 33 (1962) contains a major qualification of the extent to which price manipulators through quota shortfalls are punishable. The Article ensures that the decision to sanction a member depends on whether the country with the shortfall can get the numbers in its favour in the ICO vote. As I have already shown, the voting system favours the large bilateral oligopolies so it is very unlikely that in such a vote Brazil would not be able to get the assistance of its bilateral oligopolist partner, the United States. The third limitation of the Agreement which modifies the operation of the sanction Articles is the fact that the entire Agreement is designed to work on supply only, so there is no possible way that Articles 32 and 33 can sanction importers. Geer (1971:180) notes that importers can contribute to price instability -- price manipulation in my terms -- by holding stocks to depress prices. But the Agreement has no authority at all on the demand side of the equation.

The agreement works, even through its sanction articles, to reinforce or at least accommodate existing power centres at the external level i.e., the bilateral oligopoly of Brazil and the United States. The role of the domestic state is crucial in masking this simple fact. The role of the domestic state, because it has a formal equivalence with other states, masks the fact that the price-quota connection is not direct and that the actual operation of the sanctions on price manipulation can only benefit large exporters and importers. The formal equivalence embodied in the state makes it appear that all states can manipulate prices equally and that they will also be equally sanctioned. Similarly, the membership of the domestic state and the policing of quotas at state boundaries reinforces the view that importer/exporter cleavage is the most important in coffee relations. In fact, collusion between big exporters and big importers is facilitated through the operation of the agreement but because the domestic state has been co-opted as a midwife to facilitate this collusion and to deliver small producers and small importers to the bilateral oligopolies, the collusion is not revealed.

At the internal level -- and again the internal/external differentiation structurally present in the modern state makes the identification of such levels plausible -- the Agreement also operates to reinforce existing power centres. It does this mainly by recognising the internal sovereignty of the state in domestic society and not predetermining its nature. The reality of state internal sovereignty has implications for importers and producers as well as for the role of the ICO itself. For the state in producer countries the advantage is that it can participate in the ICO without undermining its own power to regulate internal coffee trade.

The ICA has been institutionalised within small producer countries. What is most important in the institutionalisation process is that government membership in the ICO ensures that the power of the state (small producer or otherwise) would be enlisted to reinforce the ICO. It has been shown that the ICO could not possibly have operated without the co-operation of member states, and not member firms or individuals in member countries. In fact the participation of governments in the agreement generated a certain legitimacy for the agreement by reinforcing the importer/exporter cleavage and by giving the appearance of a formal equivalence among participants. This equivalence was based on the fact that all the members were states. The role of the state goes beyond the generation of legitimacy, however, for the small producer state plays a vital role as midwife in the regulation of international coffee. The small producer state allows regulation to proceed through its special qualities of territoriality, sovereignty and its internal/external differentiation. Further, the role the small producer state plays in the flow of international coffee is that of agent in dominance of the bilateral oligopoly of Brazil and the United States. In other words, the small producing member state has been co-opted through regulation to secure the interests of the dominant bilateral oligopoly.

The ICA is built upon the myth of formal equivalence among members, a myth perpetuated by United Nations backing of the agreement and by the Agreement's liberal form. The form of organisation embodied in the apparent representativeness of the voting system promises broad participation in its politics. This gives small producers the illusion of the possibility of achieving structural change to world coffee relations through the mechanisms of the Agreement. But the form the Agreement adopts tends to have the effect of reinforcing existing coffee relations. Liberal forms tend to institutionalise and formalise structural differentiation among participants. At the same time, by broadening the basis of political participation, they hold out the promise that adjustment mechanisms can be adapted to achieve shifts in power relations. In fact, as we have seen, the changes that have been made to the various agreements have been functional ones, designed to provide technical solutions to problems rather than an alteration of power relations. Thus the agreement does not allow for the possibility of seriously curtailing the power of the dominant bilateral oligopoly.

Conclusion

The study has demonstrated that the enduring social structure in an industry arises out of production. In the colonial coffee industry of Papua New Guinea the two main classes in the industry were the white planters and the smallholders. The study exposed many important features of the hidden abode of production of these two main classes. The significance of the size of the unit of production, of the different forms of labour used on different production units – – wage labour on plantations, family labour on smallholdings – – the capacity of planters for investment and accumulation, and the need of smallholders to balance food production, food purchases and commodity production within the household were all surveyed, and their significance for the organisation of production was shown. But most importantly, it was shown that for both units of production there were severe limits on their development at the level of production. Coffee planters are limited by the production of absolute surplus value. Smallholders are limited by the simple reproduction 'squeeze', which at the level of production takes the form of the intensification of labour devoted to coffee vis-à-vis food and at the level of exchange takes the form of declining terms of trade for the household. The limits to the development of smallholders and planters are not altered with independence even though white plantations were taken over by two black class fractions, the *petit bourgeoisie* and the big peasantry.

The limits on development of the main producing classes and their distinctive class locations determines the course development and underdevelopment take beyond the production level. The fundamental fact is that antagonistic classes are in different forms of production. Planters cannot directly exploit the subordinate class in the industry, the smallholders, at the point of production, as they can wage labour. Surplus (not surplus value) has to be appropriated by the dominant class by extracting land or labour from the household, by appropriating surplus in the form of monies or other assets of the household and by monopolising the marketing outlets for the smallholder crop or in other ways turning the domestic terms of trade against the smallholder producer.

It has been shown in the book that the market for the coffee industry in Papua New Guinea, both in the colonial and the post-colonial periods, has not been marked by significant government intervention. This fact does not mean that the domestic coffee market is free or competitive. But it does mean that dominant classes have to rely more on market power than on state power if they are to exercise significant control over the flow of coffee in the domestic market. This control was achieved by white planters when they set up the industry and was inherited and extended in the post-colonial period by the *petit bourgeoisie* and the big peasantry. The strategy adopted by the dominant classes has been to become vertically integrated (from coffee buyer to exporter), in the coffee industry and to buy and sell plant and equipment so that they can control each pinch point in the industry.

In the Arabica coffee industry in Papua New Guinea, I have identified three main pinch points: the coffee buyer, the processing (from parchment to green bean), and the exporter. I have shown how surplus is appropriated from smallholders at the coffee buyer pinch point when processor-tied buyers pay smallholders the price of low-quality parchment without testing it for quality. I have argued that in the processing and exporting of coffee bought from coffee-buyers there is nothing to prevent its being graded at the higher quality level. Surplus is also appropriated from the smallholder at the processing pinch point. This is an indirect result of restricting the number of processing plants. I have shown that the argument that overcapacity exists at the processing pinch point is a fiction. But the fact that the number of processing plants is restricted assists processors to tie smallholder production to particular factories, and in the production of cherry to processing firms owned and operated by the management agencies. Many processing plants and exporters are also vertically integrated. This further reduces competition in the industry and increases the power of the dominant class in the coffee industry. At the exporter level, surplus is mainly appropriated through the operation of the stabilisation fund. This occurs less as a result of the extraction of a levy from growers to finance it than from the fact that when a bounty is paid back to the industry at a time of low prices, it is paid back to exporters. Few in the industry seriously believe that the bounty reaches the smallholder by this process.

The distribution of power in an industry is vitally affected by the role of the state. Its role in the colonial and post-colonial coffee industry in Papua New Guinea presents, at first, a not unfamiliar paradox. On the one hand, the state appears to be an instrument in the hands of the dominant class. For example, the Department of Agriculture, Stock and Fisheries (DASF) did assist well-off farmers in its early extension period, and the Coffee Marketing Board (CMB) did assist the white planters to co-opt a budding middle peasantry into the coffee industry. There are enough examples of this kind throughout the book to suggest that both the colonial and the post-colonial state in the coffee industry reinforced existing class locations and appropriation of surplus at the various pinch points. However, there are also enough counter-examples to show that the state in the coffee industry was not an instrument in the hands of either the *petit bourgeoisie* or the big peasants in the contemporary period. For example, in the colonial period DASF did not use the full coercive power of the state to prevent smallholders from planting coffee as the planters requested, and in the post-colonial period the Department of Primary Industry (DPI) has been virtually ignored by the dominant classes in the industry.

How can the form and function of such a state be explained? I have called the state form in the coffee industry of Papua New Guinea a Bonapartist state, neither an instrument in the hands of dominant classes nor masters over all social actors. The Bonapartist form highlights the fact that state action takes place within a system of social action. State policies are always subject to modification by class struggle, and may even become irrelevant in this process. In the coffee industry of Papua New Guinea, the state's specialist agricultural branches, DASF in the colonial period and DPI in the post-colonial period, played a minor role in the coffee industry. There is a huge gap between what these branches of the state claim as their own achievements and what are in fact the outcomes of social action. For example, I assess the claim that DASF assistance was vital for the growth of the coffee industry and find it to be exaggerated. I also analysed the 20-hectare developments of the post-colonial period and show that DPI was unable to play the co-ordinating role it set itself. I analysed the politics of setting up the Coffee Marketing Board (CMB) and its post-colonial predecessor, the Coffee Industry Board (CIB), as examples of the way in which Bonapartist state forms became established. I showed that setting up these boards was a political process which involved recognition of the limits of the state in shaping regulatory functions. These functions do not include state marketing because this would compromise the market power of the dominant classes, but they do include the establishment of a range of protective devices for the industry as a whole, such as the stabilisation fund.

The dynamics of power are shown in two case studies, the 20-hectare coffee development programme and the 1986 coffee rust outbreak. The 20-hectare study shows that smallholders have voluntarily handed over land and labour to dominant classes, in their guise as management agencies. The smallholders may not have lost their land forever, and the 20-hectare development may not fail, but the point is that only luck, in the form of high international coffee prices, can save smallholders from becoming completely dependent on management agency use of 20–hectare land. The study shows how the best intentions of state policy-makers can go wrong. If they can ignore power relations in a Bonapartist state where dominant classes have control over pinch points in the marketing chain, their aim to assist smallholders will not be achieved.

The case study of the coffee rust outbreak in 1986 shows the emergence of a new potentially more powerful, alliance made up of the CIB, the *petit bourgeoisie* and some influential white planters, who returned as managers of their previously–owned plantations. The vehicle for this alliance was a newly formed association, the CIA, modelled on the colonial HFSA. Their struggle to control smallholders, beyond the use of market mechanisms, caused them to adopt coffee rust as a pretext. However, this approach alienated big peasant interests, who saw the CIB/CIA alliance as a threat to local growers. Interestingly, the Highlands premiers joined the big peasant groups in a combined defence of local interests. The resulting conflict created new divisions in coffee politics but offered little solace to smallholders, who remained powerless and were potentially the victims of any major industry reorganisation.

Coffee is an export commodity, so any study of a coffee producing country must place this in the context of the flow of world coffee. Coffee is unusual in that it is highly regulated through the world's largest surviving international commodity Agreement. The study shows that the regulatory type and form of international capital as embodied in the ICO discriminates against small coffee–producing countries like Papua New Guinea. This discrimination operates in two main ways. First, it freezes quota shares on an historical basis, providing advantage to the bilateral alliances of big importers and big exporters, which dominate the Agreement. Big exporters are assured of their market share and since 1976, big importers have been assured of supply. Second, the agreement co–opts small producer states to police the operation of the Agreement. This can be expensive and carry obligations which are not in the interest of large producers in the co–opted state. An obligation on this type can be found in the stockholding provisions of the 1976 Agreement.

An important feature of the regulatory form and type of international coffee capital is that it is politically indeterminate: i.e., the control of marketing and regulation which exists at the international level does not have to be replicated in the domestic market of the member country. This is just as well, for no member country would tolerate ICO interference in its sovereignty. The domestic marketing arrangements in a coffee–producing country are also usually a product of that country's history. Hence marketing arrangements differ from country to country. In the case of coffee, the ICA confounds analysts because it has been structured around the distinctive features of world coffee trade, specifically the importance of taste and the history of trading relations in the industry.

The study of the coffee industry in Papua New Guinea gives no comfort to those who see socialism and self-reliance as a solution for underdevelopment. The call for self-reliance is only partly applicable to international coffee relations. The ICO does discriminate against small producing countries but the principal agents in this discrimination are fellow producers and the country's own state. How can self-reliance improve this situation? Inside Papua New Guinea the idea of a coffee industry organised on socialist lines is entirely fanciful. Who would be the agents of such a change? Smallholders are not communalists; they are peasants. They are not directly exploited, so they have no basis for conscious, mobilised class action in support of socialism. Also, the capitalist state proves to be a most subtle form of power. Its agents are themselves capable of advocating socialism while at the same time simply extending the system of appropriation. Because of the complexity of the analytical task, let alone the liberating one, I have not been able to suggest in this book how the slogans of self-reliance and socialism can be replaced with any concrete mobilisation strategy. There is still much theoretical work to be done before any such strategy materialises. However, the book does endorse the call for the 'defence of peasant political space', as Holmquist (1980) put it some years ago, and it shows that this defensive task is urgent in peasant societies.

Bibliography

Books and Journal Articles

Adams, F.G. and Klein, S.A. 1978. *Stabilizing World Commodity Markets* Lexington: D.C. Heath and Company.

Afflick, I. 1981. "A Commercial Bank: Papua New Guinea Banking Corporation". In M.A.H.B. Walter, ed. *What Do We Do About Plantations?* Boroko: IASER.

Aland, F.P. "Land Tenure, Settlement and Land Usage". In B. Densley, ed. *Agriculture in the Economy Volume 1.* Port Moresby: Department of Primary Industry.

Alavi, H. 1972. "The State in Post-Colonial Societies: Pakistan and Bangladesh". *New Left Review* 74.

——— . 1982. "State and Class Under Peripheral Capitalism". In H. Alavi and T. Shanin, eds. *Introduction to the Sociology of "Developing Societies".* London: Macmillan.

Allen, B. 1982. "Some Thoughts on Rural Extension and Under Development." A paper read to a symposium on Comparative Studies in Development, Ormond College, University of Melbourne.

Almond, G. and Coleman, J., eds. 1960. *The Politics of Developing Areas.* Princeton: Princeton University Press.

Althusser, L. and Balibar, E. 1979. *Reading Capital.* London: Verso.

Amin, S. 1974. *Accumulation on a World Scale.* Sussex: The Harvester Press.

——— . 1976. *Unequal Development.* Sussex: The Harvester Press.

Anderson, D. 1977. *An Economic Survey of Small Holder Coffee Producers -- 1976.* Port Moresby: Department of Primary Industry.

Andrews, B. 1982. "The Political Economy of World Capitalism: Theory and Practice". *International Organizations* 36 1.

Ashton, C. 1978. "The Leahy Family". In J. Griffin, ed. *Papua New Guinea Portraits.* Canberra: Australian National University Press.

Bagchi, A. 1982. *The Political Economy of Underdevelopment.* Cambridge: Cambridge University Press.

Baker, D.J. 1977. "PNG Review". *Australian Quarterly.*

Ballard, J. n.d. "Political Parties in Papua New Guinea". Draft chapter for H. Fukui, ed. *Political Parties of Asia and the Pacific*. Greenwood Press.

_____ . ed. 1981. *Policy-Making in a New State -- Papua New Guinea 1972-77*. St Lucia: University of Queensland Press.

Banaji, J. 1977. "Modes of Production in a Materialist Conception of History". *Capital and Class* 3.

Baran, P. 1973. *The Political Economy of Growth*. Harmondsworth: Penguin.

_____ and Sweeney, P. 1966. *Monopoly Capital*. Harmondsworth: Penguin.

Barnes, H. n.d. "Women in Highlands Agricultural Production". In D. Denoon and C. Snowden, ed. *A Time to Plant and a Time to Uproot*. Port Moresby: Institute of Papua New Guinea Studies.

Barrie, J.W. 1956. "Coffee in the Highlands". *Papua and New Guinea Agricultural Journal*, 2 1.

Bates, R.H. 1981. *Markets and States in Tropical Africa*. Berkeley: University of California Press.

Becker, D. 1983. *The New Bourgeoisie and the Limits of Dependency: Mining, Class and Power in "Revolutionary" Peru*. Princeton: Princeton University Press.

Beckford, G. 1983. *Persistent Poverty -- Underdevelopment in Plantation Economies of the Third World*. London: Zed Books.

Beckman, B. 1980. "Imperialism and Capitalist Transformation: Critique of a Kenyan Debate". *Review of African Political Economy* 19.

_____ . 1981. "Imperialism and the "National Bourgeoisie". *Review of African Political Economy*, 22.

_____ . 1982. "Whose State? State and Capitalist Development in Nigeria". *Review of African Political Economy* 23.

Bernstein, H. 1971-2. "Modernisation Theory and the Sociological Study of Development". *Journal of Development Studies* 8.

_____ . 1977. "Notes on Capital and Peasantry". *Review of African Political Economy* 10.

_____ . 1979. "African Peasantries: A Theoretical Framework". *Journal of Peasant Studies* 6 4.

_____ . 1979. "Sociology of Underdevelopment vs. Sociology of Development?". In D. Lehmann, ed. *Development Theory*. London: Frank Cass.

_____ . 1981. "Notes on State and Peasantry: The Tanzanian Case". *Review of African Political Economy* 21.

_____ . 1982. "Industrialization, Development and Dependence". In H. Alavi and T. Shanin, eds. *Introduction to the Sociology of Developing Societies*. London: Macmillan.

Bienefeld, M. 1982. Tanzania: Model or Anti–Model? In M. Bienefeld and M. Godfrey, eds. *The Struggle for Development*. Chichester: John Wiley and Sons.

_____ and Godfrey, M., eds. 1982. *The Struggle for Development*. Chichester: John Wiley and Sons.

Bilder, R.B. 1963. "The International Coffee Agreement: A Case History in Negotiation". *Law and Contemporary Problems* 28 2.

Block, F. 1977. *The Origins of International Economic Disorder*. Berkeley: University of California Press.

_____ . 1977. "The Ruling Class Does Not Rule: Notes on the Marxist Theory of the State". *Socialist Revolution* 7 3.

_____ . 1980. "Beyond Relative Autonomy: State Managers as Historical Subjects". In R. Miliband and J. Saville, eds. *The Socialist Register 1980*. London: Merlin Press.

Bluett, N. 1967. "Marketing Boards Proposals for Handling the Surplus Crop". *New Guinea Highlands Bulletin* January.

_____ . 1968. "Administrator Opens New Office and Boardroom for Coffee Board". *New Guinea Highlands Bulletin* January.

Bolton, D. 1985. *Nationalization – – A Road to Socialism? The Case of Tanzania*. London: Zed Books.

Boschen, G. 1978. "West German Consumption Stays Stable". *Coffee International* 5 2.

Bradby, B. 1980. The Destruction of Natural Economy in H. Wolpe. *The Articulation of Modes of Production*. London: Routledge and Kegan Paul.

Brenner, R. 1977. "The Origins of Capitalist Development: A Critique of Neo–Smithian Marxism". *New Left Review* 104.

Brewer, A. 1980. *Marxist Theories of Imperialism: A Critical Survey*. London: Routledge and Kegan Paul.

Brown, C.P. 1980. *The Political and Social Economy of Commodity Control*. New York: Praeger.

Bukharin, N. 1972. *Imperialism and World Economy*. London: Merlin Press.

Bureau of Agricultural Economics. 1961. *The Coffee Industry in Papua New Guinea – – An Economic Survey*. Canberra: BAE.

Butler, R. 1974. "The Unstoppable March of the Solubles". *Coffee International* 1 2.

_____ . 1979. "On Solubles". *Coffee International* 6 6.

Byres, T.J. 1982. "India: Capitalist Industrialization or Structural Status". In M. Bienefeld and M. Godfrey, ed. *The Struggle for Development*. Chichester: John Wiley and Sons.

Calvert, M. 1974. "Winter of Discontent". *Coffee International* 1 3.

Caporaso, J. 1980. "Dependency Theory: Continuities and Discontinuities in Development Studies". *International Organization* 34 4.

Cardoso, F. 1982. "Development Under Fire". In H. Makler, A. Martinelli and N. Smelser, ed. *The New International Economy*. Beverly Hills: Sage.

_____ and Faletto, E. 1979. *Dependency and Development in Latin America*. Berkeley: University of California Press.

Cartledge, I. 1978. *A History of the Coffee Industry in Papua New Guinea*. Port Moresby: Coffee Industry Board.

Chan, J. 1978a. *Statement on the Coffee Industry Draft Hansard*, 17 August.

_____ . 1978b. *Primary Industries in Papua New Guinea After Independence*. Development Studies Centre Occasional Paper 12. Canberra: Australian National University.

_____ . 1982. "Election Talk". Port Moresby: University of Papua New Guinea.

Chase-Dunn, C. 1981. Interstate System and Capitalist World-Economy: One logic or two? In W. Hollist Ladd and J. Rosenau, "World Systems Debates". *International Studies Quarterly* 25 1.

Chatterton, P. 1974. "The Historical Dimension". In P. Sack, ed. *Problem of Choice - - Land in Papua New Guinea"s Future*. Canberra: Australian National University Press.

Chilcote, R. 1981. *Theories of Comparative Politics - - The Search for a Paradigm*. Boulder: Westview Press.

_____ . 1982. *Dependency and Marxism - - Towards a Resolution of the Debate*. Boulder: Westview Press.

_____ and Edelstein, J.C., eds. 1974. *Latin America: The Struggle with Dependency and Beyond*. Cambridge Mass.: Schenkman Publishing.

Cliffe, L., Coleman, J. and Doornbos, M.R., eds. 1977. *Government and Rural Development in East Africa - - Essays on Political Penetration*. The Hague: Martinus Nijhoff.

Coleman, J. 1960. "The Politics of Sub-Saharan Africa". In G. Almond and J. Coleman, eds. *The Politics of Developing Areas*. Princeton: Princeton University Press.

_____ . 1977. "The Concept of Political Penetration". In L. Cliffe, J. Coleman and M.R. Doornbos, eds. *Government and Rural Development in East Africa - - Essays on Political Penetration*. The Hague: Martinus Nijhoff.

Conyers, D. 1976. "History of Provincial Government Part III -- Opposition as Impact Felt". *Post Courier* November 9.

Cowen, M. 1981a. "Commodity Production in Kenya's Central Province". In J. Heyer, P. Roberts, G. Williams, ed. *Rural Developments in Tropical Africa*. London: MacMillan.

_____ . 1981b. "The Agrarian Problem: Notes on the Nairobi Discussion". *Review of African Political Economy*. No. 20.

Crane, G. 1982. "The Taiwanese Ascent: System, State, and Movement in the World Economy". In E. Friedman, ed. *Ascent and Decline in the World System*. Beverly Hills: Sage.

Daoudi, M. and Dajani, M. 1983. "Contending Approaches to Social Change and Political Development -- A Comparative Analysis". *The Indian Political Science Review* 17 2.

Decker, J.A. 1940. *Labor Problems in the Pacific Mandates*. London: Oxford University Press.

De Lepervanche, M. 1972. "Social Structure". In P. Ryan, ed. *Encyclopedia of Papua New Guinea*. Carlton: Melbourne University Press.

Denoon, D. and Snowden, C. n.d. *A Time to Plant and a Time to Uproot -- a History of Agriculture in Papua New Guinea*. Port Moresby: Institute of Papua New Guinea Studies.

Densley, B. ed. 1977. *Agriculture in the Economy -- A Series of Review Papers*. Port Moresby: Department of Primary Industry.

"Development Banking Institution in P-NG Proposed". *New Guinea Highlands Bulletin*, October, 1965.

Dick, G. 1977. *Knowledge and Performance in Village Coffee Production*. UPNG: M.Ed. Thesis.

_____ . 1978. "A History of Coffee Planting in the Mt. Hagen Area". *History of Agriculture, Working Paper No. 24*. Port Moresby: UPNG/Department of Primary Industry.

Dinham, B. and Hines, C. 1983. *Agribusiness in Africa*. London: Earth Resources Research.

Donaldson, M. 1980. "Class Formation in Papua New Guinea: The Indigenous Bourgeoisie". *Journal of Australian Political Economy* 7.

_____ and Good, K. 1977. *A Working Paper on the Political Organisation in PNG; The Situation of the Eastern Highlands*. Socialist Seminar, University of Papua New Guinea.

_____ and Good, K. n.d. "The Eastern Highlands, Coffee and Class". In D. Denoon and C. Snowden, ed. *A Time to Plant and A Time to Uproot*. Port Moresby: Institute of PNG Studies.

_____ and Good, K. "Draft Chapter on the Eastern Highlands". *History of Agriculture Discussion Paper No. 30*. University of PNG and Department of Primary Industry.

_____ and Good, K. n.d. "Rural Capitalism and the Post Colonial State". Draft chapter in an unpublished work.

Dos Santos, T. 1970. "The Structure of Dependency". *American Economic Review* 60 1–2.

Downs, I. 1964. "The Story Behind the Quota Increase". *New Guinea Highlands Bulletin* April.

_____ . 1964. "Prices Should Remain Reasonably Firm". *New Guinea Highlands Bulletin* July.

_____ . 1965. "Types and Varieties of Arabica Coffee". *New Guinea Highlands Bulletin* April.

_____ . 1967. "Lets stop this Economic Suicide". *New Guinea Highlands Bulletin* April.

_____ . 1969. "Fertilizing Coffee". *New Guinea Highlands Bulletin* January.

_____ . 1978. "Kiap, Planter and Politician: A Self-Portrait". In J. Griffin, ed. *Papua New Guinea Portraits*. Canberra: Australian National University Press.

Dyson, K. 1980. *The State Tradition in Western Europe*. Oxford: Martin Robertson.

Edwards, A. 1975. *The Potential for New Commodity Cartels*. London: Economist Intelligence Unit.

_____ . 1977. "The Stabilisation of the International Coffee Market". *Food Policy* 2 3.

Ellis, F. 1983. "Agricultural Marketing and Peasant–State Transfers in Tanzania". *The Journal of Peasant Studies* 10 4.

Emerson, R. 1966. "National Building in Africa". In K. Deutsch and W.J. Foltz, eds. *National Building*. New York: Atherton Press.

Emmanuel, A. 1972. *Unequal Exchange: A Study of the Imperialism of Trade*. New York: Monthly Review Press.

English, A.N. 1974. "The Distorting Special Deals". *Coffee International* 1 3.

Erb, G.F. 1975/76. "Commodity Issues in the 1970's". *Foreign Trade Review* 10 4.

Evans, P. 1985. "Review Essay: After Dependency: Recent Studies of Class, State and Industrialization". *Latin American Research Review* 20 2.

Fine, B. and Harris, L. 1979. *Rereading Capital*. London: Macmillan.

Finney, B.R. 1973. *Big Men and Business*. Canberra: Australian National University Press.

Finney, R.S. 1971. *Would Be Entrepreneurs? A Study of Motivation in New Guinea*. New Guinea Research Bulletin No. 41. Canberra: New Guinea Research Unit.

Fisher, B.S. 1972. *The International Coffee Agreement, A Study in Coffee Diplomacy*. New York: Praeger.

Fitzpatrick, P. 1978. "Really Rather Like Slavery: Law and Labour in the Colonial Economy in Papua New Guinea". In E.L. Wheelwright and K. Buckley, ed. *Essays in the Political Economy of Australian Capitalism Volume Three*. Sydney: ANZ Book Co.

_____ . 1980. *Law and State in Papua New Guinea*. London: Academic Press.

_____ . 1982. "The Making and Unmaking of the Eight Aims". Port Moresby: Waigani Seminar.

Ford, D.J. 1978. "Commodity Market Modelling and the Simulation of Market Intervention: The Case of Coffee". In F. G. Adams and S.A. Klein. *Stabilizing World Commodity Markets*. Lexington, Mass.: D.C. Heath and Company.

Foster-Carter, A. 1976. "From Rostow to Gunder Frank - - Conflicting Paradigms in the Analysis of Underdevelopment". *World Development* 4 3.

_____ . 1978. "The Modes of Production Controversy". *New Left Review* 17.

Frank, A.G. 1969. *Capitalism and Underdevelopment in Latin America*. Harmondsworth: Penguin.

Frankel, B. 1983. *Beyond the State? Dominant Theories and Socialist Strategies*. London: Macmillan.

Freund, J. 1968. *The Sociology of Max Weber*. New York: Pantheon Books.

Frobel, F. 1982. "The Current Development of the World Economy: Reproduction of Labor and Accumulation of Capital on a World Scale". *Review* 4.

Furtado, C. 1964. *Development and Underdevelopment*. Berkeley: University of California Press.

Gallagher, K. 1977. "Taking a Cautious Look at the Future". *Coffee International* 4 2.

Galli, R., ed. 1981. *The Political Economy of Rural Development: Peasants, International Capital and the State*. Albany: State University of New York Press.

Galloway, T. 1973. The International Coffee Agreement. *Journal of World Trade Law* 7.

Garnaut, R. 1981. "The Framework of Economic Policy–Making". In J. Ballard, ed. *Policy–Making in a New State*. St Lucia: University of Queensland Press.

Geer, T. 1971. *An Oligopoly – – The World Coffee Economy and Stabilization Schemes*. New York: Dunellen.

Gerhard, H.W. 1963. "Commodity Trade Stabilization Through International Agreements". *Law and Contemporary Problems* 28 2.

Gerritsen, R. 1981. "Aspects of Political Evolution of Rural Papua New Guinea: Towards a Political Economy of the Terminal Peasantry". In R. Gerritsen, R.J. May, and M.A.H.B. Walter. *Road Belong Development: Cargo Cults, Community Groups and Self–Help Movements in Papua New Guinea*. Working Paper No. 3. Canberra: Department of Political and Social Change, Research School of Pacific Studies, Australian National University.

Gibbon, P. and Neocosmos, M. 1985. Some Problems in the Political Economy of "African Socialism". In H. Bernstein and B. Campbell, eds. *Contradictions of Accumulation in Africa*. Beverly Hills: Sage.

Gittins, M.B. 1978. "London Futures Market – – The Philosophy and the Operation". *Coffee International* 5 1.

Godfrey, M. 1980. "Editorial: Is Dependency Dead?". *IDS Bulletin* 12 1.

Goldring, J. 1978. *The Constitution of Papua New Guinea*. Sydney: The Law Book Co.

Goldsworthy, D. 1983. "Political Analysis and Development Studies". *Politics* 18 1.

Gomes, L. 1978. *International Economic Problems*. London: MacMillan.

Good, K. 1979. "The Class Structure". In A. Amarshi, K. Good and R. Mortimer. *Development and Dependency: The Political Economy of Papua New Guinea*. Melbourne: Oxford University Press.

______ and Donaldson, M. 1980. *Development of Rural Capitalism in PNG – – Coffee Production in the Eastern Highlands*. Occasional Paper No. 1. Boroko: Institute of PNG Studies.

Goodman, D. and Redclift, M. 1981. *From Peasant to Proletarian: Capitalist Development and Agrarian Transitions*. Oxford: Basil Blackwell.

Goodman, R., Lepani, C., Morawetz, D. 1985. *The Economy of Papua New Guinea: An Independent Review*. Canberra: Development Studies Centre, Australian National University.

Goulbourne, H. 1979. "Some Problems of Analysis of the Political in Backward Capitalist Social Formations". In H. Goulbourne, ed. *Politics and State in the Third World*. London: Macmillan.

Gregory, C.A. 1982. *Gifts and Commodities*. London: Academic Press.

Griffin, J., ed. 1978. *Papua New Guinea Portraits*. Canberra: ANU Press.

Grossman, L.S. n.d. "From Subsistence Affluence to Subsistence Malaise: Cash Cropping and the Subsistence System in the Highlands of PNG". *History of Agriculture Discussion Paper No. 46*. Department of Primary Industry University of PNG.

Haarer, A.E. 1962. *Modern Coffee Production*. London: Leonard Hill.

Habermas, J. 1976. *Legitimation Crisis*. London: Heinemann.

_____ . 1979. *Communication and the Evolution of Society*. Boston: Beacon Press.

Hamilton, N. 1982. *The Limits of State Autonomy: Post-Revolutionary Mexico*. Princeton: Princeton University Press.

Hart, K. 1982. *The Political Economy of West African Agriculture*. Cambridge: Cambridge University Press.

Harvey, D. 1982. *The Limits to Capital*. Oxford: Basil Blackwell.

Hasluck, P. 1975. *A Time for Building*. Melbourne: Melbourne University Press.

Hassall and Associates. 1982. *Review of the Papua New Guinea Coffee Marketing System -- Final Report*. Prepared for the Papua New Guinea Coffee Industry Board.

Hayer, T. and Watson, C. 1985. *Aid: Rhetoric and Reality*. London and Sydney: Pluto Press.

Heinz, K. 1979. "Notable German Increase". *Coffee International* 6 3.

Hess, M. 1983. "In The Long Run... Australian Colonial Labour Policy in the Territory of Papua and New Guinea". *The Journal of Industrial Relations* 25 1.

Higgott, R. 1978. "Competing Theoretical Perspectives on Development and Under-development: A Recent Intellectual History". *Politics* 13 1.

_____ . 1982. "The State in Africa: Some Thoughts on the Future Drawn from the Past". In T. Shaw. *Africa Projected From Dependence to Self-Reliance by the Year 2000*. London: Macmillan.

Hindess, B. and Hirst, P. 1975. *Pre-Capitalist Modes of Production*. London: Routledge and Kegan Paul.

Hinsley, F.H. 1966. *Sovereignty*. London: C.A. Watts & Co.

Hintze, O. 1973. "The State in Historical Perspective". In R. Bendix et.al., eds. *State and Society*. Berkeley: University of California Press.

Hollist Ladd, W. and Rosenau, J.N., eds. 1981. "World Systems Debates". *International Studies Quarterly* 25 1.

Holmquist, F. 1980. "Defending Peasant Political Space in Africa". *Canadian Journal of African Studies* 14 1.

Holzknecht, H. and Holzknecht, S. 1976. "Party Versus Personalities: The Markham Open Electorate". In D. Stone, ed. *Prelude to*

Self-Government. Canberra: Research School of Pacific Studies and University of Papua New Guinea.

Hoogvelt, A.M.M. 1982. *The Third World in Global Development.* London: Macmillan.

Hopkins, T. 1982. "Notes on Class Analysis and the World System". In T. Hopkins and I. Wallerstein, ed. *World-systems Analysis -- Theory and Methodology.* Beverly Hills: Sage.

_____ and Wallerstein I., eds. 1982. *World System Analysis -- Theory and Methodology.* Beverly Hills: Sage.

Howlett, D. 1967. *A Geography of Papua New Guinea.* Melbourne, Nelson.

_____ . 1973. "Terminal Development: From Tribalism to Peasantry". In H.C. Brookfield, ed. *The Pacific in Transition: Geographical Perspectives on Adaptation and Change.* London: Arnold.

_____ . 1980. "When is a Peasant not a Peasant? Rural Proletarianisation in Papua New Guinea". In J.N. Jennings and G.R. Lange, eds. *Of Time and Place.* Canberra: Australian National University Press.

_____ , Hide, R. and Young E. with Arba, J., Bi, H. and Kaman, B. 1976. *Chimbu: Issues in Development.* Development Studies Centre Monograph No. 4. Canberra: The Australian National University.

Hyles, G.W. 1981. *A Survey of the Papua New Guinea Plantation Sector -- Some Implications and Alternatives for the Future.* M.A. Rural Development, School of Development Studies, University of East Anglia.

Iangalio, M. 1976. "Wabag Open Electorate". In D. Stone. *Prelude to Self Government.* Canberra: Research School of Pacific Studies and University of Papua New Guinea.

International Coffee Agreement 1962. Reprinted as an appendix in T. Geer 1971.

International Coffee Agreement 1968. Reprinted as an appendix in T. Geer 1971.

International Coffee Agreement 1976. 1976. New York 31 Jan-31 July 1976. London: Her Majesty's Stationary Office.

"Introduction: The State and State Theory in Western Europe". *Kapitalistate.* No. 10/11 1983.

Ivashchenko, A. and Orlov, Y. 1976. "Expansion of the Coffee and Cocoa-Bean Processing Industries in the Developing Countries". *Foreign Trade* USSR 6.

Jackson, D. 1981. *The Distribution of Incomes in Papua New Guinea.* Port Moresby: National Planning Office.

Jessop, B. 1977. "Recent Theories of the Capitalist State". *Cambridge Journal of Economics* 1 4.

_____ . 1982. *The Capitalist State*. Oxford: Martin Robertson.

Johnson, H.G. 1976. *Economic Policies Towards Less Developed Countries*. Washington: Brookings Institution.

Kasfir, N. 1983. "Introduction: Relating Class to State in Africa". *The Journal of Commonwealth and Comparative Politics* 21 3.

Katz, S. 1980. *Africa and Social Class: A Critique of Relevant Theories*. Montreal: McGill University, Centre for Developing Area Studies.

Kay, G. 1975. *Development and Underdevelopment: A Marxist Analysis*. London: Macmillan.

_____ . 1979. *The Economic Theory of the Working Class*. London and Baskingstoke: Macmillan.

Kesselman, M. 1973. "Order or Movement? The Literature of Political Development as Ideology". *World Politics* 26 1.

Khan, Kabir-Ur-Rahman. 1979. "International Coffee Agreement 1976 -- Issues of Selectivity Regulation and Reciprocity". *Food Policy* 1 1.

Kimber, A.J. "Current Recommendations on Arabica Coffee Management". Prepared for the PNG Coffee Industry Board.

King, P. 1984. "Papua New Guinea - - Political Chronicle". *Australian Journal of Politics and History* 302.

Kirschen, L. 1974. "The Year of the Indicator". *Coffee International* 1 3.

_____ . 1977. "When the Bonanza Comes to an End". *Coffee International* 4 2.

_____ . 1978. "The ICO"s Trigger Formula". *Coffee International* 5 6.

_____ . 1979. "Is There the Will to Cope With Yet Another Crisis?". *Coffee International* 6 3.

_____ . 1980. "International Coffee Organization - - A New Agreement - - But Will it Stick?". *Coffee International* 7 6.

Knetsch, J. and Trebilcock, M. 1981. *Land Policy and Economic Development in Papua New Guinea*. Port Moresby: Institute of National Affairs Discussion Paper No. 6.

Krasner, S. 1973. "Business Government Relations: The Case of the International Coffee Agreement". *International Organisation* 27.

Kreye, O. 1981. "Dependency in the 1980s". In C. Saunders, ed. *The Political Economy of New and Old Industrial Nations*. London: Butterworth.

Kula, G.R. and Clarkson, D. 1980. "Coffee Disease in the Western Highlands". *Harvest* 6 4.

Kurian, G.T. 1982. *Encyclopedia of the Third World Volume III*. New York: Facts on File.

Laclau, E. 1971. "Feudalism and Capitalism in Latin America". *New Left Review* 67.

Lam, N.V. 1981. "The Economics of Plantations". In M.A.H.B. Walter, ed. *What do we do About Plantations*? Boroko Papua New Guinea: IASER.

——— . 1984. *The Commodity Export Sector in Papua New Guinea*. Boroko: Institute of Applied Social and Economic Research, Monograph 22.

Lea, D.A.M. and Chaudhri, D.P., eds. 1983. *The State and Rural Development*. London: Methuen.

Lenin, V.I. 1964. *Development of Capitalism in Russia*. Moscow: Progress Publishers.

Leys, C. 1975. "The Overdeveloped Post-Colonial State: A Re-Evaluation". *Review of African Political Economy* 5.

——— . 1977. "Underdevelopment and Dependency: Critical Notes". *Journal of Contemporary Asia* 7 1.

——— . 1978. "Capital Accumulation, Class Formation and Dependency". In R. Miliband and J. Saville, ed. *The Socialist Register 1978*. London: Merlin.

——— . 1980. "Kenya: What Does "Dependency" Explain?" *Review of African Political Economy* 17.

——— . 1982a. "African Economic Development in Theory and Practice". *Daedalus* 111 2.

——— . 1982b. "Accumulation, Class Formation and Dependency: Kenya". In M. Fransman, ed. *Industry and Accumulation in Africa*. London: Heinemann.

Lipton, M. 1981. "Agricultural Finance and Rural Credit in Poor Countries". In P. Streeton and R. Jolly, ed. *Recent Issues in World Development*. Oxford: Pergamon Press.

MacBean, A. 1966. *Export Instability and Economic Development*. Cambridge, Mass.: Harvard University Press.

MacWilliam, S. 1984. "Electoral Politics and State Power". *Yagl-Ambu* 11 2.

McKillop, B. 1981. "Managing Plantations in Papua New Guinea Today: Who wants to be the Labourer?" In M.A.H.B. Walter, ed. *What Do We Do About Plantations*? Boroko Papua New Guinea: IASER.

McKillop, Williamson & Associates Pty Ltd. 1982. *DPI Manpower and Training Review – – Final Report to the Government of Papua New Guinea*. McKillop Williamson and Associates Pty Ltd in association with Sloane, Cook and King Pty Ltd.

Mair, L.P. 1948. *Australia in New Guinea*. London: Christophers.

Maker, H., Martinelli, A. and Smelser, N. 1982. *The New International Economy*. Beverley Hills: Sage.

Malecki, E.S. 1981. "The Capitalist State: Structural Variation and the Implications for Radical Change". *The Western Political Quarterly* 2.

Mars, P. 1981. "Political Determinants of Revolutionary Change in the Third World". *Social Praxis* 8.

Marshall, C.F. 1972. "Coffee - - The Market in 1971 and the Present Position". *Bank of London and South American Review* 6 1.

_____ . 1973. "Coffee What Future For Cooperation?". *Bank of London and South American Review* 7 1.

_____ . 1974. "Coffee 1973: A Year Without Quotas". *Bank of London and South American Review* 8 1.

_____ . 1975. "Coffee in 1975 - - The Brazilan Frost and a New Agreement". *Bank of London and South American Review* 9 1.

_____ . 1977. "Coffee in 1976 - - The Post Gelidal Boom". *Bank of London and South American Review* 11 1.

_____ . 1978. "Coffee in 1977 - - The Peak and the Descent". *Bank of London and South American Review* 12 1.

_____ . 1979. "Coffee in 1978 - - A Precarious Balance". *Bank of London and South American Review* 13 1.

_____ . 1980. "Coffee in 1979 - - The Effect of the Bogota Group". *Bank of London and South American Review* 14 1.

_____ . 1981. "Coffee in 1980". *Bank of London and South American Review* 15 1.

_____ . 1982. "Coffee in 1981". *Bank of London and South American Review* 16 1.

Marx, K. 1954. *Capital Volume One* Moscow: One Progress Publishers.

_____ . 1959. *Capital Volume Three* Moscow: Three Progress Publishers.

_____ . 1973. *Surveys from Exile. Political Writings - - Volume 2.* Harmondsworth: Penguin Books.

Meillassoux, C. 1972. "From Reproduction to Production: A Marxist Approach to Economic Anthropology". *Economy and Society* 1 1.

Meyer, J.W. and Hannan, M.T., eds. 1979. *National Development and the World System: Educational, Economic and Political Change, 1950–1970.* Chicago: University of Chicago Press.

Miller, A.S. 1963. "Foreword, International Commodity Agreements". *Law and Contemporary Problems* 28 2.

Mitio, R. 1981. "Papua New Guinea Coffee Plantations." In M.A.H.B. Walter, ed., *What Do We Do About Plantations?* IASER Monograph 15, National Research Institute, Waigani, Papua New Guinea.

Momis, J. 1982. *Election Talk.* Port Moresby: University of Papua New Guinea.

Mortimer, R. 1975. "Social Science and the Peasant. A Case of Academic Genocide". Port Moresby: Public Lecture, University of Papua New Guinea.

Munnell, J. 1981. "The Villagers" View of the Plantation Redistribution Scheme". In M.A.H.B. Walter, ed. *What Do We Do About Plantations*? Boroko Papua New Guinea: IASER.

Msuya, M. 1979. *Coffee in the Economy of Tanzania and the Implications of Membership in the International Coffee Agreement*. Madison: PhD Thesis, University of Wisconsin.

Murray, K. 1980. *Small Holder Coffee Paper*. Delivered to Coffee Industry Board Workshop Goroka.

Mwandha, J., Nicholls, J., and Sargent, M. 1985. *Coffee: The International Commodity Agreements*. Farnborough: Gower.

Nabudere, D. 1977. *The Political Economy of Imperialism*. London: Zed Press.

Nursey-Bray, P. n.d. "Class Formation and Post Colonial State Theory in Africa". *Africa Quarterly* 20 3-4.

O'Connor, J. 1973. *The Fiscal Crisis of the State*. New York: St Martin's Press.

O'Donnell, G. 1980. "Comparative Historical Formations of the State Apparatus and Socio-Economic Change in the Third World". *International Social Science Journal* 23, 4.

Offe, C. 1976. "Political Authority and Class Structures". In P. Connerton. *Critical Sociology*. Harmondsworth: Penguin.

______ . 1981. "The Attribution of Public Status to Interest Groups: Observations on the West German Case". In S. Berger, ed. *Organizing Interests in Western Europe: Pluralism, Corporatism and the Transformation of Politics*. Cambridge: Cambridge University Press.

Offiong, D. 1982. *Imperialism and Dependency*. Washington D.C.: Howard University Press.

Onimode, B. 1982. *Imperialism and Underdevelopment in Nigeria*. London: Zed Press.

Ougaard, M. 1982/3. "Some Remarks Concerning Peripheral Capitalism and the Peripheral State". *Science and Society* 66 4.

Overseas Development Group. 1973. *A Report on Development Strategies for Papua New Guinea*. University of East Anglia.

Oxenford, I. *Guide to PNG Development Bank Policy on 20 Ha Arabica Coffee Development*. Port Moresby: PNG Development Bank.

Palma, G. 1981. "Dependency: A Formal Theory of Underdevelopment or a Methodology for the Analysis of Concrete Situations of Underdevelopment". In P. Streeton and R. Jolly, eds. *Recent Issues in World Development*. Oxford: Pergamon Press.

Papua and New Guinea. 1970. *Report of A Board of Inquiry Investigating Rural Minimum Wages Under the Native Employment Ordinance 1958–1968, Minimum Wage Fixing Machinery and Related Matters The Cochrane Report*. Port Moresby: Government Printer.

_____ . 1970. *The Structure of Unskilled Wages in Papua and New Guinea The Isaac Report*. Port Moresby: Government Printer.

_____ . Department of Agriculture Stock and Fisheries. 1970. *Project Pamphlets -- Coffee*. Port Moresby: Territory of Papua and New Guinea.

_____ . 1974. *Strategies for Nationhood, Policies and Issues, December 1974*. Port Moresby: Central Planning Office.

Papua New Guinea Central Planning Office Programmes and Performance 1975/76. Port Moresby: Government Printer.

Papua New Guinea. 1976. *National Development Strategy*. Waigani.

Papua New Guinea Coffee Industry Board. *Annual Report and Financial Statements*.

_____ . 1979. *An Outline of the Powers, Functions and General Operations of the Papua New Guinea Coffee Industry Board*.

_____ . 1980. *Coffee Growing in Papua New Guinea*. Port Moresby: Office of Information.

_____ . 1982. *An Outline of the Powers, Functions and General Operations of the Papua New Guinea Coffee Industry Board*.

Papua New Guinea Coffee Marketing Board. 1972. *Guidelines for Registration of Coffee Processing Facilities*.

Papua New Guinea. n.d. Department of Eastern Highlands, Office of Agriculture. *Coffee Development Scheme Eastern Highlands* Province. Goroka.

Papua New Guinea Department of Primary Industry. 1977. *Farming Notes --Arabica Coffee*. Port Moresby: Department of Primary Industry.

Papua New Guinea Development Bank. *Annual Reports and Financial Statements*.

_____ . n.d. *Coffee Development Policy -- Eastern Highlands Province*.

_____ . n.d. *Finance to Coffee Development, Policy Statement by Oxenford and H. Lavaki*.

Papua New Guinea Institute of Applied Social and Economic Research. 1982. "Review of Public Sector Equity Investments with particular focus on the Investment Corporation of Papua New Guinea". Paper for the Minister of Finance.

Papua New Guinea Institute of National Affairs. 1978. *The Structure and Adequacy of the Financial Institutions in PNG*. Discussion Paper No. 2. Port Moresby.

Papua New Guinea National Party. 1982. *Policies -- National Party*. Mt Hagen: Michael Mel.

Parker, R.S. 1966. "The Growth of Territory Administration". In E.K. Fisk, ed. *New Guinea on the Threshold*. Canberrra: Australian National University Press.

Parkin, F. 1979. *Marxism and Class Theory: A Bourgeois Critique*. London: Tavistock.

Pasingan, E. *Brief Report on Eastern Highlands Province, 15 October 1981*. Port Moresby: Department of Decentralisation, Legal and Corporate Services Unit.

Paulias, N.E. 1977. *Problems of Rural Development and Growing Inequalities in the Highlands of Papua New Guinea*. The Hague: Master of Public Administration Thesis, The Institute of Social Studies.

Payer, C., ed. 1975. *Commodity Trade of the Third World*. London: Macmillan.

_____ . 1982. *The World Bank*. New York and London: Monthly Review Press.

Petras, J. 1982. "The Peripheral State: Continuity and Change in the International Division of Labour". *Journal of Contemporary Asia* 12 4.

Pettman, R. 1979. *State and Class, A Sociology of International Affairs*. London: Croom Helm.

Pincus, J. 1967. *Trade, Aid and Development*. New York: McGraw Hill and Co.

Poulantzas, N. 1978. *Political Power and Social Classes*. London: Verso.

_____ . 1980. *State: Power: Socialism*. London: Verso.

_____ . 1980. "Research Note on the State and Society". *International Social Science Journal* 32 4.

Quinn, P.T. n.d. "Agriculture, Land Tenure and Land Law to 1971". In D. Denoon and C. Snowden ed. *A Time to Plant and a Time to Uproot*. Port Moresby: Institute of Papua New Guinea Studies.

Rader, M. 1979. *Marx's Interpretation of History*. New York: Oxford University Press.

Radi, H. 1971. "New Guinea Under Mandate". In W.J. Hudson, ed. *Australia and Papua New Guinea*. Sydney: Sydney University Press.

Rangarajan, L.N. 1978. *Commodity Conflict*. London: Croom Helm.

Read, K.E. 1959. "Leadership and Consensus in a New Guinea Society". *American Anthropologist* 61.

Reahy, M. 1959. *The Kuma*. Melbourne: Melbourne University Press.

Rey, P.P. 1982. "Class Alliances". *International Journal of Sociology*. Summer.

Reynolds, C. 1981. *Modes of Imperialism*. Oxford: Martin Robertson.

Riggs, F. 1981. "The Rise and Fall of Political Development". In S. Long, ed. *The Handbook of Political Behaviour*. Vol. 4. New York: Plenum Press.

Roden, C. 1977. *Coffee*. London: Faber and Faber.

Rondinelli, D. 1979. "Administration of Integrated Rural Development Policy: The Politics of Agrarian Reform in Developing Countries". *World Politics* 31 3.

Rowley, C.D. 1965. *The New Guinea Villager: A Retrospect from 1964*. Melbourne: F.W. Cheshire.

Ruttan, V. 1974/75. "Integrated Rural Development Programs: A Skeptical Perspective". *International Development Review* 17 4.

Sack, P. 1974. *Problem of Choice: Land in Papua New Guinea's Future* Canberra: ANU Press.

Salisbury, R. 1962. *From Stone to Steel*. Melbourne: Melbourne University Press.

Sandbrook, R. 1975–76. "The Crisis in Political Development Theory". *Journal of Development Studies* 12.

Samoff, J. 1982. "Class, Class Conflict and the State in Africa". *Political Science Quarterly* 97 1.

Secher-Marcussen, H. and Torp, J.E. 1982. *The Internationalization of Capital*. London: Zed Press.

Shand, R.T. 1972. "Coffee Industry". In P. Ryan, ed. *Encyclopedia of Papua and New Guinea*. Melbourne: Melbourne University Press.

_____ and Straatmans, W. 1974. *Transition from Subsistence: Cash Crop Development in Papua New Guinea*. New Guinea Research Bulletin No. 54. Port Moresby and Canberra: New Guinea Research Unit and the Australian National University.

Shivji, I. 1976. *Class Struggles in Tanzania*. London: Heinemann.

_____ . 1980. "The State in the Dominated Social Formations of Africa: Some Theoretical Issues". *International Social Science Journal* 30, 4.

Skeldon, R. 1976. "The Growth of Goroka". *Towards an Interpretation of the Past and a Warning of the Future*. IASER Discussion Paper No. 6. Port Moresby.

Skocpol, T. 1976. "Wallerstein's World Capitalist System: A Theoretical and Historical Critique". *American Journal of Sociology* 82 5.

Smith, D.W. 1975. *Labour and the Law in Papua New Guinea*. Development Studies Centre Monograph No. 1. Canberra: Australian National University.

Smith, T. 1979. "The Underdevelopment of Development Literature: The Case of Dependency Theory". *World Politics* 21 1.

Somare, M. 1975. *Sana*. Port Moresby: Nuigini Press.

Standish, B. 1976. "New Mem for an Old Society: The Chimbu Regional Campaign". In D. Stone, ed. *Prelude to Self-Government*. Canberra: Research School of Pacific Studies and the University of Papua New Guinea.

_____ . 1978. *The "Big Man" Model Reconsidered: Power and Stratification in Chimbu*. IASER Discussion Paper No. 22. Boroko: Institute of Aplied Social and Economic Research.

_____ . 1978. "So Far What Have We Learned". *Post Courier* October 2.

_____ . 1979. *Provincial Government in Papua New Guinea, Early Lessons from Chimbu Monograph* 7. Institute of Applied Social and Economic Reseach.

_____ . 1981. "'Maunten Na Barat': Policy-Making in Chimbu Province". In J. Ballard, ed. *Policy-Making in a New State -- Papua New Guinea 1972-77*. St Lucia: University of Queensland Press.

_____ . 1983. "Power to the People, Decentralization in Papua New Guinea". *Public Administration and Development* 3 3.

Staples, R. 1978. *"The State", Integrated Rural Development and Local Government in Papua New Guinea*. Development Studies Discussion Paper No. 25. University of East Anglia.

Stewart, R. 1981. "Pluralist Theories of the State". Seminar Paper. Department of Political Science The Faculties A.N.U.

_____ : 1982. "Historical Materialism and the State". Paper presented at Sociology Association of Australia and New Zealand Conference, University of New South Wales.

_____ . 1984a. "Autonomy, Dependency and the State". In R. May, ed. *Social Stratification in Papua New Guinea*. Working Paper No. 5. Australian National University: Department of Political and Social Change, Research School of Pacific Studies.

_____ . 1984b. "Coffee, Candidates and Class Struggle: The 1982 National Election for Goroka Open Electorate, Eastern Highlands Province, Papua New Guinea". *Yagl Ambu* 11 2.

Stone, D., ed. 1976. *Prelude to Self-Government*. Canberra: ANU Research School of Pacific Studies and the University of Papua New Guinea.

Strathern, A.M. 1972. *Women in Between: Female Roles in a Male World, Mount Hagen, New Guinea*. London: Seminar Press.

_____ . 1982. "Tribesmen or Peasants". In A. Strathern, ed. *Inequality in New Guinea Highlands*. Cambridge: Cambridge University Press.

Streeten, P. and Elson, D. 1971. *Diversification and Development: The Case of Coffee*. New York: Praeger Publishers.

Stuckart, C.E. 1977. "The International Coffee Agreement". *Law and Policy in International Business* 9.

Sundhaussen, U. 1977. "Ideology and Nation Building in Papua New Guinea". *Australian Outlook* 31 2.

Sundrum, R.M. 1983. *Development Economics*. Chichester: John Wiley and Sons.

Sunkel, O. 1972. "Big Business and Dependencia". *Foreign Affairs* 50 3.

Tammur, O. 1976. "How We'll Divide the Taxes". *Post Courier* November 3.

Tariff Board -- Australia 1965. Inquiry Re Coffee.

Taylor, J.G. 1979. *From Modernization to Modes of Production*. London: Macmillan.

Taylor, C.L. and Jodice, D.A. 1983. *World Handbook of Political and Social Indicators*. Third Edition. New Haven and London: Yale University Press.

Terray, E. 1972. *Marxism and Primitive Societies*. New York, Monthly Review Press.

Territory of New Guinea Report for 1953/54 -- 1969/70. Commonwealth of Australia.

Territory of Papua Report for 1953/54 -- 1969/1970. Commonwealth of Australia.

Tew, B. 1977. *The Evolution of the International Monetary System, 1945/77*. London: Hutchinson.

Thomas, C.Y. 1984. *The Rise of the Authoritarian State in Peripheral Societies*. New York and London: Monthly Review Press.

Tilly C., ed. 1975. *The Formation of National States in Western Europe*. Princeton, New Jersey: Princeton University Press, Princeton.

Townsend, D. n.d. *Agricultural Innovation in a Peripheral Area: Finschhafen District of the Morobe Province*. PNG: University, Department of Primary Industry. History of Agriculture: Working Paper No. 22.

_____ . 1977. "The 1976 Coffee Boom in Papua New Guinea". *Australian Geographer* 13.

Townsend, J. 1982. "The Study of Development: Some Introductory Questions and Observations". Australian National University: Department of Political and Social Change, Research School of Pacific Studies.

United Nations Centre on Transnational Corporations. 1981. *Transnational Corporations in Food and Beverage Processing*. New York: United Nations.

United Nations Conference on Trade and Development. 1983. *Studies in the Processing, Marketing and Distribution of Commodities*. New York: United Nations.

Urry, J. 1981. *The Anatomy of Capitalist Societies -- The Economy, Civil Society and the State*. London: Macmillan.

Von Fleckenstein, F.W. 1975. "Observations on Coffee Marketing in the Eastern Highlands". *Yagl Ambu* 2 2.

Wallerstein, I. 1975. "Class Formation in the Capitalist World Economy". *Politics and Society* 5 1.

_____ . 1979. *The Capitalist World Economy*. Cambridge: Cambridge University Press.

Walter, M.A.H.B. Ed. 1981. *What Do We Do About Plantations*? Boroko: Monograph 15 Institute of Applied Social and Economic Research.

Ward, A. 1977. "The Land Question in Independent Papua New Guinea". *Journal of Administration Overseas* 16 1.

Ward, R.G. 1971. "Internal Migration and Urbanisation in Papua New Guinea". In M. Ward, ed. *Population Growth and Socio-Economic Change*. Canberra: New Guinea Research Bulletin No. 42 ANU.

_____ and Proctor, A., eds. 1980. *South Pacific Agriculture -- Choices and Constraints -- South Pacific Agricultural Survey 1979*. Canberra: Asian Development Bank.

Wassermann, V. 1973. "Breakdown of International Coffee Agreement". *Journal of World Trade Law* 7.

Waters, A.R. 1974. "The Economic Reason for International Commodity Agreements". *Kyklos* 27.

Weber, M. 1980. *Basic Concepts in Sociology*. New Jersey: The Citadel Press.

Wellman, F.L. 1961. *Coffee*. London: Leonard Hill Books Ltd.

Wesley, R. 1980. "Coffee Industry in Papua New Guinea". *Bank of Papua New Guinea, Quarterly Economic Bulletin* September.

West, F.J. 1958. "Indigenous Labour in Papua New Guinea". *International Labour Review* 77 2.

Wheeler, M. 1979. *Coffee Development Plan Including Coffee-Model Budget 20 HA Clan Block Planting*. Port Moresby: Department of Primary Industry.

_____ and Wyatt, S.L. 1978. *Agricultural Stabilization Funds in Papua New Guinea*. Port Moresby: Marketing Section, Department of Primary Industry.

White, A. 1977. *Possible Organisations of the Cattle Industry*. Port Moresby: Paper presented to a Department of Primary Industry Seminar on developing the Cattle Industry.

Williams, G. 1981. "The World Bank and the Peasant Problem". In J. Heyer, P. Roberts, G. Williams, ed. *Rural Development in Tropical Africa*. London: Macmillan.

Wingti, P. 1982. "Standing by Our Principles in Tough Times". The Eight Point Plan and the National Goals: Performance, Problems and Prospect After a Decade. Port Moresby: University of Papua New Guinea.

Wolfers, E. 1976. "Towards Self-Government The Perspective of 1971". In D. Stone. *Prelude to Self Government*. Canberra: Research School of Pacific Studies and the University of Papua New Guinea.

Wolpe, H. 1980. *The Articulation of Modes of Production*. London: Routledge and Kegan Paul.

World Bank. 1978. *Papua New Guinea: Its Economic Situation and Prospects for Development*. Washington, D.C.: The World Bank.

_____ , Projects Department, Agriculture Division II, East Asia and Pacific Regional Office. 1981. *Country Sector Report, Papua New Guinea - - Agricultural Services Review*. Report No. 3161. Washington: World Bank.

Wright, E.O. 1979. *Class, Crisis and the State*. London: Verso.

Yorgason, V. 1976. "The International Coffee Agreement: Prospect and Retrospect". *Development and Change* 7 2.

Ziemann W. and Lanzendorfer, M. 1977. "The State in Peripheral Societies". In R. Miliband and J. Saville, eds. *The Socialist Register 1977*. London: Merlin.

Interviews

Interviews were conducted in Port Moresby and Goroka, Papua New Guinea in 1982, 1986 and 1988.

Officers were interviewed from the following departments, government agencies and private companies:

ANGCO Pty Ltd

Coffee Industry Board

Department of Commerce

Department of Decentralisation

Department of Finance

Department of Lands

Department of Primary Industry National

Eastern Highlands Provincial Government

Gouna Development Corporation

Hassall and Associates Pty Ltd

National Planning Office

National Plantation Management Agency

Papua New Guinea Development Bank

Interviews were also held with electoral candidates standing in the 1982 Goroka Open electorate and with business group members on 20-hectare coffee development projects.

Archives and Files Consulted Included

ANGCO Pty Ltd – – Project Budgets
Department of Commerce, Goroka – – Business Group Legislation
Department of Lands – – File 68/1996
Department of Primary Industry, Port Moresby
Eastern Highlands Provincial Government
- Cabinet Submissions
- Eastern Highlands Provincial Government Budget
- Rural Land Development Grant, File 8–6–8
- Agricultural Policy, Coffee, File 27–1–3

National Plantation Management Agency – – Project Budgets
Papua New Guinea Development Bank
- Project Requests for Loan Progress Payments

Periodicals Consulted Included

The Age
Australian Financial Review
Bank of Papua New Guinea Quarterly Economic Bulletin
Business Week
Coffee International
Daily News Brief PNG
Department of Finance Quarterly Summary of Economic Conditions PNG
FAO Production Yearbook
F.O. Lichts

International Coffee Organisation Quarterly Statistical Bulletin on Coffee
Household Expenditure Survey 1975/76 PNG
National Parliament Debates PNG
New Guinea Highlands Bulletin
Papua New Guinea Times
Post Courier
Reserve Bank of Australia Quarterly Statistical Bulletin
Reuters Coffee Newsletter
Rural Industries Bulletin PNG
Summary of Statistics PNG
South

Index

For Product Safety Concerns and Information please contact our EU representative GPSR@taylorandfrancis.com
Taylor & Francis Verlag GmbH, Kaufingerstraße 24, 80331 München, Germany

www.ingramcontent.com/pod-product-compliance
Lightning Source LLC
LaVergne TN
LVHW021619091026
849796LV00027B/326
* 9 7 8 0 3 6 7 1 5 7 7 8 4 *